Part 1

Rebooting the Bible

The astonishing story of a 1900-year-old rabbinical conspiracy to corrupt the Bible's ancient history and thwart belief in Jesus as the Messiah.

S. DOUGLAS WOODWARD

Other Books by the Author

ARE WE LIVING IN THE LAST DAYS?

DECODING DOOMSDAY

BLACK SUN, BLOOD MOON

POWER QUEST, BOOK TWO: THE ASCENDANCY OF ANTICHRIST IN AMERICA

POWER QUEST, BOOK ONE: AMERICA'S OBSESSION WITH THE PARANORMAL

LYING WONDERS OF THE RED PLANET

BLOOD MOON: BIBLICAL SIGNS OF THE COMING APOCALYPSE

THE NEXT GREAT WAR IN THE MIDDLE EAST

IS RUSSIA DESTINED TO NUKE THE U.S?

MISTAKEN IDENTITY: THE CASE AGAINST THE ISLAMIC ANTICHRIST

UNCOMMON SENSE: A PROPHETIC MANIFESTO FOR THE CHURCH IN BABYLON

With Douglas Krieger and Dene McGriff

THE FINAL BABYLON: AMERICA AND THE COMING OF ANTICHRIST

With Anthony Patch, Josh Peck, and Gonz Shimura

REVISING REALITY: A BIBLICAL LOOK INTO THE COSMOS

With Benjamin Baruch and Jeffrey Nyquist

THE NEW TACTICS OF GLOBAL WAR

With Gary Huffman

THE REVEALING: UNLOCKING HIDDEN TRUTHS ON THE GLORIFICATION OF GOD'S CHILDREN

REBOOTING THE BIBLE

IN TWO PARTS

PART ONE: Exposing the Second Century Conspiracy to Corrupt the Scripture and Alter Biblical Chronology

(To be published separately)

PART TWO: Reconciling Primeval Biblical History with Archaeology and Alternate History

S. Douglas Woodward

FAITH HAPPENS

OKLAHOMA CITY

Rebooting the Bible

Part One – Exposing the Second Century Conspiracy to Corrupt the Scripture and Alter Biblical Chronology

Faith Happens Book LLC. Oklahoma City, OK 73142

www.faithhappensbooks.com www.faith-happens.com

Unless otherwise noted, scripture taken from the Septuagint was translated by Sir Lancelot Charles Lee Brenton, initially published by Samuel Bagster & Sons, London, in 1844. Brenton's translation was based predominantly on Codex Vaticanus. A recent publication was produced by Zondervan, June 1, 1982. ISBN-10: 0310204305. The reader may access the Septuagint for free at Biblestudytools.com/lxx.

Other quotations marked ESV are taken from *The Holy Bible, English Standard Version*, copyright © 2001 by Good News Publishers. Scripture quotations marked KJV are taken from *The Holy Bible, King James Version.* If not otherwise designated, the scripture being cited is the ESV.

Use of extended quotations from other authors is considered fair use. Use of photographs and figures from third parties are public domain unless otherwise noted.

Boldface and italics appearing in scripture quotations are due to the author's emphasis and are not in the original.

Figures marked © S. Douglas Woodward are copyrighted, 2018, by S. Douglas Woodward and may be used if covered by fair use.

Interior page design and typesetting are by the author.
Cover design by Daniel Wright. daniel@createdwright.com

ISBN: 9781790589227

First Edition v. 1.0   Printed in the United States

TABLE OF CONTENTS

TABLE OF FIGURES

PREFACE

It is the Western World's most celebrated book, published in two volumes – the Old and New Testaments. Thanks to the beautiful language employed, it established the English language more profoundly than the writing of Shakespeare. No book has impacted the world more. No published manuscript has sold better. And yet, few think it free from flaws. It remains a thoroughly human book.

It was based upon *The Bishop's Bible* of 1569. 47 scholars, all members of the Church of England, worked collectively to create it. These scholars referenced other Bibles created by Luther, Tyndale, and Knox. When finished, it entered the public domain in 1611. Earlier Bibles in the Church of England were slowly phased out throughout the seventeenth century.

Its **New Testament** used the *Textus Receptus (TR)* as its Greek source text. The TR was initially translated by Erasmus in 1516. The TR would be revised by Lachmann in 1831, Trelles several times from 1857 to 1879, and von Tischendorf who would edit eight different versions. Revisions were necessary not because of poor grammar, but due to better rendering of the Greek as determined through additional manuscripts that came to light as the years advanced.

Its **Old Testament** considered Jerome's Vulgate (ca. 400 A.D.) disseminated in the fifth century by the Western (Roman Catholic) Church. And to a lesser extent, it referenced the Septuagint, a Greek translation of the Hebrew Old Testament translated by 70 scholars in Alexandria, Egypt, beginning 300 years *before* the crucifixion of Christ. This Septuagint (abbreviated LXX, the Roman numerals for *seventy*), remains the Bible of the Orthodox Church to this day. Besides the Bishop's Bible,

The Geneva Bible and Tyndale Bible would also contribute to its marginal notes, many which included alternate readings and factors adding to the variations of meaning the translators wanted the reader to consider. The scholars who completed the translation understood that any adaptation to another language introduces possible misunderstandings from what the original author intended when first written. Based upon their preface to this book, they believed others would come later and revise the translation to make it more fitting for future ears.

When it was completed, like the Septuagint and Vulgate, it contained supplemental texts to the more well-known and widely accepted biblical books. We call this collection, the *Apocrypha*. A century or so later, the *Apocrypha* would be dropped from its published version. The Hebrew Bible did not include it, and Protestant Reformers chose the Hebrew Bible to become its standard. Afterward, to evangelize the world, Protestant scholars would begin creating translations for almost all languages.

It was revised many times. Those revisions were performed by additional scholars beyond the original 47. These revisions were completed in 1629, 1638, 1762, and 1769. The most popular edition from 1769 was produced by Dr. Benjamin Blayney. Today's published versions of this revered Bible are primarily based on Blayney's revision.

Of course, I am talking about the *King James Bible*.

King James' name was not originally connected to this Bible. It was an "authorized version" just as *The Great Bible* and *The Bishop's Bible* had been authorized by Henry the VIII and his daughter, Queen Elizabeth I respectively, during the previous century. Dropping his name might have been appropriate since King James led a life of debauchery and was a known bisexual. He hardly deserved such a distinguished namesake.

For some, the mandatory usage of *The King James Bible* is a hedge against secularism and apostasy. In our world today, many conservative churches continue to argue vehemently that the KJV is the only trustworthy source, for it is the only Bible deemed to have the "imprimatur" of the Lord.[1] They feel God not only supernaturally inspired the original autographs of the biblical writers, but he also supernaturally inspired its preservation. As one advocate told this author, "Without God's inspired preservation, the inspiration of the autographs is meaningless."

For conservative Evangelicals, there can be no compromise. (I hesitantly label these brothers and sisters *Fundamentalists* to contrast but not to disparage.) These brethren believe *The King James Version* and only this version constitutes the Word of God. All other versions contain errors and fall short.[2] This judgment is not based on literary quality. It is judged that this Bible is the only writ that the LORD in Heaven supports. Those who advocate a different English Bible are often considered reprobates and apostates. Since God inspired the KJV – and only the KJV – true Christians must accept its full inspiration unflinchingly.

Closely tied to the commitment to the King James Bible, is the advocacy of a belief in "the Young Earth" – a view that the world was created just a bit over 6,000 years ago. The Bible does provide a chronology within its genealogies in Genesis chapters 5 and 11. And this chronology was supported by the research of Bishop James Ussher, not long after publishers

---

[1] Technically, an imprimatur is a license by the Roman Catholic Church to license a religious or ecclesiastical book. I use the term loosely to underscore an officially approved Bible by Fundamentalist churches rather than Catholic.

[2] There are 450 languages into which the Bible has been translated and 500 versions of the Bible in English alone. Is only one English version acceptable?

released the KJV to the public. This traditional conservative position demands that the universe (including humanity) was created in six, twenty-four-hour days, precisely six millennia ago. It took place on the first Rosh Hashanah, in 4004 B.C., when God created all that is. To believe otherwise – that the world is billions of years older than this – is to trust in secularism and evolutionary science, while denying the Word of God is literally true. Until little more than a century ago in America, most Evangelicals believed this. Science became our enemy.

It is often argued as a justification for this restrictive view that the people of God must have an *absolute and unchanging Word from God* – and that Word must be without the human capacity for error. In other words, for the people of God to be wholly equipped as His Saints, the Scripture must be accurate, in whole and in part, as well as free from any taint of obscurity.

Undoubtedly, the preservation of God's Holy Word involves conceptual complexities. Since it was written by human authors and has been passed down by human means, God's Word must be seen to be a human enterprise. And yet, just as Christ Jesus was both human and divine, the Word of God in Scripture also provides God's revelation to us. So, since all Evangelicals agree that the Bible is the Word of God, *how can we articulate the method by which God preserves His Word through time?* There are, indeed, numerous issues to address when attempting to arrive at a satisfactory resolution to the Bible's dual nature – that is, its *human* and *godly* character. But at this juncture, allow me to provide what may seem to be an overly simplistic explanation of the two competing perspectives that conservative Christians hold concerning the *preservation of the Word of God in the Bible*:

1. **Alternative one:** The Spirit of God preserves the Word of God presented through the Bible *by inspiring only one specific version which believers must declare is God's Word.* This text was published at one particular time in one particular language with no changes allowed whatsoever. And it has been decided by some that God preserves His Word in English through the KJV. *Tradition* mandates this version is the only acceptable, inspired translation.

2. **Alternative two:** The Spirit of God providentially preserves the Word of God presented through the Bible *from the work of scholars who study the text, applying reason and science to detect the authentic, original words and meaning as intended by the author.* If God preserves His Word in this manner, human agents (i.e., scholars), must demonstrate *evidentially* which text or meaning is most authentic to what was first written millennia ago.

The methodology of alternative one is this: Corrections to spelling or grammar must be rejected, archaic language must be accepted and not modernized. Newly discovered manuscripts that might identify the original wording should be ignored. Hence, discoveries like the Dead Sea Scrolls are to be dismissed. A new codex, like *Codex Sinaiticus (dated to the fourth century A.D.),* is disregarded. Thus, defending the Bible means blocking all attempts to alter it while overturning all claims to flaws in its contents, whether it's spelling, grammar, historical accuracy, or scientific knowledge. Finally, newer versions are banned since they alter the words of the accepted version. The Bible should be "frozen" as is, in the version tradition demands.

The methodology of alternative two is this: Scholars detect, through reason and investigation, which wording (i.e., "reading") is most likely to be authentic to the original work. Newly discovered manuscripts provide new insights into the wording of the original. Publishers may employ scholars to research and translate the Hebrew, Aramaic, and Greek texts that clarify the language of the Bible conveying a meaning of God's Word that is able to communicate effectively to us today. A good example: Erasmus used seven manuscripts in creating the TR. A modern Bible utilizes approximately 5,900 manuscripts. Many linguistic tools exist to help the textual critic determine with high probability, the authentic language of the author. And newly preferred words clarify its meaning for modern readers. Such texts point out spurious additions or changes through time. Therefore, we can conclude, "The more manuscripts, the better. We are better able to discern the original."

However, before we sally forth to prove the thesis of this book, the reader should acknowledge God's Word shines best through the purest glass possible. If we close our mind to any effort to purify the medium in which God has revealed Himself, namely the Bible, then my campaign is defeated at the outset.

This is so because the argument this book puts forth is that the King James Version was created using the Masoretic Text (MT), and therefore, *was corrupted long before today*. It happened nineteen centuries ago. This corruption was intentional. It was carried out by those rabbis who survived the destruction of Herod's Temple. Roman authorities granted them permission to create an academy in the town of Jamnia (Javneh), on the coast near Tel Aviv. There, changes were made to the original Old Testament, that focused on two areas: First, the Messianic passages of the Old Testament; and secondly, two chronologies in Genesis, chapters 5 and 11. As this book will lay out carefully, the rabbis, headed by Rabbi Akiba ben Yosef, sought to recreate Judaism while at the same time quashing the rival cult known as Christianity. Rabbinic authorities decided to obscure specific passages that supported Christian evangelists who preached Jesus of Nazareth was the promised Messiah.

At Jamnia, these rabbis created an alternate *Vorlage*, or original scripture, from which a new Greek translation would be created that contradicted the Greek Septuagint, hoping to replace this Greek Bible used by Christian apostles and teachers, especially for the Jewish communities globally. After three centuries had elapsed, and with some help from the Christian patrons Origen and later Jerome, the rabbis ultimately succeeded, at least to a meaningful extent. This would lead to one Latin and three new Greek versions based upon this Vorlage. The "revised" Vorlage differed from the original Bible, compiled (so tradition tells us) by Ezra and then safeguarded by Nehemiah and the other courageous Jews that returned from the Babylonian Empire in the fifth century B.C. (circa 445 B.C.). This new rabbinic (corrupted) Hebrew Vorlage was created about 100 A.D., while the later Greek versions were originated before the end of the *second century A.D.*, and the Latin Vulgate, approximately 400 A.D. The Septuagint's Pentateuch was finished 380 years before the rabbinic Vorlage and 680 years before the Vulgate.[3]

You see, the Septuagint had been translated in Alexandria, Egypt, from the authentic Hebrew Vorlage brought from Jerusalem for the translation. Why did the Hebrew Vorlage differ? For the rabbis, the prophecies concerning the Messiah as translated in the Septuagint easily applied to Jesus. They rejected Jesus was the Messiah. Nevertheless, Christians believed it was obvious that Jesus had fulfilled the prophecies of Moses, David, Isaiah, and the other ancient prophets. Additionally, because the tradition of the Jews held that the Messiah would

---

[3] The remainder of the Septuagint Bible (which included several additional historical books like 1, 2, and 3 Maccabees) was finished ca. 125 B.C.

arrive near the time Jesus appeared on the scene, the *timing of the Messiah's arrival* had to be altered so that Jesus would not be identified as the Christ. Thus, over one thousand five hundred years (1,500) were cut out of the original Genesis genealogies/chronologies. And another 130 years or so were deleted by the rabbis in the timing laid out in Daniel's prophecy of the 70 "weeks" of years.[4] Their efforts amount to a conspiracy to disqualify Jesus as the Christ. To accomplish this, Rabbi Akiva and his disciples at Jamnia obscured the Messianic prophecies and the chronology of Genesis from Adam to Abraham.[5] Given the New Testament authors used the Septuagint 90% of the time when quoting the Old Testament, perhaps ironically, *Christianity preserved the meaning of the original Hebrew* in these specific passages (and quite a few others as we will show).

Getting back to whether the *King James Bible* stands as the sole trustworthy version of the Bible, this book will demonstrate that the MT was more than tampered with about 1,511 years before the KJV was completed in 1611. And since the KJV Old Testament is based on the MT, it is incoherent to hold the view the KJV was flawlessly inspired by God. Once demonstrated that the razor-sharp prophecies of Messiah were surreptitiously dulled in the "revised" Hebrew Vorlage at Jamnia, to argue the KJV remains free from taint becomes *more than moot*. This is so because the variances introduced go to the heart of Christianity's claim that Jesus is the Christ.

A second important point is this: If Evangelicals wish to select the *Bible that most closely conveys the original work of its*

---

[4] This was accomplished in the *Sedar Olam Rabbah* as we will discuss.

[5] Oftentimes, Evangelicals assert that a "council" was held at Jamnia where the official canon was decided. This book makes no such claim, only that the rabbinic academies were responsible for the canon determination and the changes.

Hebrew authors, it is the Greek Septuagint and not the Hebrew or Latin versions that we should adopt as our primary text. This is despite the fact that all Protestant Bibles (and most of the Latin Vulgate) began with what would become known as the altered rabbinic Masoretic Text. This doesn't mean that the Septuagint has no blemishes nor does it mean that the Hebrew should be abandoned. Not at all. Only specific passages differ between these other versions. But they are concentrated in two critical places: Messianic prophecy and ancient biblical chronology. If Protestants should seek the authentic Word of God, it requires we lay claim *again* to the Greek Bible of the early Church, its exclusive Bible for over 500 years before the Vulgate slowly began to replace it in the Western Chuch. Once we do, *we possess the authentic biblical witness to the year of Creation as set forth in Genesis, the date of the Great Flood, the birth of Abraham, and, with the analysis this author provides in the pages that follow, the year of the Exodus and the Conquest of Canaan.* This book will break the code on how the Septuagint unlocks these mysteries and offers a complete chronology reaching from Jesus Christ to Adam.

[NOTE: While academics can (and should) debate the original wording of the Septuagint, research shows that academics almost never assume any ulterior motives influenced the changes made in the proto-Masoretic as this author asserts. My point in response: One cannot determine the original wording of the passages in question, *without suspecting that there was a rabbinic conspiracy to alter the text as this book contends.*]

It is not my intention to weaken the faith of conservative Christians. Instead, I wish to strengthen it by showing beyond a reasonable doubt that the Bible offers clarity on who the Messiah is and when he would come offering the Kingdom of God to the Jews. And please note, this book does not criticize the KJV

New Testament since its citations of the Old are almost always drawn from the Septuagint and not the Hebrew.

This book will argue forcefully that the rabbis at the end of the first century A.D., and on into the second, were deliberate in their attempt to weaken the Christian message of salvation by faith in Jesus Christ, favoring instead the newly scribed Oral Tradition (a huge addition to the original Mosaic law). This Oral Law remains subject to criticism being that it is without biblical support. No such law existed dating from the time of Moses. Where this "oral law" appears referenced in the New Testament, Jesus condemns it, calling it only the "tradition of men," specifically of the Pharisees (who would become the rabbis of the second century). But that debate constitutes a separate matter for a different study.

I will no doubt be accused of anti-Semitism for scorning the foundation of what I believe is a new Judaism, differing from the Old Testament Temple religion. However, this book is not an anti-Semitic diatribe. Like many evangelicals, I wish only the very best for the land of Israel and Jews everywhere. Indeed, if there is any superior race, history testifies that it is the Jewish race, given its seemingly indomitable culture, brilliant minds, and contributions to the world in so many fields. As one influenced by dispensationalism during my early years of research, I still argue that Yahweh continues His plan for the Jews which includes the nation of Israel today.

The scope of my critique is limited to what happened in the second century.[6] My "indictment" addresses one specific aspect of the original objectives of the Jamnia Academy. That targeted challenge is to the clandestine goal of Rabbi Akiba. In other words,

---

[6] Of course, as an Evangelical Christian, I disagree with Judaism since it rejects Jesus as its long-awaited Messiah. I still pray for the peace of Jerusalem, and hope that one day all Jews will accept that Jesus is their Christ.

the problem this author has is not so much that Judaism was reinvented by the rabbis. Instead, it is that this school altered the Bible to confuse other Jews and lead them away from their true Messiah. Except for Jewish converts to Christianity, the Jewish people missed the day of God's visitation. I hope that by identifying the rabbinic conspiracy alleged in this book, it will reopen for many Jews the question whether Jesus was indeed their promised Messiah, by highlighting the many Old Testament prophecies that speak to the historical identity of the Messiah – Jesus of Nazareth. This offering is presented to all Jews, so that they may see for themselves that Yahweh kept His promise two thousand years ago by granting them a deliverer and redeemer. Our Redeemer liveth (Job 19:25).

Finally, there is another bonus I offer which will be taken up mostly in Part 2 of *Rebooting the Bible*. Once we ascertain the correct dates of the events in Genesis, we discover the findings of Archeology are reconcilable with the Bible. The added 1,500 years included in the Septuagint's timeline (and confirmed by other ancient witnesses we will identify), suddenly line up the Bible's chronology with the findings of Egyptology and Mesopotamian Archeology. The foundation for this reconciliation is laid here in Part 1. But it remains a vast subject unto itself and requires a second volume to be published near summertime, 2019. This sequel will also include an examination of the many extra-biblical works that Christians have been introduced to and enthusiastically embraced over the past decade. And it also will consider the claims of alternate history that might span beyond the date the Bible proclaimed when Adam and Eve were created and lived in Eden.

So, to be clear, this first book is part of a two-book project. To recap, Part 1 examines why and how the conspiracy of

Jamnia altered the biblical text, how it eventually led to a fateful mistaken choice made by Protestants, and how it obscured the actual time when the most vital events in Genesis took place. To achieve this objective, this book concludes with a necessary and thorough analysis of (1) the Exodus and (2) the outset of the Conquest of Canaan since their respective dates are the gateway to the earlier Genesis chronologies. That is to say, Abraham is the bridge between primeval biblical history (in the first eleven chapters of Genesis) and the biblical account that comprised the rest of the Bible. I am hopeful Part 2 will be available within 9 months of this volume. A draft of the outline for Part 2 is provided as Appendix 6 in the back of this book.

May God bless those who read and prayerfully consider these words.

S. Douglas Woodward
Oklahoma City, Fall, 2018.

REBOOTING THE BIBLE

PART ONE: Exposing the Second
Century Conspiracy to Corrupt the
Scripture and Alter Biblical Chronology

Introduction:
REBOOTING THE BIBLE

"History would be a wonderful thing, if only it were true"
(Leo Tolstoy).

Where We Find Ourselves

When it comes to the question of origins, Christians believe that we have the inside track in this quest. And we do. We know a great deal about the past. The Christian faith is drawn from the renowned actions of the Bible's heroes and saints, our Lord Jesus chief among them. Unfortunately, we have been fooled into believing a great deal of hogwash about earlier times, what many label antiquity but which we may also properly designate as "primeval."

We might say that having the inside lane hasn't kept us from selecting the wrong road. That's why we need to exit the current highway we traverse and head in a new direction. What we believe about ancient history needs to be recast. And this begins with a *reboot* of how we understand our Bible. We must reconsider our framework for the Bible's *primeval* account. Primeval means, "relating to the earliest ages... of the world or human history." (Merriam-Webster) It is this very early history this book hopes to set aright and reinvigorate our worldview. The first step in our quest: To discover how the Bible was tarnished 1,900 years ago. Once we do this, we will understand why a reboot or "reset," using computer terms, is mandatory.

1

Over the past 200 years or so, secularism has championed positivistic explanations for sacred texts. Today, many well-known best-selling authors offer examples from a very different place. It seems spacemen were our forebears. All human achievements are explained by unseen extraterrestrials behind the scenes. However, whether from a perspective of naturalism that denies supernatural agents, to a fantastical point of view that considers every wonder in our past proving visits from ancient aliens, we need to call "balderdash" on both. (I could think of a more modern term, but this book is targeted for those who value modesty and decorum.)

We need to push back on unjustified conclusions drawn from empirical data gathered from what archeologists dig up. And we need to distance ourselves from unscientific biases that make us look foolish. At the same time, we need to colorize a black and white past. Therefore, we must address ancient biblical history, with our touchstone the birth of Abraham. And then, we will work our way all the way back to Creation – and maybe – beyond. Part 1 explains why we must challenge conventional chronology, whether we are dealing with biblical scholars or academics that express no love for the scriptures. Part 2 recasts the vital stories of primeval history, which requires a corrected chronology if we are to accomplish this goal.

History is undertaught in both religious and secular schools. And for any reader familiar with my work, that reader knows most of what all of us have been taught is not only inaccurate, it was written *intentionally* wrong. That is, our instruction fed us false lines, fake stories, and clouded our minds with pabulum. Since supposedly no child could be left behind, with too few exceptions, *all children missed the bus*. Our kids are incredibly unaware of what happened in days gone by. I know this in part because I teach college students – lots of them. Their energy is contagious. And while children are our future, too few kids know much about our past.

So while they are smart about many things, they know very little about anything happening before the Kardashians and Kanye. For the most part, our public education system has failed us. It has undoubtedly failed them. This declining education system in America combines with the "Mockingbird Media" established by the CIA in the 1960s, to promote politically correct propaganda to the public.

However, so-called "Fake news" is not new. We have lived with it for half a century. In stealth, it grows more menacing, falsely shaping the public's perception of reality, essentially brainwashing "we the people" into what the Shadow Government wants us to believe. Tragically, what it communicates only faintly resembles the truth about the past, and even less, what's really *happening* in the world today.

When it comes to what we were taught about the Bible, because of which source text we rely upon and how it was tampered with long ago, in many of its passages, our Bible fails to say what it initially did. This is not to claim that God inspired error in the biblical text. Instead, it expresses that He entrusted His Holy Word to the hands of humanity. More than once, as it regards Protestants and their Bibles, those hands faltered. God's truth was tainted. Part 1 of demonstrates when and how this mistreatment transpired as well as to how the record can be set right, in recovering the original meaning of the Old Testament and its timeline. Part 2 intends to *dig into the primeval history, the days before Abraham,* and show how the Bible and Archeology can be synchronized. Additionally, this author hopes to establish a pathway for others to explore *alternate primeval history,* that we might discover together what may have happened in those ancient days that accepted history ignores.

Unaware of the Error in Our Ways

To clarify before I lose many of my readers: *I believe in the infallible Word of God and inerrancy of its autographs.* But what happened to the Bible two millennia ago, is the greatest untold story of religious history. It remains a monumental deception. And almost no one, even well-studied Jews and Christians, know about these failures nor the duplicity of numerous founding leaders. In the pages that follow, this author aims to shine a light on these covert operations undertaken in bad faith; for these actions have done us much harm.

The falsehood about which I write was baked into the biblical text Protestants used over the centuries, but mainly since the sixteenth century. It matters because it weakens our faith and makes evangelizing unbelievers more difficult. This is especially so regarding our Jewish friends. And there are many implications due to our neglect to learn the truth.

To enumerate: We are guilty of…

- *Supporting inaccurate translations of the biblical text in no small number. In particular, many messianic passages in the Masoretic (Hebrew) text are not what the Holy Spirit inspired the biblical authors to write;*

- *Ignoring the findings of Archeology like the discovery of the Dead Sea Scrolls and the Ugaritic Texts – giving them too little place to inform our beliefs about and understanding of the Bible;*

- *Nurturing an anti-intellectual bias that implicates good science and justifies poor biblical exegesis. We label knowledge dangerous and blind faith virtuous;*

- *Professing a super-spiritual persona built upon the false premise that we only need one book – the Bible – to be the sole guide for living in this world. Evangelicals might not burn books today, but far too many pay them no mind. Nationally, we are a population practicing illiteracy. In our Evangelical churches, we lack interest in history, science, and politics. Instead, we focus on "feel-good" messages and avoid challenges to our protected view of the world. We Evangelicals, especially in America, began following Baal some time ago.*

- *Ascribing near-canonical status to apocryphal and pseudepigrapha works outside the biblical canon – which while helpful, in some cases, may be blatantly wrong.*

Because we Protestants believe the Bible is the Word of God, we have never heard how the Old Testament was altered to undermine its the messianic prophecies and salvation by grace. Likewise, its chronology was changed because it testified to the early Church that Jesus was the Christ. Because of these premeditated modifications to the authentic Word of God, our understanding of the past – from the Creation to the conquest of Canaan – has been severely impaired. This needs to be corrected.

That's why this book has found its way into your hands. It's time to set the record straight – to get us all on the same page. It's essential we commit ourselves to revisit our beliefs about the Bible. Although it will be unpopular and uncomfortable, we must inspect what we hold sacred, to consider that what we thought was free from taint isn't.

Where We Must Venture

To reconsider the times long since passed, we need to go back in time. How far? All the way back to Genesis, chapter one. That far back. And here's how we will organize our quest.

For the most part, Part 2 will focus on the first eleven chapters of Genesis. We touch on what happened at the beginning of the Bible's story (recall Genesis means *beginnings*) and consider whether this planet started spinning less than 10,000 years ago. We investigate whether the Bible supplies an accurate chronology. However, we will only glance at the debate over *The Young Earth vs. The Gap Theory* – for although significant, *Rebooting the Bible* doesn't seek to prove either to be solely correct. Our focus will be on what comes about *after Genesis 1*, conventionally seen as a 4,000-year period from Adam to Christ. The "corrected chronology" this study presents is neutral on which theory is most likely true, although it admittedly supplies a shot in the arm to the view the world is less than 10,000 years old.[7]

We recall that Noah built a giant ark (300 cubits long, 50 cubits wide, and 30 cubits high) through which he and his family weathered the world's worst *perfect storm*. But, since the global population outside the ark (both human and animal, birds included) was reset to zero, does it mean that we should call Noah our ancestor? Yes, it certainly does.

Consequently, after the Flood, Noah and his kids restarted humanity. That part of the story remains especially crucial because most Christians still don't know why God went to the extreme to destroy all land-life on the earth. The background to "why the Flood" is unlike anything we can imagine except in our worst nightmare. It involves chimeras and giants, angels corrupting the human genome, and demons appearing for the first time – and from that point forward – sanctioned to harass

---

[7] For the record, I currently believe the so-called Gap Theory is the correct way to interpret the ages before Adam and Eve. But that position is not essential to the revised chronology presented in these pages.

and deceive humanity. This is a challenging subject, to say the least. Happily, we can count on some sophisticated help from a scholar or two that will ease us over the speed bump we might label, "The Incredible Hybrid Humans, the Nephilim."

After Noah's Ark was grounded, we recall that the father of humanity, Noah, grows a vineyard, and drinks too much wine. His son Ham takes advantage of the situation (one of the more controversial episodes of the Bible's flood account), and as a result, Noah curses Ham's son (and his grandson) Canaan, commencing a fraternal conflict enduring through the ages. But what was the sin of Ham? It will surprise you. But the critical point up for discussion has more to do with the replenishment of the world, instead of what Ham did to his parents.

Then we will take up the man, the myth, the legend we call *Nimrod*. Yes, he was a real, live historical figure. And we can spot him amid the annals of the past as constructed by secular Archeology from Iraq, however treacherous such activity might be today. Was Nimrod the first "transhuman?" What difference does it make if he was? We will examine whether Nimrod was in fact, the rabble-rouser that led to the Tower of Babel incident. We will consider whether he was only an archetype of the evil one to come or will one day reappear during the *end times* as the embodiment of Antichrist. Like H.P. Lovecraft's *Cthulhu* who slumbered (suspended in the blackened depths of the darkest ocean), we will ask whether Nimrod lurks in the bottomless pit, described in Revelation 9 until his moment arrives to haunt humanity one final time.

Then we will set the table, the so-called "table of nations" that is, from Genesis, chapter 10. Through its contents, we will take a look-see to where everyone went after God enforced His mandate to humanity to multiply and replenish the earth.[8] You see, it looks as if the LORD had to force the issue by confusing the languages of humankind so we would quarrel, get in big dustups, then split them up – literally – scattering to-and-fro over God's green, and recently very well-watered earth.

Meanwhile, almost 800 years later, back in Sumer near Uruk (Spoiler alert: Fans of the *Book of Jasher* won't like the biblical chronology offered here), God places his historic call to Abraham in the famous city Ur of the Chaldees, presumably occupied by the infamous Chaldeans. But when exactly did Abraham live? Was he a contemporary of Nimrod as the *Book of Jasher* supposes? When did he first visit Egypt? When did his son Jacob (Israel) migrate the clan to the land of the Pharaohs? How many were in that clan? How long did the Israelites remain there? How many years were the Hebrews enslaved to the Egyptians? You may think you know the answers, but I can promise that only a few readers actually do.

That will bring us to the Exodus and the incident following: *The conquest of Canaan.* This period is most important because once the timing has been rightly established, for the first time the biblical testimony aligns with Mesopotamian and Egyptian Archeology. As it stands right now, by believing in the "conventional chronology" as set forth by the King James Bible, we cannot reconcile secular Archeology with the Bible. Yet, with a corrected chronology based upon the original biblical record, *the two can be synchronized.* Consequently, if we really care about our witness to the world and our ability to convince others that the

---

[8] It seems humans were clannish and didn't want to disperse, thinking they had a better chance to make a name for themselves if they hung out together.

Bible provides an accurate and reliable historical account, must no longer hold to a false history protected by traditic while conflicting with science and an authentic scripture.

First Things First

However, before we study what this author equates as the executive summary of the years from 2,200 B.C. to 5,600 B.C. – that is, the stories from *the Creation to Abraham* – we must employ the much-maligned tool we call *textual criticism.* In other words, to uncover what the Bible really said about antiquity in its initial chapters, we must revisit the testimony of its originators to verify what they recorded about the ancient world.

Call me curious, but I want to know (and I trust the reader does too) how many years ago it was when the monumental biblical events took place. Just to chronicle them here rhetorically once again for the reader: When God breathed life into Adam, how long was it before the Flood of Noah happened? Then, how many years elapsed after the Flood before the Tower of Babel was built on a plain in Shinar? After Nimrod, how many sunrises and sunsets occurred before Abraham became the most prominent forebear of the Israelites, the people of Israel and Judah? His story is indeed the tale of "the plan for man," specifically when that plan shifted to God's strategy for humanity's redemption. Abraham's biography recounts vital incidents in Canaan, for him, and his son and grandson (Isaac and Jacob). But the scene eventually shifts to Egypt where Abraham's descendants grow into an enormous population, that despite being enslaved to the Egyptians, threaten them. Although Hebrew slavery became essential to Egypt's economy, Yahweh delivers the Children of Israel through Moses. But when, exactly, did Moses lead the Children of Israel out of Egypt? We have to know this date because all of the events before the Exodus tie back to it.

You see, to create a corrected timeline we must parse the painstaking work of the scholars. However, it all begins with an investigation into the biblical sources. We must learn about (what is known as) the *Vorlage of the Bible*; that is, the earliest assembled text (ca. 450 B.C., in the time of Ezra and Nehemiah) of most if not all of what became the accepted Old Testament.[9] For it's from this Hebrew Vorlage that the *Greek version of the Old Testament*, the *Septuagint*, was created ca. 280 B.C. (The Septuagint is abbreviated *LXX* for the 70 scholars who supposedly developed the translation migrating the original Hebrew into Greek.) Why should we take such care in this investigation? Because we must understand the issue of *"which Vorlage"* because nothing less than the truth of the Bible is at stake.

You see, the LXX and MT differ in numerous crucial passages. Vital to our thesis, the *chronology of the Septuagint varies dramatically from that which is provided by the Masoretic Text (MT)*. The MT was compiled about 400 years after (ca. 110 A.D.), the LXX (ca. 280 B.C.). This "proto-MT" would one day become the "official" (i.e., canonized) Hebrew Bible, aka the Old Testament, through efforts led by Rabbi Akiba during the time of the famous Jewish rebel, Simeon Bar Kokhba (executed in 135 A.D.)

---

[9] The role of Ezra is debated among scholars. Some regard him as the author of the Torah, others see him as a later writer of the Books of Chronicles. He was clearly a champion of the Torah. The Talmud considers him the father of Judaism. Ezra is known as Esdras in the Septuagint. His Greek name was shortened to Ezra in the English world. The Documentary Hypothesis, or JEPD Theory, so detrimental to the authority of the Bible, saw Ezra in a redactor role. We can bet the priesthood assembled the scrolls and held them in the Temple. Since the Temple was destroyed in 586 B.C. by Nebuchadnezzar, the scrolls had to be secured outside of the Temple itself.

As you will see, this study is far from boring, because conspiracies play no small part swaying how our Bible was assembled. We're not just talking about selecting the books and placing them in their preferred order, but in numerous instances, the engineering process included altering the original words. Trust me: *This story is one almost no one knows.* And the few who know about it, undervalue the reasons why it's so significant that *all Christian and Jewish communities learn the truth.*

And the story delivers on drama and intrigue. To peek behind the curtains (and to peak your interest), here's this story in a nutshell:

Second-century rabbis deliberately altered the biblical text 1,900 years ago to twist what the original authors wrote.

You may protest and ask, "Why would these holy sages taint the Hebrew Old Testament? Didn't they believe it was sacred? It was their holy book after all. What could motivate them to take such drastic measures? Put simply: They decided if certain passages weren't materially changed, their ancient religion and race were both finished, *for a conquered people – minus their land, their language, and their faith – won't survive.*

As the first century A.D. was coming to a close, Rome destroyed the Jewish Temple, maintaining its draconian rule. The culture was in flux. Judea and Syria were fueled by Christians evangelists spreading the teaching of Jesus Christ like wildfire. Feeding this fire was the Greek Septuagint that by then had already become *the Christian Bible.* Jesus' Apostles brandished it as a powerful weapon, causing a revolution in the Spirit and in the political structure. Gone was the Sanhedrin. The Pharisees and Sadducees remained in a struggle for local control.

11

The rabbis, successors to the Pharisees, feared the wording in messianic passages of the Psalms and the Prophets. These passages made too strong of a case for *Jesus being the Messiah.* Additionally, the LXX was now the Bible of the Jewish Diaspora (the dispersion of Jews from 700 B.C. forward). This added insult to injury. The rabbis saw plainly that the Jewish people needed their own Greek Bible that watered down the wording of Isaiah, David, and other prophets. From Rabbi Akiba's standpoint, this "Jewish-only" Bible must weaken the prophecies concerning the Messiah.

A prime example was Psalm 40:6. The writer of the New Testament Book of Hebrews quoted the verse as written in the LXX, *"Sacrifice and offering thou wouldest not,* **but a body hast prepared me;** *whole burnt offering and sacrifice for sin thou didst not require."* Not only did this passage downplay Temple ritual, the Psalm also speaks of a *human body prepared by God for the Messiah,* which would provide the perfect sacrifice. For a rabbi, it was unthinkable that God would take on flesh. The incarnation was an abomination. Consequently, the verse had to be changed. Soon it read, *"Sacrifice and offering thou didst not desire; mine ears hast thou opened."* (Psalm 40:6, King James Version) As in other passages we will cover, not only are vital attributes of the Messiah downplayed or dismissed here, the sacrificial death of the Messiah (strongly hinted at in the passage), is replaced with a continual focus on keeping the law. Given the rabbis sought to replace the priesthood, their words were not randomly chosen.

But you still may ask, "Why did the Jews need a Greek Bible?" You see, by the time of Jesus Christ, only a few Jews throughout the world understood Hebrew; so, they needed a Bible in their everyday language which by then had become *Koine Greek.* Surprisingly, this was even true in Judaea. Since

Akiba saw that a new Greek translation was needed to counter the Septuagint, a modified Hebrew Vorlage must first be created, to facilitate a new Greek translation. This meant the Hebrew Vorlage had to be "updated" – obfuscating biblical passages buttressing the case for Jesus. The Bible must be rid of prooftexts Christians used to proselytize Jews. Therefore, Akiba created a new Hebrew Vorlage – different from what was used 350 years earlier by Alexandrian Jews when creating the LXX. Consequently, *the most significant textual revision of all time was finished,* led by none other than the father of Rabbinic Judaism, Rabbi Akiba ben Yosef.

This new Hebrew Vorlage, now hand-crafted from refashioned *copies* of the original Hebrew, became the forerunner of the Masoretic Text (henceforth often referred to as the proto-MT or the proto-Masoretic Text). Akiba's efforts (and those of his succeeding disciples for the next 100 years), were directed to eradicate this rapid-growing, heretical cult known as *Christianity.* So, even after Bar Kokhba was dead and buried and could no longer pretend to be the awaited Messiah, the Rabbis continued to put him forth as a messianic figure, displacing Jesus as the preferred messianic candidate as far as Jewish orthodoxy was concerned. Therefore, Christianity had to be stopped at all costs. What better way to hamper Christianity's growth than to undermine "the Christian Bible" by creating a new Greek Bible for Jews, purportedly based on the authentic, *original* Hebrew Vorlage? Since so few Jews knew Hebrew (including the Church Fathers save *Origen*), slipping in changes to launch the "new and improved" Hebrew Vorlage, was no trouble at all. When the "official canon" was finally settled ca. 110 A.D, the altered Vorlage was part and parcel of the go-forward plan.

13

The Implication for the Protestant Bible

Unfortunately, this means we Evangelicals must face the fact that the King James Version (KJV), based predominantly on the Masoretic Text, has carried forward these "modifications" in its Old Testament. Our current day Bibles include these errors (with a few other adjustments we will discuss). The KJV – although first published in 1611 – continues to this day to be the standard Bible for many if not most Protestants.

So, what difference does it make? The chronology of the Masoretic Text (as presented in Genesis chapters 5 and 11) and popularized through the KJV for over 400 years, is flat wrong. In fact, it is off by almost 1,500 years. Plus, *prophecies regarding the Messiah* as presented in the Old Testament (not just the KJV but virtually every Protestant Bible), have been watered down. With few exceptions, all Protestant Bibles follow the MT. Since the chronology also contributes to the case for Jesus Christ (as we will demonstrate later), the timeline was altered too – and dramatically so. The unintended consequences for Jews and Christians were not that significant. But over the last 200 years, during our modern era, this corrupted chronology has become a big problem. It became so since the science of Archeology started unearthing artifacts contradicting the dates supplied by the Masoretic Text. However, when we begin to explore Archeology and how it does sync up with a "rebooted Bible" – a major objection to biblical history and veracity is eliminated.[10]

---

[10] The challenges Christian apologists face with evolution must be dealt with in a different way than conflicts we might have with Archeology, Anthropology, and their interpretation of history. Archeology is an empirical study. It looks at recorded history aka 10,000 years ago, not 13 billion years. It surfaces tangible "hard facts" (for the most part) to establish whether a biblical supposition can be confirmed or contradicted. It is this realm that we are addressing in this book.

If my allegations are upsetting to you, please be patient. As scientist Brian Greene says, "Exploring the unknown (and the unfamiliar) requires tolerating uncertainty." I know I am stepping on some sacred foundations of faith. I also realize that what I am saying may strike you as anti-Semitic. This is far from the truth. I am reaching out to Jews and Christians alike.

When given a chance, the Septuagint untangles several messes made by the KJV's faulty chronology. We should evaluate the LXX from this standpoint, for many other relevant sources confirm the LXX while contradicting the MT. The Samaritan Pentateuch,[11] the Dead Sea Scrolls, Josephus' testimony in his *Antiquities of the Jews,* quotations from the writings of the Church Fathers, and early Jewish historians who relied upon the LXX *before* the time of Jesus. These sources represent solid witnesses confirming the assertions made here. Indeed, you will be puzzled that the Masoretic chronology, popularized by Bishop James Ussher (1581-1656), became the dominant biblical timeline once you've reviewed all the evidence.

Right up front, *again*, let me affirm that I believe in biblical inerrancy. Furthermore, allow me to say the King James Version stands without equal as the most influential book of all time in the Western World. Tens (if not hundreds) of millions have been saved by the Gospel as presented within its pages.

---

[11] The Pentateuch consists of the first five books of the Bible: Genesis, Exodus, Leviticus, Numbers and Deuteronomy. Scholarship varies widely upon authorship and the timing of when it was written. Tradition holds it was Moses. Liberal scholars believe it was created during the Babylonian captivity circa 600 BCE. The Samaritan Pentateuch requires much more explanation and will be discussed in the chapter dealing with the Septuagint's chronology.

On the other hand, please recognize the fact that the Septuagint was the Bible of *all* Christian Churches for its first four centuries (including later "splinter groups" such as Roman Catholics and the Eastern Orthodox!) In fact, for the Eastern Orthodox, the LXX never stopped being their Bible. And make note that the LXX was quoted 80% of the time by New Testament writers.[12] (The actual number is 90% if we include those passages where the LXX and MT agree.) So, we should hold the Septuagint in the highest regard – perhaps seeing it superior to the KJV's Old Testament.[13] And, generally speaking, even Jewish scholars judge it a more precise rendering of the original Hebrew Vorlage.[14]

This matters a great deal, for once we have established the foundation for the correct chronology of the Bible, we are better equipped to engage in dialogues with modern critics who challenge the Bible's historical accuracy and overall veracity. Furthermore, we can better align biblical chronology with the accepted findings of countless archeological discoveries in

---

[12] This comment should be clarified. The Vorlage, the Hebrew Text behind the Septuagint translation, is included in this statement. Matthew, for instance, cites a Hebrew source that corresponds to the Septuagint version, indicating that it was the Vorlage text being cited, not the version of the text that became the Masoretic Text.

[13] Be mindful, the KJV's New Testament does not have the same problem – for the KJV cites the original Greek New Testament, and the Old Testament verses cited by the New Testament writers follow the Septuagint nine out ten times. And the rabbis did not have the means or opportunity to corrupt the Old Testament as quoted by authors of the New. Happily.

[14] Notwithstanding, there were challenges the original translators faced migrating Hebrew idioms into "good Greek." A small example, "God is our Rock" could give an impression to Greeks that God was in a rock. No doubt, ancient Hebrew gave the *Hebrew-to-Greek* translators some real challenges.

Mesopotamia, Egypt, Israel, and elsewhere. Finally, we can intelligently consider other theories about "pre-history,"[15] those alternate views of human origins popular in today's world that date to 10,000 B.C. We introduce this controversial topic next.

Alternative History and the Origin of Homo Sapiens

Depending upon what we believe about the possibility we aren't the first highly advanced civilization on this blue globe – the *third rock from the sun* – we need to consider artifacts from *pre-history* with more than a little respect. Admittedly, pop-archeology is trumped up and commercially exploited to ridiculous lengths. Furthermore, and unfortunately, it is wedded to extensive speculation about *extraterrestrials*. Additionally, it's important to acknowledge that the marriage of aliens and the myths of antiquity offer a dangerous and deceptive alternative to conventional Theism. My pejorative epithet for this modern religion is, "The Gospel According to ET." This myth replaces the god of Christians and Jews with *creator* spacemen named Enlil and Enki, hailing from Planet X (aka Nibiru, as put forth by the late author Zecharia Sitchin). Are Enlil and Enki more believable as ancient gods who made us what we are today? Despite the widely touted views presented on TV by "ancient astronaut theorists," the artifacts fall short of proving ETs exists – and even less, that they merit our worship. These ETs, with few exceptions, seek no disciples.[16]

---

[15] Although we will not spend time on semi-deified spacemen as the cause of these "effects." (See the author's book, *Lying Wonders of the Red Planet: Exposing the Lie of Ancient Aliens*, for an exposé on what's wrong with this particularly pesky new myth for denying the Biblical account of the LORD God's creation of heaven and earth.)

[16] See the website presenting the work of Dr. Michael S. Heiser on this topic, Sitchin is Wrong (http://www.sitchiniswrong.com). Additionally, I should

More to the point, the physical (shall we say terrestrial?) findings of respected scientists who literally get their hands dirty, don't necessarily seek to replace the God of Heaven with "extraterrestrials from the stars." There are numerous incredible discoveries from the recent past which seemingly rewrite what we know about antiquity. Curiously, such discoveries imply startling possibilities which might precede biblical chronology by 3,000 to 5,000 years – even after we replace the conventional chronology based on the Masoretic Text and the work referenced above of Bishop James Ussher – with that derived from the LXX.[17]

As we will see, these surprising findings, assigned by alternate researchers to *pre-history*, don't necessarily conflict with primeval biblical chronology. And yet, if we Christians are to acknowledge their efforts, we must have a theory for how they "fit into" our worldview – without refuting the Bible. This book opens the door to this study. Others must go through it.

Nevertheless, it's significant that a whole lot of digging has been going on since the science of Archeology began. And what's been dug up has radically changed our knowledge of the past. Plus, it has significant implications on the religious

---

comment that there are disciples, like Dr. Steven Greer, who adopt the all-too-common view, that ET is our friend, seeking our good, and the advancement of all. This is an optimistic based on selected research, mostly ignoring "abductions."

[17] Ussher's chronology is the backbone of the argument advanced in prophetic circles frequented by this author that the world is 6,000 years old, that Christ will return and reign in the seventh millennium (hence, any day now!) This chronology will be discussed in depth later. The chronology developed from the Septuagint will add a significant additional timespan, solving several thorny timing issues in the process arising from inconsistencies within the MT upon which Ussher (and many other Evangelical chronologies) have been based.

texts to which we ascribe sacred status. Archeology, i.e., digging up the past, offers empirical evidence to confirm what texts from antiquity tell us.[18] When conflicts often arise, it isn't that the science is wrong although that is indeed possible. More of the time, the conflict arises because we haven't understood what the Bible tells us about its historical context.

Consequently, discovering ancient artifacts is a valuable business. And unless we are inclined to dismiss such findings out of hand due to one of the reasons highlighted at the outset of this introduction, Christian scholarship must reconcile these discoveries with the biblical record. For this author strongly believes that we must dialogue with our culture. We must earnestly contend for the faith. (Jude 3) To be sure, this apologetic emphasis comprises yet another reason behind the writing of this book. For we all are to do the work of an apologist, in our own way, with those we meet and know. *"Be prepared to give a reason for the hope that is within you."* (1 Peter 3:15, paraphrased)

Archeology's First Archeologist

Ironically, Archeology's story starts with Babylon's last king, Nabonidus (556 BCE to 539 BCE), who commenced a program to repair the ancient temples in Mesopotamia. Nabonidus wished to identify with past Babylonian glories (just as Saddam Hussein did with his Muslim hero from the time of the Crusades, Saladin).

I said *ironically*, so let me explain. First, Nabonidus's son was Belshazzar. Yes, that Belshazzar, who toasted his guests

---

[18] This is not to miss the point that most archeologists, while they do not adopt ancient astronaut theory, are hardly inclined to let biblical texts guide their interpretation of what has been discovered.

with the chalices from Solomon's Temple destroyed a few decades earlier by his ancestor Nebuchadnezzar.[19] His crassness so upset the LORD we worship, that Belshazzar and his party guests witnessed some *supernatural* graffiti, i.e., the "handwriting on the wall." As if that wasn't enough entertainment for the evening, the host's knees knocked loudly. And then (so Daniel recounts) Belshazzar soiled his britches from sheer terror.

But back to the father, Nabonidus of Babylon, humanity's first archeologist. Nabonidus was co-regent with his son Belshazzar. For many years, unbelievers criticized the biblical account claiming that Belshazzar (of whom Daniel writes) did not exist in historical records. However, eventually, the situation of the tandem kings was uncovered – thanks to archeologists. It turned out that the party host was king too. He was one-half of the father-son duo responsible for the downfall of the Neo-Babylonian Empire. How so? Nabonidus was away from Babylon when the Medes and Persians (aka the Achaemenid Empire) snuck under Babylon's city walls which crossed over the Euphrates. While the banquet boomed throughout Babylon and the band played on (with whatever instruments were common to Babylonians), the Media-Persian king, Cyrus the Great, conquered Nabonidus' empire *without firing a shot*. (Excuse my stylistic anachronism – *without shooting an arrow*.) It seems Nabonidus was always away from home. He was searching for some new artifact that could further enhance his commitment to philanthropy for history's sake. But this time his absence cost him dearly. In this instance, his trekking about as the world's first archeologist (satiating his search for historical artifacts "between the two rivers" of the Tigris and Euphrates,

---

[19] The Temple treasure and the vessels used in the Temple were brought to Babylon by Nebuchadnezzar when he destroyed Solomon's Temple in 586 BCE.

i.e., the meaning of *Mesopotamia*), proved ill-advised and horribly timed. One could point out that, as so many parents learn when they leave home without adult supervision, kids throw wild parties. And Belshazzar holds the record for achieving the most disastrous consequence ever for turning his father's residence into an unauthorized and tragic bash for his friends.

Consequently, we must put into proper perspective all modern-day searches into antiquity. And here's how: We begin with what the Bible says. Then we put new discoveries into a biblical context. And we should eagerly do so, for if empirical data merits our paying attention, it could strengthen what we believe about biblical history and open our minds to other convincing reasons to have confidence (while growing wiser, to boot). In so doing, we build an apologetic that might interest unbelieving scientists and researchers outside the biblical fold, to rethink the Bible's message and embrace Jesus Christ as Savior. Then, many other skeptics might find faith.

Going One Step Beyond

Gobekli Tepe in Turkey purportedly dates to 10,000 B.C. The pyramids and the Sphinx at Giza, although dated by establishment Egyptologists to the early dynastic period of Egypt – ca. 2850 to 2750 B.C. – offer strong evidence that they were constructed long before The Great Flood of Noah, *perhaps dating to the same timeframe as Gobekli Tepe*. Plus, we read at least a half-dozen times a year, that yet another pyramid has been discovered in a faraway place with a strange sounding name,[20] sometimes more substantial than the Giza pyramids. Their purpose

---

[20] Lyrics from an old song, covered by Sam Cooke: "Faraway places with strange sounding names – Faraway over the sea – Those faraway places with strange sounding names – Are calling, calling me."

still escapes those who study monuments, since they mutter the ludicrous explanation that these are mere Pharaonic tombs.

Just think. All that work for a place to bury a body. Even the Pharaoh's mummy. And then we learn that "The body is missing." Say what? No mummy? No sarcophagus? A reasonable person from any age (but apparently not a Ph.D. in ours), would say that providing an innocuous reason such as that for the pyramids is incredulous if not idiotic. There must be a whole lot more to it than a place to bury a dead king. Offering such a weak rationale for doing impossible work way beyond our means today, smacks as a lack of imagination.

The real "Pyramidiots," so-called, are those scholars who hold to that inane viewpoint. This epithet is hardly deserved by Graham Hancock or Robert Bauval who have been disgraced by orthodox academics employing this moniker, jealous they aren't selling boatloads of books like Hancock and Bauval. [21]

So, if not a tomb, what function did the builders of the Giza Pyramids intend? In short, the purpose of both monument complexes appears to embody acquired knowledge that has been set in stone, meant to last through any cataclysm, so that survivors down the line wouldn't have to learn everything all over again, the hard way. In effect, these remarkable edifices were the world's most elaborate time capsules.

You may recall that Gobekli Tepe after it was built, was *buried* in a dirt hill (called a *tell* – also spelled *tel* – from Aramaic meaning *mound*), to both hide and protect it for millennia. This strategy seems to have worked perfectly. It had remained hidden for 12,000 years if the age assigned to the site (by orthodox

---

[21] These are perhaps the two most well-known "alternative" researcher/writers who have contradicted established academia, but which we will consider as serious possibilities. The epithet "Pyramidiots" was coined to be directed at them.

academia) is correct. The only problem is, once again, scientists haven't yet figured out precisely what the "knowledge transfer" was that the creators of Gobekli Tepe had in mind when transmitting it to future generations of, presumably, other humanoids.[22] Perhaps this knowledge was being passed down from one civilization to the next in anticipation that the destruction of the originator's culture was imminent. This apparent impending cataclysm hitting (no pun intended) at the end of the *Pleistocene period* is all the rage in alternate history books today.[23] And deservedly so I might add.

However, this semi-benign rationale doesn't satisfy another alternative historian, Joseph P. Farrell, one of my personal favorites, who argues the Giza site resembles a military array with the oldest and grandest Pyramid of Giza serving as a weapon of mass destruction created by a not so friendly "high civilization" an eon ago.[24] Its purpose: To target objects in space; perhaps celestial bodies like planets! Absurd? Maybe. Astonishingly, when many more facts are known, it just might supplement the story of the Bible and our universe.

We also know today that scores of megalithic cities lie under hundreds of feet of water just offshore in India, the Mediterranean, in Japan, and in the Caribbean near Cuba. As I awoke today, another ancient submerged city was

---

[22] Which was likely not the created sons of God, beginning with Adam, who possessed a spirit which could commune with God.

[23] See Graham Hancock's *Fingerprints of the Gods* and *Magicians of the Gods*; Brien Forester's *Aftershock: The Ancient Cataclysm that Erased Human History*; and Brian M. Fagan's *The Seventy Great Mysteries of the Ancient World: Unlocking the Secrets of Past Civilizations*, to name but a few. We will discuss these books and others later. The Pleistocene period supposedly lasted from 2.6 million years ago to just 11,700 years ago, right when the calamity appears to have occurred.

[24] Farrell, Joseph P. *The Giza Death Star*, Adventures Unlimited Press, 2001.

purportedly discovered off the coast of Portugal (April 28, 2018). Evidence mounts that the cradle of civilization we call the Fertile Crescent in Mesopotamia may not be the genesis of the *first* advanced civilization – *Zep Tepi* ("the first time"), as the ancient Egyptians called it. Additionally, the artifacts archeologists are finding today suggests a "high civilization" existed then, rather than simple-minded megalithic humans still living in caves. This advanced culture (Atlantis?) may have met its untimely demise ca. 10,000 B.C. All of these "mega-megaliths" suggest that the beginnings of civilization may not be in Egypt or Mesopotamia after all.[25] Indeed, the cultures which occupy interest in Archeology today, like Egypt and Sumer, could be in some sense, impoverished remnants – meager legacies – to the grandeur that came before.

It is therefore not out of the question (in my view) that an advanced civilization existed on earth before Adam awoke to find Eve by his side. If so, the quest becomes, for workmen so inclined, *to integrate this possibility into our biblical worldview*. For God is the "first cause" of everything in the universe.[26]

Admittedly, this isn't an easy task. But the proper approach is not to deny these primeval facts could be true just because we don't want to upset the tranquility of our revered belief system. At the same time, I also believe *since there is an additional 1,500 years in biblical history that Ussher didn't grant*, many odd things may have happened during the 2,000 years before Noah entered the Ark. After all, this is the period when the Nephilim walked the earth (Genesis 6:1-4). Many smart, well-informed biblical

---

[25] Mei, Armando. " 36,400 BC: The historical time of the Zep Tepi theory." *Ancient Origins*. Retrieved April 28, 2018, from http://www.ancient-origins.net/ancient-places-africa/36400-bc-historical-time-zep-tepi-theory-002617.

[26] This harkens to the *Cosmological Argument* of Thomas Aquinas.

scholars today believe these giants (aka Rephaim) had a hand or two in the making of these unexplained megalithic structures and in passing technologies down to humanity in defiance of God. The non-canonical *Book of Enoch* says just that. Fallen angels instructed humanity on forbidden techniques of many kinds – from cosmetics to the weapons of war.[27]

Therefore, we will conclude this book wrestling with this superbly provocative subject. Admittedly, we don't know too many facts about this *time before time*. So, any conclusion we draw amounts to some "high octane speculation" as author Joseph P. Farrell colorfully labels it. As we walk through the sequence of events and the evidence provided through Archeology and ancient texts (despite what orthodox academics or alternate-history researchers may opine about humanity's timeline and its ultimate meaning), we who hold

---

[27] Alternate historian, Andrew Collins considers these matters in his study commencing with the Book of Enoch. His book, *From the Ashes of Angels*, discusses a race of beings from the heavens, the arrival at the end of the last ice age, of Fallen Angels – aka Watchers – and their hybrid offspring, the Nephilim. Concerning the "technology transfer" from angels to humans, he writes:

> In between taking advantage of our women, the 200 rebel angels spent their time imparting the heavenly secrets to those who had ears to listen.

> One of their number, a leader named Azazel, is said to have 'taught men to make swords, and knives, and shields, and breastplates, and made known to them the metals (of the earth) and the art of working them', indicating that the Watchers brought the use of metal to mankind. He also instructed them on how they could make 'bracelets' and 'ornaments' and showed them how to use 'antimony', a white brittle metal employed in the arts and medicine. To the women Azazel taught the art of 'beautifying' the eyelids, and the use of 'all kinds of costly stones' and 'coloring tinctures', presupposing that the wearing of make-up and jewelry was unknown before this age. In addition to these crimes, Azazel stood accused of teaching women how to enjoy sexual pleasure and indulge in promiscuity - a blasphemy seen as *'Godlessness'* in the eyes of the Hebrew story-tellers. Other Watchers stood accused of revealing to mortal kind the knowledge of more scientific arts, such as astronomy, the knowledge of the clouds, or meteorology; the 'signs of the earth', presumably geodesy and geography, as well as the 'signs', or passage, of the celestial bodies, such as the sun and moon. Their leader, Shemyaza, is accredited with having taught 'enchantments, and root-cuttings', a reference to the magical arts shunned upon by most orthodox Jews.

Collins, Andrew (1997). *From the Ashes of Angels: The Forbidden Legacy of a Fallen Race.* Retrieved August 11, 2018 from, https://www.bibliotec-apleyades.net/vida_alien/alien_watchers13.htm.

25

the Bible to be God's infallible Word, must give such theories due consideration, while at the same time bringing wild speculations about ETs back down to earth.

"It is the glory of God to conceal a matter; but the honor of kings to search out a matter." (Proverbs 25:20, KJV) In so doing, we hope to reconcile the Bible with bold (but unproven) new theories about ancient civilizations, breathing new life into a combined biblical and natural history. Thus, the unsuspecting unbeliever may find an unexpected path to faith. We should certainly hope so.

"We shall not cease from exploration, and the end of all our exploring will be to arrive where we started and know the place for the first time." *T.S. Elliot*

Chapter One:
THE CREATION OF THE ALEXANDRIAN SEPTUAGINT

Ancient Alexandria – Where Our Story Begins

I T WAS CALLED THE "PEARL OF THE MEDITERRANEAN." FOUNDED IN 334 B.C. BY ALEXANDER THE GREAT, ALEXANDRIA – EGYPT'S MOST VITAL CITY BECAME THE CENTER OF knowledge and learning for the ancient world. Destroyed by fire in 48 B.C. by the armies of Julius Caesar (and possibly Caesar himself when he burned his own ships in Alexandria's bay during the civil war with Pompey),[28] the *library of Alexandria* housed over 500,000 scrolls made of papyrus – created nearby

Figure 1 - The Library of Alexandria

from the reeds of the Nile. Its volumes were sourced from the book markets of cities such as Rhodes and Athens. Supposedly,

---

[28] When the enemy endeavored to cut off his communication by sea, he was forced to divert that danger by setting fire to his own ships, which, after burning the docks, thence spread on and destroyed the great library. – Plutarch (40 – 120 A.D.) from his Life of Caesar.

ships that sailed into the Alexandrian harbor were ordered to deliver their books (scrolls or codices) for copying at the library – one of its essential functions. Legend has it that Mark Anthony gave Cleopatra over 200,000 manuscripts from Pergamum. (Cleopatra and my wife don't have this in common; that is, appreciating books as gifts. I learned long ago such presents are not something that my wife much enjoys – too impersonal – she prefers jewelry. I can't blame her. But I like books.).

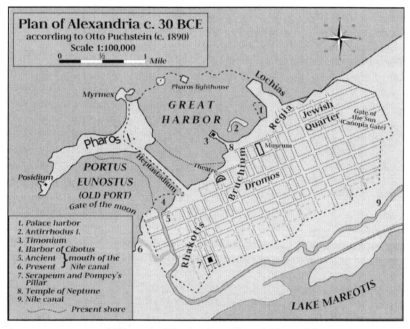

Figure 2 - The Ancient City of Alexandria

The great minds of the ancient world studied there including Euclid, Archimedes, Eratosthenes, and Aristarchus of Samos. The library consisted of many rooms, a courtyard, lectures halls, and even a zoo for exotic animals. Ever since its creation, the library and its grounds became the prototype for for universities and their campuses everywhere. One other thought: Given the intelligence that studied there, the entrance exam must have been a lollapalooza.

The quest for knowledge of antiquity became the mission of one of four generals under Alexander the Great, Ptolemy I, aka Soter. His co-regent son, Ptolemy II, *Philadelphus*, ruled the "Greek" North African empire from 283 B.C. to 246 B.C. The library project was organized by Demetrius of Phaleron, a student of Aristotle, who lost favor with Philadelphus (due to some ill-advised palace intrigue) and was banished to the desert where, supposedly, he died of a snake bite two years later. Rumor has it that it was not an accidental death.

Figure 3 - The Lighthouse of Alexandria, Artist Rendering, © Emad Victor Shenouda

One of the seven wonders of the world was the Lighthouse of Alexandria on the island of Pharos. The Lighthouse was 100 meters high (nearly 400 feet). To reach it, one was required to walk across the *Heptastadion*, a giant causeway built by the Ptolemies. The word *Heptastadion* tells us that the causeway was seven *stadia* long (also known as a *mole*, but not a blemish on the skin – or a Mexican food novelty[29]). A *stadia* is 180 meters long. With some quick math, this means the *mole* was three-quarters of a mile or almost 4,130 feet. As we will soon see, this causeway would become a brisk morning walk for some talented people soon to be mentioned.

---

[29] *Mole* comes from the French and is a unit of measurement. It is the root word for *molecule*.

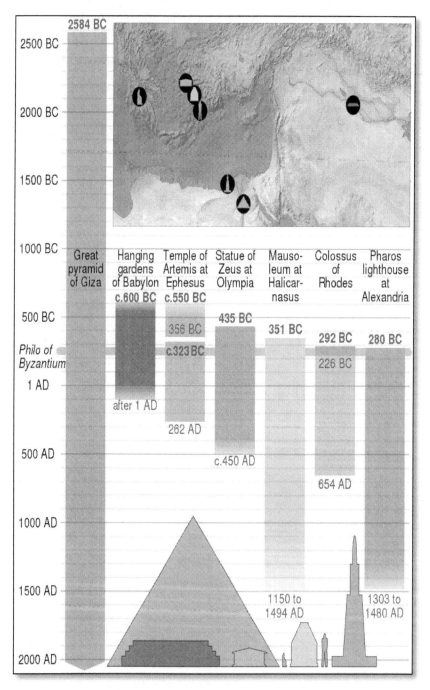

Figure 4 - The Seven Ancient Wonders of the World © Nicolas M. Perrault

A quick aside. The lighthouse was one of the "Seven Ancient Wonders of the World." Other than the Giza Pyramid which is still with us today (*extant* as the scholars say), the Lighthouse of Alexandria despite suffering significant damage from earthquakes throughout its lifetime of almost 1,800 years (280 B.C. to 1480 A.D.), constituted one of the longest lasting of the seven ancient wonders. The price tag for this project came in at a total cost of 800 talents, approximately 60,000 lbs. or 960,000 ounces of gold. With the gold spot price averaging $1,300/oz. from 2009 to 2018, that would be a price tag of $1.248 billion in US dollars. For comparative purposes, the latest aircraft carrier in our Navy's fleet (USS Gerald R. Ford), costs about 10 times this amount, just under $13 billion).[30]

Alexandria would be foundational to the Greek Orthodox Church and the Coptic Christians of Egypt. Armed with these facts, we can move on to how the Septuagint was created in Alexandria and why it would become so crucial for the next 600 years once Christianity gained its footing in the ancient world. (Incidentally, Julius Caesar recounted how holding the Lighthouse and the Isle of Pharos was the key to defeating Pompey in 48 B.C. Pompey, who had conquered Jerusalem for the Romans in 63 B.C. would be assassinated soon after his defeat at the hands of Caesar.[31]) Of course, Julius himself would meet the same fate at the hands of Senator Brutus and a few others.

---

[30] For a more in-depth study of the topics mentioned here, please see Wikipedia articles on *Alexandria, The Lighthouse of Alexandria, the Library of Alexandria, and the Heptastadion of Alexandria*, from which this author drew most of these fun facts for the reader's edification.

[31] Pompey the Great (106 – 48 B.C.) is an important figure in the history of Judah. Pompey's conquest of Judea and the taking of the Temple was discussed extensively by Josephus. When the Temple was defiled by his soldiers who

How the Septuagint Got Its Start

Like all major projects, it took money to make it happen. Happily, Ptolemy II – Philadelphus, apparently talked his father, Ptolemy I – Soter, into obtaining a copy of the Hebrew Bible for the great Library in Alexandria. This was likely the idea of Demetrius of Phaleron (not long before he was sent into desert regions of Egypt). After all, the Law of Moses was an item even for those that weren't committed to Yahweh but were committed to learning. And since Moses was once Egypt's favorite son, at least for a short time, it seemed only right that the scrolls of the Jewish scripture should be copied and included in the library. But how did this happen? There is the famous *grand legend,* and then, there is the more likely *truth about what happened.* We will discuss both.

The legend is built around a controversial document in its own right, the *Letter of Aristeas.* [32] As the story goes, Aristeas provided an account of the miraculous creation by 72 scribes from Jerusalem who were invited to come to Alexandria and create a Greek version of the Hebrew Bible. Supposedly, 72 scribes came bringing a sacred copy of the authetic and complete original of the scrolls of the Pentateuch (the first five books of the Bible) possibly assembled by Ezra and Nehemiah.

---

attacked the Temple area unhindered by the Jews since it was their Sabbath, Pompey attempted to make amends by having the priests of the Temple purify it afterwards and bring offerings to God. Then, Pompey put Hyrcanus II back in charge as High Priest. Aristobulus II had been a nuisance to Pompey. He would eventually be assassinated in Rome in 50 B.C. by Pompey's agents. The rule of the Hasmonean Dynasty would continue but now in Roman hands. Judea had been a semi-independent state within what was called *Syria* by the Romans. About 26 years later, King Herod, of New Testament fame, would overthrow the Hasmoneans in 37 B.C. See https://en.wikipedia.org/wiki/Hasmonean_dynasty.

[32] See Appendix 2, The Letter of Aristeas, for a shortened version of the letter providing highlights as summarized here.

These scrolls were purportedly written in gold letters. According to Aristeas (in his aforementioned letter addressed to his brother Philocrates), these 72 were dispatched from Eleazer the High Priest, to Ptolemy I. The contingent comprised six scribes from each of the twelve tribes; that is, representing all 12 original Hebrew tribes. (This is alledged to be true even though most of the tribes had already been scattered during the Assyrian War of 721 B.C. by Shalmaneser V.) As the reader may recall, the northern ten tribes were removed from Israel, either being killed, resettled, or forcibly scattered. Subsequently, the Northern Kingdom assimilated into other peoples throughout the Assyrian Empire. Peoples originating elsewhere were relocated into "Ephraim" (the land of Israel) to colonize the land. These were the mixed race known as the Samaritans. Whether there were in fact 72 scribes, or only 70, is a matter of some debate. Since the Septuagint is known as the creation of the 70, tradition is more likely correct. Indeed, as the name is *Septuagint*, and the familiar abbreviation is LXX (70 in Roman numerals), we are safe to assume 70 constitutes the correct number.[33]

Upon arrival in Alexandria from Jerusalem, Aristeas tells us the 72 were presented with gifts and a feast lasting several

---

[33] It should be noted that 70 may have been accepted as the final number because it had biblical precedent and spiritual significance. 70 elders went with Moses up into Mount Sinai and 70 elders helped Moses govern the people:

"After this, Moses went up, along with Aaron, Nadab, and Abihu, and the seventy of the elders of Israel; and they saw the place where the God of Israel stood. Under His feet was, as it were, a paved work of sapphire stone and the appearance of heaven's firmament in its purity." (Exodus 24:9-11, LXX)

"So the Lord said to Moses, "Gather to Me seventy men from the elders of Israel, whom you yourself know to be the elders of the people and officers over them; bring them to the tabernacle of testimony, so they may stand there with you. Then I will descend and talk with you there. I will take of the Spirit upon you and put Him upon them; and they shall help you bear the wrath of the people, that you yourself may not bear them alone." (Numbers 24:16-17, LXX)

days. King Ptolemy II Philadelphus quizzed the scribes for a lengthy period about the Hebrew scriptures; afterward, he was satisfied that the work should move forward. When it came time to get down to work, according to one account, the scribes walked every morning across the Heptastadion to Pharos Island. Another story has them working separately in different rooms with little cots (which Justin Martyr states he saw when visiting Alexandria almost 400 years later). After 72 days, they came forth and – miraculously – all had prepared the same translation *with the exact same words, down to the letter!* All were in awe including King Ptolemy. The story is recounted by Philo of Alexandria, Flavius Josephus, and even by St. Augustine. What is perhaps most surprising, given what we will learn later about the *Talmud*, is that it also tells of the miraculous translation. From the Talmud, we read:

> King Ptolemy once gathered 72 Elders. He placed them in 72 chambers, each of them in a separate one, without revealing to them why they were summoned. He entered each one's room and said: "Write for me the Torah of Moshe, your teacher." God put it in the heart of each one to translated identically as all the others did.[34]

We believe that this first section, referred to in English as "the Law" was indeed created by 70 scribes although one expert in the Septuagint and the Dead Sea Scrolls, Emanuel Tov, proposes that only the scribes did the work as asserted in another portion of the Talmud.[35] As to timing, there is ample evidence that the Pentateuch of LXX was ready within a year or less after

---

[34] From the *Tractate Megillah*, pages 9a-9b. Included also, fifteen specific unexpected translations made by the scribes translating the Hebrew into Greek.

[35] Tov, Emanuel, "The Septuagint Translation of the Hebrew Bible: Its Nature and Importance for Scholarship," p. 5. See http://accordancefiles1.com/products/introlxx1.pdf, p. 1, citing *Soferim* 1.5.

the work began ca. 285 B.C.[36] Upon completion, the work was reviewed by the King, the Library, and the Jewish inhabitants of Alexandria. It received rave reviews. The Jews of Alexandria could hardly have been more approving, now having their scripture in the only language they knew – Greek. Poor Demetrius of Phaleron, the project organizer and possibly the lead librarian (or curator) at Alexandria, was nowhere to be found. He would not witness the completion of the LXX as he never returned from his mandated time off in the desert.

Figure 5 – The Bubastite Portal of Shishak (or Shesanq) at Karnak. The wall inscription shows Israelite captive cities including Megiddo. Jerusalem is not mentioned. As we will discuss in Chapter 6, Egyptology's supreme chronological blunder, important to our study, connects directly to this.

---

[36] "The fact may, however, be regarded as certain, that prior to the year 285 B.C. the Septuagint version had been commenced, and that in the reign of Ptolemy Philadelphus, either the books in general or at least an important part of them had been completed." Brenton, Lancelot, *The Septuagint Version of the Old Testament, according to the Vatican Text,* Translated into English (London: Samuel Bagster, 1844). See http://www.bible-researcher.com/brenton1.html. Barry Setterfield, who we will cite numerous times in the pages ahead, indicates that 282 B.C. is the most common date for the completion of the Books of Moses. He derives this date from Josephus' Life of Moses (2.25-44). Many related that 250 B.C. is the accepted timeframe, but 282-285 B.C. has more scholarly support.

Another reason why this copy of the Pentateuch was created in Alexandria was that the Jewish Quarter there was extensive, constituting a significant portion of the city's population. In other words, it was a smart political move by the King. Many Jews called Alexandria home and wanted their Bible. If the King could provide it, he would be loved. From the introduction to his 1844 English translation of the Septuagint, scholar Sir Lancelot Charles Lee Brenton (1807 – 1862) stated,

> Amongst other inhabitants of Alexandria, the number of Jews was considerable: many appear to have settled there even from the first founding of the city (324 B.C.), and it became the residence of many more during the reign of the first Ptolemy. Hence the existence of the sacred books of the Jews would easily become known to the Greek population.[37]

Contemporary scholars Jobes and Silva, in their writing, *Introduction to the Septuagint*, also confirm this fact. "Papyri from Elephantine show an established Jewish community there [in Egypt] as early as 495 B.C.E. After Alexander's conquest of the Persian Empire [331 B.C.], Alexandria became the home to a large Greek-speaking Jewish population."[38]

Intriguingly, H. B. Swete, another scholar of the LXX, in his *Introduction to the Old Testament in Greek* (writing over 100 years ago), proposed that the Jewish population in Egypt may have put their roots down long before the early date Jobes and Silva allow. Swete suggested Israelites may have begun to inhabit Egypt because of the tenth-century war with Shashank (also reputed, wrongly as we will see, by Egyptologists who regard

---

[37] Ibid. para.5.

[38] Jobes, K.H. & Silva, M. *Invitation to the Septuagint*, Baker Academic, 2000. P. 34.

him to be Pharaoh Shoshenq I of the 22nd dynasty). That is, Swete follows convention asserting this figure to be one and the same as the Shishak of 1 Kings 14:25 and 2 Chronicles 12:2, in the tenth century B.C.[39] Swete indicates that the names of captive cities and hostages from Judea appear upon the walls of the temple at Karnak (The Bubastite Portal, as shown in Figure 5).[40] Swete also notes that Isaiah, writing in the eighth century B.C., foresaw a Hebrew influence in Egypt from this fascinating prophecy below, likely referencing the Giza pyramids and a future Egypt that will call upon the name of Yahweh:

> [19] *In that day there will be an altar to the LORD in the midst of the land of Egypt, and a pillar to the LORD at its border.*

> [20] *It will be a sign and a witness to the LORD of hosts in the land of Egypt. When they cry to the LORD because of oppressors, he will send them a savior and defender and deliver them.*

> [21] *And the LORD will make himself known to the Egyptians, and the Egyptians will know the LORD in that day and worship with sacrifice and offering, and they will make vows to the LORD and perform them. (Isaiah 19:19-21), ESV]*

Additionally, Swete makes note that Jewish mercenaries fought in a campaign against Ethiopia by Psammetichus I of Egypt's thirteenth dynasty (c. 650 B.C.) Later, we learn how Alexander, perhaps influenced by the warm reception he received from the High Priest at Jerusalem,[41] was favorable toward the

---

[39] This is the conventional view. We will learn this is the greatest case of mistaken identity in archeology. *Egyptian chronology gets off on the wrong foot due to this fact, a fault that may mean its timing is off by hundreds of years.*

[40] Swete, H.B., *Introduction to the Old Testament in Greek*, p. 13-14. Christian Classics Ethereal Library. 1989. Cambridge University Press, 1914. First Edition, 1900, p. 13-14.

[41] Flavius Josephus, the noted Jewish historian of whom we will make a number of references in our study, offers a colorful but logical story of what

Jews. He saw them as key to marrying East with West (which is entirely accurate). We know Jews in the fourth century B.C. choose to serve in his army. Plus, not only did Alexander make a special place for the Jews in Alexandria, according to Strabo, he granted them full citizenship.[42]

Hebrew Was Dying 200 Years Before Christ's Birth

However, what is seldom understood is, in fact, just how little Hebrew was spoken and written by Jews anywhere in the Greek Empire, let alone the Roman Empire which followed.

---

happened, especially given the fact that Soter, soon to be Ptolemy I living in Alexandria, would have been front and center to witness what happened between Alexander and the Jewish High Priest. Here is a summary of Josephus' account:

[11.330] And when the Phoenicians and the Samarians that followed him thought they should have liberty to plunder the city, and torment the high-priest to death, which the king's [earlier] displeasure fairly promised them, the very reverse of it happened;

[11.331] for Alexander, when he saw the multitude at a distance, in white garments, while the priests stood clothed with fine linen, and the high-priest in purple and scarlet clothing, with his mitre on his head, having the golden plate whereon the name of God was engraved, he approached by himself, and adored that name, and first saluted the high-priest.

[11.332] The Jews also did all together, with one voice, salute Alexander, and encompass him about; whereupon the kings of Syria and the rest were surprised at what Alexander had done and supposed him *disordered in his mind.*

[11.336] And when he (Alexander)... had given the high-priest his right hand, the priests ran along by him, and he came into the city. And when he went up into the temple, he offered sacrifice to God, according to the high-priest's direction, and magnificently treated both the high-priest and the priests.

[11.337] And when the *Book of Daniel* had showed him wherein Daniel declared that one of the Greeks should destroy the empire of the Persians, he supposed that himself was the person intended. And as he was then glad, he dismissed the multitude for the present. [Emphasis mine]

Josephus' full story is fascinating and worthy of review. It can be found at the following address: http://www.livius.org/sources/content/josephus/jewish-antiquities/alexander-the-great-visits-jerusalem/.

[42] Ibid. p. 15. In his introduction, Swete continued to provide extensive commentary on the Jewish presence in Egypt beyond these points.

Indeed, by the time of Jesus, Greek was the *lingua franca* of the world from India to England, even within Judea. In the first century A.D., Hebrew had become the language of only the elite in Jerusalem, the infamous adversaries of Jesus, the Scribes and Pharisees. In Jerusalem, Greek was as common as Aramaic.

While many in our day use Hebrew nomenclature to identify Him, the Messiah was more likely known as Jesus than Joshua/Yeshua. Jesus is the Greek form of the name; Joshua, the Hebrew. Christos was the common title for Messiah, not Mashiach. *Jesus Christos* was how the Church knew Him. And God was known as *Kyrios* (Lord), not *Yahweh* or Jehovah. Why? Because this was how the LXX had it.[43] The LXX, as we will continue to show, was the Bible of the Jews for 300-400 years after the LXX first came into being. As for the Christians, it would endure as its sole Bible for 500 years or more until Jerome's completed Vulgate (created for the Western Church ca. 400 A.D. became fully adopted by the Roman Church. (Recall: Rome governed all Christian churches until the Great Schism of 1054).[44] For the Church in Constantinople (the Eastern Church, now known as the Orthodox Church), the Septuagint remains their Bible to this day. They regard the LXX as inspired through the ongoing stewardship of the Church. *This study will argue only that Protestants should esteem the LXX as frequently the more accurate Jewish scripture despite its translation into Greek.*

---

[43] Due to the so-called Hebrew Roots Movement, many perceive they are more respectful and consistent to the New Testament by using the Hebrew form, Mashiach Yeshua. But *Jesus Christ* would have been closer to how he was spoken of in the first century and thereafter.

[44] Although Rome was the official capital of Christendom, with the Bishop of Rome (later to become the Pope governing the Church), when the Emperor Constantine moved his capital to Byzantium (which later became Constantinople and today, Istanbul) he made it his home and the center of the faith. Thus, Byzantium became the dominant city of the soon to be "Christianized" Roman Empire (officially made so in 380 A.D., through the Edict of Thessalonica).

Regardless, was the LXX truly created by the Jerusalem 70? Lancelot Brenton doesn't necessarily think so, although his final verdict seems ambiguous. He states that despite the various versions of the Aristeas account, "The basis of truth which appears to be under this story seems to be, that it was an Egyptian king who caused the translation to be done, and that it was from the Royal Library at Alexandria that the Hellenistic Jews received the copies which they used." He seems to disagree with those who suppose that the LXX became a dire necessity for the Jewish community in Egypt, leading the Jewish scholars in Alexandria to pool their efforts and create the text. And yet, he downplays the possibility that the project was completed by visiting scholars from the Holy City. After all, such legends are not permitted by academics like Brenton, even though he completed his writing 150 years ago in less skeptical times:

> In examining the version, itself, it bears manifest proof that it was not executed by Jews of Palestine, but by those Egypt: - there are words and expressions which plainly denote its Alexandrian origin: this alone would be a sufficient demonstration that the narrative of Aristeas is a mere fiction. It may also be doubted whether in the year 285 B.C. there were Jews in Palestine who had sufficient intercourse with Greeks to have executed a translation into that language; for it must be borne in mind how recently they had become the subjects of Greek monarchs, and how differently they were situated from the Alexandrians as to the influx of Greek settlers.[45]

Emanuel Tov, a contemporary and highly regarded Jewish scholar of the LXX, disagrees with Brenton's opinion that the translation was purely an Egyptian affair. Admitting that some words might smack of an Alexandrian Greek form like *sabbata*

---

[45] Brenton, op. cit., para. 13.

for the Hebrew *Shabbat* or *shabti* in Aramaic (i.e., Sabbath in English), "Jewish exegesis is visible wherever a special interpretation of the LXX is also known from rabbinic literature."[46] While that may seem obvious, he goes on to assert:

> Such exegesis reveals the Palestinian background of at least some of the translators... The LXX translation was a Jewish venture, created for Jews and probably also for Gentiles. It was used by Jews in their weekly ceremonial reading from Scripture and served as the base for the philosophical-exegetical works of Philo (a contemporary of Jesus), and the historical-exegetical writings of Josephus."[47]

Finishing the Translation of the Greek Bible

While we may believe that the first five books of the Old Testament (and possibly the book of Joshua) were completed as early as 282 B.C., the question arises as to when the rest of the Hebrew Bible was translated, completing the Alexandrian Septuagint (also known as the "Old Greek" (OG)). Swete points out that even Aristeas, as enthusiastic as he was about the sacredness of the LXX, does not mention the rest of the books beyond the Pentateuch. The church fathers, such as Irenaeus or Justin – to name but two – had no misgivings about the quality and veracity of the Septuagint. Only when we come to Jerome (342 – 420 A.D.), just before the beginning of the fifth century A.D., do we see doubt raised about the accuracy of the Greek LXX and its "inferior" quality to the Hebrew version. (We will address the "quality" issue momentarily). Swete states,

> The canon of the Prophets seems to have scarcely reached completion before the High Priesthood of Simon II (219–199

---

[46] Tov, "The Septuagint Translation of the Hebrew Bible," p. 5.

[47] Ibid.

B.C.) [in Jerusalem] If this was so in Palestine, at Alexandria certainly there would be no recognized body of Prophetic writings in the reign of the second Ptolemy [Philadelphus]. The Torah alone was ready for translation, for it was complete, and its position as a collection of sacred books was absolutely secure.[48]

But Swete continues with certainty that the completion of the LXX occurred no later than 132 B.C.[49] His verdict arises from the prologue to the *Book of Sirach* (in the LXX's deuterocanonical[50] books), in which we read that "the Law, the Prophets, and the rest of the books" were already current in a translation.[51] Swete indicates the statement by the author of the *Book of Sirach* vouchsafes the *Hagiographa* had been translated *by 132 B.C.*

Swete supplies more detail evidence for the completion of the *Tanakh* in the second century B.C. He indicates that the scholar Freudenthal had demonstrated a reference to the Greek version of *Chronicles* in the middle of the second century B.C. A footnote in the book of the Greek text of Ester states that the work was brought to Egypt in the fourth year of Ptolemy and Cleopatra[52] (Ptolemy VI Philometor, 186 − 145 B.C.) and was circulating in Alexandria. The Greek, 1 Maccabees, was likely written in the first century B.C. (within 100 years of the

---

[48] Swete, op. cit., p. 28.

[49] This was stated as the writer arriving in Egypt in the 38th year of Euergetes (what was 132 B.C.)

[50] This word means "what comes second" in the canon, meaning "of lesser rank." That would be known as the *Apocrypha* in Catholic Bibles. It is part of the LXX but excluded from Protestant Bibles.

[51] The *Hagiographa* is the third section of the Hebrew Bible (the "Tanakh"). We know it as "the writings." The Jews refer to this as "Ketuvim" (in addition to the Law and Prophets, Torah and Nevi'im," respectively, in their Hebrew form).

[52] In Egypt, the Kings or Pharaoh's were called Ptolemy, while the queens, Cleopatra. So, this Cleopatra is not the troublesome character made famous as the consort to Mark Anthony during the reign of Julius Caesar.

history it records).[53] Swete comments, "On the whole, though the direct evidence is fragmentary, it is probable that before the Christian era Alexandria possessed the whole, or nearly the whole, of the Hebrew Scriptures in a Greek translation."[54]

Once we move into the first half-century A.D., there are many citations of the LXX by *Philo* (contemporary to Jesus' earthly life). As soon as we enter the second portion of the first century AD, the New Testament as well as *Flavius Josephus* demonstrate a liberal use of the LXX. The New Testament undoubtedly uses the Septuagint for 80% of its Old Testament quotations. Thus, the LXX was widely accepted and became the Bible of Christianity, but also it served as the Bible for Jews everywhere including many in Judea.

Evidence from the Dead Sea Scrolls

Then, if we turn to the evidence from various fragments (mostly from the Dead Sea Scrolls – DSS), we obtain physical proof of the "B.C." completion of the LXX. Author and scientist, Barry Setterfield, provides a helpful list of the papyri fragments:

> Fragments of this Greek text include the John Rylands Papyrus 458, which dates from the 2nd century BC, and papyrus Fouad 266 which originated about 100 B.C. In addition, other fragments of this Greek text include 2nd century BC fragments of Leviticus and Deuteronomy (Rahlfs nos. 801, 819, and 957, and (first) century BC fragments of Genesis, Exodus, Leviticus, Numbers, Deuteronomy, and the Minor Prophets (Rahlfs notes: 802, 803, 805, 848, 942, and 943.[55]

---

[53] 1 and 2 Maccabees were written in Greek originally, not Hebrew.

[54] Swete, op. cit. p. 29.

[55] Setterfield, Barry. "The Alexandrian Septuagint History," March 2010, p. 2-3. Retrieved on May 22, 2018

What role do the Dead Sea Scrolls play in validating the Septuagint's use in Judea before Jesus? Martin Abegg, Peter Flint, and Eugene Ulrich recap the assembly and translation of these DSS manuscripts in *The Dead Sea Scrolls Bible*:

> The Dead Sea Scrolls have changed all that. Among the Hebrew manuscripts found at Qumran are what we might call proto-Septuagintal manuscripts; that is, these Hebrew manuscripts are the base texts that were ultimately translated into the Greek Septuagint.
>
> What we learn by comparing the Hebrew base text to the Greek version of the Septuagint is that the translators were very good and faithfully translated the Hebrew text. Why, then, are there differences between the Septuagint and the Masoretic Text? The answer is that the Septuagint is a translation of a slightly different Hebrew text than the Masoretic Text.[56] In a sense, this gives greater authority to the Septuagint. As a great biblical text scholar and editor-in-chief of the Dead Sea Scroll publication team, Emmanuel Tov has remarked, "The Masoretic Text is no longer the center of our textual thinking."
>
> In many cases, *where there's a variation, the text of the Septuagint is to be preferred.* Let's take a couple of outstanding examples. In Deuteronomy 32, the Masoretic Text talks about how God is distributing land to the various nations. According to the Hebrew text in its Masoretic version, God is distributing these lands according to the sons of Israel.[57] This doesn't make much sense because some of the geographical areas are obviously not Israelite and the distribution

---

fromhttp://setterfield.org/Septuagint_History.html. Regarding Rahlfs, this reference is to Alfred Rahlfs, a German scholar, 1865 – 1935, who completed a significant translation of the Septuagint. His notes, known as "sigla" were scribal abbreviations for text clarifications. These are still used. He remains one of the lasting authorities on the Septuagint.

[56] See the following discussion on *vorlage*.

[57] Those familiar with Michael Heiser's, *The Unseen Realm*, will recognize this mistake in the Masoretic Text. The LXX has it right. As we will see in the next chapter, the Masoretic Text was the subject of intentional alteration. This change was probably chosen to emphasize "the Jewish preference" of God.

(was) occurring before there was an Israel. The Septuagint, however, does not read, "according to the sons of Israel" but "according to the sons of God." This makes a lot more sense, but it's not hard to understand that it would be objectionable to the later rabbis. For most scholars, however, the reading of the Septuagint is to be preferred.[58] [Emphasis mine]

Abegg et al., provides an excellent discussion on the Septuagint's importance. These scholars supply five primary reasons:

1. The Septuagint was translated from an earlier form of the Hebrew text than the Masoretic Text (MT). While the LXX may have problems in its translation of the copy of the Hebrew text its translators used [Author's comment: possibly even one generational copy removed from the autographs in such instances as Ezra, Nehemiah, or Zechariah, as there was (sic) only around 200-250 years between these autographs and the LXX]. [59]

2. The Septuagint provides examples of Old Testament books in strikingly different forms in a few cases. Jeremiah in the LXX is 13% shorter than in the MT Jeremiah.

3. The Septuagint is the Hellenistic Bible of the old world before Christianity began. It gives us insights into how the Greek world understood God's revelation through the Scripture.

4. The LXX is the Bible of the early Christians. It supplies insights into how the apostles and the writers of the New Testament understood the meaning of the Old Testament and the next generation of writers (aka the Church Fathers) did exegesis.

5. The Septuagint set the template for the arrangement of the biblical books in the modern Bible. It employed a fourfold

---

[58] Abegg, Martin, Flint, Peter, Ulrich, Eugene. *The Dead Sea Scrolls Bible*. Harper One, 1999.

[59] The rabbis assembled the first official version of the Masoretic text almost 350 years after LXX. In "textual criticism" the older the better. The more time and copies, the greater the probability errors or "comments" by the copyists have crept into the text. We will see this dramatically in the MT later.

arrangement as follows: Pentateuch, Historical Books, Poetical Books, and Prophets. In some cases, the order of the books within these groupings differ, but the essential structure remains. Additionally, the deuterocanonical books contained in some modern Bibles established the so-called Apocrypha which was included in the Catholic Bible and continues in today's Septuagint in the Orthodox Church.[60]

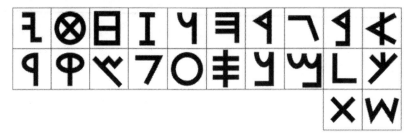

Figure 6 - The Paleo-Hebrew Alphabet
Modern Hebrews' "square characters "are used well before the time of Jesus, but become standard ca. 100 A.D.

The Samaritan Pentateuch

We should reveal another source of evidence here, which comes from the Samaritan Pentateuch (abbreviated by scholars as SP).[61] This version of the Torah was written in the Samaritan alphabet. It is in fact considered an Aramaic alphabet but resembles the old Hebrew characters (known as the proto-Hebrew alphabet, which also resembles the Phoenician, i.e., Canaanite alphabet). The old Hebrew alphabet appears more akin to the Aramaic and today's Arabic than the block letters which came into common use with the rabbinical schools

---

[60] Abegg et al, op. cit., location 190 in Kindle edition. We will repeat this analysis in the next chapter with a slightly different twist.

[61] Recall that the Samaritans were of mixed blood. These were members of the 10 northern tribes that could remain in the Kingdom of Ephraim after the Assyrians defeated Ephraim (Israel) ca. 712 B. C. Over time they intermarried with peoples relocated there by the Assyrians to "colonize" Palestine and resituate the population of other conquered enemies.

beginning at the end of the first century A.D.) It is recognized that it was this "old Hebrew," which the copy of the Temple text utilized, that was brought to Egypt and became the basis for the Septuagint translation.

As to the SP itself: We know this version came into existence when Sanballat left with his followers during his dispute with Nehemiah.[62] Critical to our study: *the chronology in the SP follows the chronology of the LXX and Josephus.*

Emanuel Tov remarks that the LXX originated from a Hebrew text that differed from what wound up being the basis for the Masoretic Text (MT). (This will become an important matter for us to examine later.) Tov says,

> Some of these differences are minor, while others involve a whole paragraph, chapter, or even book. All of these copies contain "Scripture." In our analysis of Hebrew Scripture, we ought to supplement the data of MT with valuable information included in the LXX, some Qumran (DSS) scrolls, and the Samaritan Pentateuch (SP).[63]

Paul D. Wegner notes the SP differs from the MT in approximately six thousand places. Most of these are minor spelling differences or grammatical changes. On the other hand, 1,600 of these differences in the SP (between the SP and the MT) *agree*

---

[62] This story comprises the major plot line of the book of Nehemiah. Sanballat was the Achaemenid (Persian) governor of the region in Palestine within which Jerusalem lay. He challenged Nehemiah, not wanting Jerusalem's walls rebuilt. The dating of this event is established to be late fifth century, perhaps 444 B.C. He built a temple to YHWH on Mount Gerizim (recall Jesus' conversation with "the woman at the well" in John 4), in part because the Jewish priesthood that had migrated to Jerusalem with Ezra was still loyal to Baal. However, he remained Nehemiah's and the returning Jew's enemy.

[63] Tov, "The Septuagint Translation of the Hebrew Bible," p. 14.

with the LXX. Thus, in many instances, the source for one appears to be the source for the other.

Wegner concludes that "The Samaritan Pentateuch is valuable for the study of Old Testament textual criticism since it is a separate tradition from an early period, but its sectarian tendencies must also be considered when dealing with a text that may be affected by those views."[64] In other words, the Samaritans made changes to authenticate their religious views.

The witness of the previously scholar and translator Lancelot Brenton reinforces the same phenomenon:

> In examining the Pentateuch of the Septuagint in connection with the Hebrew text, and with the copies preserved by the Samaritans in their crooked letters, it is remarkable that in very many passages the reading of the Septuagint accord with the Samaritan copies where they differ from the Jewish. We cannot here notice the various theories which have been advanced to account for this accordance of the Septuagint with the Samaritan copies of the Hebrew; indeed, it is not very satisfactory to enter into the details of the subject, because no theory hitherto brought forward explains all the facts or meets all the difficulties.[65]

In other words, the matter can't be resolved as quickly as saying that one's translation's oldest source (known as its *Vorlage[66]*) matches or doesn't match another's. In the instance of the

---

[64] Wegner, Paul D. *The Journey from Texts to Translation*, Baker Academic, (1999), p. 188. The differences will be explored in depth in Chapter 3.

[65] Brenton, op. cit. He fails to consider the work of the Holy Spirit in working through biblical writers, translators, and copyists to preserve the text's meaning. I address the preservation of the biblical text in Appendix 5 of this book. But consider here that it might be *the meaning of the Scripture* which is preserved.

[66] (Wikipedia) "A vorlage, from the German for prototype or template, is a prior version or manifestation of a text under consideration. It may refer to such

LXX and the Samaritan Pentateuch, there are times when the LXX agrees with the Hebrew, but in more cases, it coincides with the SP. Many scholars believe that the first Vorlage of the LXX and the SP were the same. When it comes to the Vorlage for the Masoretic Text which came into its own about 350 years later than the Septuagint, it appears to many experts *that it used a different Vorlage!* Emanuel Tov confirms the same conclusion in his comment:

> In all (the cases reviewed in Jeremiah, Deuteronomy, 1 Kings, Joshua, 1 Samuel), the LXX reflects different editorial stages of Hebrew Scripture from that included in MT (Masoretic Text) and some Qumran (DSS) scrolls in the literary analysis of Scripture. The relatively large number of editorial differences from MT in the LXX should probably be ascribed to the early date of the Hebrew manuscripts from which the translation (of LXX) was made and to their deriving from circles different from the ones embracing MT.[67]

So we are led to conclude there are considerable differences between the LXX and MT. These differences are likely because the LXX used older Hebrew texts (closer to the original) than the MT. (See Figure 15, in the following chapter on page 102).

In a subsequent chapter, we will consider why it appears that the MT, even before the time of Christ, was well on its way

---

a version of a text itself, a particular manuscript of the text, or a more complex manifestation of the text (e.g., a group of copies, or a group of excerpts). Thus, the original-language version of a text which a translator then works into a translation is called the Vorlage of that translation. For example, the Luther Bible is a translation of the Textus Receptus. So, in this case the Textus Receptus is the Vorlage of the Luther Bible." See https://en.wikipedia.org/wiki/Vorlage. (The Textus Receptus will be discussed later. In a few words, it comprises the primary source from which most New Testament versions were created).

[67] Tov, Emanuel. "The Septuagint as a Source for the Literary Analysis of Hebrew Scripture," p. 20. Also included in *Exploring the Origins of the Bible*, Baker Academic, Craig A. Evans and Emanuel Tov, editors, 2008.

to modification by Pharisaic forces to intensify the "sacred separateness" (to coin a phrase) of the Jewish people from the Gentiles (aka "the nations") as well as the Jewish view of God and His revelation. It is the view of this author that the LXX and the SP are indeed based on one or more separate Hebrew *Vorlages* which were the subject of "tweaking" (modification) by the Pharisaic sect. As we will see in the following chapter, this trend would help establish the Rabbinic schools (initially located near Jamnia) at the end of the first century A.D. and on into the second. In part, these academies, as they were called, were created and the text of the Bible altered, to weaken the case for Jesus of Nazareth to be the Christ (i.e., Messiah). Subsequently, the resultant text and the official Jewish canon became the basis for Rabbinic Judaism and would result in the Mishnah and the Talmud. But there's more.

Ironically, this Masoretic Text would one day overturn the Septuagint as the preferred text of the Bible for the Christian Church. There are many reasons (as this book has already presented) that the LXX should, in most cases, receive preeminence over the MT, especially when considering biblical chronology. This stands out as a fantastic part of the story and one that has enormous implications when considering the "Hebraization" of the Christian Bible to the detriment of the Church. This is so since *the Masoretic Text, and not the Septuagint, became the basis for all Protestant Bibles* (a practice this book wishes the Church to reconsider). While it is a literary masterpiece and arguably the most important book ever published in the Western world, the King James Version (KJV) has blemishes. While not a primary contention of this book, suffice it to say here that Protestant scholars seem reluctant *to bring out that there was intentional corruption of the text by Rabbinical Judaism as it began to retaliate against the "Christian takeover" of Judaism.* Although understandable for several reasons we will acknowledge, we should not miss the point: *As the MT Bible grew in its acceptance at the expense of the LXX, our Scripture lost elements which provided a stronger case for Christianity as well as a more accurate chronology of antiquity.* We will present this *evidence* in the next chapter.

Is the LXX a Poor Translation of the Hebrew?

The final topic we will address in this chapter concerns whether the Septuagint should be shunned or at least downplayed because *it is of lesser literary quality than the Masoretic Text.*

The argument goes that the Alexandrian translation amounted to a poor effort, carried out by Hellenistic translators who didn't understand Hebrew well, or by non-Hellenistic Palestinian Jews that weren't up to the task. In the case of the supposed scribes who came to Egypt (as Aristeas contends), the argument asserts that these scribes may have been experts in Hebrew, but when it came to Greek, they didn't understand the language well enough to complete a proper Greek translation. Ergo: Because the Greek is dissed by many scholars as missing the meaning of the Hebrew (both ancient and modern day as we will see), it is seen as a mistake to follow the Septuagint as the primary source for rituals, biblical readings, and doctrine.

Perhaps the earliest statement of doubt about the accuracy of LXX comes from a source we mentioned earlier, the *Prologue to the Son of Sirach*:

> You are invited, therefore, to a reading with goodwill and attention, and to exercise forbearance in cases where we may be thought to be insipid with regard to some expressions that have been the object of great care in rendering, for what was originally expressed in Hebrew does not have the same force when it is in fact rendered in another language. And not only

in this case, but also in the case of the Law itself and the Prophets and the rest of the books the difference is not small when these are expressed in their own language. [Emphasis mine]

Jesus, the son of Sirach who translated his grandfather's work ca. 130 B.C. (which is part of the LXX, *Ben Sira*), tells us that the LXX was virtually complete by his time, but he (coming freshly from Judea), was not enthralled with its translation. It didn't have the same feeling as the Hebrew. As a Jew, his view is understandable, but is it fair? While Ben Sira questioned the LXX based on its accuracy to the Hebrew, Lancelot Brenton (see page 48) offers his criticism because the style of the Greek employed wasn't the same quality as classical Greek.

First, Brenton notes that the LXX was written in the Alexandrian dialect, not the "attic" dialect of Alexander the Great (the dialect of Athens). The loftiness of Homer and other notable Greek writers was absent. The form of Greek used for the LXX was *Koine*, and specifically, the conversational style used in Alexandria. "This Alexandrian dialect is the idiom in which the Septuagint version was made."[68] "In examining the version itself, it bears manifest proof that it was not executed by Jews of Judea, but by those of Egypt – there are words and expressions which plainly denote its Alexandrian origin."[69]

Brenton offers an even more critical comment when he says,

The variety of the translators is proved by the unequal character of the version: some books show that the translators were by no means competent to the task, while others, on the contrary, exhibit on the whole a careful translation. The Pentateuch is considered to be the part of the best executed, while

---

[68] Brenton, Sir Lancelot Charles Lee, "An Historical Account of the Septuagint Version," from *The Septuagint Version of the Old Testament*, according to the Vatican Text, Translated into English (London: Samuel Bagster), 1844.

[69] Ibid.

the book of Isaiah appears to be the worst... It would be, however, too much to say that they translated with dishonest intention; for it cannot be doubted that they wished to express their scriptures truly in Greek, and that their deviations from accuracy may be simply attributed to the incompetency of some of the interpreters, and the tone of mental and spiritual feeling which was common to them all.[70]

Brenton notes that the writers of the New Testament relied heavily on the LXX, but did, on occasion, reference the Hebrew where they must have felt it was more accurate or powerful:

The use, however, which the writers of the New Testament have made of the Septuagint version must always invest it with a peculiar interest; we thus see what honour God may be pleased to put on an honestly-made version, since we find that inspired writers often used such a version, when it was sufficiently near the original to suit the purpose for which it was cited, instead of rendering the Hebrew text *de novo* [afresh] on every occasion.[71]

And finally, Brenton's best left-handed praise for the LXX:

Thus, whatever may be our estimate of the defects found in the Septuagint, its inadequate renderings, its departures from the sense of the Hebrew, its doctrinal deficiencies owing to the limited apprehensions of the translators [Brenton suggests it might be due to these translators having been recently converted from paganism... overlooking that they were Jews] – there is no reason whatever for our neglecting the version, or not being fully alive to its real value and importance.[72]

Why was he so critical? Brenton's comments could arise from an academic perspective or from an arrogant viewpoint.

---

[70] Ibid.

[71] Ibid.

[72] Ibid.

After all, he would not be the first scholar to challenge the Greek of the Bible for being "common" as that, this author believes, was often the method God used to shame the elite. As Paul taught, *"But we preach Christ crucified, unto the Jews a stumbling block, and unto the Greeks foolishness. But unto them which are called, both Jews and Greeks, Christ the power of God, and the wisdom of God."* (I Corinthians 1:23)

The Challenges of Translation 2,400 Years Ago

Now, in contrast to the embarrassment that Brenton apparently felt representing the Septuagint, let's consider the work of a scholar or two who challenge the argument that the LXX is a poor translation and less worthy of use by Christians to derive the truth about antiquity and specifically "Salvation History" (*Heilsgeschichte*).[73]

It must be remembered that when the 70 translated the LXX almost 2,400 years ago, there were virtually no tools that translators use, such as a lexicon. While translation had been done regularly for legal purposes (such as translating contracts and correspondences), converting a significant work such as the Hebrew Bible, was without precedent. The LXX was the first massive translation ever undertaken that we know about. The Library at Alexandria was in the business of storing, copying, and translating documents to fill their institution. Since it was almost destroyed entirely in 48 B.C., we are not a party to what may have been accomplished in the way of earlier larger-scale

---

[73] *Heilsgeschichte* is a German word used by theologians to incapsulate the work of God to redeem humanity. Although English is a Germanic language, we are fortunate that the King's English doesn't resemble German too much. Speaking and spelling such complicated compound German words would be tough.

translations. Indeed, it would be safe to say that translating Hebrew was probably not a regular duty of those employed there.

Secondly, the purpose of the LXX was to provide the Jews of Alexandria a copy of their Bible for practical use in worship, study, and for spiritual discipline. The mission set forth by Ptolemy I to the Library wasn't to create the *Iliad* or *Odyssey*.

Thirdly, the nature of the books of the Bible varies greatly. Some are poetic, some are pure history. It would not and should not be expected that translations appear to be either "freer" or "literal." Any translation requires making idioms of one language mean essentially the same thing in another language. Even in English, if Americans are talking to Brits, the words we use, especially our slang, cannot be translated literally. For instance, in jolly old England, we hear terms like the *lift* (the elevator), the *boot* (a trunk in a car), and many more words that are almost undecipherable unless we have a translator that knows the meaning of the varying expressions. George Bernard Shaw is falsely attributed as having once said, "The English and the Americans: Two great peoples separated by a common language." This quote originated in fact with Oscar Wilde.[74] But we get the point regardless of who said it.

In her academic paper which delves into this subject in considerable detail, "Towards a Comprehensive Explanation for the Stylistic Diversity of the Septuagint Corpus," Marieke

---

[74] From the Quote Investigator: "In 1887 the Irish playwright and wit Oscar Wilde published a short story called "The Canterville Ghost." While describing one of the main characters, the narrator included a comical remark contrasting England and America that was similar to the saying under examination." Indeed, in many respects, she was quite English, and was an excellent example of the fact that we have really everything in common with America nowadays, except, of course, language.

Dhont, at the University of Cambridge, Faculty of Divinity (Ph.D., 2016) delivers an impressive counter-argument to the challenge of the LXX being "bad Greek." From the abstract of her paper we read,

> No two translations within the Septuagint corpus are the same: some texts have been translated "literally," others "freely," some are written in "good," others in "Hebraizing" Greek. Scholars studying the translation technique of the Septuagint have generally been focusing on individual books, or on groups of books that appear to be closely related, such as the Pentateuch or the Minor Prophets. The diverse character of the books in the Septuagint has made it difficult to see these translations as part of a literary corpus in which texts all relate to one another. However, these books all belong broadly to the same context, namely that of Greek-speaking Jews in the Hellenistic era.[75]

To paraphrase, Dhont points out that no two translations in the LXX are exactly the same. Some are more "literal" (word-for-word translation) while others are more "free" (unrestricted in the selection of words used). She explains, "Literalism pertains primarily to following the word order of the source text, quantitative representation, and stereotypical word choices. Freedom tends to be explained as the absence of these features."[76] A translation is considered to be "good" if it isn't slavish to literalism but finds ways to express something that means the same, but literally is not the same. She indicates that scholars throughout the centuries have questioned the peculiar nature of the Greek in the Septuagint translation. Critics

---

[75] Dhont, Marieke. "Towards a Comprehensive Explanation for the Stylistic Diversity of the Septuagint Corpus." See https://www.academia.edu/ 36258376/ Towards_a_Comprehensive_Explanation_for_the_Stylistic_Diversity_of_the_Septuagint_Corpus.

[76] Ibid., p. 1.

have wrongly supposed that writing good Greek meant the translator wasn't hung up on translating a phrase literally, word-for-word. Bad Greek in the LXX would be forcing a phrase to indicate what the words literally mean, even though they don't really convey the same idea. Indeed, the original meaning might be mistaken in a word-for-word translation.

Dhont talks of "interference" from the source language upon the language into which it is being translated. This means that flaws can creep into a translation from a failure to recognize the fact that *the way we say something isn't the right way to say it in another language*. Idioms in non-native languages often fail to be translated properly. For instance, in English, we say "let's go shopping" while in Spanish the phrase is "*ir de compras*" which literally means, "to go of buying." If we heard the sentence, "Tammy and her mom were at the store, to go of buying," we might wonder, "Were Tammy and her mother going to go buying the store or going to go buying something in the store?" Such "interference" in translation would be "bad." If we understood that Tammy and her mom were going shopping for an item of clothing, then no problem. We get the idea because the idiom communicates "slang" *we are used to*. (In fact, ending a sentence with a preposition like I just did, is poor grammar – but it's the way we talk and is acceptable "bad English.")

However, Dhont states that regarding the peculiarity of the LXX Greek, "It has been demonstrated that the language of the [LXX] Pentateuch corresponds to the vernacular [ordinary] language of contemporary non-literary papyri. In that regard, the Greek of the Septuagint is not out of the ordinary and should not be regarded as 'bad' Greek."[77] That is, says Dhont, just because the Greek was usual, "everyday Greek," does not

---

[77] Ibid., p. 2.

make it wrong. That is, it might not be "flowery"or sophisticated in style; but it can still be correct.

Dhont notes that it has been assumed that the LXX is flawed because the translators were still learning Greek. That can't be proven to be true or false. That is like saying that second-generation Chinese growing up in America can't speak impeccable English. As we pointed out earlier in this chapter, it is entirely possible that Greek-speaking Jews had been living in Alexandria for hundreds of years and knew Greek as their mother tongue. It would also be predicted that there would be many Jewish scholars in Alexandria well-versed in Hebrew.

Nor should we assume that becoming competent in any given language means that the cultural norms of those who speak this language natively have been adopted while ancestral or community standards have been forsaken. Asserts Dhont, "The further the translator moves away from the Semitic form, the closer he gets to Greek culture. This line of thought, however, does not reflect the reality of any complex multicultural environment. Jews did not become less Jewish because they had started to speak Greek."[78] Today, English and French Jews continue to keep Passover but not in Hebrew. They are Jewish as well as English or French.

Much of what the translator feels appropriate to translate is in fact based upon what is deemed by the translator to be acceptable by his or her audience. These expectations also are guided by the type of book being translated. A book that is more poetic can be acceptably translated more "freely" while a book devoted to recounting laws must be translated more "rigidly" (or literally). A well-chosen style reflects its contents.

---

[78] Ibid., p. 5. There are those that argue the LXX, because it was written in Greek, absorbed pagan tendencies concerning the nature of the person of God. This theory would make for a good dissertation.

DEEP DIVE:
Formal Equivalence vs. Dynamic Equivalence

In translation, experts speak of two forms: *Dynamic equivalence* and *formal equivalence*. Noting their precise definitions can be helpful to our discussion. An article by Michael Marlowe describes the science of translation by citing Eugene A. Nida, from his book, *Toward a Science of Translating* (1964). Selecting a few pertinent quotes from Nida:

Formal equivalence focuses attention on the message itself, in both form and content. In such a translation one is concerned with such correspondences as poetry to poetry, sentence to sentence, and concept to concept. Viewed from this formal orientation, one is concerned that the message in the receptor language should match as closely as possible the different elements in the source language. This means, for example, that the message in the receptor culture is constantly compared with the message in the source culture to determine standards of accuracy and correctness...

A translation of dynamic equivalence aims at complete naturalness of expression and tries to relate the receptor to modes of behavior relevant within the context of his own culture; it does not insist that he understand the cultural patterns of the source-language context in order to comprehend the message. Of course, there are varying degrees of such dynamic-equivalence translations. One of the modern English translations which, perhaps more than any other, seeks for equivalent effect is J.B. Phillips' rendering of the New Testament. In Romans 16:16 he quite naturally translates "greet one another with a holy kiss" as "give one another a hearty handshake all around."[79]

Nida indicates that over the past half-century, dynamic equivalence is becoming the preferred method of translation.

---

[79] Marlowe, Michael. "Dynamic Equivalence Defined." Bible Researcher. July 2009. Citing Nida, Eugene A. *Toward a Science of Translating.* Leiden: E.J. Brill, 1964. Retrieved from http://www.bible-researcher.com/nida1.html.

Furthermore, the *freestyle* versus *literal style* cannot be accounted for by *assuming some books are more authoritative than others*. Dhont points out: "Contemporary translation studies have shown that translating is a socio-cultural activity. This implies that translators have to deal with culture-bound constraints – that is, notions regarding what a translation should (not) be and/or could (not) be, known as norms…" and she adds, "any given rendering is the result of a plethora of factors that influenced the translator's choices."[80] Dhont asserts that the analysis of the translation process essentially counters the "wisdom" of a scholar like Brenton (who is hardly alone) when he criticizes the quality of the LXX's Greek or its faithfulness to the Hebrew based upon unprovable prejudicial premises from which his (dated) criticism sprang. Additionally, Dhont suggests "increased attention to Greek usage and style within Jewish compositions could have motivated Jewish translators to distance themselves from formal representation of the Semitic source text." Remember, cultural norms change over time – the LXX was translated over a 100-to-150-year timeframe. Consider how much language norms have changed in America from the time of World War II until today. This is not only true regarding the language used on the street, it is also true when composing legal briefs, contracts, prose, and poems. The Septuagint comprises a translation undertaken by many distinct persons, many types of material, and a process lasting over a century – dedicated to one particular locale. It is no wonder the text does not meet the standards of Greek and Hebrew scholars looking back 2,400 years ago, who critique the nature of its style as if the purpose of the Scripture was identical to the meaning

---

[80] Ibid. p. 8.

of an epic like *The Odyssey* – composed by one author over a portion of a single lifetime.

The point of this analysis is not to uphold the Septuagint as an authoritative source to be followed exclusively instead of the Masoretic Text. No, the end sought is to properly appreciate the nature of God's revelation to us in its earliest forms. Thus, we should take into account the history of the Bible including the LXX. Textual criticism, when it is performed correctly, secures the best opportunity to "get it right."

Textual criticism is the *human side* of the "preservation of the text." Just as the LORD God chose to convey His Word initially through inspired writers of the Holy Bible, He also preserves His text, in part, through the science of textual criticism. Like its first penning, the Bible uses human agents in the process. This is what Yahweh strongly prefers. After all, He is about the process of growing us into His glorious image – and this requires our participation.

"And we all, with unveiled face, beholding the glory of the Lord, are being transformed into the same image from one degree of glory to another. For this comes from the Lord who is the Spirit." (2 Corinthians 3:18, ESV) [81]

So, is the Septuagint the Word of God? Of course. There is no rule that the Word of God lies solely within the Septuagint or the Masoretic Text. That the New Testament writers relied principally on the LXX should be case enough for that to be so. Since it was composed almost 250 to 400 years before the MT

---

[81] For an extensive study on the transformation of humanity into our glorfied state, see the author's book, *The Revealing: Unlocking Hidden Truths On the Glory of God's Children*, co-written with Gary Huffman, Oklahoma City, Faith Happens Books, LLC.

was officially established by Judea's rabbinic academies ca. 100 A.D., only adds force to the argument. That there are three nearly complete Greek codices (*Codex Alexandrinus, Codex Vaticanus,* and *Codex Sinaiticus*) dating between 600-700 years before the single codex used for the Masoretic Text (the *Leningrad Codex – 1008 A.D.*), vouchsafes another critical source.[82] And, as we will see in the next chapter, the MT would become a means to displace the LXX even though the LXX was the more authentic witness to the Word of God as originally inspired. The Septuagint would be subject to no less than two significant plots (one Jewish and one Christian) to weaken Christianity's argument that Jesus was the real, long-awaited Messiah of the Jews (unto whom the Gentiles would be drawn as well). These plots threatened the truth of humanity's redemption and the timing of profound events in our history. *This partially successful plot has, up until now, corrupted popular awareness of true biblical chronology.* We will address the Jewish conspiracy in the next chapter and the Christian scheme in successive sections that follow. In our quest to know how God spoke through the

---

[82] From https://www.gotquestions.org/Codex-Sinaiticus-Vaticanus.html, we read, "*Codex Sinaiticus,* was found by Count Tischendorf in 1859 at the Monastery of St Catherine on Mount Sinai. Portions of the manuscript were found in the monastery dump, and a larger portion was presented to Tischendorf by one of the monks. It (comprises) about half of the Old Testament in the Septuagint version and the full New Testament. It has been dated to the *second half of the 4th century* (A.D.) and has been highly valued by Bible scholars in their efforts to reconstruct the original biblical text. Sinaiticus has heavily influenced the translation work of modern Bible versions. Though it is considered by some scholars to represent an original form of the text, it is also recognized as the most heavily corrected early New Testament manuscript. *Codex Vaticanus,* also known as "B," was found in the Vatican library. It is comprised of 759 leaves and has almost all of the Old and New Testaments. It is not known when it arrived at the Vatican, but it was included in a catalog listing in 1475, and it is dated to the *middle of the 4th century* (A.D.)." [Emphasis added]. Alexandrinus is dated between 400-440 A.D. and is in a British library along with Sinaiticus.

biblical authors, the LXX demands our highest respect and a good portion of our study. To discover the truth about the creation, the birth of humanity, the Great Flood, the Exodus, and so on, we must "reboot the Bible." Many of the findings of Archeology can now be much better squared with God's truth.[83] Therefore, we should have the ultimate motivation to search out the Septuagint diligently. To misquote Mulder from X-Files, "The truth is 'in' there." But we must concentrate as we explore the past here, like investigative historians, to find out the real facts. *Time is of the essence.*

Colonel Mark M. Boatner once said that "Truth is hard enough for historians to discover and convey in their writings, but some readers resent their going to the trouble."[84]

No doubt some readers will resent the arguments posed in this book too. But if one speaks truth to be popular, especially in spiritual matters, that one has ignored the history of religion and its prophets.

---

[83] The "facts" are still subject to a never-ending process of research. I do not mean to say that what Archeology or Anthropology hold to be true, actually is. But both are assuredly invaluable pursuits Christians should honor. Rightly conceived and vigorously pursued, they may provide evidence that what the Bible teaches is true. They certainly can be true and often lead us to verify the Bible.

[84] Col. Mark M. Boatner, "The American Revolution: Some Myths, Moot Points & Misconceptions," *American History Illustrated, Vol. III,* #4, July 1968, P. 20. Cited by Gruber, Daniel. *Rabbi Akiba's Messiah: The Origins of Rabbinic Authority* (p. 6). Elijah Publishing. Kindle Edition, p. 3.

Chapter Two:
RABBI AKIBA, THE BAR KOKHBA
REVOLT, & THE LXX ATTACK BEGINS

The Jewish Wars – The First Was Not the Worst

JESUS HAD PREDICTED IT. *"You see all these, do you not? Truly, I say to you, there will not be left here one stone upon another that will not be thrown down."* (MATTHEW 24:2) AND THERE WERE CONSEQUENCES.

The generation of Judeans who rejected Jesus of Nazareth as "the anointed one," i.e., the Messiah, came close to annihilation. Christians through the ages believed their destruction was Godly retribution – for the Jews did not honor *"the day of (their) visitation."* (Luke 19:44) Ancient Jewish prophets also foresaw judgment as the outcome for Messiah's rejection.[85] The day of visitation was a common Hebrew idiom for God's presence to save His people, but more often, *to judge them.*

Most of us know that the siege against Jerusalem lasted three and one-half years, beginning in 66 A.D. and concluding on the 9th of Av, August 30, A.D. 70., the same day of the month as the day Solomon's Temple was destroyed by Nebuchadnezzar in 586 B.C. The Jewish historian Josephus records that over

---

[85] "And what will they do in the day of visitation? for affliction shall come to you from afar: and to whom will ye flee for help?" (Isaiah 10:3, LXX) "The days of visitation are come, the days of recompense are come; Israel shall know it." (Hosea 9:7, KJV. See also Micah 7:4; Jeremiah 11:23; 46:21, 23:12; 51:18.)

1.1 million civilians perished and 97,000 were sold into slavery during *The Great Revolt,* the first Roman-Jewish war.

Few know a curious detail of the story: Josephus was himself an actor in the event. At the order of Vespasian, he attempted to mediate between the Romans and the Zealots, who occupied the Fortress of Antonia on the Temple Mount, (adjacent to the second Temple, i.e., Herod's Temple). Josephus would be unsuccessful and struck by an arrow for his trouble. By the end of July, 70 A.D., the fort fell to the Romans. One month later, the Temple was captured, and the city set ablaze. Soon the fire spread to Herod's Temple. Despite efforts to save the Temple by the Roman general, it was not

Figure 7 - The stones thrown from the fortress of Antonia by the Romans, at the West Wall.

salvaged. Soon, stones were separated to get at the gold which had melted into the cracks between its massive stones. Jesus' prophecy from 38 years prior (like other Jewish prophets who foresaw this outcome 600 years before it occurred), was fulfilled. Not one stone was left upon another. Only the retaining wall of the hill remained.[86] But this war, plus the battle at Masada a short time later, concluded only the first of three Roman – Jewish Wars. And as bad as it was, it was not the worst.

The Second and Third Roman-Jewish Wars

The second war was a shorter affair but almost as deadly, known as *The Kitos War*, 115-117. Its setting varied with points across the Mediterranean. It did not involve the land of Judea to any great extent – only the northern city of Lydda, late in the war was included. This conflict arose at the time when the Roman Emperor Trajan had led his armies into Mesopotamia, successfully pressing a campaign there against the Parthian Empire (aka Arsacid or Persian Empire, 247 B.C. – 224 A.D.) During his campaign near the Persian Gulf, populations of the Jewish diaspora began rioting in several cities around the Empire. The provocation that triggered it may have been a Jewish "poll tax" instituted after The Great Revolt. The Jews slaughtered the Romans at their respective garrisons in Cyprus, Egypt, and Cyrenaica (aka Cyrene, a city in ancient Libya).[87] The Jews were supposedly responsible for killing 460,000 Greeks. We read of this from a summary by the Roman senator/historian, *Dio Cassius:*

> Meanwhile the Jews in the region of Cyrene had put one Andreas at their head and were destroying both the Romans and the Greeks. They would cook their flesh, make belts for themselves of their entrails, anoint themselves with their blood, and

---

[86] A recent argument has been put forth by author, researcher, explorer, Bob Cornuke in his book, *Temple*, that argues the Temple was not adjacent to Antonia, but existed about 500 yards to the south in the area known as "the City of David." This is the same view originally argued by Ernst Martin decades earlier.

[87] Simon the Cyrene, was known as the cross bearer of Christ. Cyrene had been known as the Athens of Africa based upon a school of philosophy founded there by Aristippus, a disciple of Socrates.

wear their skins for clothing. Many they sawed in two, from the head downwards. Others they would give to wild beasts and force still others to fight as gladiators. In all, consequently, two hundred and twenty thousand perished. In Egypt, also, they performed many similar deeds, and in Cyprus under the leadership of Artemio. There, likewise, two hundred and forty thousand perished. For this reason, no Jew may set foot in that land, but even if one of them is driven upon the island by force of the wind, he is put to death. Various persons took part in subduing these Jews, one being Lusius [Quietus, from whom the name *Kitos* is derived], who was sent by Trajan.[88]

Notice the tensions reported in our featured city from the previous chapter, Alexandria. It seems the city experienced a series of pogroms by the Greeks against the sizeable Jewish community there, beginning in 38 B.C. It isn't clear exactly why. Apparently, the former good times there ended abruptly.

But the third war, known as the *Bar Kokhba Revolt*, was a truly massive conflagration that dwarfed the first two Roman – Jewish Wars. And the consequences of these wars reverberate down to our day not only because this firmly established the relocation of the Christian movement away from Jerusalem as its home base (i.e., to Rome, Ephesus, Corinth, and other cities), but also because of what was happening behind the scenes with a rabbi best known as *Akiba* (aka Akiva).

Rabbi Akiba ben Josef would become a leader at the academies near present-day Tel Aviv in a village known as *Yavne* (in the first century – *Javneh*, in the Bible, Jabneh, and in English, **Jamnia**), during the period from 90 A.D. to 136. And, importantly (to be taken up shortly), the fact is that *Rabbi Akiba*

---

[88] *Dio's Rome, Volume 5*, Book 68, para. 32.

would endorse and support the warrior Simeon Bar Kokhba. Akiba's backing included a declaration he was the Messiah. This proclamation comprised a crucial aspect of the unfolding disaster.

Where Rabbinic Judaism Began

Originally, Jamnia had been a Canaanite city founded circa 2000 B.C. It held little import during the two millennia before Christ. However, after the destruction of the Second Temple, Jamnia would become *the center for restructuring Judaism* – to be known as *Rabbinic Judaism*. This new form of Judaism centered on writing down the legendary "Oral Law." This tradition became the crux of the revised Judaism. This project was the *Talmud* (recorded in two flavors, *Palestinian* and the more influential *Babylonian*), whereby the oral law would overtake the written law (Torah) as the dominating influence driving the theology, ritual practice, and culture of the Jewish religion. How important was this new take on Judaism? In a word: *Very.*

Jews today might disagree with this author's summation, but in effect, *Judaism became a distinctive religion, quite different from what it was before.* However, many modern-day Jewish scholars confirm my point of view. The old Judaism emphasized the Temple, the Priesthood, and the written Law of Moses. But instead of emphasizing the words of God in the *Tanakh* (the full Bible – the Law, the Prophets, and the Writings), the emphasis shifted to the *Mishnah* – an oral law supposedly given to Moses on Mount Sinai at the same time as the written law. However, according to the rabbis, this oral law always existed having been secreted away until the end of the first century A.D. – then its greater part was unveiled. Afterward, it was put forth by the emerging rabbinic order.

69

Certainly, the fact the Temple was razed created a crisis. The priesthood, the Scribes, and Sadducees were "history" too. Harry Freedman in his book, *The Talmud: A Biography*, summarized the situation between the Sadducees and the Pharisees with these words:

> The Sadducees had done well under Roman occupation, and many of the ordinary people resented their wealth and privilege. The people found they had much more in common with a group of pious scholars who observed conditions of strict ritual purity, abstaining from forbidden foods and distancing themselves from objects that Moses had declared impure because they carried a taint of death or decay. They called themselves Pharisees, or Separatists. In due course their leaders would go by the title rabbi, or teacher.[89]

Only these Pharisees-cum-rabbis survived. Soon, their prior moniker would fade away. So instead of the emphasizing the Tanakh, as we noted earlier, Rabbinic Judaism henceforth would stress the Mishnah, and later its completion in the massive *Talmud*. It became their primary focus. The rabbis asserted they amounted to nothing more than a mere evolution of Jewish teachers dedicated to their respective flocks. This position understates the truth, however, since the rabbis relaunched Judaism, not in an *evolutionary model, but with an intensified, revolutionary method.*

Shaye Cohen points out that, "at no point in antiquity did the rabbis clearly see themselves either as Pharisees or as the descendants of Pharisees," but the identification was

---

[89] Freedman, Harry. *The Talmud: A Biography.* London: Bloomsbury Publishing Plc., 2014, p 15.

revealed, "for the first time only in an early medieval text, the *scholia* to the Scroll of Fasting."[90]

But I am getting ahead of the story. Retreating to the Bar Kokhba revolt, the largest of the three Jewish Wars, it's how the revolution fits into the story of Rabbi Akiba, and especially *Akiba's attack on the Septuagint*, to which we are most attuned.

Figure 8 - Walls of the Ancient Fortress at Bethar

Simon Bar Kokhba, the Leader of the Pack

Just how grand in scope was the third Roman – Jewish War? It was massive. It would eventually involve 12 Roman Legions, and perhaps as many as 50 auxiliary units, totaling over 60,000

---

[90] Cited by Gruber, Daniel. *Rabbi Akiba's Messiah*. Version 1.3.0. Hanover, NH: Elijah Publishing. Kindle Edition. (2014), p.23. He goes on to explain that the reason the Rabbis wished to be seen as "sages" and "sages of Israel" and not Pharisees was because they did not wish to be labeled a sect like the Christians (at that time) or the Essenes. He says, "Pharisees, which literally means 'separatists,' was the opprobrious epithet hurled by opponents." From Cohen, Shay J.D., "The Significance of Yavneh: Pharisees, Rabbis, and the End of Jewish Sectarianism," *Hebrew Union College Annual 55*, 1984, p. 40.

soldiers plus consorts which, when combined, exceeded 120,000 Roman personnel. The total contingent fighting in Judea equaled *one third of Rome's armies.* The scope of this war was four times larger than the fabled first Jewish War.

Author Daniel Gruber in *Rabbi Akiba's Messiah,* which we will review carefully throughout this chapter and the next, opines the same as this author, documenting the following about the third Roman – Jewish War. Specifically, he writes:

> The Bar Kokhba Revolt against Roman … equaled, or surpassed, these previous two tragedies [Roman – Jewish Wars 1 and 2] in the numbers who were killed, starved to death, or led into exile and slavery. In other ways, the Bar Kokhba Rebellion was a greater tragedy than either the destruction of the First or the Second Temple.[91]

From the standpoint of the Roman military, the specific 12 Legions engaged at different times were the following:

1. Legio III Cyrenaica
2. Legio X Fretensis
3. Legio VI Ferrata
4. Legio III Gallica
5. Legio XXII Deiotariana
6. Legio II Traina
7. Legio X Gemina
8. Legio IX Hispana
9. Legio V Macedonica
10. Legio XI Claudia
11. Legio XII Fulminata
12. Legio IV Flavia Felix

---

[91] Gruber, Daniel. *Rabbi Akiba's Messiah.* Version 1.3.0. Hanover, NH: Elijah Publishing. Kindle Edition. (2014), p.1. Gruber's comment reflects the fact that, after the Third War with Rome, Jews were no longer able to remain in the land, live in Jerusalem, and their land itself would be renamed *Palestine.*

Jewish militia has been estimated at up to 400,000 plus 12,000 more who comprised Bar Kokhba's personal guard. The war led to 580,000 civilian deaths, most of the militiamen, the destruction of 50 fortified towns and 985 razed villages. The Romans also suffered huge losses.[92] At war's end, Jerusalem would be plowed entirely, and the Temple Mount so wholly destroyed, suspicion could arise that Solomon's and Herod's temples never existed at all on their shared location.

Arguably, the Jews became the worst of all Roman subjects, unrelenting in their opposition to Roman law and religion. Jews would be forbidden to live in or near what had been Jerusalem. The city built on its spot would be created by the Romans, for the Romans, and those to whom the Romans allowed to reside there. It was renamed *Aelia Capitolina*. We know that *Aelia* was the first name of Emperor Hadrian, hence it was a tribute to him. After that, the land was called *Palestina* (Palestine) and not Judea. To add insult to injury, Palestina referred to the *Philistines*, the ancient enemies of the Jews. Such is the history whose consequences persist down to our day.

The last stand for Simon Bar Kokhba was at his fort, *Bethar* (also spelled, Betar and Beitar), near Bethlehem. (See Figure 8 picturing the ruins of Bar Kokhba' s stronghold).

Another surprising fact that few know: The destruction of the stronghold and the end of the revolt was on Tisha B'Av – the 9th of Av – *the very same date as the destruction of the two Temples.* And the uprising lasted for three and a half years. This

---

[92] These numbers are from Dio Cassius' history and Talmudic sources as cited in Wikipedia. See https://en.wikipedia.org/wiki/Bar_Kokhba_revolt. If we were to inflate these losses, pro rata, to modern populations, it would amount to over three million Jewish deaths, three times more than America's Civil War.

provides yet another prophetic curiosity, the length of the revolt – 42 months, seems foreshadowed in Daniel and Revelation. This was also the length of the first Roman-Jewish war (not counting the Battle of Masada).

Figure 9 - Bar Kokhba, a watercolor by Arthur Szyk, 1927.
The Arthur Szyk Society, (www.szyk.org)

Samuel Abramsky, in an article on Bar Kokhba within *Encyclopedia Judaica*, contends, "In Jewish tradition, the fall of Bethar was a disaster equal to the destruction of the First and Second Temples." That it fell on the 9th of Av too is astounding. Indeed, this event marked the end of Judea as the Jewish homeland. After that, Jews famously wandered worldwide for a home. This bitter defeat ended the hope of national sovereignty for Israel until 1947-1948, when, under the British Mandate, the United Nations voted to partition Transjordan, carving out land for a new Jewish nation in the region still called Palestine. As this is written in May 2018, 70 years have passed since Israel was officially reestablished. And, though the United Nations seems to challenge Israel unrelentingly today, 70 years ago it seemed eager to placate the Zionists who sought a Jewish homeland. After 1812 years, Israel was reborn.

Gruber relates that the third war with Rome caused the final split between Jews and Christians as well as leading to a Judaism *fundamentally altered in its nature and its religious ethos.* And this event set the path for the brutal, immediate, and continuous persecution of Jews for centuries on end, long after Christians were accepted by the Roman Empire with the coronation of Constantine in 306 A.D. For the record, Constantine lived from 272 to 337 A.D.

The pivotal question is, "Why did Rabbi Akiba support Bar Kokhba?" Gruber cites Franz Rosenzweig (1886 – 1929, a German Jewish Theologian), who stated this same puzzlement with these poignant words, "Why did even the wisest teacher of his age (Akiba) fall for the false messiah, Bar Kokhba, in the time of Hadrian?"[93]

We are told that these two personalities could not have been more at odds. But Gruber's thesis (at the core of our delving into this topic), contends Akiba primarily sought to *disprove Jesus of Nazareth was the Jewish Messiah.* If so, given Akiba was at the heart of founding Rabbinic Judaism, it shines a light

---

[93] *Judaism Despite Christianity*, Edited by Eugen Rosenstock-Huessy, U. of Alabama Press, University, Alabama, 1969, p. 159. Cited by Gruber, op. cit. p. 3.

upon the fundamental premises of "the new Judaism" established early in the second century.[94]

There are almost no standard histories of Akiba or Bar Kokhba and virtually nothing offered by the aforementioned Roman historian Dio Cassio (who wrote over 100 years after the fact). However, there are traditions, both from the Talmud and from the Church Fathers, supporting the idea that Akiba was vital to the rise of Bar Kokhba, by naming him "Son of the Star." (Note: his real name was *Simeon ben Kosevah* – also spelled *ben Kosiba*.) This appellation referenced messianic prophecy, and two prophecies in particular: *"A scepter… shall not depart from Judah "*(Genesis 49:10)[95] and *"A star will come out of Jacob and a scepter arise out of Israel."* (Numbers 24:17) In other words, Akiba named ben Kosevah, "Bar Kokhba" which meant "Messiah." And yet, did Bar Kokhba deserve such a acclamation ?

---

[94] While it may seem a technical point, there was no "standard" or "normative" form of Judaism for decades after the Temple was destroyed. The idea had been put forth by a scholar named G.F. Moore early in the twentieth century, that Rabbinic Judaism was "normative" already in the first century. But other scholars have since demurred. "It is difficult to realize that for fifty years that conception (of Moore's) formed a major obstacle on the study of archaeological data, because the literary evidence produced by 'Normative,' that is, Rabbinic, Judaism seemed to make no room for what archaeologists had revealed. Today I cannot think of a single important scholar of the history of Judaism who conceives Rabbinic Judaism to have been 'normative' in a descriptive, historical sense." Neuser, Jacob. *A Life of Yohanan ben Zakkai*, Ca. 1-80 C.E., *Studia Post-Biblica*, Leiden, 1970, p. 25, quoted in David E. Aune, "Orthodoxy in First Century Judaism? A Response to N. J. McEleny," *JSJ, Vol VII*, No. 1, June 1976, p. 3. Cited here by Gruber, *Rabbi Akiba's Messiah*, p. 23.

[95] This reading of Genesis 49:10 is traditional, from the Masoretic. The LXX actually personifies the meaning much more, pertaining to the man who is to be called Messiah. *"A ruler shall not fail from Judah, nor a prince from his loins, until there come the things **stored up for him**; and **he** is the expectation of nations."* As so the Douay-Rheims Bible which follows the LXX, *"The sceptre shall not be taken away from Judah, nor a ruler from his thigh, till **he comes that is to be sent, and he shall be the expectation of nations.**"*

Gruber cites Israeli scholar Hugo Mantel who concluded, "Simeon Bar Kokhba was merely an heir and disciple of the rebels in the days of the Temple, and the rebels and zealots, in turn, continued to fight for the cause of the Hasmoneans..."[96] In other words, like the Maccabees almost 300 years prior, Bar Kokhba fought for Judean sovereignty. He was not a legitimate candidate for the messiah, although there are hints as to why some may have thought so. And, as we will see later, Akiba's interest in proclaiming Bar Kokhba "Messiah" was to offer up an alternative to Yeshua, as icing on the cake, topping his other efforts to spurn Christian claims about Jesus Christ.

Figure 10 - A Third Temple Built by Bar Kokhba? On his Freedom Coins minted during the early portion of the revolt.

Surprisingly, a few Talmudic references fuel some scholarly debate as to whether Bar Kokhba had a hand in rebuilding a *third Temple* in Jerusalem during the first two years of the revolt (132-33 A.D). Gruber provides several reasons to wonder:

> There are some references in the rabbinic writings to a Bar Kokhba temple. In the Talmudic tractate Ta'anith, we are told, "It has been taught: When Turnus Rufus the wicked destroyed

---

[96] Hugo Mantel, "The Causes of the Bar Kokhba Revolt," *JQR, #3-4*, Philadelphia, 1968, p. 278. Cited by Gruber, op. cit., p. 32, 38.

the Temple, R. Gamaliel was condemned to death." Turnus Rufus was one of Hadrian's officials. Unless Bar Kokhba had rebuilt the Temple, there would not have been one for Turnus Rufus to destroy. It is not, however, necessary for us to know whether Jerusalem was captured, and the Temple rebuilt to determine why Rabbi Akiba proclaimed Bar Kokhba the Messiah. Nor is it necessary to know the immediate cause of the rebellion.[97]

Gruber argues there are so many collateral factors that reveal the motivation of Akiba, and yet we have so little history to justify Bar Kokhba's significance. What remains important is that Judaism's foundation had been thoroughly upset. Said Dio: "Thus, nearly the whole of Judaea was made desolate, an event of which the people had had indications even before the war. The tomb of Solomon, which these men regarded as one of their sacred objects, fell to pieces of itself and collapsed and many wolves and hyenas rushed howling into their cities."[98]

We should also note: The comment of *Maimonides*, aka *Ramban* (1135 – 1204), the most famous Torah scholar in the Middle Ages: "Rabbi Akiva was a great sage, one of the authors of the Mishnah, yet he was the right-hand man of Ben Koziva, the

---

[97] Gruber, op. cit., p. 35. There are conflicting assertions about the whole matter of what Temple, if any, was rebuilt on the Temple Mount. Dio Cassius says the revolt occurred because Hadrian had built a temple to Jupiter on the Mount. Epiphanius (a fourth century bishop in Cyprus) stated that Hadrian had only made up his mind to build a city and name it after himself. Eusebius, the noted Church Historian also writing in the fourth century presents yet a third view: "Hadrian's Year 20 (AD 136) [that] Aelia was founded by Aelius Hadrianus; and before its gate, that of the road by which we go to Bethlehem, he set up an idol of a pig in marble, signifying the subjugation of the Jews to Roman authority." Eusebius, *Chronicon Pascale*, cited in Yadin, op. cit., p. 258. Cited by Gruber, op. cit., p. 37.

[98] Gruber, op. cit., p. 40.

ruler, whom he thought to be King Messiah. He and all the sages of his generation imagined Bar Kokhba to be King Messiah until he was slain, unfortunately. Once he was slain, it dawned on them that he was not [Messiah]."[99] Perhaps having built a third temple, however unimpressive, warring for three and one-half years, and coming to a calamitous end on the 9th of Av, might explain why some thought him the Messiah.

Was Akiba Really Important to Rabbinic Judaism?

The Talmud states that "When R. Akiba died, the glory of Torah ceased." (Sotah 49a). Freedman asserts, "Akiva is the best known and most highly regarded of all the rabbis. Legends and stories about him abound."[100] Louis Ginzberg (1873 – 1953), a conservative Talmudic scholar, wrote in *The Jewish Encyclopedia*, this summary of his importance:

> The greatest tannaim [scholars and teachers] of the middle of the second century came from Akiba's school, notably Meir, Judah ben Ilai, Simeon ben Yohai, Jose ben Halafta, Eleazar ben Shammai, and Nehemiah. Akiba's true genius, however, is shown in his work in the domain of the Halakah; both in his systematization of its traditional material and in its further development... Our Mishnah comes directly from Rabbi Meir, the Tosefta from R. Nehemiah, the Sifra from R. Judah, and the Sifre from R. Simon; but they all took Akiba for a model in their works and followed him." (Sanh. 86a) We are told that, "All are taught according to the views of R. Akiba."[101]

---

[99] Maimonides, Moses. *Mishneh Torah*, (Yad Hazakah), Ed. Philip Birnbaum, Hebrew, New York, 1985, p. 327. Gruber, op. cit., p 50-51.

[100] Freedman, Harry. Op. cit., p. 23.

[101] *The Jewish Encyclopedia, Vol. I*, p. 305-306, citing Jer. Shek. 5:1, 48c. Cited by Gruber, op. cit., p. 57-58.

According to the *Encyclopedia Judaica*, Aquila, one of Akiba's most noteworthy pupils, created a new Greek translation that closely followed Akiba's exegesis. This "Akiba-endorsed" Old Testament became the accepted Old Testament for the Greek-speaking Jewish diaspora, eventually displacing the Alexandrian LXX. This is a strategic point to which we will return. Louis Finkelstein (1895 – 1991), another noted Talmud scholar wrote, "The later Talmudists rated these achievements so high that they declared Akiba had saved the Torah from oblivion. They ranked his work [equal to] the discovery of the Law in the days of Josiah and Ezra."[102] In the Talmud, praise is heaped upon Akiba in many places. One such acclamation pointed out Akiba's persistence in assembling the early *Talmud*:

> To what may Akiba be compared? To a peddler who goes about from farm to farm. Here he obtains wheat, their barley, and in a third place, spelt. When he comes home, he arranges them all in their respective bins. So Akiba went about from scholar to scholar, getting all the traditions he could; and then he proceeded to arrange them in an orderly granary.[103]

Gruber pulls together the most vital points of Akiba's importance, including the title "the father of Rabbinic Judaism." Before Akiba, there were many "Judaisms," but after he finished his work, *there was only one*. While he compiled and edited what went before, "his disciples completed the work with what came later. Their work, the whole Talmud, is a natural extension of the purpose, system, and procedure that he put together."[104] For Gruber, the Talmud is "a declaration of rabbinic authority."

---

[102] Finkelstein, Louis. *Akiba: Scholar, Saint and Martyr*, Atheneum, NY, 1978, p. 156. Cited by Gruber, op. cit., p. 58.

[103] B. Gittin 67a, Abot of R. Nathan 18, 34a. Cited by Gruber. op. cit., p. 57.

[104] Gruber, op. cit., p. 57.

Furthermore, Gruber concludes that "The magnitude of the accomplishments of "the father of rabbinic Judaism" appears poignantly if we ask the simple question, "What is a rabbi? And then compare the answer found in the Tanakh to that found in the Talmud."[105]

Foreshadowing Akiba's lasting influence: His legacy eventually caused the Alexandrian Septuagint to be forsaken by most Christians – both Catholics as well as Protestants. In other words, it would be Akiba's foundational work for the Masoretic Text (MT) that would eventuate in the neglect of the Alexandrian Greek Old Testament for all Western churches. And with this loss, *accurate biblical chronology would be remarkably distorted with its timespan significantly reduced.* From an apologetic standpoint, this constitutes a great tragedy few Christians appreciate.

What Makes a Rabbi a Rabbi?

Akiba's goal was more than to provide a commentary on the Torah. In fact, the Torah would take a back seat to the Talmud. The Talmud was the book that captured all the wisdom of sages and from the Jewish perspective, all the knowledge of the ages. Rabbis now would be seen as scholars and sages. Before the Talmud, Jewish leaders were prophets, priests, and kings. There were the Sanhedrin, the Scribes, and the Sadducees. But the new Judaism no longer needed these positions nor those holding such titles. We see this in the Second Temple texts. Jewish leaders were not called rabbis. Indeed, Philo and Josephus did not use the title. Thus, a new meaning for the word *rabbi* had been invented by the academies in Jamnia.

---

[105] Ibid., p. 57.

After Akiba, the term *rabbi* would be applied to great leaders like Moses and Ezra even though the Torah called them priests (or Levites), and Ezra, a scribe. "Rab" was a designation of a chief, such as Daniel who was the "rab" prefect over all the wise men of Babylon – the Chaldeans. But *rab* was never associated with sages and scholarship. Gruber states we find the word rabbi 150 times in the Tanakh; however, there it can apply to Gentiles as well as Jews. It is attached to the wise men of Persia, Babylon, and Egypt.

> It is also used for skilled artisans of different types, those considered wise in heart or learned in the law of God, whether king or counselor, son or servant. For that matter, Elihu the son of Barachel tells Job, "It is not the rabbim [רבים/'great' or 'many'] that are wise [yekhcamu/יחכמו], nor the aged that discern judgment.[106]

Gruber asserts that there is no place or position for rabbis (as final authorities) in the Bible. They are never mentioned. He cites Stuart Cohen who summarized the situation with these words, "As a group, rabbis were unable to claim a historically sanctioned locus standing within any of the traditional frameworks of Jewish government."[107] Rabbi no longer just meant teacher – it now meant *authority*. The rabbi would become the epicenter for governance. Gruber argues:

> The preeminent role assigned to the Rabbis and to the system that surrounded and supported that role must be attributed to Akiba. Under Akiba's leadership, the Rabbis became an elite revolutionary party which transformed itself from a group of unauthorized outsiders into the holders and/or guardians of all authority in heaven and earth.[108]

---

[106] Gruber, op. cit. p. 63.

[107] Cohen, S.A. p. 151. Cited by Gruber, op. cit., p. 63.
[108] Gruber, op. cit., p. 66.

Figure 11 - A page from the Vilna Edition of the Babylonian Talmud, Tractate Berachot, folio 2a

So, should Rabbis be treated with such high regard? According to the Talmud, the Rabbi is seen as the final authority. "Even God Himself cannot contradict (him)."[109] Gruber collates many other significant aspects of the place of rabbis based upon his extensive research:

- He who marries his daughter to a sage, partners with a scholar, or supplies financial benefit from his estate, "is regarded by Scripture as if he had clung to the divine presence."[110]

- "They sustained life in this world, and their teachings provided the way of entry into the world to come."[111]

- R. Joshua b. Levi said, "Whoever makes derogatory remarks about scholars after their death is cast into Gehinnom."[112]

- "Every man who forgets a single word of his Mishnah what he has learned [from the Rabbis], Scripture accounts it unto him as if he had forfeited his soul."[113]

We learn that not only does the absolute authority and high regard of rabbis alter the nature of Judaism as established by Moses and the Prophets, the written codification and vast expansion of the Oral Law after Akiba became the knowledge rabbis held exclusively to themselves; it was not for the ordinary people because it was complicated and would cause controversy. Recall, 'knowledge is power' (said Francis Bacon). And Oral Law was the hinge upon which Judaism swung, opening the doorway for a new path forward.

---

[109] Ibid. p. 63.

[110] Ket. 111b. Cited by Gruber, op. cit. p. 64.

[111] Ibid., p. 64.

[112] Ber. 47b. Cited by Gruber, op. cit., p. 65.

[113] Ab. 3.9, cf. Men. 99b & Gerhardson, Memory and Manuscript, op. cit., p. 168. Cited by Gruber, p. 66.

The Oral Law, Privileged Knowledge, and Rabbinic Authority

Gruber provides an extensive study into the rabbinic tradition of the Oral Law and *why it does not have the support of the written Torah of the Bible*. Gruber begins this matter with this revealing passage from the Talmud:

> "When Moses ascended on high he found the Holy One, blessed be He, engaged in affixing coronets to the letters. Said Moses, 'Lord of the Universe, 'Who stays Thy hand?' [I.e., 'is there anything wanting in the Torah that these additions are necessary?'] He answered, 'There will arise a man, at the end of many generations, Akiba b. Joseph by name, who will expound upon each tittle heaps and heaps of laws'. 'Lord of the Universe', said Moses; 'permit me to see him'. He replied, 'Turn thee round'. Moses went and sat down behind eight rows (and listened to the discourses upon the law). Not being able to follow their arguments he was ill at ease, but when they came to a certain subject and the disciples said to the master 'Whence do you know it?' and the latter replied 'It is a law given unto Moses at Sinai' he was comforted. Thereupon he returned to the Holy One, blessed be He, and said, 'Lord of the Universe, Thou hast such a man and Thou givest the Torah by me!' He replied, 'Be silent, for such is My decree.'"[114]

We learn here about *halakha* – an elaborate interpretation of Torah. Through it, rabbis may derive an infinite number of interpretations ("heaps and heaps of laws"). *This was something Moses didn't know but would learn from Akiba.* Here also, we learn that Akiba is the originator of Oral Law, not Moses as rabbis today suggest. And Akiba and his disciples weren't interested in Moses' thoughts. In fact, Moses must sit "eight rows

---

[114] Menahoth 29b, p. 190, p. 190n. Cited by Gruber, op cit., p. 87.

back" behind other listeners (i.e., "in the peanut gallery.") Consequently, Moses is inferior to Akiba in Rabbinic Judaism.

Thus, not only is there no regard for Jesus. The respect for Moses is lacking as well. *For it is not Jesus who is seen as the second Moses (cf. Deuteronomy 18:15), it is Akiba!* "Such is the verdict of this Talmudic appreciation of Akiba. But a second Moses meant a *new foundation of Judaism,* for it had been Moses who had first established Israel as a nation."[115] [Emphasis added] Jacob Neusner (1932 – 2016), an ordained Jewish rabbi and professor at Dartmouth with degrees from Hebrew University (Masters) and Columbia (Ph.D.), in his book *Early Rabbinic Judaism,* points out how the halakhas don't need to be grounded by Torah. There need be no relationship to Scripture whatsoever. Indeed, the rabbis can invent laws not justifiably tied to the Bible at all.

> Perhaps the exegetes took for granted that the bed-rock convictions of the laws also were assumed by the Scriptures. But they still have not shown us where in Scripture they locate those laws or principles, and I think the probable explanation is that they could not (and did not care to). That is why they remind us that *Ohalot* [the second tractate of the Order of Tohorot in the Mishnah] has much law but little Scripture.[116]

Gruber adds, "Implicit in the doctrine of a parallel "Oral Law" given at Sinai is the recognition that much of Halakhah cannot be tied to the written Torah in any way at all."[117] Gruber

---

[115] A comment by Ehrhardt on Sanh. 37a. Cited by Gruber, op. cit. p. 87.

[116] Neusner, Jacob. *Early Rabbinic Judaism,* p. 27. Cited by Gruber, op. cit., p. 88.

[117] Neusner, op. cit., p. 27. Cited by Gruber, p. 88.

clarifies that it's not so much that these early rabbis would claim their law is a separate revelation from Moses, but they have authority to forbid what the Torah permits and to permit what the Torah forbids.[118] There is very little here the Bible commends.

So, when did this Oral Law historically commence? Different sages offer various answers to that question. Some say during the time of the Hasmoneans (Kiddushin 66a and Yoma 28b). Others asserted it went all the way back to Abraham before the written Torah was even given to Moses. According to Gruber, R. Nahman ben Isaac, writing several centuries after Jesus Christ, "maintained that only the Pharisees could or would transmit the Oral Torah. No one else would. *It was not in possession of all Israel.* With the destruction of the Pharisees, the world would be desolate, as it was before God gave it form. It would be without the Oral Torah."[119] [Emphasis added]

In other words, by creating a basis for authority, the Pharisees transformed themselves into sages, the rabbis, the "keepers of the Oral Law." Like Priests in other religions, they held private knowledge (think *gnosis* as in *Gnosticism*), that empowered them because *only they knew it.* "The Rabbis made themselves the creators and administrators of an Oral Law claimed to be given to Moses... [However] neither Torah nor Tanakh as a whole, provide any basis for the doctrine of an Oral Law."[120]

Do contemporary rabbis emphasize the place they were given in the *New Judaism* founded in the second century? Not in America. Today's Judaism is not so authoritarian.

---

118 Gruber, op. cit., p. 89.

119 Gruber, op. cit., p. 91.

120 Ibid., p. 96.

Nowadays, rabbis emphasize "Oral Law" as *oral tradition*. Authority *beyond* the synagogue isn't relevant in modern-day politics.

> [Modern] sources all speak in terms of tradition or an "oral tradition." None of them speak of an "Oral Law." We thus have indications that in the time of Josephus and Philo oral transmission was looked upon as the characteristic medium of Pharisaic tradition. Though Josephus and Philo mention Pharisaic tradition, they do not mention an "Oral law."[121]

Figure 12 - Rabbi Akiba

The Jewish experts are certainly aware, however, of the nature of Judaism's new beginnings in the second century A.D. Akiba crafted a new rule for interpretation which he called, "Inclusion and Limitation."

Louis Finkelstein contended, "Akiba was trying to change the complexion of the inherited law. To accomplish this [change] he had to find an authority superior to that of his predecessors and accepted by everyone. Only one instrument could fulfill those requirements – Scripture itself."[122] Still, this

---

[121] Ibid. p 98. Gruber cites three sources for this assertion: Hayim Halevy Donin, *To Be a Jew*, Basic Books, 1991, p. 26. Additionally, J.M. Baumgarten, "The Unwritten Law in the Pre-Rabbinic Period," *JSJ, Vol.III*, Oct. 1972, p. 15. And one quotation by Elman which states the circumstances plainly: "Oral Torah is what the sages of Israel and Keneset Yisra'el innovated by their own perception of heart and mind of the will of God, and that is the understanding that God apportioned to them according to the limits of their capacity." Yaakov Elman, "R. Zadok HaKohen on the History of Halakha," *Tradition: A Journal of Orthodox Jewish Thoughts, Vol. 21*, No. 4, p. 15. Cited by Gruber p. 99.

[122] Finkelstein, "Akiba," op. cit., p. 139. Cited by Gruber, op. cit., p. 103.

linkage was tainted by the fact that the plain meaning of scripture didn't matter. It was just for "optics."

Here is Gruber's summary of Finkelstein's observations regarding Akiba's method of scriptural interpretation– what we would critically label *eisegesis.*

1. Akiba's agenda was "read into" the Bible.
2. The logic and grammar of the text were not significant.
3. Accepted interpretive methods were no longer relevant.
4. And yet, to accomplish his goals, he must tie his agenda and method to scripture "for appearance's sake," i.e., to make it acceptable to those seeing the Bible as the true authority.

Eliezer Berkovits condenses the rabbinic interpretative rule as follows: "Sound reasoning overrules an authoritative text… Because of logical argument, a new meaning was forced upon the biblical text violating its linguistic content."[123] Gruber comments, "What the text actually said was not relevant to the discussion and could no longer be considered." Furthermore, for Akiba, *apart from the words of the sages, Israel could not understand the Torah.*

Thus, Akiba's method put distance between God's Word in the Torah and the people at large. Thus, the rabbi serves in a similar role as a priest in Catholicism, the necessary mediator to *effectuate* the relationship between God and humanity.[124] In other words, rabbis alone could link man to God. Without the rabbi, God and humankind remain separate and apart.

---

[123] Berkovits, Eliezer. *Not in Heaven: The Nature and Function of Halakha,* Ktav Publishing Co., NY, 1983, p. 5, 7. Cited in Gruber, op cit., p. 113.

[124] Ibid., p. 105. These mediators "connect" God with humanity.

It was at Jamnia (Javneh) that the Hebrew canon was settled. It was Akiba who played the pivotal role in fixing the canon, and even the text of Tanakh. "Akiba was the one who definitely fixed the canon of the Old Testament books," said Louis Ginzberg in *The Jewish Encyclopedia*.[125] Akiba put certain books in the canon others might not and withheld some books others preferred not to be included. This should not be surprising given what we've learned. Talmudic Judaism sees Akiba as a lawgiver *greater than Moses!*[126] Settling on which books were canonical and what the text really said, was his prerogative.

Freedman cites Finkelstein who provides this summation of Akiba's importance to Judaism:

> Akiva ranks in depth of intellect, breadth of sympathy and clarity of vision with the foremost personalities of the Hebrew tradition, Moses and Isaiah amongst the prophets, Maimonides, Crescas and Spinoza amongst the philosophers. He dominates the whole scene of Jewish history from the period of the Second Isaiah, about 540 B.C.E. until the rise of the Spanish school of philosophers, about 1100 C.E.[127]

So why should Christians care? *Akiba's position of authority and interpretive method became the basis for his altering Scripture.* You see, if the Bible's wording didn't suit Akiba, he (and his disciples) would merely change it to what would. And, as we will document, these unwanted (and unwarranted) changes eventually found their way into the Protestant Bible's Old Testament.

---

[125] Ginzberg in *The Jewish Encyclopedia*, *Vol. I*, op. cit., p. 305-306, citing Je. Shek. 5:1, 48c. Cited by Gruber, op. cit., p. 109.

[126] Gruber, op. cit., p. 109.

[127] Finkelstein, Louis. *Akiba: Scholar, Saint, and Martyr.* New York: Jason Asronson Inc., 1936, p. ix. Cited by Freedman, op. cit., p. 24.

But Did Akiba Alter the Tanakh?

Gruber states, "Once the canon was fixed, it became possible to endeavor to standardize the text of the different books that were included."[128] Richard Longenecker comments, "Prior to the standardization of the consonantal text at Jamnia there probably existed more versions and recensions of the Old Testament that are now extant, as the discoveries at Qumran [the Dead Sea Scrolls] seem to indicate."[129] Gruber then cites Harry Orlinsky 1908 – 1992), editor-in-chief of The New Jewish Publication Society's translation of the Torah in 1962.

> The rabbinic literature itself, in quotations from the Bible, exhibits more frequently than is generally realized, readings that differ from those preserved in our so-called 'Masoretic' texts, readings that are not due to faulty memory and that crop up in Hebrew manuscript… The standardization of the text, to whatever extent that occurred, offered an opportunity for those doing the "standardizing" to choose those variations which were most in accord with their own beliefs.[130]

As we related in chapter one, Greek was the standard language of Jews in the Diaspora. Far more Jews spoke Greek than Hebrew. Indeed, outside of Judea, other than a few elites and scholars, no one understood Hebrew. According to Paul Davis, "Greek terms were used to designate such essentially Jewish institutions as the *Sanhedrin*, and it has been claimed that more

---

[128] Ibid., p. 109.

[129] Longenecker, Richard N. *Biblical Exegesis in the Apostolic Period*, Eerdmans, Grand Rapids, 1975, p. 143. Cited by Gruber, op. cit., p.110.

[130] Orlinsky, Harry. "The Masoretic Text: A Critical Evaluation," from *The Canon and Masorah of the Hebrew Bible*, ed. Sid Z. Leiman, Ktav publishing House, NY, 1974, p. 852. Cited by Gruber, op. cit., p. 114.

than 1,100 Greek terms are used in the Talmud."[131] Even *syna-gogue* is a Greek word. Another scholar doing epigraphical research, noted that in Beth-Shearim, Northern Israel, out of 209 inscriptions, 175 are in Greek and only 34 in Hebrew or Aramaic.[132]

Since the Septuagint included the Apocrypha, which might be used by Jewish Christians to argue on behalf of Jesus' Messiahship, it had to go! Furthermore, because it was the LXX from Alexandria, the Hebrew Bible (in Greek) most Jews in the world used, a new Greek Bible must be developed which didn't contain the Apocrypha nor too many prophetic scriptures worded in such a way that the anticipated Messiah could be easily seen to have been the late Jesus of Nazareth. Thus, Gruber contends:

> The previous texts were all written before there were rabbis. Aquila's, or Akiba's, version, was not more "Jewish" than the other texts, for they were all written and used by Jews. Aquila's version would simply have been one newly produced to support the teachings of his own particular sect. As Ginzberg pointed out, it was Akiba's idea, and "A careful examination of the translation... shows that it follows Akiba's exegesis." Akiba's exegesis did not follow the text of Tanakh.[133]

In short, *Akiba felt free to alter the Torah when it suited him.* Gruber states: "The Rabbis are the source of their own authority to annul the Torah. They gave this power to themselves. They gave to their own laws the same binding power as the laws of Torah. Actually, they ascribed greater authority to their

---

[131] Davies, Paul cited by Gruber, op. cit., p. 111. Reference to Davies 'work appears to be lost.

[132] Gruber, op. cit., p. 114.

[133] Ibid., p. 112. Ginzberg citation fr. *Encyclopedia Judaica, Vol. 2.* p. 489-490.

own laws than to the laws of Torah, for they claimed that their laws took precedence over what is written in Torah."[134] Their new laws superseded the old. Barry Setterfield makes this statement which serves to summarize the previous pages and to provide a foundation for the discussion in the next section:

> (Rabbi Akiba) had a passionate hatred of Jesus and he admired Bar Kokhba. Rabbi Akiba ended up supporting Bar Kokhba as the Messiah. Akiba came with a purpose in mind: to give Rabbinical Judaism complete control over every aspect of Jewish life. This process did not happen overnight. However, over a period of time, this was achieved by Akiba and the Council of Jamnia.[135]

It is too much to say that, by itself, the beginning of Rabbinic Judaism changed everything. Or that Akiba by himself was the sole forebear of "Neo-Judaism's" future impact. But four centuries of academies in Babylon and Palestine, coupled with another 300 years or so of editing, organizing, and collating, completed the process with a thoroughness demonstrated in the large 15 volumes of the Talmud that resulted, ca. 800 A.D. We can easily acknowledge that the Talmud comprises a "magnum opus" no other religion can match in respect to its founding holy book. As we will discuss in Appendix 5 at this book's end, it's full of great wisdom on many matters. However, *it obscures the only way to salvation.* Additionally, by altering the Torah and superintending the Talmud, the rabbis built a greater chasm between Judaism and Christianity. While Christianity's

---

[134] Ibid., p. 127. Gruber cites Baumgarten, op cit., p. 22 n.5, "on the authority of the sages to nullify biblical laws." "' Wherever a man makes a condition which is contrary to what is written in the Torah, his condition is null and void,' [Kid. 19b] but not wherever a Rabbinic scholar makes such a condition."

[135] Ibid. p. 127.

Church Fathers would undoubtedly intensify the hatred, Akiba and Bar Kokhba initiated the animosity at the outset, establishing a fervent feud still felt today.

Judaism's Great Divide

The principles of *Talmudic Judaism* comprised a complete makeover of *Temple Judaism*. As such (perhaps it goes without saying), Talmudic Judaism is less compatible with Christianity than the principles of Temple Judaism. For Jesus' opposition to the Judaism of his day wasn't due to the rituals in the Temple as prescribed by Mosaic Law, for these rituals foreshadowed the meaning of His sacrifice, and they were God-given laws. Jesus did not come to destroy the Law but to fulfill it. (Matthew 5:17) Instead, Jesus' opposition first lay with the Sadducees that made a mockery of Temple worship as they sought to grow rich through Temple tithes and, on the Temple steps, sell animals for sacrifice. Jesus did not oppose Temple rites, He challenged unrighteousness outside the Temple. *"The zeal of thine house hath eaten me up."* (Psalm 69:9, LXX, cf. John 2.17)

In the second place, His opposition lay with the Pharisees who sought to extend the law into nooks and crannies that placed excessive burdens of the common man and woman. The Pharisees constructed laws that only they could keep, excluding the masses from practicing the presence of God. But Jesus simplified the Law for His followers, prioritizing what was most important, anticipating that He would send His Spirit to enable His followers to help keep His law. This they would do as they studied His word, supported one another, and placed their trust in Him. Nevertheless, although made entirely available for the ordinary person to apply (unlike the Talmud), His law was even harder to follow – absent His ongoing grace and enabling Spirit.

So, although the Sadducees grew extinct as Temple worship ended in 70 A.D., the Pharisees persisted. Evolving into
the rabbis, the Pharisees morphed only slightly. With their Sad-
ducee rivals now out of their way – that is, since Temple worship was over – the Pharisees still had two splinter sects to overcome. The first, *the Zealots* who had started the Great Revolt, fell
prey to Rome. The second sect of concern was *the Essenes*. They
were monastic purists that took keeping the law to the extreme.
They secluded themselves at Qumran (and from their former
Pharisaic colleagues who were "not quite holy enough"), alleg-
ing Temple worship had become corrupted.[136]

Figure 13 - WOE UNTO YOU, SCRIBES AND PHARISEES,
James Tissot Broolyn Museum, (2008)

---

[136] "But both scholars and laypeople would do well to remember that during
the entire Qumran period, the Pharisees and Sadducees were as much 'sects' as
the Essenes were!" Abegg at al., op. cit., Kindle Edition. Loc. 244. The Essene' legacy is, of course, the Dead Sea Scrolls of which we will have much more to say. An
outstanding paper on the Essenes can be found at Heritage History on the Essenes.

Regarding the outcome, one commentator supposes, "Many of the Essenes perished in the wars against the Romans. Many of the survivors probably became Christians."[137] Perhaps. In any event, Qumran appears to have been deserted late in the first century A.D. or early in the second, based upon the dates of the diminishing manuscripts preserved in the Dead Sea Scrolls.

On the other hand, the next sect whom the Rabbis addressed, proved impossible to suppress – this sect would not succumb to their persecution (either in the second half of the first century or the first half of the second). That sect was Christianity. The Apostles, under the guidance of Peter, James, Paul, and many other lesser-known leaders had also transformed Judaism into a distinctly different religion. Christianity proclaimed the Messiah had come. *His death was not the end of Judaism, but its fulfillment.* As Jesus said, *"I did not come to abolish the law, but to fulfill it."* (Matthew 5:17-20, paraphrased)

That the Temple worship did not continue fulfilled Jesus' prediction, and it also proved what he taught concerning His mission was true. The Law and the Temple were given to direct us to the God-man, the Messiah Jesus. After that, the Temple resided within all believers – God now dwelt within.

Rabbinic Judaism took a much different path. It downplayed the Law of Moses (this author believes) by multiplying the Oral Law. The Oral Law had been limited – it amounted to the "traditions of men." (Mark 7:8; Colossians 2:8)

---

[137]Upper Biblical Studies for All, "The Essenes who were they?" Retrieved June 15, 2018, from https://mjseymour1959.wordpress.com/the-essenes-who-were-they/.

DEEP DIVE:

JESUS' CRITICISMS OF THE PHARISEES – FROM THE GOSPEL OF MATTHEW

THE SIX WOES OF HYPOCRISY

They taught about God but did not love God. They would not enter the Kingdom and couldn't lead others there either. They were blind guides. (Matt. 23:14)

1. **They preached about God, but they converted persons to a dead religion**, making their converts twice as fit for Hell as they were themselves (Matt. 23:15)

2. **They taught that oaths sworn on the Temple and its altar were not binding**, but if sworn of its gold ornamentation – or a sacrifice on the altar – they were binding. Jesus' point: The Temple and altar were made sacred by God. So how could they teach oaths sworn on lesser objects could be binding? (Matt. 23:16-22)

3. **They obeyed minutiae about the laws they made up**, while neglecting the "weightier things" of the Torah such as justice, mercy, and faithfulness to God. (Matt 23:23-24)

4. **They presented a holy, clean appearance only on the outside** by showing restraint in carnal matters externally, while inside they were unclean, full of worldly desires, greed, and self-indulgence. (Matt 23:25-26)

5. **They proclaimed themselves holy and set apart by being "keepers of the law"** while their inner persons were unrighteous. They were full of wickedness and evil. They were like "whitewashed tombs" with dead men's bones inside (which would make them unclean "despite the white"). (Matt. 23:27-28)

6. **They claimed, unlike their ancestors, they never would have persecuted or killed the prophets.** Yet, they *were the offspring of the prophets* – with murderous blood in their veins. (Matt: 23:29-36) This was proven when, along with the Romans, they crucified the Messiah, the Son of the Living God. (Acts 2:22-36)

97

It was the source of Jesus' criticism of the Pharisees. (See the "Deep Dive" above.) For the rabbis, being close to God only came through keeping His law, as they interpreted it. In contrast, Christians accepted the truth that God desired to live in their hearts – *they were the new Temple*. God dwelling within would enable them to live out the Law, not to acquire righteousness; but to demonstrate a right standing with God and ultimate loyalty to Him as they brought their thoughts and actions captive to the obedience of Christ. (2 Corinthians 10:5)

Thus, at the end of the Roman – Jewish Wars, Judaism had split into two religions: Rabbinic Judaism and Apostolic Christianity. Rabbinic Judaism would build its new religion by creating a new text – part one, the *Mishnah* and then part two, the *Gemara* (together they constitute the Talmud, although in some instances, the Gemara and Talmud are seen to be synonymous). Christians would follow the leading of the Holy Spirit individually, participate in community, and obey their leadership. This would feature bishops anointed by apostles then later by other bishops (known as *Apostolic Succession*) while the community would anoint overseers with spiritual gifts (*charismata*) of the Spirit. (Romans 12:3-8; 1 Corinthians 12:27-31)

So, how then would Rabbinic Judaism rid itself of Christianity? Akiba elected to *attack its principal text; namely, the Septuagint from Alexandria.* How did he do this? And is it speculation to think this course of action was a deliberate attack plan?

The Attack on the Septuagint

Setterfield comments:

> The changes we find dating from the time of the Council of Jamnia are deliberate. There are too many… in specific places to be the result of accumulated errors by isolated copyists over the centuries or millennia. Evidence of the many changes

dispels any impression that Akiba's scribes were careful "not to lose a jot or tittle," as rabbinic tradition has indicated. That is simply not true. Akiba and his colleagues had a specific agenda to fulfill and they left no stone unturned to accomplish that.[138]

Setterfield cites a paper by Dr. S. H. Horn (Ph.D. in Archeology from Andrews University), who wrote:

Figure 14 - A 2018 colorized version of the Arch of Titus
© Created by Biblical Archeology

Retrieved 6/14/18 from https://www.biblicalarchaeology.org/wp-content/up-loads/arch-of-titus-restoration.jpg

However, the facts – that a unified [Hebrew] text suddenly became the standard at the end of the first century and that not one copy of a divergent text survived, except the Dead Sea Scrolls (already hidden when Jamnia convened), clearly indicate that the Council of Jamnia must have taken action in this matter. Moreover, the fact that Aquila, one of Akiba's pupils, soon… produced a new Greek translation that slavishly translated the 'new' unified Hebrew text for the use of the Diaspora Jews, gives credence to the idea that Akiba must have been a key influence in the standardization of the Hebrew text.[139]

---

[138] Setterfield, Barry. "History of the Septuagint." Retrieved 4/28/18 from www.setterfield.org/Septuagint.History.html, p. 5.

[139] Horn, S.H. "The Old Testament Text in Antiquity, *Ministry*, (November 1987), p. 6. Cited by Setterfield, op. cit., p. 5.

Aquila's new Greek Bible was completed ca. 128 A.D., three decades after Jamnia. His translation was not based on the original Hebrew Temple "Vorlage" used at Alexandria 400 years earlier. Instead, it was based on a "new version" of the Hebrew text prepared at Jamnia's academies. This new Hebrew version, from which Aquila's new Greek Bible was translated, would one day become known as the *Masoretic Text*.

Unfortunately, as we have stated several times already, it's this version that would become the basis for Protestant Bibles down to our day (the impact of these alterations will be covered in the next chapter along with a brief overview of the textual transmission process that continued past the second century).

Additionally, we should recognize that *Akiba's Hebrew Vorlage was not the same one used in Alexandria.* It is possible that the Temple scrolls had been taken as spoil by the Romans (they appear to be identified in the Arch of Titus in Rome, along with other Temple artifacts, celebrating Titus' victory, see Figure 14). That Aquila "slavishly" followed the Hebrew, indicates that Aquila was careful that the text the rabbinic school had created, would be followed "to the letter." The Rabbis were nothing if they were not rigid; thus, the version they created was rigidly fashioned too.

As we discussed in the last chapter, a "good translation" translates idioms which mean one thing in one language, to say the same in the other, while particular words may differ. This was not the way of the Pharisees. Akiba used copies of copies to create his Hebrew version. Then Aquila used Akiba's Hebrew version to create his Greek translation that would become the new Greek standard for the Diaspora's use, from a much more recent set of texts. After that, it would be the accepted "standard Bible" for Greek-speaking Jews – instead of the "Old Greek" Alexandrian LXX.

While simplified, Figure 15 illustrates the flow of the two textual lineages pertinent to our study. First, we see the Septuagint (created beginning ca. 250-280 B.C., most likely from a fourth-century copy of the authentic Temple Vorlage); and secondly, a nascent Hebrew version developed by Akiba and the Jamnia academy. It was composed from Hebrew manuscripts, possibly diluted through two or more generations of copies later than the OG Vorlage (i.e., likely *without the Temple Vorlage*). Akiba's version was completed ca. 110-120 A.D., 400 years after the LXX and 600 years from the Vorlage used by creators of the LXX, an extremely long gap in a day when copies were made by hand scribing. In fact, many scholars believe that Ezra and Nehemiah assembled the temple Vorlage, ca. 450 B.C., not long after a small contingent of Jews returned from Babylon – led by Zerubbabel and Joshua – to begin work on the Second Temple (which wouldn't be officially declared complete until King Herod finished his modifications and additions almost 500 years later). So, the point is this: The LXX was likely created from a first generation copy of the original Vorlage, only 170 years after Ezra. *Consequently, the chance that errors crept into the LXX was significantly less than with the Masoretic Text.*

Indeed, the New Testament cited the LXX in the latter half of the first century A.D., only four to five decades before Akiba formulated his new Hebrew edition.[140]

---

[140] "It was only from the second century CE onward that one type of Judaism— that of the Pharisees and their descendants, the Rabbis— became standard for the Jewish people as a whole." Abegg et al, op. cit., Kindle Loc. 244.

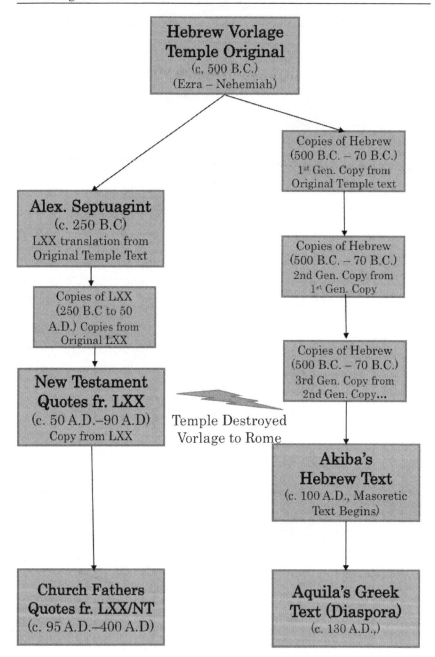

Figure 15 - Differing Pathways to Judeo-Christian Holy Books
Simplified for Illustrative Purposes
Note: *The Masoretic Text will continue to change for over 800 more years.*
© *S. Douglas Woodward*

DEEP DIVE
Justin Martyr's Allegations in
Dialogue with Trypho the Rabbinical Jew.

The Dialogue with Trypho is an apologetic work in which Justin seeks to persuade a (likely fictional) rabbi (Trypho) that he should recognize Jesus as the answer to the Law, bringing salvation to Jews and to all humankind. The book was likely penned ca. 160 A.D. only a few decades after Akiba completed his intentional corruptions accomplished at Jamnia. What follows are selections from the *Dialogue.* Justin addresses numerous examples of how the rabbis were altering the Bible to keep their flocks from learning that Jesus of Nazareth was the promised Messiah.[141] First, regarding Isaiah's prophecy of a virgin conceiving and bearing a Son (Isaiah 7:14):

"Behold a virgin shall conceive and bear a Son," spoken of Him. For, if the one of whom Isaias spoke was not to be born of a virgin, to whom did the Holy Spirit allude when He said: "Behold, the Lord Himself shall give you a sign: Behold, a virgin shall conceive and bear a Son"? If He was to be born of human intercourse like any other first-born son, why did God solemnly announce that He would give a sign which is not common to all first-born? What is truly a sign, and what was to be an irrefutable proof to all men, namely, that by means of a virgin's womb the First-born of all creatures took flesh and truly became man, was foreknown by the Prophetic Spirit before it took place and foretold by Him in different ways, as I have explained to you... But here, too, you dare to distort the translation of this passage made by your elders at the court of Ptolemy, the Egyptian king, asserting that the real meaning of the Scriptures is not as they translated it, but should read, "Behold a young woman shall conceive," as though something of extraordinary importance was

---

[141] Thank you to Stephen Rudd for identifying and commenting on these passages in *The Dialogue.* See Rudd, Steve. "The Septuagint LXX Greek Old Testament and Tanakh." Bible.ca. 2017.

signified by a woman conceiving after sexual intercourse, as all young women, except the barren, can do… And, especially when it was prophesied that this would happen, you should not venture to mutilate or misinterpret the prophecies, for in doing so you do no harm to God, but only to yourselves.'" [142]

Next, we see Justin reference the account as told in the Letter of Aristeas, regarding the 70 elders who made a "correct" translation of which the rabbis changed words and deleted passages:

"'I certainly do not trust your teachers when they refuse to admit that the translation of the Scriptures made by the seventy elders at the court of King Ptolemy of Egypt is a correct one and attempt to make their own translation. You should also know that they have deleted entire passages from the version composed by those elders at the court of Ptolemy, in which it is clearly indicated that the Crucified One was foretold as God and man, and as about to suffer death on the cross.[143]

"They have also deleted these words from Jeremiah: "I was as a meek lamb that is carried to be a sacrificial victim; they devised counsels against Me, saying: Come, let us put wood on His bread, and cut Him off from the land of the living, and let His name be remembered no more." Since this passage from the words of Jeremias is **still found in some copies of Scripture in the Jewish synagogues (for it was deleted only a short time ago),** and since it is also proved from these words that the Jews planned to crucify Christ Himself and to slay Him, and since He is shown, as was likewise prophesied by Isaias, as led like a lamb to slaughter, and in accordance with this passage He is marked as "an innocent lamb," they are so confused by such words that they resort to blasphemy."[144]

---

[142] Justin Martyr. Dialogue with *Trypho the Rabbinical Jew* 84, 150 A.D.
[143] Ibid., 71.
[144] Ibid. 72.

This textual lineage could undergo changes for the next 800 years or so (despite the meticulous Masoretes).[145] The LXX much less so. If true, the Temple Vorlage (the original scrolls) had been carted off to Rome by Titus as one of the many spoils from the Jewish Temple, the "original" Temple Vorlage was lost to them. The rabbis would have to assemble their rabbinic version from copies of copies unless they chose to translate the Greek LXX back to the Hebrew, an unlikely approach. Then they would destroy all other copies, treating them as spurious. *What wasn't known was that **The Dead Sea Scrolls** had been hidden by the Essenes and would survive despite Akiba's textual purge.*

Abegg, Flint, & Ulrich, in their introduction to *The Dead Sea Scroll Bible*, confirm this author's assertion of the superiority of the LXX's accuracy through the following critical assessment:

The Septuagint is important for several reasons:

- First, almost all the books it contains were translated from an earlier Hebrew or Aramaic form. ... This means that the Septuagint gives readers a window on an ancient Hebrew form of the Old Testament that is earlier than the time of Jesus.

- Second, the Septuagint sometimes offers striking evidence of different ancient forms of biblical books (for example, Jeremiah is about 13 percent shorter in the Greek than in the Masoretic Text) as well as different ancient readings in specific passages.

- Third, because the Septuagint was the Bible of Hellenistic Judaism, it offers important insights into how Greek-speaking Jews used and understood Scripture.

---

[145] The Masoretes were noted for their scribal scrutiny to avoid errors. See the next chapter for a description on the Masoretes and scriptural transmission.

- Fourth, since the Septuagint is quoted in the New Testament and was used by early Christian authors, it constitutes the Bible of the early church and helps to explain early Christian exegesis of Scripture.
- Finally, the Septuagint contains the books of the Old Testament in the fourfold arrangement that is found in modern Christian Bibles: Pentateuch, Historical Books, Poetical Books, and Prophets (though the specific order of books sometimes varies between Septuagint manuscripts).
- It is from the Septuagint that most modern Bibles have adopted this grouping and that Catholic Bibles have included the deuterocanonical books (or Apocrypha).[146]

To paraphrase and abbreviate the five key reasons cited by Abegg as to why the LXX is essential:

1. Its translation was much earlier than the Masoretic.
2. It contains more books and many variant readings.
3. From the LXX, we learn how Greek Jews used the Bible.
4. The LXX was the Old Testament used by the New.
5. It arranges the books of the Bible (the same as today's) in a four-fold structure: Law, History, Poetry, & Prophets.

We can also add that in most cases the deuterocanonical books (i.e., the so-called *Apocrypha*), are separated from the canonical texts. The Latin *Vulgate* (which we will briefly discuss in the next chapter), will follow this lead in many respects. Protestants Bibles (most notably the King James Version and all modern versions like the New American Standard, New International Bible, English Standard Version, etc.) drop the Apocrypha – following Akiba's approach – but not the OG.

---

[146] Abegg et al, op. cit., Kindle Loc. 177.

Regarding point number four, as we have said previously, the Church Fathers (e.g., Irenaeus, Tertullian, and Justin Martyr) used the LXX, seldom referencing the Hebrew (since – except for Origen – their knowledge of Hebrew was little more than mine!) It was the Church's exclusive Bible for almost 300 years (until Jerome's Latin *Vulgate*). It remains the Bible of the Eastern Orthodox Church today among several other branches of Christendom (e.g., Coptic and Syriac Churches). And as argued here, it was subject to less corruption (due to the ravages of time and transmission errors) as well as due to alterations made by the Jamnia Academy.[147]

Danish biblical scholar Mogens Muller contends that:

Historically the Septuagint should be endowed with special significance considered as a translation, because to some circles of Greek-speaking Jewry, it replaced the *Biblia Hebraica*, and thus became their Bible. Because it was accepted as conclusive evidence of the biblical revelation, it was used by the authors of the New Testament writings, and accordingly came to have a decisive impact on the theology of the New Testament. In a historical perspective, it became, to an even greater extent than the *Biblia Hebraica*, the Old Testament of the New Testament. This circumstance is fundamental insofar as this translation as a witness to the handing on of traditions represents a reappraisal of the basic content of the Old Testament. According to Robert Hanhart, it even expresses a more profound appreciation for the Old Testament's testimony of revelation (i.e., than the Hebrew). [148]

---

[147] As mentioned earlier, the matter of the preservation of the text and biblical "inerrancy" will be taken up in Appendix 5 at this book's conclusion.

[148] Muller, M: *The First Bible of the Church*, Sheffield Academic Press, 1996, p. 115-116. Hanhart published a German version of the LXX in 2006.

In the next chapter, we delve into the differences between the two distinctive textual traditions and their historical progression into complete codices (viz., a whole Bible intact and bound inside a single cover).

Figure 16 - The Caves at Qumran, the Location of the Dead Sea Scrolls

One particular distinction important to this study: The LXX's ancient chronology, contrasting with the truncated timeline of the Masoretic Text. That also follows in a later chapter. However, here we must address one final subject before we proceed: The Dead Sea Scrolls and the light they shed on the Septuagint's accuracy.

The Dead Sea Scrolls and the Septuagint

The Dead Sea Scrolls (DSS) fall into two groups: *Group one* contains the DSS written before the Temple was destroyed in 70 A.D. (approximately 250 B.C to 70 A.D.); and *Group Two*, those partial texts that were written after 100 A.D. The Essenes occupied the caves of Qumran beginning ca. 150 B.C. They brought with them documents from the previous 100 years, and they created copies of various texts during their "undisturbed" stay, from 150 B.C. to 68 A.D.[149] A few Essenes likely survived after this date.

- *Group one* includes over 170 manuscripts from eleven Qumran caves and fragments from Masada. This collection contains fragments and scrolls from the Pentateuch and the Book of Job. They were written in pre-exilic, paleo-Hebrew text – the same alphabet used in the Samaritan Pentateuch (which generally follows the LXX).

- *Group two* encapsulates documents hidden after 100 A.D. According to Dr. Horn, these documents are found at other locations (not Qumran): Wadi Murabba'at, the Nahal Hever, and the Nahal Se'elim. These are second-century texts which follow the Proto-Masoretic – but not the Septuagint.[150]

Abegg's summary analysis of the contents of the DSS shows that parts of every book of the Jewish and Protestant Old Testaments are there, the only exceptions being Esther and Nehemiah. Books included in the LXX (and later the Vulgate) were present too: Tobit, Ben Sira (Ecclesiasticus), and the so-called "Letter of Jeremiah." Abegg et al. also posit that the Essenes viewed the books of *1 Enoch and Jubilees as canonical Scripture*. In Part 2 of *Rebooting the Bible*, we will evaluate, to a limited extent, a number of the more popular books in this category, known as *pseudepigrapha*.

Abegg notes that most various fragments found among the DSS are the Psalms (37 manuscripts), Deuteronomy (30

---

[149] Abegg et al, op. cit., p. 14-15.

[150] Horn op. cit. quoting Y. Aharoni, *Israel Exploration Journal*, 11 (1961), pp.22-23, and Yadin, Israel *Exploration Journal*, 11 (1961), p.40. Cited by Setterfield, op. cit. p. 6.

manuscripts), and Isaiah (21 manuscripts). Interestingly, he also points out:

> If we count the number of times an Old Testament passage is quoted or referred to in the New Testament, the same three books turn up most: The Psalms (cited about sixty-eight times), Isaiah (sixty-three times), and Deuteronomy (thirty-nine times).[151]

Dr. Horn compares scrolls of the DSS' *Book of Samuel* from the LXX and from the Masoretic with these words:

> In an article dealing with one of the Samuel scrolls from Qumran Cave 4, Frank Cross informed the scholarly world of new developments in our understanding of the pre-Masoretic Text form. Cross showed that this particular manuscript agrees more with the Septuagintal than with the Masoretic Text.[152]

Setterfield quotes the *Biblia Hebraica* which admits the greater accuracy of the LXX: "Recent Aramaic findings among the Dead Sea Scrolls read most closely with the LXX, and not with the Masoretic Text… This suggests that the older LXX may be more accurate than the newer Masoretic Text which was given to Jerome."[153] And Setterfield points out that Jerome used the Masoretic Text for the greater part of his Latin translation (the *Vulgate*) because his Jewish friends argued that it was more accurate than the "old Alexandrian Septuagint" used at the time by the third century Christian Church. That

---

[151] Abegg et al, op. cit., Kindle Loc. 266.

[152] Horn, op. cit., p. 6-7. Cited by Setterfield, op. cit., p. 6. Frank Moore Cross (1921 – 2012) was Professor Emeritus at Harvard, most notable for his work interpreting the Dead Sea Scrolls. He had previously been Professor of Old Testament at the Harvard Divinity School and Hebrew Professor at Harvard from 1958 – 1987.

[153] *Biblica Hebraica*, "The Septuagint." Cited by Setterfield, op. cit., p. 6.

was a *most unfortunate error*. We will learn about the impact of this significant mistake.

And one more supportive citation provided by Setterfield:

In a review of some of this scholarship, Hershal Shanks notes that "many Hebrew texts [are available] that were the base text for Septuagintal translations..." Further, he [Shanks] notes that what "texts like 4QSama show is that the Septuagintal translations are really quite reliable [and] ...*gives new authority to the Greek translations against the Masoretic Text.*" [Emphasis added]

Quoting Frank Moore Cross (a co-author of the book under review), Hershal continued, "We could scarcely hope to find closer agreement between the Old Greek [Septuagintal] tradition and 4QSama than actually is found in our fragments."[154]

Conclusion

If we seek the most accurate Old Testament available today, the verdict must be *the Alexandrian (OG) Septuagint*. It was the Church's Bible for hundreds of years, it has the best textual support, and it offers splendid backing for the affirmation that Jesus Christ is the Messiah. Additionally, it was the intent of Rabbi Akiba ben Josef and the Jamnia Academy to muddle the biblical testimony that God Himself would come in the flesh as our Redeemer. Thus, the *most essential attribute of the Messiah* was rejected by Rabbinical Judaism – that is, the Messiah was not just "anointed" – He was *a member of the Godhead*.

For the rabbis, the Messiah was no more than their mighty warrior and political leader who would fulfill the promises of

---

[154] Hershal Shanks, *4QSama - The Difficult Life of a Dead Sea Scroll*, Biblical Archaeology Review, Vol 33 No 3, May/June 2007, p. 66-70. Cited by Setterfield, op. cit., p. 7.

the Kingdom to the land of Israel. But the Messiah, like Bar Kokhba, would never be more than *human*.

Christian testimony stands utterly divergent: The Christ would be more than a political ruler and conqueror – He would be an incarnated deity. To reiterate, he would not be just any deity, *He was the Angel of God of the Old Testament, the Second Person of the Trinity, Jesus Christ, the Logos, and the Only Begotten of the Father.* The LXX, much more than the Masoretic Text, makes this claim more clearly as the next several chapters demonstrate.

Chapter Three:
THE BATTLE FOR THE SEPTUAGINT

Inspecting the Scene of the Crime

A S SHOULD BE APPARENT TO THE READER BY THIS POINT, THERE ARE MANY REASONS TO SUSPECT THAT THE TEXT PROTESTANTS AFFIRM AS THE AUTHORITATIVE STANDARD was intentionally corrupted by the rabbinical academies in the early second century. In contrast, the Septuagint, whose Pentateuch translation was completed in the middle of the third century B.C. in Alexandria, Egypt, had escaped this textual sabotage. As we will see, Messianic prophecies in the Old Testament were, at least in part, spoiled. However, two caveats:

- First, I affirm the supernatural, providential preservation of the text. This is a complex subject and is addressed separately in Appendix 5. Many readers may wish to stop at this point and review this material, for it must be kept in mind as I take up the matter of how the MT was corrupted, and yet, through His providence, God preserved His Word.

- Secondly, that although this author is expressing sharp criticism of the rabbinical school and their intentional changes to the text – my condemnation remains limited to the rabbis of the first and second centuries. Although today's Judaism traces its ancestry to this movement in Jamnia; nevertheless, I consider Judaism constituting the greatest religion of the world apart from Christianity; for it springs from the same fountain as the faith of the Christian Church.

113

And we must sympathetically acknowledge how reasonable it is that Jewish leadership would *seek a new path forward* with their Temple destroyed, their nation in ruins, and the basis for their religion vanquished. Freedman comments:

> In Yavneh, the Pharisees were faced with a stark reality. Unless they could find a way to save the religion that now lacked its Temple and sacrificial cult, their civilization would disappear. The proud, independent Israelite culture with its rich biblical and prophetic heritage would be eradicated, their people would become just another subjugated nation under the Roman thumb. [155]

Consequently, I am not without sympathy for the situation the Jewish nation found itself in after Rome destroyed its Temple. However, as a Christian, it's hard to overlook that Messiah Jesus was rejected by the national Jewish leaders who called for His crucifixion. Despite that fact, this author remains a strong supporter of Israel and its right to exist in its ancient homeland. I affirm a belief that the return of the Jew to the land of Palestine is a partial fulfillment of Bible prophecy. Nevertheless, what happened between 70 A.D. and 135 A.D. was a tragedy that put Judaism on a two-millennia-long collision course with Christianity and, as we have seen, tainted the Holy Scripture for both religions. As a conservative Evangelical with high regard for the inspiration and authority of the Bible, altering the Word of God as Rabbi Akiba ben Josef and his second-century disciples did, remains unforgivable. I realize that to attack Akiba amounts to attacking Judaism.[156] However, it is the case that not all of Judaism supports the Talmud and rabbinic Judaism as authentic.

---

[155] Freedman, op. cit., p. 18-19.

[156] On a personal note, Rabbi Daniel Lapin has been a fantastic and caring friend, advising me on numerous points of Judaism. I am hopeful this work will not alienate him. He is a "mensch" (he taught me this word).

(An example is the Karaites.[157]) So, I call on Christians not to overlook the fact that the Jewish race should not be condemned because their Torah-centered religion shifted to a Talmudic one. Nor should we hold Jews today responsible for what happened in 30 A.D. *We should love the ancient people of God, pray for their redemption, and hope the dry bones (Ezekiel 37) come back to life soon.*

Despite Textual Errors, We Can Restore God's Word

In addition to intentional alteration, we have to be mindful that time altered the original words of biblical texts, with editorial "glosses" and omitted words or lines. Even without considering the Akiba alterations, errors could have crept into a greater extent with the MT than the LXX. The Vorlage of the LXX was likely from the fifth century B.C., while the MT Vorlage originated in the third or second century B.C.[158] Regardless, as demonstrated in the last chapter, the most significant damage to the Masoretic Text occurred in Jamnia (Judea), before the Bar Kokhba Revolt of 132-135 A.D.[159]

---

[157] "Karaites maintain that all of the divine commandments handed down to Moses by God were recorded in the written Torah without additional Oral Law or explanation. As a result, Karaite Jews do not accept as binding the written collections of the oral tradition in the Midrash or Talmud." See Wikipedia, https://en.wikipedia.org/wiki/Karaite_Judaism.

[158] Paul Wegner notes that, "D. N. Freedman has dated the present form the Masoretic text [presumably manuscript fragments] between the third and second century B.C. based on its *orthography* (primarily the number of *matres lectionis.*" ["mothers of reading" which designated long vowels specifying which word the consonants intended to compose.] D. N. Freedman, "The Masoretic Text and the Qumran Scrolls: A Study in Orthography," *Textus 2* (1962): 87-102, reprinted in *QHBT*, 196-211. Cited by Wegner, op. cit., p. 171. However, please note since the rabbis would have destroyed the DSS, they did not have access to these earlier manuscript fragments. It would be reasonable to suppose their copies would be from first or second-century copies rather than second or third-century copies that Freedman asserts are those discovered at Qumran in 1948.

[159] This assertion is a supposition with which many argue. However, it is difficult to prove outright. The Dead Sea Scrolls offer evidence "both ways." In some cases, the accuracy is remarkable, but in many instances, changes are quite

Having said that, this chapter will explain why Akiba's influence had a detrimental impact on the usage and transmission of the OG LXX.

Finally, as illustrated in the preceding chapter in considerable detail, there are numerous Jewish scholars and textual experts who confirm that the rabbinic school had "method, means, and opportunity" to alter the text. (*Note: I am relying heavily on Jewish scholars to press my case against Akiba – not many Christian ones*). And these rabbinic "sages" did so with "malice," primarily crafting an Old Testament and a written Oral Law that enforced rabbinic authority and new content for a "Neo-Judaism." Secondly, the sages weakened those scriptures that gave quarter to the claims of Christians. That is, they altered the passages that most clearly identified Jesus as the Christ, and that He was the long-expected Messiah, the King of the Jews. We will see this evidence "in spades," throughout this chapter and the two that follow immediately after.

Warning: Readers who are wedded to the King James Version or any other text (which is based on the Masoretic textual legacy – as all Protestant Bibles are), prepare yourselves for a shock. Remain open-minded and tighten the chinstrap on your "Berean hat."[160]

To begin: There is some good news and bad news. First, the bad news. Many of us must sacrifice our assurance in one and

---

apparent. And some findings, as we will discuss concerning Theodotion's Greek *recension* [a "rewrite" of a previous text] offers some unexpected surprises.

[160] "*Then the brethren immediately sent Paul and Silas away by night (from Thessalonica) to* **Berea***. When they arrived, they went into the synagogue of the Jews. These were more* **fair-minded** *than those in Thessalonica, in that they received the word with all readiness, and searched the Scriptures daily to find out whether these things were so. Therefore, many of them believed, and also not a few of the Greeks, prominent women as well as men.*" (Acts 17:10-12, NJKV, emphasis added)

only one inspired version; namely, believing the KJV to be a pristine text, fully inspired by God down to the very English words, all without error.[161]

However, here's the good news: We can restore God's Word to "full strength" by *giving place to the original Septuagint and the science of textual criticism.* In my opinion, the LXX as we have it today is not perfect. It differs from the autographs. But its authenticity exceeds the Masoretic. And, as you will soon see, it clearly offers a much stronger case for the deity of Jesus Christ.

Therefore, we should be tuned into the fact that it is in Jesus Christ, *not a particular Bible version,* that we trust. For if we seek after the truth ingrained in the closest rendering of the author's original words, it is time we read the Septuagint attentively and respectfully, finding the increased certainty it provides, as it often offers superior validation for who the Messiah really is.

From the Rabbis to the Masoretes to a Codex

Higher textual criticism, often seen correctly as a plague upon biblical truth, doesn't offer us much help.[162] However, "lower" textual criticism comprises a much different story. It helps us know what words the original text most likely contained. It has

---

[161] I oversimply the process here. But this statement follows the typical view of a fundamentalist understanding of "the preservation" of the text. To arrive at the "autographs" – we must rely heavily on textual criticism, for both the LXX and the MT, as I go on to say in the segment on textual transmission and as we discuss in Appendix 5: *The Preservation of the Bible* at this book's conclusion. Note: Eastern Orthodox believers affirm that the LXX is also fully inspired by God, and when interpreted through the Church, reflects an "inerrant" Scripture. Perhaps so.

[162] Higher textual criticism brings anti-biblical assumptions to the text, primarily a rejection of miracles, that God's revelation is "existential" and not propositional, and a rejection of virtually all evangelical (biblical) doctrinal views. But textual criticism is part of God's providence, working through humans to discover the original texts, and is an essential aspect of the preservation of the text.

greatly helped overcome challenges in the text during the past 200 years or so, due to its meticulous examination of hundreds (if not thousands) of manuscript fragments newly discovered during those past 200 years – fragments that are very old (aka "early") for both the LXX and the MT. This certainly includes the Dead Sea Scrolls, but many other discoveries have also impacted the process we call *textual transmission*. To appreciate this, we must understand the progression leading up to the codices of the Old Testament, what these codices are, where they were discovered and obtained, and how they served as the basis for modern versions of the Bible we revere today.

First off, we know that scribes continued to copy the texts of the Hebrew Bible from the second century to the end of the fifth century. It is highly likely that all the adjustments to the Bible that the rabbis felt must be made, had been made before the end of the second century. Polemically speaking, "the damage had been done." Thenceforth, for the Jews, accuracy in the MT became paramount. Around the fifth to sixth century, a group of scribes came into being called the *Masoretes* (from which the MT gets its name). Wegner states that the Masoretes inherited the scribal traditions of their predecessors but increased the rigor around their copying process by using a series of counts to ensure that no letters were added or lost. But when we hear of how meticulous these scribes were, we need to remember that they were excruciatingly careful to prevent accidental changes in the text AFTER the changes made at Jamnia were already in place. We also need to make special note that these meticulous practices did not come into play UNTIL the time of the Masoretes. Wegner gives us the details:

> There were two major venues of Jewish scholarship, one in Babylon and one in Palestine. Following the Islamic conquest of Palestine in A.D. 638, Tiberias once again revived and became

the chief center for Jewish textual studies. From about A.D. 500 to 800 the Masoretes added vowel points, accents, and the *Masorahs* [Masorahs equal *metadata*] (to help safeguard the text from error), as well as many scribal corrections.[163]

Wegner explains that there were two families responsible for copying – the Ben Asher and Ben Naphtali families. Although once considered rivals with differing textual traditions, only eight minor consonantal differences materialized through the years, although "vowel pointing" (vocalization hints) varied. Going all the way back to DSS manuscript fragments, it can be verified that ancient scribes made notations (little diamonds) above letters or words in doubt, to call attention to possible scribal errors in the text. The Masoretes did this too. Eventually, as to these two separate methodologies, the Ben Asher tradition became the de facto winner while the Ben Naphtali tradition faded away.

Collections of the various books in the Hebrew Bible were assembled in a codex instead of a scroll. This wasn't new. This practice had been commonplace for over a thousand years. The codex, you may recall, involves "stitching together" *leaves* or pages to assemble a book instead of a scroll. Nevertheless, the first complete codex of the Hebrew Bible would not be discovered *until the eleventh century A.D.*, several hundred years after the Masoretes began their work; 900 years after Akiba altered the text; and over 1,100 years from the copies of the text used in constructing this proto-Masoretic Text.

Verse numbering had initially taken place with the Latin Vulgate, ca. 1200 A.D. This numbering process found its way into the Hebrew for the first time about 130 years later (1330).

---

[163] Wegner, op. cit., p. 172-172.

Now, as to the printed *Hebrew* Bible (post-Gutenberg that is), a complete Bible (Old Testament) was published in 1488 while the first Rabbinic Bible was printed in 1517 with commentary. As stated earlier, the first complete pseudo-ancient Hebrew Bible in existence today (extant) is the **Leningrad Codex** (*Codex Leningradensis*) dating to about 1008 A.D. It is, as the name indicates, kept in Leningrad in its Public Library. Wegner states,

> The Dead Sea Scrolls provided texts of the Old Testament approximately one thousand years earlier, and their impact was explosive on the field of textual criticism. Careful study of these manuscripts has helped to confirm that the Hebrew text we possess is very accurate; differences are minimal between a good number of the Dead Sea Scroll manuscripts and manuscripts from about A.D. 800 to 1000. However, even the Dead Sea Scrolls reveal a certain amount of diversity in the Old Testament in the centuries right before Christ. Some texts found near Qumran appear to follow more closely the Samaritan Pentateuch, others tend toward the Septuagint, and still others reflect the Masoretic Text.[164]

However, when we count the differences between the versions, the numbers aren't that small. For instance, the Samaritan Pentateuch (SP), which we mention in the next chapter, differs from the MT in 6,000 places.[165] It also varies with the LXX, but in far fewer places – only about 1,600 instances. As explained in a previous section, the Samaritan Pentateuch's tradition begins at the time of Nehemiah's dispute with Sanballat around 450 B.C. Those Samaritans who followed Sanballat's

---

[164] Ibid., p. 187-188.

[165] However, it should be admitted some significant differences exist in the text between the SP and the MT due to *partisan differences vital to Samaritans* which have to do with seeking legitimacy for their alternate holy sites and rites.

lead, relocated their holy place away from Mount Zion in Jerusalem to Mount Gerizim in Samaria.[166]

To advance one thesis of this book, we must make note of this particular timing and here's why: We know that the Hebrew Vorlage, from which the SP textual tradition began, made use of the same proto-Hebrew script (similar to the Aramaic cursive script which the ancient Hebrew Vorlage used, see Figure 6 – The Paleo-Hebrew Alphabet). Modern Hebrew "square characters" were used well before the time of Jesus but became standard later, ca. 100 A.D. The square characters were characteristic of Babylonian, Aramaic, and later, Hebrew.

When we consider the alterations in the text pertinent to the implied chronology of Genesis 5 and 11[167] which occupy our attention in the next chapter, the *SP generally agrees with the LXX and not the MT*. The Vorlage for the SP and the LXX might have been the same. The MT Vorlage (many generations of copies) arises hundreds of years after the Hebrew Vorlage which was used when creating the SP and LXX. Logically (and evidentially), *the MT was altered* and not the other way around.

Many critics suggest that the LXX's translators living in Alexandria (Egypt), altered the Genesis' chronology to synchronize Hebrew history with the Egyptians, due to "historical envy" (as to whose history is the oldest). This argument is frequently put forth to justify why the MT has different genealogical records so that its dates are held out to be sacrosanct,

---

[166] Site of the famous encounter between Jesus and "the woman at the well" recounted in John, chapter 4.

[167] The chronology of interest is the period from the Creation to the Flood (Genesis 5) and then from the Flood to Abraham (Genesis 11).

121

protecting the KJV from "expressing erroneous information." Specifically, critics of the LXX contend, "there was no reason for the scribes copying the [Hebrew] MT to alter the intervals in Genesis 5 and 11; therefore, the MT must be right."[168] LXX naysayers make these anachronistic statements without considering the timing associated with each of these three versions – that is *when their respective Pentateuch was initially created.*

To press the point further: Critics of the LXX are apparently unaware of the MT makeover we've covered in this book. We know the Genesis genealogies as they appear in the LXX and SP differ from the MT in several entries. Specifically, almost all the ages of the Patriarchs when they died are the same in all versions, but what is different is the age when the Patriarchs "begat the next entry in the genealogy." The son mentioned is often misunderstood to be the first-born son. But the son through whom the Messiah would one day come was not necessarily their first-born. Because this fact amounts to yet another controversy (this one between Bible believers and those who doubt the historical record of the Scripture), we must explore these details. Indeed, we will show evidence from Archeology in Part 2 that provides pieces of scientific data supporting the LXX's timeline – enabling us to reconcile the timelines of the Bible and Archeology – demonstrating that the genealogies recorded in Genesis 5 and 11 provide a sequential, unbroken lineage yielding a reliable chronology. This corrected chronology (which is *the inspired, original Genesis chronology*)

---

[168] Bishop Ussher (1581–1656) did his chronological calculations not long after the KJV was published, using its Masoretic-text based version without awareness of what had happened to corrupt the MT, and why the LXX was more accurate. Ussher calculated 6,000 years of history using the MT/KJV. The original records contained within the LXX provide for substantially more years.

overturns the popular chronology associated with the "Bishop Ussher" timeline. Unfortunately, "KJV only" advocates and those contending for a "Young Earth" base their position upon Ussher's math and research. [169] This is most unfortunate. The chronology of the KJV, which is identified with Bishop Ussher and the Young Earth theory, do not need to be linked. In other words, we can throw away the Bishop Ussher chronology and still argue for a Young Earth. And we can throw away the KJV chronology and still contend for an infallible Bible. These connections need to be broken.

Let me emphasize this again to be clear: *These factors do not have to be linked, but they are in every single presentation I have seen from those who contend for the "Young Earth."* The Septuagint timeline would benefit the Young Earth argument in many ways which, as I said, will be covered in Part 2. So, Young Earth presentations should stop using the KJV chronology, and begin using the LXX timeline, which adds (as we will document) over 1500 years to the biblical timeline of Genesis 1.

The Transmission of the LXX and Christian Texts

While the proto-MT codex (containing almost all biblical books) is dated to the year 1008, there are three Greek (i.e., Christian) codices that predate it by 600-700 years. Once again, the number and dating of codices support the verdict that the LXX more closely resembles the autographs of both the Old

---

[169] To foreshadow: It turns out the reasons for the genealogical changes in the MT have to do with the rabbinic attempt to upset first and second century Christians who sought to identify Jesus as the Christ based upon "eschatological timing" of when the Messiah's "visitation" should be expected. Furthermore, after the reader carefully considers the numerous alterations in the Old Testament prophecies concerning Christ (within the MT – as conveyed in the KJV and modern Protestant Bibles) to be chronicled thoroughly in this chapter, the motive for making genealogical changes affecting chronology will become believable.

Testament. Additionally, we know that the LXX quotations from the OT cited by the NT, comprise between 80-90% of all OT references) – yet another factor strengthening the case for the LXX over the MT. It's time we learn more about codices.

Indeed, the history of these codices is intriguing. Each has its own features. We will recap their respective stories.

The first and most esteemed codex is **Codex Vaticanus**, dated to the middle of the fourth century, about 100 years after Origen (184–253 A.D.) and contemporary with Athanasius (296–373) A.D. As with all the codices, there are missing sections, although the percentage of missing portions is quite low. Codex Vaticanus is known as Codex "B," and it has been stored at the Vatican library since 1475. Since the Vatican relied upon the Latin Vulgate as its official Bible, work on this codex was discouraged. In fact, Codex B wasn't published until 1867. According to Wegner, while the Vatican made a photographic facsimile of the Codex in 1889-90, it was still not widely circulated for study by scholars.[170]

The second most highly regarded Codex is **Codex Alexandrinus.** This codex is known as Codex "A." It is dated to the middle of the fourth century, within perhaps two decades of Jerome (347 – 420 A.D.) and Augustine (354 – 430 A.D.) It is the first great "uncial" (a *majuscule* script, i.e., basically "all caps") codex that was *made available to scholars.* Its books are ordered slightly different from today's LXX. (See Appendix 3) It includes many of the "apocryphal books" plus two letters from an early Bishop, Clement of Rome (circa 95 A.D.) It contains

---

[170] Ibid.

scribal corrections, indicating it was subject to careful review during its earlier life. Wegner provides some interesting detail:

> In 1627, Cyril Lucar, patriarch of Constantinople (1621 – 1638), offered this manuscript to the English ambassador to Turkey, Sir Thomas Roe, as a gift to King James I. However, it came to England after King James had died and was instead presented to Charles I of England. Lucar probably obtained Codex Alexandrinus while he was Patriarch of Alexandria (1602 – 1621), hence its name. The codex was housed first in the Royal Library, but in 1757 it was incorporated into the British Museum in London.

Note the interesting timing here. The codex, if it had come to England a decade or so earlier, would likely have influenced the King James Bible (the KJV is the King's namesake), as the scholars working on the Bible would have had a full and worthy copy of the Septuagint before them – and not just a handful of texts following the MT. No doubt, its age would have swayed the translators toward many of the wording choices in the LXX (which we will cover shortly) which built a stronger

Figure 17 - A Panorama of St. Catherine's in front of Mount Sinai (Traditional Location)

case for the deity of Jesus Christ and the nature of His incarnation. However, King James I died in 1625, and Charles I was no help in seeing the KJV revised in accordance to the LXX as he was too busy battling with Oliver Cromwell for political control of the nation (and whether the English should be Catholic or Protestant). And I should mention in passing, that he attempted – unsuccessfully – to escape hanging (he famously went to the gallows in 1649). We can only speculate that the final form of the King James Bible might have been significantly different had the Codex arrived 15 years earlier.

Nevertheless, these chance dates give one pause. This author suspects the implication for Jewish conversion might have been momentous. The English, unlike the Swiss and the Germans, were highly supportive of the Jews' right to worship freely (Cromwell was the first "ruler" to endorse it). They supported "Restorationism" in the seventeenth century, an early form of Dispensationalism. But the timing of a Jewish "revival" was not to be.[171] England's King James Bible was printed without reference to either the Vatican's Codex B (locked in its library); or Codex A that "missed the bus" for consideration by KJV translators by a matter of 15 years or so.

Finally, the earliest of the codices, the third of three, is the most recently discovered at the traditional location of Mount Sinai on the Sinai Peninsula, at St. Catherine's Monastery. This codex is known as **Codex Sinaiticus**, aka "S," and has also been dated to the middle of the fourth century. Its unique contents include the Shepherd of Hermas and the Epistle of Barnabas which were virtually lost before this find. Like all the codices, it was written on *vellum* (calf skin – the key to the survival of the codices). It contains far more mistakes of various

---

[171] See William C., Watson, *Dispensationalism Before Darby: Seventeenth-Century and Eighteenth-Century English Apocalypticism.* Lampion Press, 2015. In his inscription inside the book cover to this author, Dr. Watson (from Denver Seminary) advised, "Don't let anyone tell you that Darby invented all this!" As to the Jewish impact the LXX might have had, the fullness of time had not yet come.

kinds than the other codices. These include poor spelling and use of vulgar language! (In this instance, vulgar may be better understood as "everyday expression" rather than dirty words![172]) Notwithstanding, its story is intriguing.

It seems that Constantin von Tishcendorf (1815-1874), a beginning lecturer at the University of Leipzig who had been instrumental in promoting *Codex Vaticanus*, was also the discoverer of *Codex Sinaiticus*. Tishcendorf had been trolling the Middle East looking for ancient manuscripts and was studying in the library at St. Catherine's in 1844 when he discovered a basket with old leaves of manuscripts thought to be destined for burning. He noted that they were ancient "book leaves" and asked only if he could have them instead of their being used as kindling for the monk's fire. The monks agreed, and the hook was set. To his detriment, he displayed too much enthusiasm, so the monks became unwilling to part with their parchments.

Over the next two decades, he made two more trips to the monastery. Finally, on the third trip (yep, "third-time is always the charm"), he struck gold. When proudly showing the steward of the library his newly printed copy of the Septuagint, the steward related that he also had a copy of the LXX, but the steward's copy wasn't so new or well bound! The steward brought out a hulking pile of loose leaves wrapped in a red cloth. This time, Tishcendorf hid his enthusiasm as he glanced through the material. With the stewards "leave," he spent the

---

[172] Vulgar is a tricky word in this context. Jerome's Vulgate, the Catholic Bible" comes from the Latin *editio vulgata* – the "common version." Vulgar means common. Plus, *Koine Greek* is "the common man's Greek." The Word of God is not meant to be a model of sophisticated linguistics. It means to tell the story of salvation and the history of God's revealing Himself to humanity, not just the elite. God's Word is "down to earth" but it intends to lift us all "to the highest heaven."

night reviewing the *stack of loose leaves*. During his "all-nighter" he carefully inspected this diamond in the rough. Early in the AM, he might have yelled out "Eureka! I've found another co-dex!" Before him lay most of the Greek Old Testament (the LXX) and a completed New Testament. And it was apparently ancient. He tried, unsuccessfully, to purchase the old LXX from the monks. He made several more attempts in the months ahead to buy what would become Codex Sinaiticus but to no avail. And yet, eventually, his persistence paid off. What money couldn't buy, kindness relinquished to him, for he finally received "S" as a gift. Not too long afterward, in 1862, "S" was published, predating the far more restrained printing and distribution of the Codex Vaticanus by just a few years.

It turns out, this unexpected treasure was held in Russia until Lenin needed money; so, it was sold to the English for £100,000. Thus, in 1933, on Christmas Day, Codex Sinaiticus came to England![173] Ironically, Lenin, the atheist, strengthened the Christian Faith by selling this valuable property for profit. Lenin, it seems, had reneged on Marxist principle, making money hawking property, and a Bible no less!

Daniel Wallace, a textual scholar, the "Indy Jones" of ancient biblical manuscripts, and professor at Dallas Theological Seminary, recently presented an informative and vital update to the truths associated with Codex S and St. Catherine's. He defends the monks there by stating they really weren't burning leaves, which was almost impossible to do (they were animal hides after all), not to mention they emitted an odious fragrance

---

[173] Ibid., 196-197.

no one would have been capable of withstanding![174] KJV-only advocates vehemently challenge Sinaiticus. Nevertheless, Wallace's work has done a great deal to demonstrate "S's" value to both Old and New Testament studies.

Other Greek Versions – Symmachus & Theodotion

Having covered as much of the topic of textual transmission via the codices as is relevant to our study, we need to backtrack and pick up another critical thread – *the other Greek versions of the Old Testament.*

There were two other recensions created in the second century (along with Aquila's recension). While neither of these is extant today, they exist in bits and pieces and can be found in fragments of many manuscripts. Plus, there are numerous references to them in the early writings of the Church Fathers.

It is customary today to talk regarding the various versions of the Greek Bible *collectively* as the Septuagint without respect to the specific version developed by any single translator. The original, the Alexandrian Septuagint, is known as the "Old Greek" or OG and therefore often abbreviated as the LXX/OG. However, this practice is most unfortunate. *The real effort must be directed at getting to the autographs, as closely as possible.* Citing Jobes and Silva, "Septuagint scholars, following the lead of Paul de Lagarde in the nineteenth century, have generally believed that there was *only one initial Greek translation of the Hebrew Scriptures* and that the recovery of that "proto-Septuagint" (Ur-

---

[174] "Tiscendorf and the Discovery of the Codex Sinaiticus." See YouTube, https://youtu.be/LVSzBGXXL1Y. Wallace is especially knowledgeable of this codex, having investigated it thoroughly and visiting St. Catherine's on several occasions. He offers strong defenses for its usefulness and validity.

Septuaginta) is the great task at hand…"[175] In contrast, another
Hebraist from a previous generation had argued that the Alexandrian version of the LXX was only one among several others
created before the birth of Christ and that it, along with the LXX,
vied for acceptance. According to this alternative viewpoint
voiced by Paul Kahle, *The Letter of Aristeas* (See Appendix 2) was
written to win consensus for the Alexandrian version. However, Kahle's argument failed to convince scholars. Says Jobes
and Silva, "Lagarde's position [not Kahle's], with some modifications, [functions] as the working assumption for most special-
ists."[176] This means the LXX/OG is the only relevant LXX for
textual scholars interested in determining its original words.

Origen, Other Greek Recensions, and the *Hexapla*

While this author has liberally attacked the second-century
rabbinic founders for changing the biblical texts to suit their
purposes, there was also one early Christian theologian who
contributed to the fate of the LXX as the universal Christian
Bible. While Justin, Irenaeus, Eusebius, and Chrysostom talked
glowingly about the original version of "The Seventy" (by
which they exclusively meant the Old Greek or Alexandrian
text), the controversial Church Father, Origen, added considerable confusion to the issue when he attempted to harmonize
the various Greek and Hebrew versions in the third century.

Origen decided that the "standard" Hebrew version
(Akiba's proto-MT version) should be the basis for "correcting"
the Greek versions. Why he made this decision is multi-faceted

---

[175] Jobes and Silva, op. cit., p. 22.

[176] Ibid., p. 22. We will mention the recension of Theodotion shortly, that
does give Kahle some empirical support. However, the overwhelming evidence
supports the majority opinion.

involving bias and bad doctrine. His multi-column version, known as the *Hexapla*, six versions of the Bible laid "side by side," consumed perhaps six thousand pages and 15 columns. It was so massive, no one could carry it (let alone copy it by hand which was the only publishing option available).

Consequently, everyone used only "column five" of his harmonized recension of the LXX, which eventually led the loss of all his notations (commentary, explanations on the variances, and rationale for his changes). Not only were subtleties lost, but important portions of the text were sacrificed. After that, the Septuagint of the third century (used by Jewish synagogues and doubtless some churches) became "Hexaplaric" which is a pejorative meaning that it *had made soup of the Greek Bible*.[177]

Typically, scholars attempt to detect the differences in versions. *Origen* cloaked the differences, obfuscating the *original*. Happily, for various text-critical reasons, the Alexandrian original is far from lost. But justice was served, so to speak, since Origen's *Hexapla* was lost when its only known copy, in Caesarea, was apparently destroyed by fire amid Mohammed's conquest of Palestine in the seventh century.

But returning to the two Greek recensions of Symmachus and Theodotion (which riff mostly on Aquila's translation): These "new and improved" recensions, like Aquila's original, were also created *in the second century*. Let's take up each in turn.

The first is Symmachus' recension. Symmachus was a Jew converted to Christianity and then back to Judaism. Although apparently double-minded, his words were well chosen. He

---

[177] Ibid. p. 23.

authored his recension between 170 – 200 of the current era. Scholars consider it, by far, the most elegant translation of all three Jewish recensions of the original Greek translation. For instance, Jobes and Silva cite Alison Salvesen who effusively asserts that Symmachus produced a Greek translation of the Hebrew Pentateuch which "combined the best Biblical Greek style, remarkable clarity, a high degree of accuracy regarding the Hebrew, and the rabbinic exegesis of his days: It might be described as a Greek *Targum* or *Tannaitic* Septuagint."[178] [Emphasis added]

Her enthusiasm does not include an evaluation of whether the recension represents the authentic Hebrew Vorlage.

While Symmachus stuck to the story as laid out by Aquila (namely, making sure that Akiba's changes remained intact), Symmachus did a much better job translating Hebrew into words Homer would have liked (i.e., terms more in line with classical Greek), making sense of Hebrew idioms with Greek equivalents. While Aquila's was a "slavish" translation, Symmachus was not so constrained. Still, he managed to maintain the meaning of the text (aka *semantics*) near Aquila's. While Symmachus found it necessary to create some new Greek words along the way to convey Hebrew ideas. Note: this practice is not frowned upon by critics today. "Jerome praised Symmachus for making his translation so intelligible – he was able to use it more than Aquila's literal translation when

---

[178] Salvesen, Alison. *Symmachus in the Pentateuch*, JSSM 15 (Manchester: University of Manchester, 1991), p. 296-297. Cited by Jobes and Silva, p.30. *Targum* refers to the Aramaic version of the Hebrew Bible, frequently used in Babylon and other Aramaic communities. *Tannaitic* refers to the Rabbinic traditions of the second century which have incurred this author's intensive criticism. Salvesen's enthusiasm for Symmachus lacks sensitivity to Christian polemics.

working on the Vulgate."[179] From the standpoint of literature, without question, the loss of Symmachus' Greek Old Testament constitutes a major loss. However, while we should appreciate that his Hebrew translation into Greek was stylistically superior to the LXX/OG, from the viewpoint of a more accurate rendering of what comprised LXX's authentic Vorlage (that is, the original used by the Old Greek), his contribution wouldn't have been helpful to the quest had it survived.

The other recension by Theodotion (a third Greek version but less inspired by Akiba's Hebrew Old Testament), was also created late in the second century. Who, pray tell, was Theodotion? He was likely a Greek convert to Judaism living in Ephesus. Regarding his recension, four essential facts stand out:

1. Theodotion often resorted to *transliteration* in order to facilitate similar pronunciation between the languages (in this case, transliteration means using Greek letters that collectively sounded the same as the pronunciation of the Hebrew word);

2. His recension of the Book of Daniel became the Church's preferred Greek translation of that prophet's work and would find its way until the Church's Greek Bible;

3. His Book of Job is one-sixth longer than that of the LXX, suggesting poetic license or more likely, another text at his disposal.

4. Theodotion likely utilized, in part, a Greek text predating the birth of Christ, different from the LXX/OG. Some have called this text, "proto-Theodotion."[180]

---

[179] Wegner, op. cit., p. 200.

[180] Jobes and Silva, op. cit., p. 27. Also, see Bruce, F.F. *The Books and the Parchment*, Pickering and Engles, 1963, p. 143. Cited by Wegner, op. cit., p. 197.

133

This last point prompted Jobes and Silva to speculate that the Theodotion fragments, "have confirmed the view that, for at least parts of the Hebrew Bible, a translation containing elements once attributed to Theodotion, was already in use before NT times. We now realize that the motive for revising the Greek versions toward a particular Hebrew text must have arisen as early as the Hasmonean period in the first century BCE."[181] Meaning, that as far as the Greek versions of the Hebrew Old Testament, there is something of a "mashup" of these latter works. Indeed, scholars talk in terms of a *Kaige* (chi-guh) set of texts that employ common methods likely shared by these translators (and a few others) who were attempting to establish a standard Greek recension of Aquila, and to a lesser extent the LXX/OG,[182] with some reliance on a first century B.C. manuscript differing from the LXX/OG. We could summarize his impact negatively by stating that Theodotion contributed to muddling the text, and thereby created more variations in the text for scholars to dissect. However, so few fragments of his version remain or were quoted that his impact has been limited.

Now, a critical comment on my sources: As we move closer to analyzing the many significant changes made in the LXX/OG, this author feels it is necessary to point out that the scholarship of Jobes and Silva (as well as Wegner), is indeed

---

[181] Perhaps as much as 100 years before the birth of Christ. Jobes and Silva, op. cit. p. 27-28.

[182] The definition of Kaige by Jobes and Silva, "Kaige (also Kaige recension). An early revision of some books in the Old Greek, characterized by a number of distinctive features, such as the consistent use of *kaige* (καίγε) to render Hebrew gam (ם, "also"). This work sought to bring the Greek translation into greater conformity with the Hebrew text that was becoming standardized in the first century of our era." Ibid., p. 372.

worthy of all the academic recognition they have garnered. However, they lack much concern for the changes imposed on the text from Aquila and his successors – changes that have certainly hampered Christian apologetics. How so? They weakened the evangelistic imperative demonstrating *how the Scripture strongly supports Jesus as the Messiah.* Of course, *why* the original texts were altered isn't their issue. They don't concern themselves with biblical inspiration and Scriptural authority. That is to say, they are aware of the variations yet offer nothing more than modest speculation for why these changes were made. They do not appear to be aware that many scholarly Jewish sources are critical of Akiba, which partially explains why so many differences exist between the LXX and the MT. We read:

> It would be fair to say that, in the majority of passages in the Hebrew Bible where a textual variant is suspected, the question comes down to a decision between the MT and the LXX. This is easily confirmed by noting the frequent use of LXX evidence in the apparatus to editions of the Hebrew Bible. And in numerous passages, it is likely (in some cases, virtually certain) that the LXX preserves a more reliable text.[183]

In a footnote to the above passage, they call out a number of these changes in the MT, where the LXX is much more likely to be the correct text or where it provides some text the MT is "missing" – as in "dropped." These variants are different from what I present in the following chapter.[184]

---

[183] Ibid. p. 163.

[184] Additionally, it should be noted there are hundreds of variations. These are but a few.

Here's their short list of the original LXX wording and then the MT variant:

1. Genesis 37:36, LXX - "Midianites" (MT Medanites");
2. Genesis 47:21, LXX – "he enslaved the people," (MT "he moved the people to the cities");
3. Exodus 8:23, LXX - "distinction," (MT numbering 8:19), "redemption;"
4. Numbers 32:17, LXX - "[as a] vanguard," (MT "hurrying");
5. Deuteronomy LXX - 33:28, "Jacob will dwell," (MT "the fountain of Jacob");
6. Joshua 19:34, LXX - "the Jordan," (MT "in Judah the Jordan");
7. 1 Samuel 8:16, LXX - "cattle," (MT "young men");
8. 2 Samuel 24:13, LXX - "three," (MT "seven");
9. 1 Chronicles 1:4, LXX - "the sons of Noah," (MT "Noah");
10. Esther 3:7, LXX - "and the lot fell on," (missing in MT);
11. Psalm 35:16 (Verse numbering in LXX 34:16), LXX - "they mocked me with mocking," (MT is uncertain or missing);
12. Ecclesiastes 9:2, LXX - "and the bad," (missing in MT);
13. Isaiah 45:2, LXX - "mountains," (MT uncertain);
14. Ezekiel 32:27, LXX - "of old," (MT "uncircumcised");
15. Daniel 9:27, LXX - "temple," (MT "wing");
16. Hosea 11:2, LXX - "me," (MT "them").[185]

Wegner, in his excellent and respected book on textual transmission (from which we have drawn in this chapter), offers the opinion of scholar R.W. Klein who admits to Aquila's suspect motivation in rendering his translation:

"**Aquila seems to have been motivated in part by a desire to expunge certain readings in the LXX which were being used by Christians for apologetic purposes**. A classic

---

[185] Ibid. p. 180.

example is his use of a word meaning 'young woman' instead of LXX's 'virgin' in Isa. 7:14)." [186] [Emphasis mine]

Klein's comment hits the nail on the head. And we will look carefully at this verse and over *26 other variations that demonstrate similar bias* besides this more well-known disparity.

Jobes and Silva point to the judgment of no less a scholar than Emanuel Tov and his ringing endorsement, "The LXX is the single most important source for preserving evidence of the literary development of the Hebrew text. The Hebrew Vorlage of the LXX/OG predates the earliest extant manuscripts of the MT by many centuries."[187] For Tov, the LXX is trusted more than the MT. But for academics, this exists only due to the long interval of time between extant texts and the end-product.[188]

In fairness, Jobes and Silva go on to provide a derivative guideline for today's textual criticism of the Bible: "The current consensus is that there were at least two distinct Hebrew text

---

[186] Wegner, op. cit., p. 199. Wegner makes note of these variations but doesn't show concern that the MT's variations might be due to poisonous motives in its creation. It is almost certain that Wegner believes in Biblical inspiration. But his academic priority keeps him from pressing for an answer that might help his reader take Akiba's ulterior motive into account. Clearly, I am at liberty to point this out to the non-technical or non-academic audience. Bless you, my audience.

[187] Ibid. p. 161.

[188] Jobes and Silva state, "Surviving manuscripts of the MT go as far back as the ninth century of our era, and the Masoretic scribes had been at work for several centuries before that. The evidence suggests that, as a whole, the MT is for all practical purposes the same Hebrew text that had emerged as the standard late in the first century of our era, but that still leaves a significant temporal gap between it and the earliest form of the text." (op. cit., p. 155) This also tells us that the differences between the LXX and the MT *owe themselves to the work done in the first century by Akiba, and not due to later scribes or the Masoretes.*

forms in circulation and that the longer versions in the MT developed from the shorter versions preserved in the LXX."[189]

Perhaps textual critics would agree to a *heuristic* that goes something like, "*The older, the better; the shorter, the better.*"

Nevertheless, while we might *excuse* LXX scholars from excessive speculating on "why there are so many differences" between the LXX and MT (especially in Messianic and salvific passages), it's harder to justify their failure to admit Akiba's widespread meddling in the text that so many Jewish scholars underscore (as documented in the previous chapter). Are they fearful that pointing out this fact could open them to charges of anti-Semitism? No doubt I will encounter this criticism despite my claims otherwise. It likely will be ignored that my criticism means to target *religious variance Christians have with Judaism,* not the race.

Origen's Contribution to the Septuagint's Setback

But not all the blame for what happened to the LXX can be dumped on Akiba's doorstep. Nor can we fault just the recensions of Aquila, Symmachus, and Theodotion whose works were motivated by Jewish concerns.

The guilt must be shared by Christians too. Indeed, more than one Christian leader created big dustups over the matter of the nature of Christ's divinity. In the early Church, this debate had an enormous impact on the fate of the LXX/OG – that is, *why the original LXX would not become the standard Bible for all of Christendom.*

---

[189] Ibid. p. 162.

To understand this aspect of the story, we turn once again to Origen, his theology, and an account of the debate. Admittedly, Origen may have had good intentions; that is, to create a tool to help in the apologetic (evangelistic) effort when speaking with "the Jews." His work, however, would backfire. Wegner writes:

Figure 18 - Origen of Alexandria

Origen claims that he compiled this work primarily to equip Christians for discussion with Jews and to protect them against the charge of falsifying the biblical texts, as he explains in a letter to Julius Africanus (c. 240). "I make it my endeavor not to be ignorant of their [Septuagint's] various readings, less in my controversies with the Jews I should quote to them what is not in their copies and that I may make some use of what is found there, even although it should not be in our Scriptures."[190] [Clarification in original]

This quotation indicates Origen's methodology was to minimize the differences in the text at the expense of losing the Septuagint's original wording since it was (no longer) found in the Hebrew MT which had become standard in his time (ca. 220 A.D.). Jobes and Silva provide this assessment:

Aware of the differences between the Septuagint and the Hebrew text, he [Origen] set out to produce an edition that

---

[190] Wegner, op. cit., p. 200.

would take those variations into account. Origen's work, however, must not be confused with the aims of a modern textual critic. He did not intend to gather variant readings and decide which was the original. Instead, his aim was apologetic and in service to the church [which wasn't], to assure that the Greek OT read by Christians accurately represented the Hebrew text known to him.[191] [Comment mine]

The contexts of the *Hexapla's* six columns:

1. The Hebrew text [as provided by Akiba's Rabbis].
2. A transliteration of the Hebrew text using Greek letters.
3. Aquila's [Greek] translation of the Hebrew Proto-MT.
4. Symmachus' Greek translation [recension]
5. The translation of the Seventy [with Origen's changes]
6. Theodotion's Greek translation [recension][192]

The transliteration (column 2), as mentioned previously, would have been useful to readers of Old Testament Scripture during Church worship when called upon, helping them properly pronounce the Hebrew words. As argued by one scholar, columns two and three taken together were to facilitate Greek speakers learning Hebrew, with Aquila's "word-for-word" version providing something of a "crib sheet" or quasi-interlinear. The three columns devoted to the Greek recensions – Aquila's, Symmachus', and Theodotion's – were to help justify the changes Origen made to the LXX/OG in column five.[193] *The actual, original LXX/OG, was not retained.*

---

[191] Jobes and Silva, op. cit., p. 39. As we will see, his doctrine was a factor in his project, but not readily admitted to his colleagues.

[192] Ibid., p. 39.

[193] Ibid., p. 45.

But the result of his project wound up being detrimental to apologetic debates and evangelistic dialogues with Jews, not just in his day but for over a millennium after. This is because Origen's watered-down version – supposedly having corrected the LXX – would "quickly became the standard OT for the Eastern churches from Antioch to Alexandria."[194] Meaning, that despite its corrupting influence, his recension became the "Septuagint of record." How so? "After his work, the name *Septuagint* could refer to the Greek text used as his base [that would be put on the back burner] and *the text he "revised" which would be published via scriptoriums.*[195]

Furthermore, Jobes and Silva confirm...

> It was copied and promoted by church leaders for centuries. It too was the "Septuagint," although it was no longer the "Septuagint" text with which Origen had started... [for] Where the Greek Bible disagreed with the Hebrew Bible, Origen felt it important to "correct" the Greek version used at that time by the church to agree with the Hebrew version used at that time by the synagogue.[196]

And Origen's diluted LXX became official:

> Justinian, who on February 8, 533, decreed the Septuagint to be the authorized version, [gave] also a nod to Aquila: "Those who read in Greek shall use the Septuagint tradition, which is more accurate than all the others... We give permission to use also Akilas' [Aquila's] translation."[197]

---

[194] Ibid., p. 45. The Septuagint of today is essentially the "Old Greek."

[195] Ibid., p. 23.

[196] Ibid., p. 43.

[197] Ibid., p. 31. No doubt for Greek-speaking Jews to use in the Synagogue.

Perhaps if Origen had noted all the differences pertinent to Christianity, he might have come to recognize the evil seed sown by Akiba and wouldn't have been so enthusiastic to eliminate those variations he obviously noted in the LXX's text (or he wouldn't have made changes). And yet, he apparently didn't seem to notice that the original wording better supported the meaning of the incarnation of Christ and salvation by grace through faith.

So, what caused Origen's quest to "correct" the text of the Septuagint? Undoubtedly, he preferred the Hebrew version presuming it more accurate (as would Martin Luther). It turns out his effort, however well-intentioned to provide a certain copy of the original writings of biblical authors, was tainted by *several doctrinal biases*. [198] We take a short look at Origen's relevant theology next.

Theology's Main Dispute In the Fourth Century

We've noted why translations (and recensions) aren't free from the beliefs and understandings of the one (or many) doing the writing and editing. Additionally, the words selected for inclusion in the new document bring to the translation their own baggage. What the chosen words mean in the minds of their nature speakers, varnish the reading and how it is understood. Jobes and Silva note, "Hebrew Ps. 1:5 reads, 'Therefore the wicked will not *stand* in the judgment," whereas the Greek has, "Therefore unbelievers will *not arise in (the) judgment*." The latter appears to convey a theological notion that only believers will be resurrected. On the surface, this appears to be the

---

[198] Origen is unfairly criticized in some matters. We discuss several following.

meaning of the text. The Greek word used, *anistemi*, means "to rise up" and is the word NT writers preferred when referencing the resurrection.

Words greatly influence specific doctrines. Words matter a lot. In "doing theology," it should go without saying that we provide a much better exegesis when we possess the original words of the author, or in this case, a translation as close in time as possible to the original, in the hopes that crucial words will not be dropped or altered.[199]

But Origen's doctrinal beliefs seem to have led to a willingness that allowed changes to Messianic passages. As we will see, the original wording clearly testifies to the *deity* of the Messiah. Plus, the words called the Messiah "Christ" in Greek, a title put to extensive use throughout the Mediterranean wherever Christians spread the Good News. Deleting "Christ" and using an alternate term, helped make the case against Jesus.

Despite scriptures to the contrary, Origen didn't subscribe to the view that the Father and the Son were One, at least not in the manner in which it is generally professed among Evangelicals. Jesus was uniquely divine – he was, in essence, the same as God the Father. Paul's teaching in Colossians 2:9 is clear, "*For in Him all the fullness of Deity dwells in bodily form*," NASB). However, Origen stressed the Son's subordinate role, and this is uncomfortable for Christians who see the Son on the very same footing as the Father. In short, the wording of his

---

[199] By citing this verse from the LXX, I am not asserting belief in the dead not rising at the last judgment. That is matter for another day. But having the original wording of the text, obviously greatly helps to correctly exegete relevant passages.

understanding of incarnation theology – a formal explanation of Christ's divinity – appeared to veer away from the accepted path of Orthodoxy.[200] And the incarnation was what Christians were grappling with as the fourth century A.D. began.

The Arian Heresy infected Christianity just as Christians were finally freed from the persecution of Rome and its Caesars. The Synod of Alexandria declared Arius a heretic in 321 A.D. Thanks to Arius and his references to Origen, Origen was (fairly or not), associated with Arianism. That is, Origen, writing a hundred years earlier, was likely the theologian upon which Arius based his viewpoint, often known as "Subordination." This view holds that *the essence of God the Father is superior to the essence of Christ.* A *subordinationist* believes Christ is divine, but that he isn't exactly equal to the Father. Christ is "subordinate" to the Father **not just in role or duty** (*"The Son can do nothing by himself; he can do only what he sees his Father doing"* – John 5:19, NIV) but in a manner of his origination too. The Son was begotten of the Father, and being begotten, this seemed to make Christ a secondary member of the Godhead. It can easily be argued that Origen did not hold to Arianism and would be horrified to learn that his thinking was taken to mean such things. However, the emphasis of his position led down a questionable path and left his genius unappreciated.

While Arianism would be condemned at the Council of Nicaea in 325 A.D., it would continue to plague the Church for centuries, and in some respects, continues down to our day (many in modern Christian liberalism hold to *Subordination* or

---

[200] We can work backwards from a Syriac copy of the LXX made in 617 by Bishop Paulus of Tella. He recorded all of Origen's changes to the LXX. So the original form of the LXX has been preserved. See Setterfield, op. cit., p. 9.

to *Adoptionism* – the latter sees the human Jesus *becoming Christ at his baptism, not at his birth).* This stands in stark contrast to the Scripture which teaches, *"Have this mind among yourselves, which is yours in Christ Jesus, who, though he was in the form of God, did not count equality with God a thing to be grasped, but emptied himself, by taking the form of a servant, being born in the likeness of men,"* (Philippians 2:5-7, ESV). The more we consider its many aspects, we realize the mystery of the incarnation is not easily explained. Origen may be a victim of his own making.

Nevertheless, his thinking was unquestionably divergent in other areas.

- He taught the pre-existence of souls; specifically, that souls lost their intense love of God in heaven and thus became flesh and blood beings, Christ being chief of these beings because His love for the Father stood out above the rest.

- Additionally, Origen denied that Christ rose in a physical body (his immortal body was spiritual but not tangible in a conventional sense). Indeed, the physical quality of spiritual existence appeared to trouble Origen, despite the fact the Scripture depicts our bodily resurrection, that God prepared a physical body for His Christ, and that God would not allow Christ's body to suffer corruption.

- Origen argued for universalism and hoped all would be redeemed. (He was falsely accused of teaching that Satan would eventually be saved, to which he called this accusation "balderdash" – or something similar, more in line with the slang of his day!)

- He also authored, for the first time in Theology, the notion of "the ransom theory of atonement" which many consider scriptural (*"For the Son of Man came not to be served but to serve and give Himself a ransom for many"* (Mark 10:45; see also 1 Timothy 2:5-6).

145

- He was very much an ascetic and a pacifist. Some regard such views heterodox too although fasting is a minor form of asceticism and pacifism has many passages in the life and teaching of Jesus offering strong support.[201]

Figure 19 - Constantine, Bishops, and the Nicaean Creed

---

[201] For a well-considered view on pacifism and the violence in the New Testament, a good article can be found at https://peacetheology.net/pacifism/8-christian-pacifism-and-new-testament-understandings-of-the-death-of-jesus/.

Origen would eventually die in 253 A.D. as a martyr (his death resulting from wounds suffered from torture during imprisonment in 250-51 A.D.) Despite all his work, personal sacrifice, and vast writings on behalf of the Church, he would be declared a heretic posthumously in 400 A.D. - a charge confirmed by Justinian in 543 - simultaneous with the Emperor's order that Origen's books be burned.

Nonetheless, Origen was famous across the Roman Empire for his lectures and knowledge of philosophy. He wrote no less than 2,000 treatises touching on almost all branches of theology. Some consider him the greatest genius the early Church produced.[202] Regardless of what we think of Origen, the heresy of Arianism would haunt the Church for at least another 1,000 years. As we will discuss next, the debate over Arianism before, during, and after Nicaea, would have an enormous impact on the obfuscation of the LXX/OG.

Arius, Eusebius, Athanasius, & Gregory Mix it Up

Arius was denounced in 321 A.D. by the Synod of Alexandria due to his denial of Jesus' deity. Disgraced, he left the Egyptian city so vital to our story, Alexandria, settling at Caesarea, in Palestine.[203] Another resident of that city was Eusebius of Caesarea, the noted historian of the early Church, a student of Pamphilus with whom he co-authored the *Defense of Origen*, and friend and counselor to Emperor Constantine. Arius was safe with Eusebius and the strong Christian community there.

---

[202] McGuckin, John A. *The Westminster Handbook to Origen*, John Knox Press, p. 25.

[203] Caesarea was the beautiful city built with a manufactured harbor by King Herod. It was center to the Roman Court in Judea/Palestine, and home to Pontius Pilate when he wasn't dealing with rioting and discord in Jerusalem.

At Nicaea, the Bishops of the Christian Church from across Asia Minor, North Africa, and Europe, accepted the wording of the Nicaean Creed in 325 A.D. In reality, however, they didn't all agree.

Constantine favored Arianism because it was easier to understand than Trinitarianism. But, after the Bishops made their decision, Constantine put his authority behind their action, threatening excommunication for anyone who didn't comply and fall into step. So, it was no surprise that everyone, but two dissenters, signed.

Nevertheless, the debate continued among the leaders of the Council for decades afterward in hopes acceptable wording could be hammered out. In 381, there were slight modifications made at a Second Council of Nicaea that quieted things down – at least somewhat.

The essential portion of the original Creed that touches on our story is as follows:

> And in one Lord Jesus Christ, the Son of God, **begotten of the Father** [the only-begotten][204] that is, of the essence of the Father, God of God,] Light of Light, very God of very God, begotten, not made, **being of one substance with the Father;**[205]

With that wording, the "subordinate" issue receded. The Creed settled, at least for the time being, the Arian debate.

---

[204] In Greek, *Monogenēs* (μονογενὴς) one of a kind, with a special relationship no one else has.

[205] In Greek, *Homooúsios* (ὁμοούσιος) was used by Origen despite the fact he had suggested that Christ was in some sense lesser in stature that the Father. To be totally fair, Origen's position remained ambiguous. For instance, this statement is quite orthodox: "Wherefore we have always held that God is the Father of His only-begotten Son, who was born indeed of Him, and derives from Him what He is, but without any beginning" (from *De Principiis.*).

Constantine exiled Arius to Illyricum (modern-day Croatia) against the wishes of his protectors, Eusebius of Caesarea and his namesake and second cohort, *Eusebius of Nicomedia*.

Soon after the council was history, in 331 A.D., Constantine asked his friend Eusebius of Caesarea to create 50 copies of the LXX. Eusebius, a man of wealth and steward of the library there, had funding and copyists available to him at the library (in a "scriptorium"), where Origen's magnum opus, the *Hexapla* just happened to be stored (Origen brought this to Caesarea 100 years earlier after being "encouraged" to leave Alexandria).

So then, from which version of the LXX would Eusebius choose for creating 50 copies? Of course, he decided on the LXX as revised by Origen (recorded in the Hexapla, "column 5"). Since the copying at Caesarea far outstripped the reproduction that Athanasius could muster back in Egypt, "the LXX according to Origen" won the day. It was distributed to Churches far and wide. This standard would of course be changed once Jerome completed his Vulgate, and the Roman Church adopted his Latin version, *influenced by the Hebrew proto-MT*.

Now, regarding Athanasius. He was a young man in 325 A.D. when he appeared at Nicaea. He was not officially invited to the conference but attended with the aging Patriarch of Alexandria, Alexander, with whom Athanasius was attached as an assistant. However, at Nicaea, Athanasius was permitted to speak. He did so eloquently on behalf of the Trinitarian point of view. His presence would set in motion a conflict with Arianism that would define him throughout his famed theological career… and get him in trouble numerous times.

A few months after the Council, the challenge began. Athanasius' patron, Alexander the Patriarch died. Athanasius was appointed head of the Church in Alexandria, (which he served from 327 to 373 A.D.) So then, he had authority (and some help). Gregory, a famed Bishop in Nazianzen, Cappadocia (central Turkey), was a strong supporter of Athanasius. Gregory was known as the "Trinitarian Theologian." In 379, Gregory became the Archbishop of Constantinople. He would serve in this capacity until his death in 389. Gregory thought very highly of his good friend Athanasius. From Gregory's Oration, xxii. 9, we read of his heartfelt and confident support:

> (Athanasius was) "fit to keep on a level with common-place views yet also to soar high above the more aspiring, as accessible to all, slow to anger, quick in sympathy, pleasant in conversation, and still more pleasant in temper, effective alike in discourse and in action, assiduous in devotions, helpful to Christians of every class and age, a theologian with the speculative, a comforter of the afflicted, a staff to the aged, a guide of the young."[206]

With his new appointment, *Athanasius likely took it upon his administration in Egypt, to make copies of the original Septuagint held in Alexandria,* now aging past the point of use, *almost 600 years since its creation.* Along with the LXX/OG, the New Testament would need to be included in the package. *It is at this moment when the Codex Alexandrinus was created* – a codex to be treasured – which would begin the rescue of the original LXX from obscurity almost 1,300 years later.

Barry Setterfield provides a lively account of what followed. I defer to his words at this point in the story:

> Arius himself was still living, and his friend Eusebius of Nicomedia rapidly regained influence over Emperor

---

[206] St. Athanasius, Christian Classics Ethereal Library. Retrieved June 29, 2018, from http://www.ccel.org/ccel/athanasius. Cited by Setterfield, op. cit., p. 9.

Constantine. The result of this was a demand made by the Emperor that Arius should be re-admitted to communion. Athanasius stood firm and refused to have any communion with the advocates of a "heresy that was fighting against Christ." In the summer of 335 AD, Athanasius was peremptorily ordered to appear at Tyre, where a council had been summoned to sit in judgment upon his conduct. The most conspicuous leaders of this Tyrian council were the two Eusebii. The council then condemned Athanasius and restored Arius to church communion. On the 6th November 335 AD, Athanasius was falsely charged by the Eusebii before Emperor Constantine and was accordingly banished to Trier in the Rhineland. About two years later Constantine fell seriously ill and was baptized by Eusebius, Bishop of Nicomedia, shortly before he died on 22 May, 337 AD. Soon after that, Athanasius was able to return to Alexandria, which remained his base of operations throughout his life.[207]

Setterfield relates that Athanasius would go through a cycle of five "banishments and restorations" during his turbulent career, as Constantine II was – like his father – sympathetic to the Arian position and under the advisement of the two "Eusebii" (as Setterfield cleverly tags them) who continued to harass Athanasius.

In summary, Athanasius would be known as the critical prosecutor on behalf of the Trinity. He would also finalize the canon for the Church in his Easter Letter of 367. Athanasius died on May 2, 373. But his legacy still shines brightly today.

What Happened to the "Old Greek" Septuagint?

During the early 1600s Cyril Lucar, the Patriarch of Alexandria, (we mentioned him earlier in this chapter) was appointed Patriarch of Constantinople in 1621 (this would be considered

---

[207] Setterfield, op. cit. p. 10.

a promotion as it was the center of the Eastern Church). *The Alexandrinus Codex had been in his safekeeping in Alexandria.* However, when he migrated to Constantinople, he took the OG LXX codex with him (most likely, **the official copy of the original**). He intended to present the Codex to King James, but the English (and Scottish) King died. Instead, the gift was received by his successor, Charles I, who agreed he would accept it, and did so in 1627.

The legend (supported by sound documentation) is that a noble lady named Thecla, *transcribed the Codex Alexandrinus.* At the end of the first folio was a colophon[208] which stated, "According to the Arabic note on folio one, the codex was written by Thecla, the martyr from Egypt, just after the Council of Nice (Nicaea) in 325."[209] Setterfield's fine narration indicates:

1. Thecla held her monastic vocation sometime after 325 when she began work on the Codex.
2. Her father founded the monastery in which she worked. He may have provided the financing for the high cost of animal skins.
3. Gregory of Nazianzen's (later, of Constantinople) letters indicates that he, Thecla, and Athanasius were contemporaries.
4. Her trinitarianism could be the reason for her martyrdom.[210]

Setterfield also mounts a compelling argument that a connection exists between all three codices:

---

[208] A colophon is a concluding piece at the end of the publication providing information about the document.

[209] OT Manuscript Series: #6 Codex Alexandrinus – Reference from Setterfield is given as F.H.A. Scrivener, *Six Lectures on the Text of the New Testament and the Ancient Manuscripts Which Contain It: Chiefly Addressed to Those Who Do Not Read Greek.* (Cambridge, MA: Deighton, Bell, and Co., 1875), p. 50-51.

[210] Setterfield, op. cit. p. 14.

Therefore, it seems that although these three Codices originated from the same scriptorium[211] over a period of 50 years, the question becomes, "Which scriptorium, and why?" After producing the 50 copies of the Bible for the Emperor, it is unlikely that the scriptorium at Caesarea would be involved in the production of three rival versions which used a different text to that of the Hexapla. Indeed, Kenyon points out that there is not the slightest evidence for them to have been produced at either Caesarea or Constantinople. Furthermore, Kenyon, Gardhausen, Ropes, and Jellicoe *all conclude that at least some of the three were written in Egypt, probably at Alexandria.* The evidence ... suggests that if one was produced at Alexandria, then probably all three were.[212]

Were all three copied over a 50-year interval in the fourth century? That is the work of textual criticism, and this supposition could provoke many challenges. Nevertheless, the connection of the Codex Alexandrinus with Thecla and Athanasius, as well as their sanctified struggles, seems beyond question. That this may be a copy one generation removed from the original OG LXX, makes one's mind reel. In conclusion, the story of our Bible is a far more dramatic epic than most of us know. It remains rich in conspiracy and intrigue.

Next, we examine a selected 27 variances this author believes were intentionally altered within the Messianic and salvific passages of the Masoretic Text – a departure from the original (and essential) words of the Old Greek Septuagint, of whose importance we have, hopefully, awakened the reader.

---

[211] A scriptorium is a room set aside in a monastery for copying scripts.

[212] Ibid., p. 15. In the final analysis, it remains Alexandria's legacy that Christian as well as Jew should revere. Its influence on us is monumental.

Chapter Four:
TAMPERING WITH THE TEXT –
COMPARING THE LXX WITH THE MT

Introducing Hard Evidence

OUR STUDY MAKES SOME SEVERE ALLEGATIONS SURE TO SPUR DISAGREEMENT, CONSTERNATION, AND CONDEMNATION FROM MANY QUARTERS OF CHRISTENDOM AND Judaism. Are these allegations provable? Is the evidence plain enough to justify the claims that rabbinical schools at the end of the first century intentionally corrupted what became the Masoretic Text? Should such corruption cause concern that our Bibles have been severely altered? Do these variances introduced into the Old Testament really matter?

This author claims the evidence is unassailable, and it does make a difference. So, now the time has come to introduce the hard evidence backing up these claims. It's also time for Protestant Christians to reclaim the LXX as our preeminent historical text. *Our Bibles must take the LXX into account with deference to many if not most of its readings.*

To prove my case, not only must we consider the history of the corrupting process (which we have done in the first three chapters), we must establish the allegations by looking at the Bible itself. In this chapter, we will evaluate numerous key variances between the Septuagint (LXX) and the Masoretic Text (MT). This is only a selection. With study, one learns there are hundreds. These can be found on the internet at numerous sites that tackle this critical fact. However, here we will consider those which pertain to the prophecies of the Messiah, His mission to the Gentiles, and the nature of the salvation He brings. All these topics served as challenges to the rabbinic leaders who wished to restrict salvation to the Jews, disprove Jesus was the anticipated Christ, and sought to emphasize *law rather than grace* as the means to achieve salvation.

In the next chapter, we will look carefully at the chronology presented implicitly in the genealogies of Genesis 5 and 11. As I will demonstrate, the same motive existed there for corrupting numerous passages resulting in *significant tampering with the Masoretic Text.*

Presenting the Evidence

Here's how we will evaluate the evidence that Rabbi Akiba and Jamnia changed the text in numerous passages of the Old Testament, regarding the Messiah, God's grace and our salvation, and the mission of the Messiah to the Gentiles:

- First, our study presents the **New Testament** (NT) verses quoting the Old Testament (OT). We employ the *English Standard Version* (ESV) for the NT which considers recent manuscript discoveries by scholars translated into modern English. *When citing the Old Testament,* the NT writers *used the Septuagint (LXX),* not the Masoretic Text (MT), 90% of the time.

- Second, we reference the *King James Version* (KJV) for the **OT as quoted in the NT**. That is, we will use the KJV to represent the *Masoretic Text's translation* of the Hebrew and Aramaic language of the Old Testament. We chose the KJV since it constitutes the standard Protestant Bible. The reader should notice how the wording differs in these passages. In some, the variance is clear-cut, others less so. The commentary provided highlights the distinction. The 27 NT passages selected are directly related to the coming of the Messiah, His attributes, the manner of His "visitation," and the means of our salvation.

- Third, we present the *Septuagint Version* to compare the KJV OT with the ESV NT. It confirms the OT LXX is the version that NT writers prefer. LXX also makes a stronger case that the Messiah is deity as Jesus of Nazareth claimed. Our point: In rendering the proto-MT, Rabbi Akiba selectively altered the text since, by the second century, the three Greek versions (Aquila, Symmachus, Theodotion) – derived from the proto-MT of Akiba – are complete and after that, the MT text is, in essence, "frozen."

To summarize, in 80% of the verses *that directly cite the Old Testament* (about 300 in all), NT authors prefer the LXX. In 10% of these, the LXX and MT agree. In the other 10%, a Hebrew version appears referenced that may align better with a copy of what was the MT Vorlage or another Hebrew source.

After reviewing these passages, the reader can decide whether or not a pattern exists demonstrating that the Masoretic Text was manipulated to obscure Christian teaching about the nature of Jesus Christ, the grace of God working through his death and resurrection to bring us salvation, and the mission of the Messiah to gather in the Gentiles.

A final word: Consider this a "Bible study," delving into the meaning of many scriptures vital to our faith. Enter into this examination open to the Spirit of God and His speaking to you.

Highlighted Differences in Text – LXX with MT

Key Salvific and Messianic Passages Altered in the Masoretic Text

1. Matthew 13:15 with Isaiah 6:10
2. Romans 9:27-28 with Isaiah 10:22-23
3. Romans 15:12 with Isaiah 11:10
4. Acts 4:25-26 with Psalms 2:1-2
5. Matthew 13:35 with Psalms 78:2
6. Hebrews 10:5 with Psalms 40:6
7. Matthew 12:20-21 with Isaiah 42:4
8. Acts 15:16-18 with Amos 9:11-12
9. Matthew 1:23 with Isaiah 7:14
10. Romans 9:33 with Isaiah 8:14 and 28:16
11. Luke 4:18 with Isaiah 61:1
12. Hebrews 1:6 with Deuteronomy 32:43
13. Genesis 49:10 – The LXX vs. MT

Other Passages with Important Variances Between the Septuagint and the Masoretic Text

14. Matthew 15:8-9 with Isaiah 29:13
15. Romans 11:34 with Isaiah 40:13
16. Hebrews 13:6 with Psalms 117:6
17. Hebrews 12:5 with Proverbs 3:11
18. 2 Corinthians 6:17 with Isaiah 52:11
19. Romans 11:9 with Psalms 69:22
20. Matthew 3:3 with Isaiah 40:3
21. Romans 3:13 with Psalms 5:9
22. Ephesians 4:26 with Psalms 4:4
23. Romans 3:12 with Psalms 53:3
24. Acts 2:25-28 with Psalms 16:8-11
25. Romans 10:15 with Isaiah 52:7
26. Hebrews 11:21 with Genesis 47:31
27. Romans 10:20-21 with Isaiah 65:1-2

Key LXX Passages Altered by the Masoretic Text

#1	Highlighting Differences in Text Matthew 13:15 with Isaiah 6:10
ESV	**MATTHEW 13:15,** "For this people's heart has grown dull, and **with their ears they can barely hear,** and their eyes they have closed, lest they should see with their eyes, and hear with their ears and understand with their heart and turn, and I would heal them.'"
LXX	**ISAIAH 6:10,** "'For the heart of this people has become gross, and **their ears are dull of hearing,** and their eyes they have closed; lest they should see with their eyes, and hear with their ears, and understand with their heart, and be converted, and I should heal them.'"
KJV	**ISAIAH 6:10,** "Make the heart of this people fat, and make their eyes heavy, and shut their eyes; lest they see with their eyes, and hear with their ears, and understand with their heart, and convert, and be healed."
SDW	The passage limits the failure of the Jews to hear the voice of God. The NT follows the LXX in conveying that the lack of compassion, deafness, and blindness is not directed by God but occurs due to everyone's choice. The Lord responds sorrowfully due to that outcome. If they would but convert (turn), "I would heal them." The KJV *commands* the failure of compassion, blindness, and deafness take place, so that **they will not be converted, nor healed** (conveying the Lord is *not* eager to heal those who disobey his laws)."

#2	Highlighting Differences in Text Romans 9:27-28 with Isaiah 10:22-23
ESV	**ROMANS 9:27-28,** "And Isaiah cries out concerning Israel: "Though the number of the sons of Israel be as the sand of the sea, **only a remnant of them will be saved,** for the Lord will carry out his sentence upon the earth fully and without delay."

LXX	**ISAIAH 10:22-23,** "And though the people of Israel be as the sand of the sea, **a remnant of them shall be saved**: For he will finish the work and cut it short in righteousness: because the Lord will make a short work in all the earth."
KJV	**ISAIAH 10:22-23** "For though thy people Israel be as the sand of the sea, yet *a remnant of them shall return*. The consumption decreed shall overflow with righteousness. For the Lord GOD of hosts shall make a consumption, even determined, in the midst of all the land."
SDW	The NT follows the LXX in associating a remnant *with salvation* whereas the KJV connects the remnant *to returning to the land*. This illustrates the notion of salvation for Jews being connected to Eretz, their land. The KJV uses the word *consumption* for translating the Hebrew word, *killayon* (Strong's 3631). A more familiar word would be *destruction*. This word is used only twice in the Old Testament. The other instance is Deuteronomy 28:65, where it is translated "failing" of eyes as in "going blind."
	Consumption in pre-modern times was associated with tuberculosis, a slow-acting, devastating, and persistent disease, seemingly incurable. It was also known as the "white plague." It is a slow death, consuming its victims little by little. Consequently, *consumption is a poor word to choose*. Destructive, yes; but slow. God will save His people quickly and make "short work" of the destruction He has decreed in the midst of the land.

#3	**Highlighting Differences in Text** **Romans 15:12 with Isaiah 11:10**
ESV	**ROMANS 15:12,** "And again Isaiah says, 'The root of Jesse will come, even he who arises **to rule the Gentiles; in him will the Gentiles hope**.'"

LXX	**ISAIAH 11:10,** "And in that day there shall be a root of Jesse and he that shall rise **to rule over the Gentiles; in him shall the Gentiles trust,** and his rest shall be glorious."
KJV	**ISAIAH 11:10,** "And in that day there shall be a root of Jesse, which *shall stand for an ensign* of the people; to it *shall the Gentiles seek*: and his rest shall be glorious."
SDW	The MT passage poses significant differences to the LXX. Instead of personifying the rule of the Gentiles with an individual, the KJV depersonalizes the subject of the passage, altering it from a person to an ensign. The Gentiles seek the ensign. It also eliminates the phrase *"rule over the Gentiles and in him shall the Gentiles trust."* These words attempt to limit the salvation of God to only the Jews. In the LXX, the root of Jesse *will rule the Gentiles.* In the MT, the Gentiles only seek the descendants of Jesse.

#4	**Highlighting Differences in Text** **Acts 4:25-26 with Psalms 2:1-2**
ESV	**ACTS 4:25-26,** "Who through the mouth of our father David, your servant, said by the Holy Spirit, 'Why did the Gentiles rage, and the peoples plot in vain? The kings of the earth *set themselves,* and **the rulers were gathered together,** against the Lord and against his Anointed.'"
LXX	**PSALMS 2:1-2,** "Wherefore did the heathen rage, and the nations imagine vain things? The kings of the earth **stood up,** and the **rulers gathered themselves together** against the Lord, and against his Christ."
KJV	**PSALMS 2:1-2,** "Why do the heathen rage, and the people imagine a vain thing? The kings of the earth set themselves, and the rulers take counsel together, against the Lord, and against his anointed."

SDW	The KJV leaves out the phrase, "rulers gathered themselves together." The ESV agrees with the KJV using the phrase "set themselves" instead of "stood up" as the LXX. The NASV translates that phrase, "take their stand" which might better communicate to the modern ear the meaning of the Hebrew *yatsab* (Strong's 3320 taking the form יִתְיַצְּבוּ -yit-yas-se-bu). We could also use modern idioms like, "rise to their feet" and "braced themselves." The kings know they face an unwinnable fight against the Messiah/Christ.

#5	**Highlighting Differences in Text** **Matthew 13:35 with Psalms 78:2**
ESV	**MATTHEW 13:35,** "This was to fulfill what was spoken by the prophet: 'I will open my mouth in parables; I will utter what has been **hidden since the foundation of the world**.'"
LXX	**PSALMS 78:2,** "I will open my mouth in parables; I will utter dark sayings which **have been from the beginning**."
KJV	**PSALMS 78;2,** "I will open my mouth in a parable: I will utter dark sayings *of old*."
SDW	In this comparison, hidden within, is the indication that the speaker (prophetically Christ, the Messiah, the Son of God), was speaking these words and the Father's plan was set from the very beginning – *the founding of the world itself.* This speaks to the dwelling of the Son of God with the Father, from eternity. The KJV diminishes the implication of the statement by indicating that this plan is only *ancient*, "**of old**." The ESV conveys that "dark sayings" are related to "what has been hidden since the foundation of the world." The salvation of the individual believer, through the Messiah's atoning death, was hidden from eternity past. This thought clearly links to Paul's teachings on the *mysteries of Christ and the Gospel* (of which there are over a dozen).

"But we **speak the wisdom of God in a mystery**, even **the hidden wisdom,** which God **ordained before the world** unto our glory." (1 Cor 2:7) (See also Ephesians 3:3-11) Once again, the reading from the KJV weakens the Scripture's testimony on the full deity of Jesus Christ. He was with God in the beginning, and "all things were created by Him." (Colossians 1:16)

#6	**Highlighting Differences in Text** **Hebrews 10:5 with Psalms 40:6**
ESV	**HEBREWS 10:5,** "Consequently, when Christ came into the world, he said, "Sacrifices and offerings you have not desired, but **a body have you prepared for me**; in burnt offerings and sin offerings you have taken no pleasure."
LXX	**PSALMS 40:6,** "Sacrifice and offering thou wouldest not, but **a body thou hast prepared me**: whole-burnt-offering and sacrifice for sin thou didst not require."
KJV	**PSALMS 40:6,** "Sacrifice and offering thou didst not desire, *mine ears hast thou opened;* burnt offering and sin offering hast thou not required."
SDW	This passage is one of the most obvious deviations from the original text. The writer of the Book of Hebrews points out that the sacrificial system of Old Testament Judaism could not blot out sin. Instead, the writer asserts that Christ was speaking to the Father prophetically in Psalms 40:6, indicating that sacrifices and sin offerings would not achieve the objective of eliminating sin; consequently, *"Thou has prepared a body for me,"* for through that body, the LORD would perform a sacrifice of Himself (through the Son) to eradicate the problem of sin forever. However, the KJV (the MS text) alters the clear reference to the incarnation of God to a phrase, "mine ears hast thou opened" asserting that learning (knowledge) will accomplish salvation. This provides a remarkably easy proof of the rabbinic corruption of the text. This reading seeks to disprove the claims of Christians and address the end of Temple worship as the essence of Judaism.

#7	**Highlighting Differences in Text** **Matthew 12:20-21 with Isaiah 42:4**
ESV	**MATTHEW 12:20-21,** "A bruised reed he will not break, and a smoldering wick he will not quench, until he brings justice to victory; and **in this name the Gentiles will hope.**"
LXX	**ISAIAH 42:4,** "He shall shine out, and shall not be discouraged, until he have set judgment on the earth; and **in his name shall the Gentiles trust.**"
KJV	**ISAIAH 42:4,** "He shall not fail nor be discouraged, till he have set judgment in the earth; **and the isles shall wait for his law.**"
SDW	This is perhaps one of the most blatant alterations of the text, illustrating that instead of salvation coming by the Anointed One, the Messiah **in whom the Gentiles will have hope**, the KJV (following the Masoretic Text) reads "the isles shall wait *for his law.*" In this one verse we see the striking difference between Christianity and Judaism. Christianity places its hope in the person of Jesus Christ who will not discard *reeds* that can't make music (since they are bruised) or *burnt wicks* (that smell and cease to function properly). Judaism, Rabbinic Judaism, places its hope for salvation in the Law. It is quite easy to imagine Akiba underscoring the need to alter this verse since it speaks so clearly to God's salvation being offered to the Gentiles, bypassing adherence to the law as a means to be made holy (sanctified). Bruised reeds and burnt wicks are discarded.

#8	**Highlighting Differences in Text** **Acts 15:16-18 with Amos 9:11-12**
ESV	**ACTS 15:16-18,** "After this I will return, and I will rebuild the tent (tabernacle) of David that has fallen; I will rebuild its ruins, and I will restore it, that the remnant of mankind may seek the Lord, and **all the Gentiles who are called by my name,** says the Lord, who makes these things."

LXX	**AMOS 9:11-12,** "In that day I will raise up the tabernacle of David that is fallen, and will rebuild the ruins of it, and will set up the parts thereof that have been broken down and will build it up as in the ancient days; that the remnant of men, **and all the Gentiles upon whom my name is called**, *may earnestly seek me*, said the Lord who does all these things."
KJV	**AMOS 9:11-12,** "In that day will I raise up the tabernacle of David that is fallen, and close up its breaches; and I will raise up its ruins, and I will rebuild it as in the days of old; **that they may possess the remnant of Edom**, and *of all the heathen*, which are called by my name, saith the LORD that doeth this.
SDW	The statement in Acts 15, at the first Church Council in Jerusalem, is a final verdict indicating that God has confirmed in numerous ways (most powerfully through the giving of the Holy Spirit), that Gentiles have equal share in the Kingdom of God. James, who was perhaps the most wedded to the traditional Jewish manner of keeping the law of God as a means to sanctification, brought great apostolic insight into the prophecy of Amos 9:11-12. Said James, *"Brothers, listen to me. Simeon has related how God first visited the Gentiles, to take from them a people for his name. And with this the words of the prophets agree, just as it is written, 'After this I will return... that the **remnant of mankind may seek the Lord, and all the Gentiles who are called by my name**, says the Lord, who makes these things known from of old.'"* James quoted from the LXX not the proto-Masoretic Text. But the KJV (MT) again flips the meaning. Instead of the Gentiles possessing the hope of God through Christ, the KJV – following the MT – indicates that the rebuilding of the temple is in order that the Jews *may possess the remnant of Edom* (Edom being a common Jewish synonym for the Gentiles), *and all the heathen*, since they are called by God's name (I believe this is only a general statement as to their Maker). This alteration argues that the Jews will rule the world and the Gentiles will answer to them, flipping the meaning of the passage.

165

SDW	Certainly, there is a difference in being *free to seek the Lord* instead of *being possessed by the Jews* at the time the Temple is restored. Once again, we have a strong indication that the Hebrew "proto-Masoretic" text was altered to conform to the new Judaism of the rabbis to resist Christians who sought to prove that Jesus was the Messiah by referring to Old Testament prophecies.

#9	**Highlighting Differences in Text** **Matthew 1:23 with Isaiah 7:14**
ESV	**MATTHEW 1:23,** "'Behold, **the virgin shall conceive** and bear a son, and they shall call his name Immanuel' (which means, God with us)."
LXX	**ISAIAH 7:14** "Therefore, the Lord himself shall give you a sign; behold, **a virgin shall conceive** in the womb, and shall bring forth a son, and thou shalt call his name Emmanuel."
MT*	**ISAIAH 7:14,** "Therefore, the Lord Himself shall give you a sign: behold, *the young woman* shall conceive, and bear a son, and shall call his name Immanuel." (Note: We are not using KJV here, but the *Jewish Tanakh 1917 for the MT*.)
SDW	Perhaps the most famous of the differences between the Septuagint and the Masoretic Texts has to do with the Virgin Birth. The Hebrew customarily uses the word *almah* for "young woman" and the Tanakh (published in 1917) chose this word. All Protestant Bibles translate the word "virgin" but which in Hebrew usually means "maiden." No doubt pressure from Christians through the ages served an ultimatum to Bible manufacturers, "Translate *almah* as **virgin** and not *maiden*; or else!" This came to pass after the Revised Standard Version translated the Masoretic, 'young woman' instead of virgin. But the issue is, "What did the original Hebrew say? Was the word changed?" In Greek, the word for virgin is "Parthenos." In Hebrew, the word for

	virgin is *betulah*. However, the ambiguity still exists since pre-Mosaic clay tablets use the word *almah* for virgin.[213]

#10	**Highlighting Differences in Text** **Romans 9:33 with Isaiah 8:14 and 28:16**
ESV	**ROMANS 9:33**, "As it is written, 'Behold, I am laying in Zion **a stone of stumbling, and a rock of offence**; and whoever believes in **him will not be put to shame.**'"
LXX	**ISAIAH 8:14 & 28:16**, "(8:14) And he will become a sanctuary and a **stone of offense and a rock of stumbling to both houses of Israel**, a trap and a snare to the inhabitants of Jerusalem." (28:16) "Therefore, thus saith the Lord, even the Lord, Behold, **I lay for the foundations of Sion a costly stone,** a choice, a corner-stone, a precious stone, for its foundations; and **he that believes on him shall by no means be ashamed.**"
KJV	**ISAIAH 8:14 & 28:16**, "(8:14) "And he shall be for a sanctuary; but for a **stone of stumbling and for a rock of offense** to both the houses of Israel, for a gin and for a snare to the inhabitants of Jerusalem." (28:16) "Therefore thus saith the Lord GOD, 'Behold I lay in Zion for a foundation a stone, a tried stone, a precious corner stone, a sure foundation: *he that believeth shall make haste.*'"

---

[213] Citing Cyrus H. Gordon:

> The commonly held view that "virgin" is Christian, whereas "young woman" is Jewish is not quite true. The fact is that the Septuagint, which is the Jewish translation made in pre-Christian Alexandria, takes **almah** to mean "virgin" here. Accordingly, the New Testament follows Jewish interpretation in Isaiah 7:14. Therefore, the New Testament rendering of **almah** as "virgin" for Isaiah 7:14 rests on the older Jewish interpretation, which in turn is now borne out for precisely this annunciation formula by a text that is not only pre-Isaianic but is pre-Mosaic in the form that we now have it on a clay tablet.

Gordon, Cyrus H. "Almah in Isaiah 7:14," *The Journal of bible & Religion, Vol. 21* (April 1953), p. 106. See https://jewsforjesus.org/ publications /issues/issues-v09-n01/almah-virgin-or-young-maiden/.

| SDW | Paul conflates two scriptures from Isaiah, both dealing with Jesus "as the rock." Isaiah 8:14 shows no significant differences other than the inference that the rock, in one verse in Isaiah, is the same rock in the other verse. In 28:16, we learn that the rock is a highly precious stone. The LXX is effusive on the value of the stone; the MT less so. The key difference arises *as to the meaning of the stone*. In the LXX and NT, the point is this: All *who believe on this stumbling block and precious stone* **will not be shamed**. In the MT, believing in the stone leads one to "make haste." I am confident the reader readily discerns the distinction here. |

#11	**Highlighting Differences in Text** **Luke 4:18 with Isaiah 61:1**
ESV	**LUKE 4:18,** "The Spirit of the Lord is upon me, because he has anointed me to proclaim good news to the poor. He has sent me to proclaim liberty to the captives and **recovering of sight to the blind**, to set at liberty those who are oppressed..."
LXX	**ISAIAH 61:1,** "The Spirit of the Lord is upon me, because he has anointed me; he has sent me to preach glad tidings to the poor, to heal the broken in heart, to proclaim liberty to the captives, and **recovery of sight to the blind...**"
KJV	**ISAIAH 61:1,** "The Spirit of the Lord GOD is upon me; because the LORD hath anointed me to preach good tidings unto the meek; he hath sent me to bind up the brokenhearted, to proclaim liberty to the captives, and the opening of the prison to them that are bound."
SDW	The principal aspect of this textual difference is *the omission of the phrase "recovery of sight to the blind."* The KJV leaves this important phrase out. Why so important? Because *making the blind man see* was one of Jesus' most striking signs. The story of the "man born blind" in John's gospel, chapter 9, no doubt made such an impression upon the Jewish leaders of that day, that this miracle resonated in Judea for decades after. As the man himself said when asked repeatedly how we was now able to see, "Now this is

remarkable! You don't know where he comes from, yet he opened my eyes... Nobody has ever heard of opening the eyes of a man born blind. If this man were not from God, he could do nothing." (John 9:30, 32, ESV) That the Masoretic Text and the KJV OT does not include this important phrase, demonstrates yet again that the translators of the proto-Masoretic Text were biased against passages that testified to Jesus Christ being the Messiah.

#12	**Highlighting Differences in Text** **Hebrews 1:6 with Deuteronomy 32:43**
ESV	**HEBREWS 1:6,** "And again, when he brings the firstborn into the world, he says, "'**Let all God's angels worship him.**'"
LXX	**DEUTERONOMY 32:43,** "Rejoice, ye heavens, with him, and **let all the angels of God worship him**; rejoice ye Gentiles, with his people, and **let all the sons of God strengthen themselves in him;** for he will avenge the blood of his sons, and he will render vengeance, and recompense justice to his enemies, and will reward them that hate him; and the Lord shall purge the land of his people.
KJV	**DEUTERONOMY 32:43,** "Rejoice, O ye nations, with his people; for he will avenge the blood of his servants, and will render vengeance to his adversaries, and will be merciful unto his land, and to his people."
SDW	Here we see two vital phrases completely dropped from the Masoretic Text, "Let all God's angels worship him" and "Let all the sons of God strengthen themselves in him." Not only are the statements deleted outright, but the intent of their deletion is rather obvious: The statements assert that the Messiah, the firstborn, is higher than the angels and strengthens all the sons of God – both humans and angels. This so utterly conflicts with the theology of the rabbis that these crucial portions of the verse were entirely stricken. On the issue of altering passages that reflect on the nature and purpose of the Messiah, "the prosecution rests." Actually, there are still many more to come.

169

#13	**Highlighting Differences in Text** **Genesis 49:10, Septuagint with Masoretic**
ESV	**GENESIS 49:10,** "The scepter shall not depart from Judah, nor the ruler's staff from between his feet, until tribute comes to him; and to him shall be the obedience of the peoples.
LXX	**GENESIS 49:10,** "A ruler shall not fail from Judah, nor a prince from his loins, **until there come the things stored up for him**; and he is the expectation of nations."
KJV	**GENESIS 49:10,** "The scepter shall not depart from Judah, nor a lawgiver from between his feet, until Shiloh come; and unto him shall the gathering of the people be."
SDW	In this passage, a well-known Messianic passage, there are significant differences between the LXX and the MT. The MT labels the ruler, "a lawgiver" (consistent with the Jewish recognition of leadership derived from law and emphasizing the Law and Moses). The MT speaks of *Shiloh*, with which many English translations agree. Gill indicates as does Barnes in their commentaries that "Shiloh" is regarded in the Jewish Talmud as a name of the Messiah, although some versions suggest not that Shiloh comes, rather, he that will rule will come to Shiloh. Why Shiloh? Shiloh was the first place where God made His name to dwell (Jeremiah 7:12) and was associated with the presence of God. Does not Shiloh convey that the Messiah equates to "the presence of God"? 1 Samuel 3:21, "The **LORD continued to appear at Shiloh**, and there he revealed himself to Samuel through **His word**." The noticeable element missing is the phrase, "until there come the things stored up for him." The ESV mentions in a footnote that "by a slight revocalization, a slight emendation (revision) yields "until he comes to whom it belongs" which follows the Syriac and the Targum (Aramaic). The phrasing "He is the expectation of nations" conveys a universal expectation, while "unto Him shall the gathering of the people be" suggests that the Messiah will gather *only the Jewish people*, without an appeal to "all the people."

Other Passages Illustrating Important Variances

#14	**Highlighting Differences in Text** **Matthew 15:8-9 with Isaiah 29:13**
ESV	**MATTHEW 15:8-9,** "This people honors me with their lips, but their heart is far from me; in vain do they worship me, **teaching as doctrines the commandments of men.**"
LXX	**ISAIAH 29:13,** "And the Lord has said, 'This people draw nigh to me with their mouth, and they honor me with their lips; but their heart is far from: but in vain do they worship me, **teaching the commandments and doctrines of men.**'"
KJV	**ISAIAH 52:11,** "Wherefore the Lord said, 'Forasmuch as this people draw near me with their mouth, and with their lips do honour me, but have removed their heart far from me, *and their fear toward me is taught by the precept of men.*'"
SDW	The quotation in Matthew follows the LXX closely while the KJV alters the text of Isaiah 52 dramatically. In the LXX, the prophet rebukes Israel's teachers for putting the notions of men in the place of God's Law. However, *"teaching the fear of God through men's precepts"* in the text of the KJV may actually flip the meaning. Instead of condemning the practice of substituting men's laws for God's Torah, the language of the KJV translation appears to sanction men teaching God's precepts to people in the manner of Akiba. *"The fear of God is the beginning of Wisdom"* (Proverbs 9:10). But Akiba's disciples superseded the authentic Law of God with men's precepts. Evangelicals recall the wording of Matthew 15:8-9, which cites Isaiah, but its wording comes from the LXX, not the Masoretic Text as followed by the KJV.

#15	**Highlighting Differences in Text** **Romans 11:34 with Isaiah 40:13**
ESV	**ROMANS 11:34,** "For who has known **the mind of the Lord,** or who has been his counselor?"
LXX	**ISAIAH 40:13,** "Who has known **the mind of the Lord?** And who has been his counsellor, to instruct him?
KJV	**ISAIAH 40:13,** "Who hath *directed the Spirit of the Lord,* or being his counsellor hath taught him?
SDW	The NT closely follows the LXX. The KJV implies an interesting interpretation of "the mind of the LORD" as *the Spirit of the LORD* which stands in contrast to the NT and the LXX. The NT sees the Spirit as the "heart" of God that can be grieved. (Eph. 4:30) The tripartite model of man – mind, soul, and spirit is often compared to Father, Son, & Spirit.

#16	**Highlighting Differences in Text** **Hebrews 13:6 with Psalms 117:6**
ESV	**HEBREWS 13:6,** "So we can confidently say, 'The **Lord is my helper,** I will not fear; what can man do to me?"
LXX	**PSALMS 117:6,** "**The Lord is my helper** and I will not fear what man shall do to me."
KJV	**PSALMS 117:6,** "*The Lord is on my side*; I will not fear; what can man do unto me?"
SDW	The New Testament follows the wording of the LXX more precisely. However, the LXX makes an assertion instead of asking a rhetorical question. The LXX is arguably more strongly worded.

#17	**Highlighting Differences in Text** **Hebrews 12:5 with Proverbs 3:11**
ESV	**HEBREWS 12:5,** "And have you forgotten the exhortation that addresses you as sons? 'My son, do not regard lightly the discipline of the Lord, nor be weary **when reproved by him.'**"
LXX	**PROVERBS 3:11,** "My son despise not the chastening of the Lord, nor faint **when thou art rebuked** of him."
KJV	**PROVERBS 3:11,** "My son, despise not the chastening of the LORD, neither be *weary of his correction*."
SDW	The New Testament follows the wording of the LXX. The KJV softens the implication of the stronger words *rebuke* or *reprove*. We might see this as weakening the personal attention God possesses for the believer and his or her individual growth.

#18	**Highlighting Differences in Text** **2 Corinthians 6:17 with Isaiah 52:11**
ESV	**2 CORINTHIANS 6:17,** "Therefore go out from their midst, and **be separate from them**, says the Lord, and touch no unclean thing: *then I will welcome you.*
LXX	**ISAIAH 52:11,** "Depart ye, depart ye, go out from thence, and touch not the unclean thing; go ye out from the midst of her; **separate yourselves**, ye that bear the vessels of the Lord."
KJV	**ISAIAH 52:11,** "Depart ye, depart ye, go ye out from thence, touch no unclean thing; *go ye out of the midst of her*; be ye clean, that bear the vessels of the Lord."

SDW	The differences in this passage are minor. It appears that Paul is quoting from a reading different from the LXX and the Hebrew version used by the Masoretic/KJV, as indicated by the phrase *"then I will welcome you."* Different readings existed before the Council of Jamnia (or the Academies), after which variant versions were destroyed by Akiba. We see variations in all three versions cited here in regard to the phrase *"be separate from them"* which differs from the LXX's translation, *"separate yourselves,"* and the KJV's *"be clean." "Be sanctified"* would be another alternative way to render the directive.

#19	**Highlighting Differences in Text Romans 11:9 with Psalms 69:22**
ESV	**ROMANS 11:9,** "And David says, 'Let their table become a snare and a trap, a stumbling block and a **retribution** for them; let their eyes be darkened so that they cannot see and bend their backs forever.'"
LXX	**PSALMS 69:22,** "Let their table before them be for a snare; and for a **recompense**, and for a stumbling-block."
KJV	**PSALMS 69:22,** "Let their table become a snare and that **which should have been for their welfare**, let it become a trap."
SDW	The KJV, following the Masoretic Text, translates the Hebrew word "shalom" (soundness, welfare, peace – Strong's 7965) with the lengthy phrase "which should have been for their welfare." There are three ways to interpret the meaning. In the first, KJV reduces the sting of the verse – "what they were served should have been beneficial, but they were intentionally tricked." The second possible meaning conveys *reproach and judgment.* Those at table are fooled into believing they will be treated like kings; instead they fall into a trap and are deceived. And finally, the last possible meaning is, "What they are to be served in the judgment" equals *what they dished out to others.*

SDW (CONT)	The passage in Psalm 69:12 and afterward prophesies the distress the Messiah will feel and his heartfelt cry that his enemies get what they deserve! This Psalm, like Psalm 22, no doubt came to mind for Jesus when he hung on the cross. We can suppose these thoughts were before Him too. *However, he withstood them and did not react with wrath or call 12 legions of angels to his aid.* (Matthew 26:53) Pauls' argument in chapter 11 of Romans, addresses the stern judgment of God upon Israel but also its eventual redemption when "all Israel shall be saved." Israel has received **retribution** for its sins, but one day, it will receive **redemption**. Exactly how this occurs, generates a considerable amount of debate, to say the least. But redemption will come to Israel.

#20	**Highlighting Differences in Text** **Matthew 3:3 with Isaiah 40:3**
ESV	**MATTHEW 3:3,** "For this is he who was spoken of by the prophet Isaiah when he said, 'The voice of one crying in the wilderness; "Prepare the way of the Lord; **make his paths straight**."'" (cf. Lk 3:4, Mk 1:3)
LXX	**ISAIAH 40:3,** "The voice of one crying in the wilderness, prepare ye the way of the Lord, **make straight the paths of our God**."
KJV	**ISAIAH 40:3,** "The voice of him that crieth in the wilderness, 'Prepare ye the way of the LORD, make straight in the desert a highway for our God."
SDW	The differences in this passage are subtle. Once again, however, it is clear that the NT follows the wording of the LXX. When comparing *"make his paths straight"* and *"make straight in the desert a highway for our God,"* the distinction doesn't stand out. The MS (KJV) inserts "in the desert" and uses "highway" instead of "paths." The wording of the KJV is admittedly more eloquent. It may not be more accurate.

SDW (CONT)	The speaker in Matthew is John the Baptist who resided in the desert. However, "to make straight Christ's path" conveys the key content of the message: *making the pathway to salvation plain*; whereas "making a highway in the desert," implies a different message. "Straight" (*euthys*, Strong's G2117) means upright, true, sincere, or "on the level." The road ahead is a "straightaway," not a treacherous curve. Rabbinical teaching can be convoluted while the gospel is *straightforward*. God doesn't throw us a curve. He is straight with us.

#21	**Highlighting Differences in Text** **Romans 3:13 with Psalms 5:9 and Psalm 140:3b**
ESV	**ROMANS 3:13,** "Their throat is an **open grave**; they **use their tongues to deceive**. The venom of asps is under their lips."
LXX	**PSALMS 5:9,** "For there is no truth in their mouth; their heart is vain; their throat is an **open sepulcher**; **with their tongues they have used deceit**." **Psalm 140:3b**: "The poison of asps is under their lips."
KJV	**PSALMS 5:9,** "For there is no faithfulness in their mouth; their inward part is very wickedness; their throat is an **open sepulcher**; **they flatter with their tongue. Psalm 140:3b**, "adder's poison is under their lips."
SDW	Once again, the NT follows the LXX. The phrase, *"The venom of asps is under their lips"* we find in Psalm 140:3, "The venom of asps is under their lips." Paul used the Septuagint and likely used an earlier version of the Hebrew scripture from that used by Akiba and later the Masoretes (or a Vorlage altered by the Jamnia rabbis), dropping the phrase "the venom of asps under their lips." That a student of Hebrew and Greek might refer to both seems more probable than merely possible.

#22	**Highlighting Differences in Text** **Ephesians 4:26 with Psalms 4:4**
ESV	**EPHESIANS 4:26,** "**Be ye angry,** and do not sin;' do not let the sun go down on your anger."
LXX	**PSALMS 4:4,** "**Be ye angry**, and sin not; feel compunction upon your beds for what ye say in your hearts. Pause."
KJV	**PSALMS 4:4,** "**Stand in awe**, and sin not; commune with your own heart upon your bed and be still. Selah."
SDW	The variances in this passage appear to be minor. However, they still indicate Paul used the LXX. The KJV in Psalms 4:4 provides distinctly different wording, "Be in awe" instead of "Being angered." This alters the admonition from the LXX. However, "Do not let the sun go down on your anger" is a creative alternative to "feeling compunction (regret, sorrow) on your bed." Perhaps it is a proverb Paul inserts referencing a reading from another version of the LXX or an alternative early Hebrew reading (not the MT). Recall, Paul warns against letting anger overwhelm your self-control, for if you do, *it gives the devil an opportunity*. This aphorism reminds us of what God told Cain before Cain slew his brother Abel. "Sin is knocking at the door; you can choose to not open it – you can still find favor with me if you do the right thing," (my paraphrase of Genesis 4:7). The ESV reads, "If you do well, will you not be accepted? And if you do not do well, sin is crouching at the door. Its desire is contrary to you, but you must rule over it." Don't let anger fester – don't meditate upon "getting even when you go to bed." Instead, "let go of the anger." "Don't let anger 'get the best of you!'"

#23	Highlighting Differences in Text Romans 3:12 with Psalms 53:3
ESV	ROMANS 3:12, "All have turned aside; **together they have become worthless**; no one does good, not even one." (See NKJV reference below.)
LXX	PSALMS 53:3, "They have all **gone out of the way, they are together become unprofitable**, there is none that doeth good, there is not even one.
KJV	PSALMS 53:3, "Every one of them is gone back; they are altogether become filthy; there is none that doeth good, no, not one."
SDW	The differences in this passage appear to be minor. However, if we look at the New King James Version for Psalm 53:3 instead of the ESV, there is a clear preference for the LXX, *"They are all **gone out of the way**, they are **together become unprofitable**, there is none that doeth good, no, not one."* The NKJV uses multiple more sources, no doubt including the LXX which the original KJV didn't utilize because alternative sources had not yet been discovered. Consequently, the New King James Version in the New Testament agrees with the LXX Old Testament, *not the King James Version Old Testament.*

#24	Highlighting Differences in Text Acts 2:25-28 with Psalms 16:8-11
ESV	ACTS 2:25-28, "For David says concerning him, '**I saw the Lord always before me**, for he is at my right hand that I may not be shaken; therefore, my **heart was glad,** and my **tongue rejoiced**, my flesh also will dwell in hope. For you will **not abandon my soul to Hades or let your Holy One see corruption.** You have made known to me the paths of life; you will make me full of gladness with your presence.'"

LXX	**PSALMS 16:8-11,** "I foresaw the Lord always **before my face**; for he is on my right hand, that I should not be moved. Therefore, my heart rejoiced and **my tongue exulted**; moreover, also my flesh shall rest in hope: **because thou wilt not leave my soul in hell, neither suffer thine Holy One to see corruption.** Thou has made known to me the ways of life; thou wilt fill me with joy with thy countenance: <u>at thy right hand there are delights forever.</u>
KJV	**PSALMS 16:8-11,** "*I have set the LORD always before me*; because he is at my right hand, I shall not be moved. Therefore, my heart is glad, and my *glory rejoiceth*; my flesh also shall rest in hope. **For thou wilt not leave my soul in hell; neither wilt thou suffer thine Holy One to see corruption.** Thou wilt shew me the path of life; in thy presence is fulness of joy; <u>at thy right hand there are pleasures for evermore.</u>
SDW	Here is yet another passage with differences that illustrate two things: (1) The LXX is still preferred over the proto-MT. (2) The reading used is not in the LXX, but it is included in both the NT and the KJV (MT). The words "at thy right hand there are delights forever" is not found in the LXX. This would likely indicate that the phrase was added in a later copy of the LXX perhaps to show alignment with a Hebrew version.

#25	**Highlighting Differences in Text** **Romans 10:15 with Isaiah 52:7**
ESV	**ROMANS 10:15,** "And how are they to preach unless they are sent? As it is written, 'How beautiful are the feet of those who **preach the good news**!'"
LXX	**ISAIAH 52:7,** "As a season of beauty upon the mountains, as the feet of one preaching glad tidings of peace, as one preaching **good news**: for I will publish thy salvation, saying, 'O Sion, they God shall reign.'"

179

KJV	**ISAIAH 52:7,** "How beautiful upon the mountains are the feet of him that bringeth *good tidings*, that publisheth peace; that bringeth *good tidings of good*, that publisheth salvation; that saith unto Zion, 'Thy God reigneth!'"
SDW	The signature message of Jesus and the Christian sect of Judaism was "good news" (*basar*, Strong's 1319, can be translated "good tidings" or "good news" (in 2 Sam 18:19, 18:20, 18:26, 18:31, 1 Chron 10:9). The KJV translated the word as "good tidings" and the NASB translated the word as "good news." Which phrase best translates *basar* in this instance is not clear-cut. But failing to use "good news" twice in the MT (KJV) could be considered intentional.

#26	**Highlighting Differences in Text** **Hebrews 11:21 with Genesis 47:31**
ESV	**HEBREWS 11:21,** "By faith Jacob, when dying, blessed each of the sons of Joseph, bowing in worship **over the head of his staff.**"
LXX	**GENESIS 47:31,** "And he said, 'Swear to me; and he swore to him.' And Israel did reverence, leaning on **the top of his staff.**"
KJV	**GENESIS 47:31,** "And he said, 'Swear unto me.' And he swore unto him. And Israel bowed himself *upon the bed's head.*"
SDW	This passage demonstrates once again that the LXX is cited although, ironically, this is one place where the LXX may have mistranslated the Hebrew word *hammittah* (Strong's 4296) which the KJV translated differently. Jacob sat up in bed and swore his blessing as he lay dying instead of leaning over his staff as the NT and the LXX record. The issue is the *mittah's* consonants, MTH, could be assigned differing vowels. (The original Hebrew did not possess any vowels written in the text). In one case it means "the head of the bed" and the other "a staff." Since Jacob was old, either translation is possible but the translation of "head of the bed" is agreed by scholars to be the appropriate rendering.

#27	**Highlighting Differences in Text** **Romans 10:20-21 with Isaiah 65:1-2**
ESV	**ROMANS 10:20-21,** "Then Isaiah is so bold as to say, 'I have been found by those who did not seek me; **I have shown myself to those who did not ask for me.** But of Israel he says, "All day long I have held out my hands to a disobedient and contrary people."
LXX	**ISAIAH 65:1-2,** "I became manifest to them that asked not for me; I was found of them that sought me not; I said, 'Behold, I am here, to a nation, who called not on my name.** I have stretched forth my hands all day to a disobedient and gainsaying people, to them that walked in a way that was not good, but after their sins.'"
KJV	**ISAIAH 65:1-2,** "I am sought of them that asked not for me; I am found of them that sought me not: I said, 'Behold me, behold me,' unto a nation that was not called by my name. I have spread out my hands all the day unto a rebellious people, which walketh in a way that was not good, after their own thoughts.
SDW	There difference here is subtle although the NT follows the LXX more closely than the wording of the KJV. The LXX translation employs an "active voice" in the manifestation of God (He made Himself plain or appeared to those that did not ask for Him) rather than being passive in the process, being found by those not seeking Him out. Paul interprets the text speaking to two different peoples: First, a people or nation that found Him even though they never sought after Him (the Gentiles), and the second, a nation (Israel), which had sought Him out in the past but became disobedient and turned away toward their sins. Of course, the LORD initiates and we respond. However, if it were not for the LORD's doing, Scripture teaches that no one would answer His call. Jesus said, *"For many are called, but few are chosen."* (Matthew 22:14, KJV)

181

Conclusion

The variances of the Masoretic Text from the Septuagint are numerous and often significant as we have demonstrated in this chapter. Therefore, allow me to share an article written by an Eastern Orthodox clergyman who points out one of the most crucial factors why Protestants ought to favor the LXX over the MT (specifically, over the KJV *Old* Testament):

> *The Septuagint text is the text that the Church has preserved.* The Masoretic Text is a text that has not been preserved by the Church, and so while it is worthy of study and comparison, it is not equally trustworthy. We have the promise that the Holy Spirit will guide us into all Truth (John 16:13), and so can indeed affirm that "Our Church holds the infallible and genuine deposit of the Holy Scriptures" ("Encyclical of the Eastern Patriarchs" of 1848).[214] [Emphasis added]

This does not mean we ignore Bibles based on the MT. *The King James quotes the LXX when it is providing Old Testament quotations in the New Testament.* That is, the KJV New Testament does not have the same problem as its Old Testament. Plus, it is helpful that the English Standard Version points out the LXX differences in marginal notes.

Nevertheless, when it comes to getting it right, the Septuagint should be regarded as the most authentic and trustworthy Old Testament in virtually all situations. Although it was translated into Greek, the evidence favors the assertion that it provides the proper meaning of the original Hebrew in a majority of cases, as written and preserved from Moses to Malachi.

---

[214] Whiteford, Fr. John, "The Septuagint and the Masoretic Text, retrieved July 6, 2018, from http://orthochristian.com/81224.html.

Chapter Five:
CORRECTING CHRONOLOGY –
THE GENESIS TIMELINE RECOVERED

The Bishop of Armagh

WHEN WE THINK OF THE CHRONOLOGY OF THE BIBLE, WE THINK OF BISHOP JAMES USSHER (1581-1656). USSHER PUBLISHED HIS FAMOUS ANCIENT CHRONOLOGY IN 1650. His chronology proposed the date of creation to be October 23, 4004 B.C., (on the first Rosh Hashanah although that day slipped over into a Sunday). Many other pre-enlightenment scholars also indicated that the age of the world, according to Scripture, was approximately the same: This includes 3761 B.C. (by Jose ben Halafta, a disciple of Akiba), 3992 B.C. (by Johannes Kepler), and Sir Isaac Newton (4000 B.C.)

Ussher relied upon the genealogies of Genesis 5 and 11, as published a few decades earlier (1611) in the King James Bible.[215] Genesis 5 and 11 both present 10 generations in a male lineage, that tells the age of the Patriarch and his age when his "child of promise" was born. As mentioned earlier, the child referenced was not the first-born child, but the child in the genealogy that led to the birth of the Messiah (as traced by Matthew and Luke in the New Testament).

---

[215] He also did an enormous amount of research across many sources of ancient history, before settling on the date published, which closely follows the MT.

There are several ways to calculate the timeline, depending upon specific fixed dates the Bible provides that are usually accepted by both biblical and secular scholars. One of those critical dates is *when the Temple in Jerusalem was destroyed by Nebuchadnezzar of Babylon*. That date is fixed on the 9th of Av (Tisha B'Av), 586 B.C. ± 1 year.[216] This day usually falls in July or August on our Gregorian calendar. From this date, calculations trace back to the split of Israel's Kingdom into ten tribes in the North (Ephraim) and two tribes in the South (Judah), which is typically set ca. 936 B.C., and then back to Solomon's Temple (four years into his 40-year reign), ca. 972 B.C. Thus, David's reign began about 1016 B.C. and Saul's reign about 1056 B.C. These dates are conventional. *Despite being the majority view, this book will establish dates about 40 years earlier*. This is the first step to right the ship regarding biblical chronology.

But after these events, the timeline blurs. The counting of time considers the period of Judges and the Conquest of Canaan following the Exodus. The length of the captivity in Egypt is much debated. Depending upon how this question is settled, the births of Abraham, Isaac, and Jacob can then be easily placed in the timeline. From Abraham, the chronology dates to the Tower of Babel incident (which can only be estimated), then the Great Flood of Noah (which is specific). Lastly, the creation of Adam

---

[216] Tisha B'Av is the saddest day of the calendar for Jews. Many horrible things happened on this date in history. The curse of this day begins with the 10 spies coming forth, circa 1500 B.C., with the bad report on taking the land of Canaan vis-à-vis the good report of Joshua and Caleb. Both the first and second temples were destroyed (586 B.C. and 70 A.D. respectively). Bar Kokhba's stronghold was captured by Rome and one year later on Tisha B'Av, Jerusalem was totally razed. In 1290, Jews were expelled from England by King Edward I; Jews were expelled from Spain in 1492, the day after Columbus set sail on his first American voyage. World War I began (1914), setting in motion many end time events according to futurist eschatology. In 1942, Polish Jews were deported for the first time to Treblinka where many would die in the Holocaust.

and Eve is set (which may or may not be the date the entire Creation was spoken into existence – that is, the universe, not just the founding pair of humans), all by the Logos, the Word of God.

Of course, most secular authorities in Archeology accept that Abraham was the father of all Semites; his estimated birth date ranges from about 2300 B.C. to 2000 B.C. Before that, academia doesn't trust the Bible's chronology whatsoever. Therefore, one of our goals in Rebooting the Bible (Parts 1 & 2) is to offer a date that can be synchronized with Archeology, something which the timelines of Ussher and the King James Bible cannot do.

The Critics of Ussher

The dating schema of Ussher found itself surrounded by enlightenment critics at the end of the eighteenth century. Charles Darwin's *Origin of Species* (1859) and *The Descent of Man (1871)* dealt near fatal blows to Ussher's Chronology. Henceforth, by the middle of the nineteenth century, theologians began to doubt the legitimacy of the chronology. Three decades later in 1890, with William Henry Green's article "Primeval Chronology" published in *Bibliotheca Sacra* (as far as Ussher's chronology was concerned), the wheels came off the wagon.

Green stated, "We conclude that the Scriptures furnish no data for a chronological computation before the life of Abraham; and that the Mosaic records do not fix and were not intended to fix the precise date either of the Flood or of the creation of the world."[217] Famous Reformed Theologian, B.B. Warfield, commented that it is "precarious in the highest degree

---

[217] Green, William H., "Primeval Chronology," *Bibliotheca Sacra*, April, 1890, p. 285-303. Retrieved 7-7-2018 from http://www.genevaninstitute.org/syllabus/unit-two-theology-proper/lesson-5-the-decree-of-creation/primeval-chronology-by-dr-william-henry-green/.

to draw chronological inferences from genealogical tables."[218] Indeed, one of the most critical areas to examine is whether the genealogies of Genesis 5 and 11 are complete and intended as a means to determine the number of years that elapsed "from Adam to Noah" and then "from Shem to Abraham." Consequently, by 1901, virtually all theologians with an academic bent no longer affirmed the conventional dating of the age of the world in correspondence with the Bible. The two Princeton Theologians identified above, Green and Warfield, naturally fell into this category. We will talk exceptions later.

Do the Bible's Genealogies Provide a Chronology?

As stated in the previous section, it has become standard practice to deny that the Bible's genealogies furnish a timeline of ancient events. This denial holds true even for most "mainstream" Evangelical theologians. In fact, one way to distinguish between "mainstream" Evangelicals and Fundamentalist Evangelicals is what they affirm about biblical chronology. The Fundamentalist hold to the "young earth" and usually embrace the Ussher chronology. Mainstream Evangelicals avoid the question or claim that such allegiance is misplaced. They argue that the Bible's authors never intended that the Genesis genealogies were to be used to calculate how many years passed from the beginning of the lineage to its concluding entry. It is suggested that the author intended something else by supplying dates for all the entries in the genealogy. What exactly that is, isn't clear.

Indeed, most authorities make a sweeping assertion that none of the Bible's genealogies yield a timeline at all.

---

[218] Warfield, Benjamin B., "On the Antiquity and Unity of the Human Race," *Princeton Theological Review 9*/(1), 1911. p. 1-25.

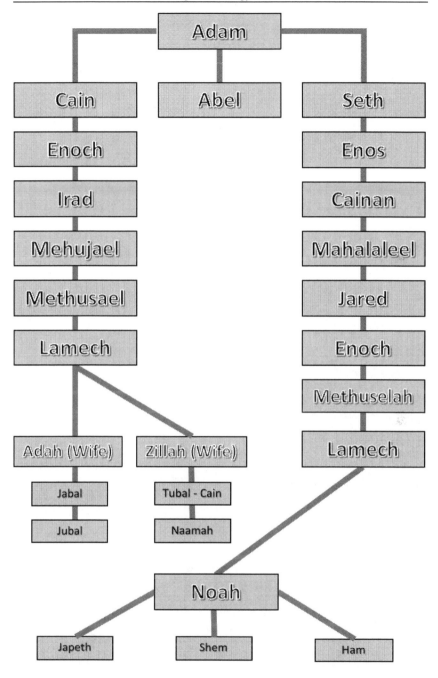

Figure 20 - From Adam to Shem, Genesis 5 Genealogy
10 Generations from Adam to Noah, 11 in Total

187

At the center of this discussion is whether all biblical gene-alogies follow the same pattern. Is it possible that the genealogies of Genesis 5 and 11 differ from other lineages given later? For example, later genealogies in Genesis, and distinct genealogies in Exodus, as well as 1 and 2 Kings (to name a few) mention the individual's name but don't give their ages. They also don't supply dates for the ages of the patriarchs when each had his son of the promise (the Messianic "thread" in the genealogy) and how long they lived (the total number of years) as the chronologies do in Genesis 5 and 11.

This author is not ashamed to argue differently.

To make my position clear, the Genesis 5 and 11 genealogies supply a precise chronology or timeline, while other lineages don't follow this pattern. In the Genesis genealogy, the total years of the Patriarch's life and his age when he had his "child of promise" matter. We will demonstrate this by looking at several tables and comparing texts. It's a bumpy ride, so hold on tight.

The Family Trees

As a baseline, let's review the family tree from Adam to Noah according to Genesis 5. We know that all the males in this list had many children, but the Bible traces the specific lineage of Israel's Patriarchs down to and including Jesus Christ.

On the previous page, we see a clear identification of the persons in the lines of Cain and Seth. Cain's line, most pre-sume, died out at the time of the Great Flood (if you believe the deluge was global), killing all terrestrial life (creeping things, birds, and human – see Genesis 6:7) except those preserved in the Ark. (Note: many Evangelicals do *not* hold to a universal flood. We will discuss this more in Part 2 of *Rebooting the Bible*).

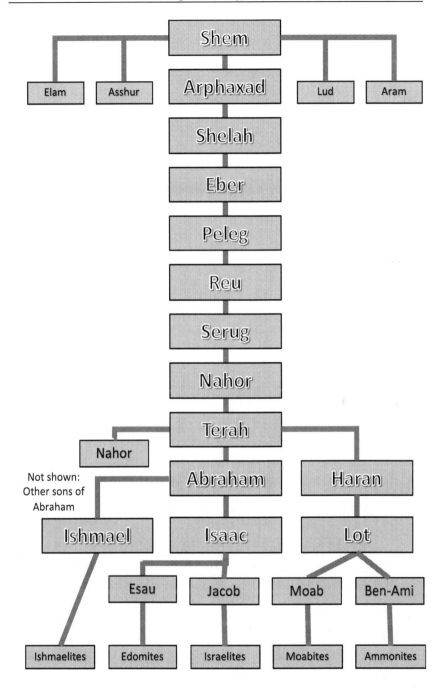

Figure 21 - From Shem to Abraham, Genesis 11 Genealogy
10 Generations from Shem to Abraham, 11 to Jacob

The second chart on the previous page provides the genealogy of Genesis 11, from Shem (one of three sons of Noah) down to the sons of Isaac, Lot, and Ishmael. The second chart intends to demonstrate the connection from Abraham to Adam, through Shem and Noah. The names in the figure also pinpoint where many of the peoples discussed in the Bible originated. We will study this more in Part 2. But to recap the beginnings of selected peoples and races to help us set the stage, let's note:

- **Elam** was father to the *Elamites* who will live in what is today Eastern Iran. The Elamites are a vital part of the story of Mesopotamia, lying just east of the Zagros Mountains. They become enemies of the Sumerians and Babylonians for a millennium.

- **Asshur** was father to the *Assyrians*. Some see Asshur as another name for Nimrod.[219] Nimrod, the son of Cush, is customarily held to be the ancient king of both the Assyrians and Babylonians, founding cities both in Assyria and Sumer. We will discuss Nimrod in Part 2 as well. It is challenging to identify Nimrod with one of the ancient Mesopotamian kings, but we will endeavor to delay this until a later chapter. *Mizraim*, another son of Ham, is considered the father of the Egyptians. Geographically, Asshur's peoples populated the land between and surrounding the Tigris and Euphrates (today's Iraq), but in ancient times, these areas were known as Sumer and Babylon.

- **Aram** was the patriarch of the *Aramaeans*, peoples that inhabit areas in Syria, Jordan, and Iraq. The language Aramaic, the language of Neo-Babylon, and post-exilic language of the Judeans (along with Greek), traces its origins back to these peoples.

- **Eber** was the father of all peoples that are called *Hebrew*, although this race is typically associated only with Jews. The Iberian Peninsula in Spain is sometimes identified with Eber as the home of the Iberian peoples. But this is not a standard view.

---

[219] Goodgame, Peter. *The Second Coming of the Antichrist*, Crane, Mo: Defender Books. (2012) We will discuss Peter's thesis on Nimrod in Part 2.

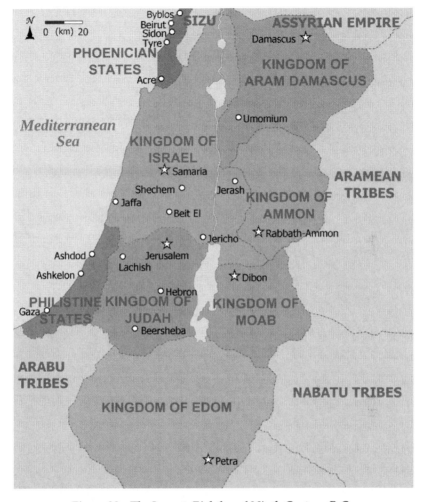

Figure 22 - The Levant, Eighth and Ninth Century B.C.

- **Ishmael,** son of Abraham and rival to Isaac, was the patriarch of the *Ishmaelites* who later become an enemy of the Jews. Ishmael is customarily seen as the father of the Arab race, although "Arab" actually means "mixture" or "mixed race."

- **Esau** was the father of the *Edomites*. The Edomites would be enemies of the Jews but likewise were exiled to Babylon by Nebuchadnezzar. The remnants of Edom later become *Idumeans* and

191

migrated to southern Judah. King Herod was much hated, in part, because he was an Idumean (Edomite). Edomites are also sometimes used in the Bible as a name *for all Gentiles.*

- **Moabites** were fathered by Lot. Their lands were east of the Dead Sea, extending from Edom to Ammon.

- **Ammonites,** also fathered by Lot, lived between Israel (during the time of Israel's 10 northern tribes), and the Aramaeans. The capital of today's Jordan is Ammon, a clear link to the past.

This recap provides several clues how the peoples of today can be traced by their common names, the names of their cities, and their uncommonly known self-designated names (such as the Egyptians who call themselves *Murz*). The table of nations (Genesis 10) identifies 70 "tribes" and, to some extent, where the members of their "tribe" migrated. Beginning in Armenia post-Flood, they spread across the globe. While academics doubt that all of humanity traces its roots to Shem, Japheth, and Ham – the three sons of Noah – they repudiate what empirical research verifies. Many studies argue this biblical truth, demonstrating their names can be seen in place names globally.[220]

Timing Differences between the LXX and the MT

Next, we must provide the preliminary data illustrating the difference in chronology implied in the genealogies. We will show that the Septuagint's genealogies in Genesis 5 and 11 are the original record of the Hebrew Vorlage by considering other witnesses who confirm both these ages and timeline *well before Akiba did his devious work.* Next, we discuss theories of how the

---

[220] I discuss the table of nations in regard to Japheth, the ancestor of Magog, in Chapter 9 of my book, *The Next Great War in the Middle East.* Faith Happens (2016). I include this in my method to identify Gog and Magog. (Ezekiel 38-39)

author of the Pentateuch (who tradition testifies is Moses), wanted his words understood by his readers.

NOTES	Patriarch	References	Masoretic (MT) Begetting Age	Remaining Years	Lifespan	Septuagint (LXX) Begetting Age	Remaining Years	Lifespan	VARIANCE
	Adam	Gen 5:3-5	130	800	930	230	700	930	100
	Seth	Gen 5:6-8	105	807	912	205	707	912	100
	Enosh	Gene 5:9-11	90	815	905	190	715	905	100
	Kenan	Gen 5:12-14	70	840	910	170	740	910	100
	Mahalalel	Gen 515-17	65	830	895	165	730	895	100
	Jared	Gen 5:18-20	162	800	962	162	800	962	
	Enoch	Gen 5:21-23	65	300	365	165	200	365	100
	Methuselah	Gen 5:25-27	187	782	969	187	782	969	
	Lamech	Gen 5:28-31	182	595	777	188	565	753	6
1	Noah	Gen 5:32, 7:11, 8:13-14, 9:28-29, 10:21, 11:10	500	350	950	500	350	950	
	Shem	Gen 11:10-11	100	500		100	500		
2	Arpachshad	Gen 11:12-13	35	403/430		135	430/330		100
3	Cainan	Gen 11:13b-14b				130	330		130
	Shelah	Gen 11:14-15	30	403		130	330/403		100
4	Eber	Gen 11:16-17	34	430/370		134	370		100
	Peleg	Gen 11:18-19	30	209		130	209		100
	Reu	Gen 11:20-21	32	207		132	207		100
	Serug	Gen 11:22-23	30	200		130	200		100
	Nahor	Gen 11:24-25	29	119		79	129		50
5	Terah	Gen 11:26, 32; Acts 7:2-4	130	75	205	130	75	205	0
	Abraham	Gen 11:28, 32, 12:1-4, 21:5, 25:7	100	75	175	100	75	175	
6	Totals:		2,106			3,492			
	Difference:		1,386						1,386

NOTES EXPLAINED	
1	Noah's begetting age is either 500 or 502; 100 years from Shem to the Flood implied.
2	Arphachshad lifesan variances are likely due to scribal errors.
3	Cainan is left out of MT, but included in Luke's genealogy of Christ.
4	The LXX provides a resolution for this variance.
5	Terah's begetting age is debated, it is either 70 or 130. 130 is used here.
6	The chronology is established by begetting age, not total lifespan

Figure 23 - Variances between MT and LXX

From the earlier recounting of the efforts of Rabbi Akiba, the reader will recall why Akiba found it necessary to corrupt the Hebrew text in Messianic prophecy. Here we see additional evidence by altering the implied chronology in Genesis 5 and 11, primarily to refute the claims of Christians that Jesus Christ was the Messiah. In the pages ahead, we will take up why Akiba believed the changes to chronology were necessary. Figure 23 illustrates that the difference between the two chronologies. The genealogies of the MT and LXX differ by 1,386 years. If only added to Ussher's timeline, the date when Adam and Eve first walked the earth, would be 5,400 B.C. instead of 4,004 B.C. Archeology will bear this out as we will see.

We will explore support for LXX's dating next and why it is evident that the original Hebrew's Vorlage must have contained the same information as the LXX, with only one or two minor alterations in the LXX through the centuries, by which the copyists sought to "correct" the previously stated dating seeing particular time-specific details erroneous. Later we will examine the critical issue of when Methuselah "brought forth" his son Enoch. This idiom sounds strange, but it is the manner by which Scripture expresses births within these genealogies. The language is not viewed favorably by MT advocates *who may use this odd wording to denounce the LXX.*

The LXX Compared to the Samaritan Pentateuch (SP)

Regarding the legitimacy and origin of the Samaritan Pentateuch, there are two theories as to how it arose:

1. The Samaritans, successors to the Ten Tribes, inherited this text after Israel was enslaved by Sennacherib (712 B.C.), or The Samaritans received the text from an Israelite priest sent by Esarhaddon (2 Kings 17:24-33) when their temple was founded on Mount Gerizim.

The scholar Gesenius believes "both Samaritan and Septuagint were formed from Hebrew manuscripts differing from one

194

another as well as from the authorized (text) of Israel, and that many willful corruptions… crept it." [221]

We know that the SP text was distinct from the Hebrew text because the Jews and Samaritans sought Ptolemy I (Soter) to settle their dispute in 300 B.C., only two decades before the LXX was translated from the Hebrew Vorlage to Greek. In the chart below (Figure 24), we see several differences between the LXX and the SP. As the notes below the table describe, some variances are due to the SP's keepers attempting to synchronize its chronology with what was recorded in a shortened version of Genesis, the Book of Jubilees (ca. 150 B.C.). However, the SP comparison strengthens the case for the LXX as it pertains to the post-Flood era. In contrast, its antediluvian record has no effect on the issue since it endeavored to be synchronized with the timeline of the Book of Jubilees, which we will discuss in Part 2.

Josephus and *Liber Antiquitatum Biblicarum*

Perhaps the most crucial testimony from other manuscripts that contain ancient chronological information that mirrors the Bible (whether from Hebrew, Greek, or Latin texts) is found in two additional sources. First is the Jewish historian Flavius Josephus, who provided a chronology derived from the Genesis 5 genealogy in his book, *Antiquities of the Jews*. Less familiar is a Latin work named *Liber Antiquitatum Biblicarum* (LAB), known in English as, *The Book of Biblical Antiquities*, which was previously misunderstood to have been a work of Philo of Alexandria (hence the author is now referred to as *pseudo-Philo*).

---

[221] From the definition of Samaritan Pentateuch in *Fausset's Bible Dictionary* (see Bible History Online).

Both accounts follow the LXX timeline very closely. These works *were completed (ca. 50-75 A.D.), several decades before Rabbi Akiba created the proto-Masoretic Text.* The work referred to as "LAB" was possibly completed during the lifetime of Jesus Christ. If the Hebrew Vorlage was available to these respective

NOTES	Patriarch	References	Septuagint (LXX)			VARIANCE	Samaritan Pentateuch (SP)			VARIANCE
			Begetting Age	Remaining Years	Lifespan		Begetting Age	Remaining Years	Lifespan	
	Adam	Gen 5:3-5	230	700	930	100	130	800	930	-100
	Seth	Gen 5:6-8	205	707	912	100	105	807	912	-100
	Enosh	Gene 5:9-11	190	715	905	100	90	815	905	-100
	Kenan	Gen 5:12-14	170	740	910	100	70	840	910	-100
	Mahalalel	Gen 515-17	165	730	895	100	65	830	895	-100
1	Jared	Gen 5:18-20	162	800	962		62	785	847	-100
	Enoch	Gen 5:21-23	165	200	365	100	65	300	365	-100
1	Methuselah	Gen 5:25-27	187	782	969		67	653	720	-120
1	Lamech	Gen 5:28-31	188	565	753	6	53	600	653	-135
	Noah	Gen 5:32, 7:11, 8:13-14, 9:28-29, 10:21, 11:10	500	350	950		500	350	950	
	Shem	Gen 11:10-11	100	500	600		100	500	600	
2	Arpachshad	Gen 11:12-13	135	330	465	100	135	303	438	
3	Cainan	Gen 11:13b-14b	130	330	460	130				-130
4	Shelah	Gen 11:14-15	130	330	460	100	130	303	433	
	Eber	Gen 11:16-17	134	370	504	100	134	270	404	
5	Peleg	Gen 11:18-19	130	209	339	100	130	109	239	
5	Reu	Gen 11:20-21	132	207	339	100	132	107	239	
5	Serug	Gen 11:22-23	130	200	330	100	130	100	230	
5	Nahor	Gen 11:24-25	79	129	208	50	79	69	148	
6	Terah	Gen 11:26, 32; Acts 7:2-4	130	75	205	0	70	75	145	-60
	Abraham	Gen 11:28, 32, 12:1-4, 21:5, 25:7	100	75	175		100	75	175	
	Totals:		3,492				2,347			(1,145)
	Difference:		LXX to SP:	(1,145)			MT to SP:	241		

NOTES: EXPLANATION
There are considerable differences in the Shem to Abraham lifespans of the Patriarchs.
In the Antediluvian period, he SP follows the MT in 6 of 9 Patriarchs.
1 The begetting age in SP is the same except for Jared, Enoch, & Methuselah.
   These three were fixed to line up with the apocryphal work, Jubilees, and to ensure
   that these Patriarchs did not live past the Great Flood.
2 The Arpachshad discrepany is likely a copyist error transposing the 330 to 303.
3 Cainan was dropped in the MT and the SP, but is in the LXX and in Luke's Gospel.
4 Shelah's remaining years were likely a copying error, another transposition of 330 to 303.
5 The begetting years in the SP agree with the LXX, but the remaining years care incorrect.
6 The variance in Terah's age goes back to the debate over whether Terah was 70 or 130 when
   he begat Abram (Abraham). Most scholars believe the 130 number to be correct.

Figure 24 – Variances Between the LXX and the SP

sources, we must ask, "Why did they select the same dating (practically speaking) as the LXX?" The answer is quite simple: The dating of the LXX followed the original, authentic Hebrew Vorlage, not the proto-Masoretic Text created at Jamnia by Akiba and his academy as the second century A.D. began.

Josephus indicated he himself translated the Hebrew text into Greek – and *not by referencing the LXX*. Said Josephus, "(These) antiquities contain *the history of 5,000 years;* and are taken out of our sacred books but *translated by me into the Greek tongue.*"[222] [Emphasis added] Since his "begetting ages" and "years remaining" match the LXX and not the proto-MT, he was using *a copy of the Hebrew other than the baseline text of Akiba.* Note His statement that the histories he records cover 5,000 years (actually, more like 5,400 years). This tells us his source was not the Old Testament as custom tailored by Rabbi Akiba. Otherwise, Josephus would have stated the Jewish timeframe from the Hebrew scriptures *was 4,000 years.* Concerning the *LAB:* It is an extant book in Latin, translated from an intermediate Greek source. The author's timeline begins with Adam and takes his reader back to King Saul (about 1050 B.C. in LAB's reckoning). There is a group of scholars who vouch for the timing of LAB and its distinctly Hebrew attributes.[223] *This additional witness virtually clinches the argument that the timeline in the LXX was the original.* As the chart on the following page illustrates, there are very few variances between the LXX, Josephus, and LAB. The simple explanation is that *they were referencing the same Hebrew Vorlage.*

---

[222] Josephus. Against Apion 1.1.

[223] Smith, Henry B. "Methuselah's Begetting Age in Genesis 5:25 and the Primeval Chronology of the Septuagint: A closer Look at the Textual and Historical Evidence." *Answer's Research Journal 10* (2017) p. 169-179. Smith cites four scholars and alludes to others. I follow Smith's data with confirmation from Barry Setterfield's paper on chronology, "Ancient Chronology from Scripture," 1999.

Patriarch	References	Masoretic (MT)			Septuagint (LXX)			Josephus			Liber Antiquitatum Biblicanum		
		Begetting Age	Remaining Years	Lifespan	Begetting Age	Remaining Years	Lifespan	Begetting Age	Remaining Years	Lifespan	Begetting Age	Remaining Years	Lifespan
Adam	Gen 5:3-5	130	800	930	230	700	930	230	700	930		700	930
Seth	Gen 5:6-8	105	807	912	205	707	912	205	707	912	205	707	912
Enosh	Gene 5:9-11	90	815	905	190	715	905	190	715	905	190	715	905
Kenan	Gen 5:12-14	70	840	910	170	740	910	170	740	910	170	740	910
Mahalalel	Gen 5:15-17	65	830	895	165	730	895	165	730	895	165	730	895
Jared	Gen 5:18-20	162	800	962	162	800	962	162	800	962	162	800	962
Enoch	Gen 5:21-23	65	300	365	165	200	365	165	200	365	165	200	365
Methuselah	Gen 5:25-27	187	782	969	167/187	782	969	187	782	969	187	782	969
Lamech	Gen 5:28-31	182	595	777	188	565	753	182/188	595	707/777	182/188	595	777
Noah	Gen 5:32, 7:11, 8:13-14, 9:28-29, 10:21, 11:10	500	350	950	500	350	950	500	350	950	500	350	950

NOTES: EXPLANATION
MT Differences due to Akiba's corruption of proto-MT text circa 100 A.D.
Methuselah's difference is due to scribal error (see Smih's article)
Lamech's variance is due to a copyist error in the LXX

Figure 25 – Comparison of MT/LXX with Josephus and LAB

This Vorlage is likely what Akiba had a copy of, but which he elected to alter to fit his purposes. One of the few discrepancies between these three sources has to do with the remaining years of Lamech after *bringing forth* his son Noah. The MT has 777 years as does one group of Josephus' manuscripts, while the other group has 707 years. The "LAB" has 777. This appears to be one instance where LXX has an incorrect number of years that may be due to a scribal error in the copying process. (See Smith's article identified below for a thorough and meticulous recounting of all the dates in each of the sources, including explanations that take into account *scribal errors due to the nature of how numbers are recorded in the Hebrew system using letters*.).

Voices Confirming MT Corruption of the Timeline

Debating the nature of the differences between the LXX and the MT isn't just a recent pastime of interested academics. It has been a hot topic for seventeen centuries! *And scholars in the early Church arrived at the same conclusion that our study deduces:* The rabbis of the first and second centuries changed the MT text in Messianic passages, but also "deflated" the Genesis 5 and 11 chronologies. Henry B. Smith Jr. informs us:

> Ephraem of Syria [306-373 A.D.] is the first known ancient source to explicitly argue that the Jewish rabbis of the second century AD deflated the primeval chronology by ca. 1300 years in their Hebrew MSS for the purpose of discrediting Jesus as the Christ: "The Jews have subtracted 600 years [in Genesis 5] from the generations of Adam, Seth, etc., in order that their own books might not convict them concerning the coming of CHRIST: he having been predicted to appear for the deliverance of mankind *after 5500 years*." Ephraem was one of

many ancient authors who claimed that the rabbis deliberately reduced the primeval chronology for messianic reasons.[224]

Prophecy students are familiar with the notion that there would be a "sabbath week" of millennia, meaning that biblical history would extend 7,000 years with the final 1,000 years being the reign of Christ – aka the Kingdom of David, or more appropriately, the Kingdom of God. Few know that this belief was widespread in Second Temple Judaism – meaning that the Messiah would appear before six thousand years had transpired. Says Smith, "Messianic chronologies were usually associated with the Days of Creation, with each day representing 1,000 years of history. In some schemes, the Messiah would arrive in the 6th millennium (5000–5999AM), and usher in the kingdom in the 7th millennium (6000AM)."[225] Smith comments that this was done by the rabbis because "reducing the primeval chronology as presently found in the MT places Jesus' life outside the time of the coming of the Messiah [That is, Jesus's coming in 1 B.C., would have been *too early* for Jesus to qualify as Messiah].[226] *But Akiba had altered the dates so that Jesus of Nazareth didn't come as the Messiah after 5,000 years!*

---

[224] Ibid. p. 1. Smith cites Hales, W. 1830. *A New Analysis of Chronology and Geography, History and Prophecy. Vol. 1. Chronology and Geography.* London, United Kingdom: C.J.G. and F. Rivington. Smith adds, there are additional citations of Ephraem's claims in Assemani (J. S. 1719. *Bibliotheca Orientalis Clementino-Vaticana. Rome: Typis Sacrae Congregationis de Propaganda Fide.*); Wacholder (Wacholder, B.Z. 1974. Eupolemus: *A Study of Judaeo-Greek Literature.* Cincinnati, Ohio: Hebrew Union College Press.) and Anstey (Anstey, M. 1913. *The Romance of Bible Chronology: An Exposition of the Meaning, and a Demonstration of the Truth, of Every Chronological Statement Contained in the Hebrew Text of the Old Testament.* London, United Kingdom: Marshall Bros.)

[225]. Beckwith, R.T. 1996. Calendar and Chronology, Jewish and Christian: Biblical, Intertestamental and Patristic Studies. Leiden, The Netherlands: Brill. Cited by Smith op. cit., p.1.

[226] Ibid., p.1.

Figure 26 - England's Great Bible of 1539

While Ephraem was the first to blame the Post-Temple rabbis *for changing the chronology of Genesis 5 and 11 to attack Jesus as Messiah*, he was hardly alone in discussing the divergencies between the LXX, MT, and SP (Justin Martyr attacked the rabbis ca. 160 A.D. for their actions). Smith identifies the following five scholars of the early Church who carried on the conversation; to wit, the corruption of the chronology by the Jews. These scholars are the Vulgate author Jerome (340-420 AD), Julian of Toledo (642-690 A.D.), Jacob of Edessa (640-708 AD), George Syncellus, a Byzantine chronologist who died in AD 810, and Armenian historian Bar Hebraeus (1226-1286 A.D.)[227]

The Evolution of the Protestant Bible

At this point, we need to pause and recap how the *Protestant Bible was married to the Masoretic Text, while the LXX was "left at the altar."* Given the suspected perfidiousness of the rabbis altering the text, it seems the Septuagint would be preferred. But this perfidy was not widely known, while other unfavorable factors *pushed Protestants to the MT and away from the LXX.*

Up until the Reformation, the LXX was considered the Bible of the Eastern Church (Greek, Arminian, and Russian Orthodox) with the Vulgate the Bible of the Western Church (Roman Catholicism). *The MT was only the Bible of Judaism.* With the reformers Martin Luther and John Calvin, the Catholic Latin Vulgate and Orthodoxy's Greek Septuagint lived in enemy territory.

Historically, "common language" (aka native vernacular) translations were created beginning with Martin Luther's German Bible published not long after his nailing 95 theses to the Wittenberg Door in 1517. His Bible influenced Tyndale to

---

[227] Ibid., p. 2.

produce his controversial English Bible. Tyndale was rewarded with a public defrocking and inhumane execution, as he was strangled to death for heresy in 1536. His martyrdom was not for doctrinal issues mind you, but for employing words in his translation that were *not*, shall we say, politically correct. Instead, his translation was seen as a threat to the King's authority.

The Great Bible of 1539 (see the figure above) was the first Bible of the Church of England, authorized by King Henry VIII. It was based on the Tyndale Bible (with objectionable features dropped), the Latin Vulgate, and Luther's German translation. Unlike Tyndale, *The Great Bible* was not derived from the Greek, Hebrew, or Aramaic texts. It relied upon the Latin Vulgate and the German Translation of Luther. *The Great Bible* would be succeeded by *The Bishop's Bible* in 1568, which would later become designated as *the principal source text for the King James*. (Note: A previous English Bible was used as a basis for the KJV).

By 1576, the entire *Geneva Bible* had been printed. Since Calvin and John Knox were both involved in its creation, *The Geneva Bible* was adopted in Scotland so strongly that the government passed a law mandating that all Scotsmen should be given the means to purchase their very own copy. (Holy welfare!)

However, the Church of England stuck with *The Great Bible* until the *King James Bible* (the Authorized Bible!) was published in 1611 and popularly adopted over the next 100 years. The *Geneva Bible* employed more profound scholarship, *making use of both Greek and Hebrew manuscripts*. It was also the first English Bible to utilize verse numbering. Early versions of the KJV included some of the marginal notes from *The Geneva Bible*, which was surprising, given concerns that its ecclesiology (its organizing principle) was Presbyterian (i.e., the local church reigns supreme, thus directly conflicting with the Church of England's hierarchical approach: Bishops presiding over all churches).

Work on the *King James Bible* would begin in 1604 and be completed seven years later. It combined the work of 47 scholars, all members of the Church of England. These translators were ordered to make sure the wording of the Bible supported the governing structure of the Church of England (*Episcopal* ecclesiology with ordained clergy). Translators based their work *on the Old Testament* using the Hebrew (MT) and Aramaic Bibles (SP). They referenced the Greek LXX only on a limited basis (as noted in their *preface* to the KJV); specifically, in cases of Old Testament texts having "a Christological interpretation" such as Psalm 22:16. The *Hebrew Rabbinic Bible* by Daniel Bomberg (1525) read, "Like lions my hands and feet" whereas the LXX read, "They pierced my hands and my feet."[228] By then, the fix was in.

An excellent overview of the King James Bible's creation is provided in Wikipedia. It indicates the KJV translators used many sources, primarily *The Bishop's Bible* (produced during the reign of Queen Elizabeth I), concerning *The Geneva Bible* for alternate readings. The General Committee of Review, according to John Bois' notes, "show that they discussed readings derived from a wide variety of versions and patristic sources; including explicitly both Henry Savile's 1610 edition of *The Works of John Chrysostom* and the *Rheims New Testament*, which was the primary source for many of the literal alternative readings

---

[228] This is another example of corruption not included in the previous chapter. It is noteworthy that the translators of the KJV tried to "fix" the text that had been altered in line with the Septuagint. Obviously, they missed a lot of passages where their adjustments to Messianic language was not fixed.

provided for the marginal notes."[229] Clearly, in composing the KJV, the translators did not work exclusively from "the original tongues."[230] Their approach was eclectic.

For the first 150 years of its printing, the KJV included the Apocrypha as did the Vulgate and the Septuagint. This is significant for some today hold the Septuagint and Vulgate in disdain because they contain "the uninspired *Apocrypha*" (not realizing the KJV *had incorporated the Apocrypha* within its binding for over a century). By 1715, this Bible came to be known as the *King James Bible*. By the mid-eighteenth century, the KJV also became the accepted Bible for scholars, replacing the Latin Vulgate.

Consequently, the Septuagint seems to have been "lost in the shuffle" as a result of the Protestant reformation breaking with the perceived "elitism" of the Catholic's Latin and Orthodoxy's Greek. And so it is that *the Church lost the original and authentic chronology of the Old Testament while the corrupted chronology of the MT became standardized.* The baby had been thrown out with the bathwater (or in this case, perhaps the reverse!) Furthermore, with the onslaught of Enlightenment skepticism, Church people desired a "sure word from God" not subject to "textual criticism" and meddlesome scholars. For four centuries that sure word grew to be the *King James Bible based on the Masoretic Text*. But this preference would one day assert that the KJV was the only, solely inspired Bible.

---

[229] See "Sources" from Wikipedia's article on the King James Version. Retrieved July 12, 2018 from https://en.wikipedia.org/wiki/King_James_Version.

[230] If the KJV is inerrant as in its translation (as some suppose), then presumably its source texts were inerrant too, although they differed from one another in the particular words which conveyed inerrant text. (Quite a challenging conundrum!) This premise actually creates more problems than it solves primarily because the supposition is easy to disprove. Find one error, it all falls apart.

In the nineteenth century, this view became enshrined in the work of Dean Burgon as a reaction to the Church of England's "Revised Version" published in 1883.[231] It is important to note, however, that the kerfuffle related to the New Testament and the use of Westcott and Hoyt's Greek New Testament revision, instead of Erasmus' sixteenth century "Received Text" or *Textus Receptus* (TR). Obliviously, the arguments over the KJV frequently center on the TR ignoring the fact that the TR contains only the Greek New Testament, which from this author's standpoint, is not my focus.[232]

At this juncture, allow me to reaffirm my commitment to inerrancy in the autographs of biblical authors and God's ongoing provision to protect the text – a requirement for ensuring the Holy Scripture rightly conveys His Word – and remind the reader Appendix 5 takes this up in great detail.

Having said that, it's time to get back to whether the Septuagint and the Hebrew Vorlage did, in fact, provide a chronology intertwined with a genealogy. Did the Vorlage supply a timeline extending from *the creation account* in Genesis chapter 1 to the *destruction of the first Jewish Temple in 586 B.C.* ± 1 one year?

This date of 586 B.C. is chosen intentionally because it's the point where biblical and secular historians reach a consensus on

---

[231] See Baptist scholar Bill Combs post on Dean Burgon and the Revised Version at http://www.dbts.edu/2012/03/21/dean-burgon-and-the-revised-version/.

[232] I will not offer arguments here for why the TR is likely not as accurate to the original autographs as Westcott and Hoyt. The issue deals with the number of manuscripts referenced in their translation. Erasmus used seven manuscripts. Westcott and Hoyt used several thousand more recently discovered texts.

the dating of biblical events. From that point forward – give or take one year – scholars don't quibble.[233]

Green's Gaps and Genealogical Name Dropping

So how does the providential protection of textual transmission address the issue of differing timelines derived from various biblical genealogies as established in our sacred texts? Once again, we return full circle and face the matter of whether *genealogies yield chronologies*. Can there be a *chronogenealogy*?

William H. Green's 1890 theological paper, from which we launched this chapter's trek, *turns out to be a watershed in Evangelicalism*. Afterward, Genesis 5 and 11 were no longer seen to be *inspired historical information*. Green argued against a "primeval chronology" in his article using the same title. Spurred no doubt by the destructive effects of Darwinism, Green mounted the then latest apology for *the separation of historical facts from spiritual truth*, a distinction that those familiar with the teaching of Francis Schaeffer will readily recognize.[234]

---

[233] A quick foreshadowing: the *Seder Olam Rabbah*, the Hebrew Language Chronology, was also created by Rabbi Akiba and his disciples in the second century A.D., conventionally associated with Yose ben Halafta in 160 A.D. It covers the time from Adam to Bar Kokhba. We will see later in this chapter that the rabbis dropped even more years to invalidate the timing proposed by Daniel (and the Christian interpretation of it), which had the Messiah appearing about the time of Jesus Christ. This endeavor amounted to "fine tuning" to fix the dates so Jesus of Nazareth wouldn't qualify to be Prince (Messiah) of Daniel 9:24-27. This demonstrates once again, that altering biblical truth was not beyond the Rabbis.

[234] Schaeffer argued that separating the two "fields" of knowledge – religious from historical – constituted an "escape from reason." His argument was that a Bible that includes mistaken history can't be trusted. For those religious or theological advocates that do trust it even though it makes mistakes, are taking the Kierkegaardian leap of faith. Therefore, Schaeffer would not accept a Bible that makes historical (or scientific) mistakes. He was not, however, a KJV-only guy.

As Henry Smith points out in the article we've referenced several times already in this chapter, the weapon often welded by MT supporters in their condemnation of the LXX is whether the LXX "got Methuselah's age wrong" when Methuselah's son, Enoch, was born to him. (Note: This Enoch is the namesake of the Book of Enoch, *pseudepigraphally* speaking, that is.[235])

Jeremy Sexton has written a superb scholarly paper on the topic of Green's article.[236] Sexton makes the point as did Henry B. Smith, that Green's seminal essay was the crossroads for distinguishing (better yet, *separating*) *genealogy from chronology*. Sexton conveys, "(Green) argued that "the genealogies in Genesis 5 and 11 were not intended to be used, and cannot properly be used, for the construction of a chronology."[237] His paper stated unequivocally that "the Scriptures furnish no data for a chronological computation before the life of Abraham."

At the beginning of Sexton's "rebuttal," he provides an impressive summary of the historical authorities using genealogies as chronology. Allow me to make use of his exact words:

> Green's proposal challenged the long-established approach to Gen 5 and 11. Biblical interpreters had been reading the genealogies as chronologies since before Christ. Jewish historians Demetrius (ca. 200 BC), Eupolemus (ca. 160 BC), and Josephus (ca. AD 93), as well as the authors of Jubilees (ca. 150 BC) and Seder Olam

---

[235] A *pseudepigrapha* is a book written using another's name, perhaps attempting to "speak in the same spirit as" the person whose name is used. It was not seeking to plagiarize, though this is confusing to modern readers. Conservative Evangelicals are unwilling to accept that pseudepigrapha can be inspired.

[236] Green, op. cit.

[237] Sexton, Jeremy. "Who was born when Enosh was 90? A Semantic reevaluation of William Henry Green's Chronological Gaps." *Westminster Theological Journal 77* (2015), p. 193-218. This article is available for study at www.biblearcheology.org and is retrievable through search words, "Enosh" and "90." I highly recommend readers interested in this subject read the article carefully.

Rabbah (ca. AD 150), used genealogies for chronological computation. Several early and medieval churchmen – for example, Theophilus of Antioch (ca. 168), Julius Africanus (ca. 218), Origen (ca. 230), Eusebius (ca. 315), Augustine (ca. 354), Bede (ca. 723), and Cedrenus (ca. 1060) – did likewise. Luther dated creation to 3960 BC, Melanchthon to 3963 BC, and "Geneva" to 3943 BC. During the interval between the Reformation and the publication of Green's essay, Ussher dated creation to 4004 BC, Vossius to 5590 BC, Playfair to 4007 BC, Jackson to 5426 BC, Hales to 5411 BC, and Russell to 5441 BC. This is merely a small sampling of those who used Genesis 5 and 11 for the construction of a chronology. By 1890 the chronological interpretation had deep roots.[238]

Sexton notes the unfortunate approbation by Walter C. Kaiser Jr., in which Kaiser stated how Green's article was "one of the finest moments in Old Testament scholarship."[239] Sexton describes the reason why Green's approach was so attractive: It proposed that all Old Testament genealogies had "gaps" where names are dropped (and generations too). The genealogies of Genesis 5 and 11 were no different. Since Ussher's dating of 2348 B.C. for the Great Flood occurred after Egypt's 1st Dynasty, dated by Egyptologists to 3000 B.C., one chronology or the other must be wrong. However, if there were gaps in the Genesis 5 and 11 genealogies, then dating conflicts are resolved.

Sexton reviews the core "proof" adduced by Green which has to do with citing familiar omissions in the genealogy of Jesus (e.g., Matthew 1:8, "Joram begat Uzziah" aka Azariah, even though Uzziah was Joram's great-great-grandson). The technical details delve into *hiphil* verb forms in Hebrew. The specific

---

[238] Ibid. p. 93-94.

[239] Walter C. Kaiser Jr., ed., Classical Evangelical Essays in Old testament Interpretation (Grand Rapids; Baker, 19712, p. 7. Cited by Sexton, ibid., p. 94.

Hebrew word is יֶלֶד (*yalad*) which can mean "to bear, give birth to, bring forth, beget, or travail" (Strong's H3205). As mentioned earlier, the English equivalent of its literal meaning in Genesis 5, when using the *hiphil* form is (however awkward it may seem in English), "he caused his sons and daughters to come forth." This is reminiscent of the argument used in the book of Hebrews that Levi was resident in Abraham's "loins" – so when Abraham tithed to Melchizedek, *so did Levi* (generations later) demonstrating (for the author of Hebrews at least) that the priesthood of Melchizedek is superior to Levi's (Hebrews 7:9-10) inasmuch as "the lesser blesses the greater." (Hebrews 7:7)

This notion also sheds light on the Trinity doctrine for we say, "the Son is begotten of the Father," meaning the Father causes the Son to be brought forth." We should grasp it is the *will* of the father which is intrinsic to the process – not by his "seed" per se. *The Father's **will** brings forth the Son **continuously** and **eternally**."*

Green counted the number of times various forms of this Hebrew word was used in Genesis 5 and 11:10-26, demonstrating that this same word is used in other biblical genealogies that prove out to have had gaps or "names dropped" (a case where *unimportant* names are being dropped, not famous ones – the pun is intended). Examples are 2 Kings 24:12-17; 25:1-7. In 2 Kings 20:18, Isaiah prophesies to Hezekiah that he will have sons (descendants) that will go into exile. These turn out to be *Hezekiah's great-great-grandson, Zedekiah, and great-great-great-grandson, Jehoiachin.* Sexton stipulates to Green's point. *Yalad* can imply and include gaps.

However, that point turns out to be moot in Genesis 5 and 11. Sexton demonstrates Green's logic is flawed for he misses the point. Given that the Patriarchs in Genesis 5 and 11 have been given specific ages when their son (or descendant) was born, *the generations of the begetting are linked one after another.* That is, these begetting ages establish an unbroken sequence. For instance, when Enosh was 90, he "brought forth" Kenan. Whether Kenan was *Enosh's son or grandson,* when Kenan was brought forth by Enosh, Enosh was 90. Even if Kenan was a great-grandson, Enosh was still 90 when this took place.

Here's the technical skinny for those who, unlike this author, know more than a *little* Hebrew:

> Who was born when Enosh was 90? The untranslatable parti-
> cle את marks קינן ("Kenan") as the direct-object accusative of ויולד
> ("he had"); a "direct-object accusative is the recipient of a transitive
> verb's action. The transitive verb ויולד describes birth. Therefore,
> Genesis 5:9 refers to Kenan's birth when Enosh was 90. [240]

That is, even if Kenan was a son or great-great-great-grandson, Enosh was 90 years old. Green acknowledges that the statement of the Patriarch's age is constant although the direct object of the action could be generations apart. *In Genesis 5 and 11, genealogical gaps don't matter because the chronology stays the same.* In other words, the timelines don't change even if the descendant identified comprises a son or a great-great-great-grandson (or, to be a bit absurd, a descendant even further "down the line"). Thus, gaps "from name-dropping" don't change the chronology. The timing stands. Of course, it may not be aligned with science or acceptable to skeptics; *but it still means exactly what the Bible says it means.*

It is interesting that the opposing point of view Sexton brings against Green had been put forth shortly after Green

---

[240] Waltke and O 'Connor, *Introduction to Biblical Hebrew Syntax,* 164, italics in original. Cited by Sexton, ibid., p. 197.

published his paper in 1890. However, this counter-point essay was not published although the editor of *Bibliotheca Sacra* promised it would be as stated in a letter to its author, June 29, 1893. Sexton quotes from this author, Smith Bartlett Goodenow, who wrote in his critical response to Green's thesis (which became the standard Evangelical position despite being wrong-headed):

> The 'begat' indicates the birth of the person named after it; and the date of that birth being given, it matters not how many unnamed generations intervene. The *chronology* is fixed and unchanged. No such anomaly is known in Scripture, or in reason, as a dating given to *an unnamed ancestor's* birth.[241]

A separate article, authored by Sexton and Henry B. Smith Jr. "Primeval Chronology Restored: Revisiting the Genealogies of Genesis 5 and 11," (an article I highly recommend that readers study as it confirms the details I provide here), we read:

> The ancient Jews, who prized their chronologies and genealogies, never would have forgiven a deliberate textual alteration of this magnitude in the foundational chronogenalogies of Genesis 5 and 11. And yet for four hundred years this corruption supposedly was not just overlooked, but adopted by all the Jewish historians of that time... Such a scenario is utterly implausible.[242]

Sexton and Smith point out before the second century A.D., no Jewish scholar used the MT dates, they only used the LXX. Why were the dates changed? To discredit Jesus as the Christ. "We propose, then, an adequate motive for Palestinian Jewish scribes to alter the sacred text, a motive that is supported by

---

[241] Goodenow, Smith Bartlett, *Bible Chronology Carefully Unfolded* (New York: Fleming H. Revell, 1896, 322, italics original.

[242] Sexton, Jeremy, and Smith Jr., Henry B. "Primeval Chronology Restored: Revisiting the Genealogies of Genesis 5 and 11." Bible and Spade 29.2 (2016).

historical and theological evidence: discrediting the Lord Jesus as Messiah." And yet, LXX scholars publishing today, with few exceptions, don't consider that it is *this motive* which is *prima facie evidence, that explains why the LXX and the MT differ.*

Did Matthew Use Genealogy to Create A Pattern?

There were other arguments made by Green that are answered in Sexton's essay. Of interest is Green's case that since each genealogy has 10 generations, it is an artificial pattern (these genealogies actually have 10 or 11 depending upon whether you count or don't count Noah – see my "family trees" on page 187 and page 189).

Green insists that since *pattern* must be critical to the author, then it also must mean the genealogy can't be historical. He argues that just as Matthew alleged there were 14 generations in each of three groups "bringing forth" Jesus (recall Matthew did not include all the generations traced back to Abraham for some undisclosed reason), the genealogy isn't meant to have historical validity – there must be a spiritual message concealed within the pattern. While Green's argument incorrectly counts the number of "Genesis generations," Green is correct that there probably is a "spiritual pattern" intended in Matthew's genealogy. Logically, however, a pattern expressed in one genealogy doesn't mean a pattern exists in all. Nor does the fact that since one genealogy doesn't intend to be historical (i.e., to provide a timeline), that all genealogies are equally indifferent to historical accuracy. So then, what might Matthew's "pattern" mean?

A plausible explanation is provided by Pastor Bob Deffinbaugh, a graduate of Dallas Theological Seminary. From his article on Bible.org, "The Origins of Jesus Christ" (Matthew 1:1-25), we read:

Genealogies were especially important to the Jewish people. Israel's king had to be a Jew, and not a foreigner (Deuteronomy 17:15). Later on, it was revealed that he must be a descendant of David (2 Samuel 7:14). When the Jews returned from the Babylonian captivity, it was important for these returned exiles to show that their roots were Jewish and could be traced through the genealogies. No one could serve as priest whose name could not be found in the genealogical records (Ezra 2:62). Bruner writes that the famous rabbi Hillel was proud that he could trace his genealogy all the way back to King David. He further indicates that Josephus began his autobiography with his own pedigree. Then there was Herod the Great, who was half-Jew and half-Edomite. Obviously, his name was not in the official genealogies, and thus he ordered that the records be destroyed. If he couldn't be found there, he did not want to be upstaged by anyone else… Matthew's genealogy is divided into three sections, each consisting of 14 names. In order for Matthew to achieve this order, he had to omit some of the names. This poses no problem because the Greek term (rendered "the son of" [*gennao*, Strong's G1080]) refers to one's descendants, who might therefore be sons, grandsons, great-grandsons, etc. The point I wish to make here is that Matthew wanted us to view his genealogy as very neat and orderly. [243]

My thinking: Matthew employs the Greek word *gennao* (ghin-nay-oh), which conveys in Greek what *yalad* does in Hebrew. He uses permissible generational name dropping. Why? *He isn't providing a chronology; he is only presenting a genealogy.* He establishes a balanced presentation of Jesus' genealogy (perhaps) to bring biblical numerology into play. My conjecture: 14 is twice times 7; 2 signifies differentiation while 7 is spiritual perfection. Jesus Christ has two natures: One is Deity

[243] Deffenbaugh, Bob. "The Origins of Jesus Christ". Bible.org. Retrieved July 13, 2018 from https://bible.org/seriespage/origins-jesus-christ-matthew-11-25.

and one is human. Likewise, 42 is 7 times 6; while 7 (again, spiritual perfection) times 6 being the number of humanity. Perhaps Matthew's hidden numerical message in his genealogy sets forth the truth, *Jesus is the incarnation of God in man.* This isn't provable, but it is reasonable.

Sexton points out yet another point that slipped past Green. Since Genesis 5 tells us that Methuselah died when the Great Flood commenced, his "aging and begetting" had historical significance. If his age and begetting age (i.e., of Enoch) had chronological meaning, why wouldn't the other entries in the genealogy of Genesis 5 also have historical value?

Sexton continues to trace other recent theologians who follow Green's lead but continue to make the same mistake. It certainly appears modern theologians seek relief from the challenge of defending the implicit genealogies of Genesis 5 and 11 with scientifically-minded skeptics. Concludes Sexton:

> We commend Green for seeking a scriptural response to the aspersions of skeptics, but we must conclude that he did not find a tenable one. A computable chronology of the human race, going back to Adam on the sixth day of creation (Gen 1:26-27; 5:1-3), is lexically and grammatically inescapable. If we suppose that the genealogies in Gen 5 and 11 do not communicate chronology, then the possibility of a chronogenalogy becomes difficult to imagine, for "no mode of speech could be contrived to give successive dates to Bible generations if those tables in Genesis be denied as such.[244]

Sexton continues his compelling argumentation in several appendices to his article. One striking paragraph there points out that the debate over the correct chronology (whether the

---

[244] Sexton, op. cit., p. 207. Sexton cites Goodenow, *Bible Chronology*, p. 323.

LXX or the MT possesses the exact timeline) has been heated throughout the Church Age.[245] He notes that Jewish histories written before Akiba's corruptions in the second century used the higher begetting ages (adding 100 years to 12 generations listed in Genesis 5 and 11).[246] This includes Demetrius, Eupolemus, and Josephus' *Jewish Antiquities*. Jerome used the MT's lower begetting ages in the Vulgate. But in his *Chronicon*, he followed Eusebius' chronology based on the Septuagint.

The Roman Church *officially regarded the Septuagint's higher begetting ages authentic* until *after the Reformation*. Here we have one of the few times that Catholics imitated Protestants – and we, unfortunately, led them astray!

While the Reformers broke with tradition as outlined earlier, other scholars followed who lived in the seventeenth, eighteenth, and nineteenth centuries that *insisted the LXX had the correct chronology*. Sexton lists twelve biblical authorities: Vossius, Pezron, Des Vignoles, Hayes, Jackson, Hales, Faber, Russell, Seyffarth, Rawlinson, Budd, and Goodenow… who "called for a return to the numbers in the Septuagint. This text-critical discussion lost steam after the publication of Green's essay, which left the begetting ages with no clear purpose."[247] Which is to say, if the begetting ages don't provide an implicit chronology there was no reason for the author of Genesis to be so explicit about something that, ultimately, didn't matter one iota.

---

[245] This debate has been, however, not a subject in popular books – a lapse this author hopes his study here will correct.

[246] There were 12 instances of adding 100, one instance of adding 50, and a difference in Lamech's age of 6 years. Finally, Cainan was left out of the MT, adding 130 years.

[247] Sexton, op. cit. p. 211-212.

We could summarize the outcome by contending there are two dissenting positions in two groups: First, there are those in Group A that continue to follow Ussher and the King James Bible ignoring the theological reasons for the Septuagint's superior chronology (buttressed by textual criticism and a list of scholarly opinions as long as our arm). We can assert this group is dominated by a non-biblical authority: *spiritual inertia,* i.e., "tradition." Secondly, there is Group B, who are followers of Green's contention that we must avoid the stated biblical chronology *since it is irrelevant to modern man and his spiritual understanding.* However, both seek to alleviate "cognitive dissonance" by adopting their respective viewpoints, hoping to eliminate criticism that might unsettle their sacrosanct belief systems. At any rate, both share the same unsatisfactory outcome: *Being wrong.*

Akiba's *Seder Olam* – More Years Trimmed

However, solid critical scholarship quietly abounds when it pertains to reckoning the real number of years covered in biblical chronology *after the destruction of Solomon's Temple.* We see this when judging the chronology advanced by second-century Jewish rabbis, the *Seder Olam Rabbah.*[248]

The assessment of the Seder Olam Rabbah resolved that Akiba's disciples rid themselves of another 165 years from the "post-exilic" period (from 586 B.C. to 70 A.D.). Instead of 656 years, the Seder Olam recognizes only 471 years. Why? Eight Persian kings after Cyrus I (that academic history recognizes),

---

[248] The Sedar Olam Rabbah details the dates of biblical events from Creation to Alexander the Great's conquest of Persia; albeit incorrectly as I show.

are glossed over by the Seder Olam, obfuscating the timing of the Messiah ("the anointed one") in Daniel 9:24-27.[249] Beginning with discussions on Genesis 5 and 11, scholarship reveals what must have been the second-century rabbis' corrupting principle. If so, it confirms the thesis of this book. And it demonstrates that *if they were willing to change the Bible and history in one area, they were equaling willing to change it in another.*

The following passage in Sexton's essay links the timeline of the Seder Olam to the Genesis chronologies by identifying that the Rabbinical *tannaim* ("masters of the law") intentionally went about altering chronologies specifically to contradict the witness of Christians concerning the timing of the Messiah. Instead of the Messiah (*Mashiach*) being "cut off" in *30 A.D.*, pointing to the death of Jesus of Nazareth (Daniel 9:26), they interpret "cutting off" (כָּרַת, *karath*, kaw-rath) refers to the destruction of the Temple *in 70 A.D.* We read:

> Interpreters have discussed what likely motivated the second-century Jews to reduce the interval between creation and Christ to less than 4,000 years (3,761 years in Seder Olam Rabbah) … The Septuagint's primeval chronology, which existed in Hebrew texts before the second century AD, puts the birth of Jesus at ca. AM 5500. Many scholars have argued that during the second century AD, the Palestinian Jews shortened the chronology in the Hebrew copies of Gen 5 and 11 to remove the life of Jesus far from the sixth millennium of the world. A similar tendency may exist in Seder Olam Rabbah's postexilic chronology, which (having been reduced by roughly 185 years) artificially lays the groundwork for the Jewish interpretation of Daniel's seventy משיח weeks (Dan 9:24-27),

---

[249] The Seder Olam states that the Persians ruled for 52 years while accepted history holds that their reign was for 207 Years (from 539 to 332 B.C.)

specifically the belief that the cutting off of the ("anointed one") in Dan 9:26 was fulfilled ca. AD 70. This manufactured timeline in Seder Olam Rabbah was apparently an attempt to undermine the Christian interpretation of Daniel's messianic prophecy. Goodenow concludes, "Since the Jews of that day did thus fabricate a false [postexilic] chronology in their attempt to defeat Christianity; the only question is, 'Did they go further, and corrupt the numbers of Genesis for the same purpose?'"[250]

The Church Fathers concluded the same as this author. To reiterate: Sexton and Smith, from the joint article referenced earlier, make that perfectly clear:

Numerous church fathers testify to the lengths to which orthodox Judaism went to discredit Jesus' Messianic office, a phenomenon also recorded throughout the book of Acts. Justin Martyr says that the Rabbis deliberately expunged or altered Messianic verses from their Scriptures in their project of discrediting Lord Jesus as Messiah (e.g., see *Dialogues.*71). According to Justin, the second-century Jews were still promulgating the lie that the disciples had stolen Christ's body from the tomb (cf. Matthew 28:13-15). Augustine writes that "the Jews, envying us for our translation of their Law and Prophets, have made alterations in their texts to undermine the authority of ours" (Civ. 15.11)[251]

The late J.R. Church, in his book, *Daniel Reveals the Bloodline of Christ*, presented in meticulous detail critical errors in the

---

[250] Sexton, op. cit. p. 216. Sexton cites Goodenow in this passage from *Bible Chronology*, 306-7.

[251] Sexton and Smith, op. cit.

Seder Olam. The primary issue he recounts: the 13 Persian kings, including eight dropped by the Seder Olam (SO):[252]

1. Darius the Mede. 538-537 B.C.
2. Cyrus. 537-529 B.C.
3. Artaxerxes (Cambyses). 529-522 B.C.
4. Darius (Artaxerxes the Great, Ahasuerus). 521-485 B.C.
5. Xerxes, son of Vashti (not Ester per SO). 485-465 B.C.
6. Artaxerxes, co-rent until 474, then king until 425 B.C.
7. Xerxes, son of Artaxerxes, one year only. 425 B.C.
8. Secundianus (second son of Artaxerxes). 424-423 B.C.
9. Ochus/Darius (third son of Artaxerxes).423-404 B.C.
10. Arsicas/Artaxerxes (son of Ochus). 404-361 B.C.
11. Ochus (son or Arsicas). 361-338 B.C.
12. Arses. 338- 336 B.C.
13. Darius. 336-331 B.C. (Defeated by Alexander the Great).

The palace intrigue among the Persian kings, described by Church, certainly stands out as it involved poisonings and assassinations to wrest the throne from one king by another. It is most memorable even if eight of these kings were omitted by the Seder Olam. Why did Yose ben Halafta exclude 164/165 years of the 207 years in which Persian kings ruled? (Note: Sexton and Smith indicate 185 years). Church cited Rabbi Simon Schwab who agreed there was a blatant omission. In his book, *Comparative Jewish Chronology*, Rabbi Schwab states:

> It should have been possible that our Sages – for some unknown reason – had covered up a certain historic period and purposely eliminated and suppressed all records and other material pertaining thereto. If so, what might have been their compelling reason for so unusual a procedure? Nothing short

---

[252] Church, J.R. *Daniel Reveals the Bloodline of the Antichrist.* Prophecy Publications, 2010, p. 245-248.

of a Divine command could have prompted...those saintly 'men of truth' to leave out completely from our annals a period of 165 years and to correct all data and historic tables in such a fashion that the subsequent chronological gap could escape being noticed by countless generations, known to a few initiates only who were duty-bound to keep the secret to themselves.[253]

Church rightly summarized the situation:

Schwab and others went on to suggest that they might have falsified the dates in order to confuse anyone who might try to use the prophecies of Daniel to predict the time of the Messiah's coming. The truth is, sometime between A.D. 135-160, Yose ben Halafta, student of Rabbi Akiva and admirer of Bar Kokhba, *changed the dating so that Daniel's seventy weeks would point to Bar Kokhba as their predicted Messiah, rather than Jesus.* He deliberately pointed generations of Jews away from Jesus, the true Messiah![254] [Emphasis mine]

If we assumed that the Sages had no ulterior motive, then we might conclude they just got all the Xerxes and Artaxerxes mixed up. But since Greek and Persian historians provide the same list we supplied on the previous page, the Sages had hundreds of years to catch their error and correct it. But they didn't. Christians know why. Hopefully, soon, many Jews will realize the same thing. The books were cooked! The Jewish calendar date of 5777 is way off. The year should be in the 7000s.

In our study, this is the last indictment we will make concerning the second-century Rabbis. There are more chronological issues to set straight, but they involve analysis of the

---

[253] Schwab, R. *Comparative Jewish Chronology*, p. 188. Cited by Church, op. cit., p. 248-249.

[254] Ibid., p. 249.

Scripture (*exegesis*), examining history, and reviewing Archeology. This is the business we take up in the chapters that follow and in Part 2 of our study.

A Complete Chronology of Genesis 5 & 11

Indeed, we have more work to do to uncover all the historical mysteries that enable us to "reboot the Bible," aligning it with current academic history for the past 7,000 years or so. We will cover new ground starting with Abraham's calling in Ur to the timing of the conquest of Canaan (the Promised Land). But before we finish Part 1 of this book with the two chapters that follow, allow me to offer the chronology developed by Barry Setterfield, a resource so helpful in launching me into this study. But note: This is not the final chronology to be presented in this book. *Mine will differ with Setterfield in several points that turn out to be vital to the overall argument.*

Setterfield develops his dates by "backing into" the time of creation. He begins by referencing the King List of Israel and Judah; then moves to the construction of the Temple of Solomon; next to the Exodus and Conquest of Canaan; then the calling of Abraham. From that point, the chronologies of Genesis 5 and 11 can be followed as set forth by the Septuagint. This established the timing of the Great Flood and from there, all the way back to the Creation account of Genesis 1.

We haven't yet covered all the data that Setterfield brings to the table. And, as the reader will see, there remain some enormous dating challenges to consider when arriving at a timeline that starts with Abraham's covenant with El (the most ancient name of God), to the conquest of Canaan which challenges the dating of ancient Egypt put forth by Egyptologists.

Before we venture there, Setterfield's chart (Figure 27) calculates the Genesis 5 and 11 *chronogenalogy*. Setterfield is a world-class scientist and mathematician, a genuine polymath whose writings are profound and provocative.

The chart (1) begins with the Patriarch's name; (2) the "begetting" (*yalad*) age of the Patriarch at his son's birth; (3) the Gregorian date of the son's birth after creation (AC, aka AM for *anno mundi*); (4) the time of the son's birth before Christ (BC); (5) the lifespan of the Patriarch in years, and finally; (6) the lifespan of the Patriarch BC. The reader should recall that many historic Christian scholars saw the creation date to be ca. 5500 BC. Setterfield calculates 5810 BC. At this point, we should reckon his dates to be one possible proposal. My chronology will contrast with Setterfield's, but I acknowledge his work upon which much of mine is built. (I provide my calculated chronology, Figure 53, on page 311.)

The critical point: The timeline of the Septuagint differs from Ussher's account by over 1,600 years. This number includes corrected dates for the period of Israelite (and Jewish) Kings, the period of the Judges, the Conquest of Canaan, and the Exodus. All of these periods must be corrected. It was one of the important goals of this book that a complete chronology could be set forth. I believe this has been accomplished with only a few approximations among several variables to be considered.

Indeed, as we move through the next chapter, it will become clear that nailing down the date of the Exodus remains the pivotal point in completing a biblical chronology. From there, we can establish the actual primeval biblical history which is reasonably well supported by secular Archeology as we will see in Part 2 of *Rebooting the Bible*.

BIBLICAL CHRONOLOGY FROM ADAM TO JOSEPH (LXX)						
Patriarch	Son	Begetting Age	Son's Birth AC	Son's Birth BC	Lifespan (Years)	Lifespan (Dates BC)
CREATION	5810 B.C.					
Adam	Seth	230	230	5580	930	5810-4880
Seth	Enosh	205	435	5375	912	5580-4668
Enosh	Kenan	190	625	5185	905	5375-4470
Kenan	Mahalalel	170	795	5015	910	5185-4275
Mahalalel	Jared	165	960	4850	895	5015-4120
Jared	Enoch	162	1122	4688	962	4850-3888
Enoch	Methuselah	165	1287	4523	365	4668-4323
Methuselah	Lamech	187	1474	4336	969	4523-3554
Lamech	Noah	188	1656	4148	777	4336-3359
Noah	Shem	500	2158	3654	950	4154-3204
THE FLOOD	2256 Yrs After Creation, about 3554 B.C.					
Shem	Arpachshad	100	2258	3552	600	3652-3052
Arpachshad	Cainan	135	2393	3417	535	3552-3017
Cainan	Shelah	130	2523	3287	460	3417-2957
Shelah	Eber	130	2653	3157	433	3287-2854
Eber	Peleg	134	2787	3023	404	3157-2753
Peleg	Reu	130	2917	2893	339	3023-2684
Reu	Serug	132	3049	2761	339	2893-2554
Serug	Nahor	130	3179	2631	330	2761-2431
Nahor	Terah	179	3358	2452	208	2631-2423
Terah	Abraham	130	3488	2322	205	2452-2247
Abraham	Isaac	100	3588	2222	175	2322-2147
Isaac	Jacob	60	3648	2162	180	2222-2042
Jacob	Joseph	91	3739	2071	147	2162-2015

NOTES: EXPLANATION

MT Differences due to Akiba's corruption of proto-MT text circa 100 A.D.

Methuselah's difference is due to scribal error (see Smith's article)

Lamech's variance is due to a copyist error in the LXX

Figure 27 - A Biblical Chronology from Adam to Joseph,
As Expounded by Barry Setterfield, Setterfield.org.

When the date of the Exodus is established, we can work back to the birth of Abraham. And once we have identified the date Abraham was born, we can follow the timeline back to Adam in the Garden of Eden. The issue will then be whether Adam and Eve were created in short order after the universe was created as the Young Earth contingent contend; or whether their special creation took place within a world that had already seen civilizations come and go. Could Creation have been a **recreation**? This too, we will take up in Part 2 to be published in the summer of 2019.

Chapter Six:
ESTABLISHING THE EXODUS –
A CHRONOLOGY CONTROVERSY, Pt. 1

The Egyptian Benchmark

W HEN WE THINK OF ANCIENT CHRONOLOGY, OUR MINDS FIXATE ON EGYPT, AND IMAGES ARISING FROM MILLENNIA PAST, LIKE THE SPHINX AND THE GIZA PYRAMIDS.

The notion that Egypt's history represents humanity's antiquity isn't just a conception made famous by films and television. This predilection is validated by the world of Archeology too. The chronology of Egypt is the benchmark for antiquity across the Mediterranean world, from Carthage in North Africa to Babylon in Western Asia. But how-

Figure 28 - The Sphinx and Pyramid of Khafre

ever ancient other civilizations are, Egypt seems still older to popular thinking. The commonly held view is that the structures on the Giza plateau date to 3000 B.C. or thereabouts.

To be more precise, two primary sources in the Western world spawn archeological efforts. While Egypt remains the first that comes to mind, Mesopotamia is not a distant second. The reason these two ancient civilizations are so prominent in the subject of antiquity is that both supply artifacts – physical proof of people and events that demonstrate these civilizations arc much more than the substance of mere myth. The physical evidence retrieved from the dust reveals their history.

The *Oxford Dictionary* defines an artifact as "an object made by a human being, typically an item of cultural or historic interest." Whereas some texts like the Bible take us to times and places older than most artifacts, such writings can be subject to more debate. In some cases, texts such may be more accurate in telling

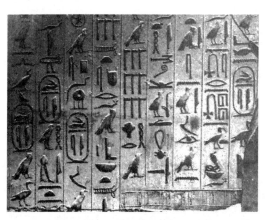

Figure 29 - The Unis Pyramid Texts

us real history (obviously) instead of myth, legend, or (tongue-in-cheek), archeologists' interpretation of ancient artifacts. However, Egyptian texts are genuinely magical and leap to fantastic and famous myths (e.g., Isis, Osiris, & Horus). Egyptian texts reside on pyramid walls and temples, such as Karnak. The oldest hieroglyph supposedly dates to 3150 B.C. from the tomb of a King at Abydos. The oldest Pyramid Text is the *Unis* text (from King Unas), estimated to date from 2353 to 2323 B.C. These Egyptian texts, from the Pyramid Texts to the Ptolemaic Texts, tell the stories of the gods, ritual practices, magic, and the like. The *Egyptian Book of the Dead* is a series of magic spells intended to help the dead for their journey in the afterlife. The Unis text falls into this category. Like the others, many of the 192 spells are written with hieroglyphs and painted on tomb walls or its sarcophagi. More spells exist on Papyri.[255]

However, in a world dominated by empirical thinking, a "hard object" always seems more reliable than a written text. Predictably, this positivistic bias infects the thought of the public. Scientists are the priests of our day. What they say, goes. This is even though honest archeologists will admit what they tell us about the past is only 10% hard data. 90% of what they write amounts to interpretation... which is chock full of speculation.

Egyptian chronology connects the many dynasties with their respective Pharaohs and what they did. The very first dynasty, according to Archeology, dates to 3100-3000

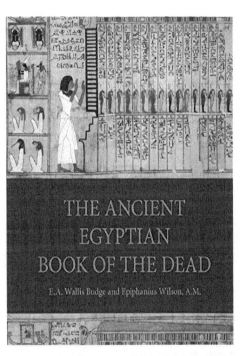

Figure 30 - A Published Copy of the Egyptian Book of the Dead

B.C. Archeologists classify history before this foundational period as "pre-dynastic." The Pharaohs of the most famous and picturesque pyramids belong to the fourth or fifth dynasty, and the three most massive monuments to the Pharaohs, Khufu,

---

[255] Karl Richard Lepsius, is the first author to publish an entire "Book of the Dead" in 1842, containing 165 spells. However, the awareness of an Egyptian Book of the Dead (EBOD) goes back to Medieval times. The work of the famous E. A. Wallis Budge of the British Museum is often associated with EBPD.

229

Khafre, and Menkare. Egyptologists, those archeologists that focus their time and effort on Egypt's past, speculate that these kings lived ca. 2600 B.C. to 2500 B.C.

In Egyptian chronology, there are three primary periods, equivalent to three kingdoms: *Old, Middle, and New.* There are also "intermediate periods." These periods are "dark" times of transition. There are pharaohs in these periods too, but they are less prominent than those of the "kingdoms." The beginning and end of each of these periods is placed along a timeline that extends from the first dynasty beginning with Menes I (aka Narmer, 3100 B.C.) to the thirtieth when Alexander the Great conquered the last *native* Egyptian Pharaoh, Nectanebo I, *in 332 B.C.* Afterwards, the Greek Ptolemies ruled from Alexandria

Figure 31 - Ramesses the Great

until they were defeated by the Romans. The death of Cleopatra (50-31 B.C.) constitutes the conclusion of Egyptian history as the benchmark of the ancient world. Afterward, the chronological context for history shifted to Rome and its Caesars. [256] The dynasties were recorded by an Egyptian Priest, *Manetho*, whose works are lost to us apart from what's quoted by others, most notably Flavius Josephus. Supposedly, Manetho was the author of *Aegyptiaca* from which we draw out the history of the Pharaohs. Like the *Septuagint's* authors, he wrote while living in Alexandria and commissioned by Soter (Ptolemy I) or Philadelphus (Ptolemy II). The reader can certainly see how *Alexandria stands head and shoulders above all other cities of the ancient world when it comes to recording our primeval history.*

From a historical point of view, the most famous of all Pharaohs is Ramesses II, aka *Ramesses the Great*. He was the third Pharaoh of the Nineteenth Dynasty. His reign was long – 60 years – dated from 1279 to 1213 B.C. He represents a crucial character because he is most often associated with the Exodus (as the "Pharaoh of the Exodus"). Academics that grant the Exodus occurred at all, believe it took place ca. 1250. It should be no wonder then that when Cecil B. DeMille created his famous film, *The Ten Commandments,* Moses battles Ramesses II – a worthy opponent. For Ramesses the Great's reign constituted the peak of the New Kingdom's empire culminating in the *Battle of Kadesh* (1274 B.C., the greatest chariot battle of all time – see Figure 32 following). However, why Ramesses became the Pharaoh of the Exodus amounts to one of Archeology's greatest blunders. Indeed, this mistake (and one other), go to the heart of our story.

---

[256] A website providing a concise but clear overview of the Egyptian chronology has been created by Michael Stecker. It is entitled, The Thirty Dynasties of Egypt. See http://mstecker.com/pages/egyptdyn_fp.htm.

Figure 32 - The Great Sesostris (Ramesses II) at the Battle of Kadesh
from The History of the World for English People, *1881.*
See https://en.wikipedia.org/wiki/Battle_of_Kadesh.

Archeology's Mistakes: Confusion with the Bible

Despite the fact secular Archeology gives little credence to the Bible, the best-kept secret of Egyptology is how it was built upon two biblical references, both of which are *misunderstandings of Bible passages*. This is the great irony of Egyptology.

The first mistake is easy to follow. It generates little debate today. The second mistake is a more significant mistake, dramatically affecting Egyptology. It is much more difficult to follow. We will explain this colossal blunder, nevertheless.

Tim Mahoney, filmmaker, along with his "consulting Egyptologist" David Rohl, describe how this mistake happened and why it affects Egypt's chronology. Rohl constitutes the driving force behind the so-called "New Chronology" in Egyptology.[257] His proposed revision of Egyptian history (which influences the dating of the chronologies of other lands) has drawn little support from academia. However, we will show Rohl is mostly correct. From his extensive effort, it appears adjusting Egyptian history (by moving it forward 150 to 200 years) makes great sense. There are just too many years in Egypt's timeline. We will explore this in the next chapter, "Establishing the Exodus, Part 2."

But first, to review the easy mistake. It is the false accusation that Pharaoh Ramesses II was the pharaoh of the Exodus. Why was Ramesses II identified as Moses' opponent? Probably due to a scribal error (or at least a misunderstanding) from Exodus 1:11.

---

[257] My research indicates (in concurrence with Setterfield), that an adjustment is necessary, mostly related to the Hyksos invasion, conventionally dated ca. 1750-1650 B.C., preceding the Exodus by 100 to 150 years. And yet, it appears more likely the Hyksos, who were likely the biblical Amorites, invaded Egypt immediately after the Hebrew Exodus, when Egypt had no army to defend its territory (it was at the bottom of the Red Sea!) Other implications can be drawn from this possibility that amplify the providence of the timing of the Exodus. Please see https://en.wikipedia.org/wiki/New_Chronology_(Rohl) for an overview of the New Chronology.

No, Rameses II Was Not the Pharaoh of Exodus

The Septuagint reads, "*And he set over them task-masters, who should afflict them in their works; and they built strong cities for Pharao(h), both Pitho(m), and Ramesses, **and On, which is Heliopolis.**"* The King James Version has a shorter version with a material difference, "*Therefore they did set over them taskmasters to af-*

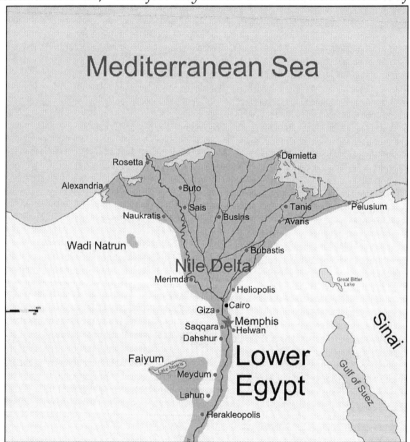

Figure 33 - The Nile Delta Showing Avaris
Wikipedia, Minister for Bad Times & Andy King, GNU Free Documentation License

flict them with their burdens. And they built for Pharaoh treasure cities, Pithom and Raamses."

Apparently, we could celebrate yet another material variation to the Masoretic Text as it drops the city of "On, which is

Heliopolis."[258] This omission (or inclusion in the Septuagint) may give us a clue, however, regarding how Ramesses becomes identified as the *Pharaoh of the Exodus*. We note the translator likely added the mention of the city of *On* aka Heliopolis. It is odd because the word "both" applies to only *two* cities, but *three* are included in this passage. Since the Septuagint translators lived in Egypt, they had "local knowledge." So, this inclusion may have been important, or it's possible the Masoretic Text dropped this clarification since Akiba's team decided it wasn't vital to the passage (perhaps since Jews around the world didn't know Egyptian geography anyway). Second, it is possible that the most accurate statement (as we will see), would have been referencing "the city of Avaris which is today Ramesses."

Ramesses was built on top of *Tell Ed-Dab'a*, identified as Avaris. Austrian Egyptologist, Manfred Bietak, who has excavated and studied this eastern area of the Nile Delta for over 30 years, has thoroughly demonstrated that Avaris was the city of the Hyksos, the western Asiatic rulers of Lower Egypt from ca. 1600 B.C. to 1500 B.C.[259] About 200 years later (most scholars say the Hyksos dominated lower Egypt for 105 years) the Hyksos were "run out" of Egypt. The Nineteenth Dynasty, that is, the Ramesside family, "buried Avaris" and built the city on fresh

---

[258] The city of *On*, Heliopolis, is known as the City of the Sun (Ra-Atum). It was occupied since the pre-Dynastic period, one of the world's oldest cities. It was the origin for the obelisks in London and New York. It is associated with Thoth, the *scribe* of the so-called *Seven Sages* of pre-dynastic Egypt, aka the *Apkallu* (familiar to fans of Dr. Michael Heiser). Thoth is often connected to Enoch, and sometimes to *Hermes Trismegistus*. In this "ancient wisdom," Enoch is the builder of the great pyramids. For a wild trip into this occult viewpoint, see https://www.matrixdisclosure.com/thoth-enoch-saurid-great-pyramid-egypt/.

[259] I will utilize the dates that are generally agreed by Barry Setterfield and David Rohl (as supplied by Tim Mahoney in his film and book, *Patterns of Evidence*). These are dates to which I concur. When dates based upon conventional Egyptology differ (which is most of the time), I will specify the conventional dates.

ground above. What isn't said in Exodus 1:11, *This spot (and at least 20 others nearby) in the eastern Delta, is where the children of Israel resided as slaves for at least 215 years (or 430 years, depending on your view of the length of the Egyptian Exile).* Their property was provided through a gift from Pharaoh to Joseph and his family. At that time, c. 1800 B.C, this location was prime real estate. As Rohl and Mahoney illustrate in the movie, there is substantial evidence for the story of Joseph lying beneath Avaris; that is, specific characteristics of graves and their contents as well as the special housing built in the style of Northern Syria (from which the patriarchs originated). As has been clearly demonstrated by

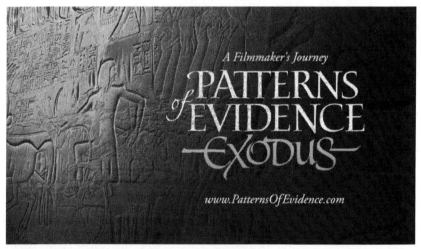

Figure 34 - The Film by Tim Mahoney, Patterns of Evidence

Bietak' s excavations (at the level below Avaris), another Asiatic people dwelt in this same place, but with different traditions from the Hyksos (i.e., the Amorites).

Tim Mahoney's fabulous *Patterns of Evidence*, a film and accompanying book we will rely upon heavily in this chapter, make it obvious that people from Canaan – more specifically, the Hebrews – populated this city, making it one of the largest cities in the world at that time. Of particular fascination: Given the extent of the evidence presented, the tombs of Joseph and his brothers may have been located there. This discovery, presuming it an accurate interpretation of artifacts from the excavation, provides solid proof for the Bible's historicity. And, more pertinent to our study here, it provides data from which we can assign a date for the Exodus.

Shaking Up the "Shishaks" and the "Shoshenqs"

However, this leads us to the second big mistake. But beware, this one is harder to follow. It originates from the research of David Rohl. He explains why the error *muddles Egyptian history*. He asserts scholars have presumed a connection from an Egyptian inscription at Karnak (with a King of Egypt known as Sheshonq or Shoshenq) with the statement mentioning Shishak I, from 1 Kings 14:25-26, *"In the fifth year of King Rehoboam, Shishak king of Egypt came up against Jerusalem. He took away the treasures of the house of the Lord and the treasures of the king's house."*

A quotation from *The Archeology Study Bible* provides a concise statement of the conventional view. It goes as follows:

> Shishak I, also known as Sheshonk, Sheshonq, or Shoshenq, founded the Twenty-second Dynasty and ruled Egypt from c. 945 to 924 B.C. His successful military campaigns into Palestine are reported not only in 1 King 14:25 and 2 Chron. 12:2-9 but also on a 25-foot (7.9-m) high triumphal relief engraved on the southern face of the Bubastite Portal, the gateway to the colonnaded first court of the grand temple of Amun at Karnak, Egypt. This relief presents the giant figure of Shishak smiting his Asiatic enemies, whom he holds captive in his hand by their hair. To the left are multiple rows of small *cartouches* [a small drawing serving as a nameplate or identifier], each containing the name of a people or city conquered during the campaign. Among the cities listed from

the northern Kingdom of Israel are Aijalon, Gibeon, Beth-shean, Rehob, Shunem, Taanach, and Megiddo. Most of the Judahite city names are illegible. Arad is mentioned several times, but no reference to Jerusalem has survived, its cartouche may be among those damaged or eroded, or Jerusalem may have been excluded from the list because Rehoboam paid the tribute Shishak demanded [giving up the gold from the Temple treasury].

In addition to the biblical account of Shishak's campaign and the relief on the Bubastite Portal, a stone fragment once belonging to a 10-foot (3-m) Victory stela was found during early excavation in Megiddo in Israel. The fragmentary hieroglyph inscription reads, "Bright is the form of (the sun-god) Re. Aman's beloved, Shishak."[260]

So, from this example, we see the conventional view equates Shishak with *Shoshenq of Karnak*. This constitutes the second major mistake. To be more specific, a Pharaoh whose military campaigned against Judah ca. 930 B.C., *was mistaken for* a Pharaoh who came up against Canaanite and Syrian enemies, when there was no Israel or Judah, perhaps around 1270 B.C. (during the time of the Judges of Israel). It turns out, this mistake doesn't muddy the waters of biblical chronology much at all, but it does tarnish Egyptian chronology.

Allow me to explain.

---

[260] *Archaeology Study Bible*, English Standard Version, Wheaton Illinois, Crossway, 2017, p. 496. This ESV references the Dead Sea Scrolls and the Septuagint, serving a wealth of information on relevant archeological finds and offering stunning illustrations. I highly recommend it.

See also Wikipedia article on Shoshenq I that asserts, "(Shoshenq I is) "presumed to be the Shishak mentioned in the Hebrew Bible, and his exploits are carved on the Bubastite Portal at Karnak." Retrieved from https://en.wikipedia.org/wiki/Shoshenq_I August 17, 2018.

Egyptology begins with Jean-Francois Champollion (1790-1832). Champollion, a child prodigy, studied Egyptian Coptic and Demotic (an Egyptian cursive script) at an early age. He was the first person to decipher the hieroglyphs on the Rosetta Stone, made official in 1824 with the publishing of *Précis*.[261] The Stele presents three languages: Greek, Demotic, and the hieroglyphs, *which, in the final analysis, were decidedly phonetic.*

Figure 35 - The Rosetta Stone (The British Museum)
By © Hans Hillewaert, CC BY-SA 4.0, https://commons.wikimedia.org/w/index.php?curid=3153928.

---

[261] The formal title of Champollion's book *was Précis du système hiéroglyphique des anciens Égyptiens.*

In 1828-29, Champollion conducted a safari of sorts, visiting locations throughout Egypt. His visit to Karnak would be, practically speaking, the founding of Egyptology. In reviewing a portion of one of the "walls of fame" at the Bubastite Portal (see Figure 33 on page 234), Champollion convinced himself the inscription told the tale of Pharaoh Shoshenq of the Twenty-Second Dynasty who was thought to have conducted a campaign in Canaan during the New Kingdom period, c. 970 B.C. In truth, Karnak's inscription does tell the story of conquest in Canaan. However, Champollion's interpretation of the hieroglyphs indicated this inscription was witness to Pharaoh Shishak of 1 Kings 14 and 2 Chronicles 12. His translation was mistaken.

Champollion believed the hieroglyphs on the Karnak wall stated, "Judah the Kingdom" (*Yudah-ha-malkuth*) when it should have been translated, "Hand of the King" (*Yad-ha-malek.*") Champollion jumped to the conclusion, wrongly, that he had found a reference to the Shishak *mentioned in the Bible*. It's not hard to see why he was eager to draw this conclusion. Early in the nineteenth century, archeologists sought proof for the Bible. Investigators from 200-years ago were biased in favor of faith. In stark contrast, today's archeologists might be accused of seeking to dismiss the Bible as "pious fiction." Times do change.

Subsequently, translating hieroglyphs would continue to improve. Eventually, Champollion's mistranslation was corrected (he lived only a couple of years past this excursion). *But the link between Shoshenq and Shishak stuck.* As a result, dating the Egyptian dynasties would be, quite probably, misstated. Which is to say, misidentifying the Egyptian Pharaoh of the Twenty-Second Dynasty with the Pharaoh mentioned in 1 Kings and 2 Chronicles *had corrupted the chronology of Egypt at its very outset.*

The Shishak Mistake Still Lingers – Unfortunately

According to David Rohl, this misconception *still underlies Egyptology*. In a presentation given by Rohl with Tim Mahoney by his side, Rohl cites scholar Eric Hornung who opines, "There are many uncertainties in the Third Intermediate Period, as crit-ics such as David Rohl has rightly main-tained, even our *basic premise of Shoshenk's campaign to Jerusalem* is not built on a solid foundation."[262]

Figure 36 - Egyptologist and Author, David Rohl

To go a bit deeper (since we've gone this far already), the tale told at Karnak is un-questionably the story of a Canaan campaign by a Pharaoh; how-ever, there were many campaigns by Phar-aohs in their quest to build their empires and enrich themselves. Rohl indicates whom he believes the Pharaoh to be, about whom the Karnak inscription was written. And his

---

[262] Hornung, Eric, et al. *Ancient Egyptian Chronology – Handbook of Oriental Studies I. Vol. 83*, Leiden, 2006, p. 13. I highly recommend Rohl's presentation, especially for those who enjoyed *Patterns of Evidence*. It delves much deeper into various matters, especially those I recount here, based on his fine work. It is enti-tled "The Biblical Exodus: Fairytale or Historical Fact? And can be viewed on YouTube (Search keyword: David Rohl).

identification appears to be a real work of genius (at least, to this non-expert). Allow me to recount it.

As we've stated, Shoshenq of Karnak, a Pharaoh of the twenty-second dynasty, purportedly links his dynasty to a period of Israel's history after Solomon, during the time of his son/successor Rehoboam (using my revised dating, ca. 970 B.C.; Rehoboam becoming King of Judah, ca. 975 B.C.)[263] Thus, this campaign against Judah was tied to 970 B.C. This premise becomes the fixed point from which all dynasties are then "backed into" (moving from that point backward) to establish their respective dates. For instance, where (when) was Ramesses II of the Nineteenth Dynasty placed in the timeline? Ramesses II stands out as one of the most renowned of all Pharaohs. As stated above, he is conventionally associated with the Exodus. He was the Pharaoh of the Battle at Kadesh. His reign dates to 1279-1213 B.C. (in conventional scholarship). So, you may ask, "What's the problem?"

The confusion arises when we learn that Rohl believes Shoshenq of Karnak is not Shishak of the Bible, *but Ramesses II*! If true, this becomes the second major mistake of Egyptian chronology, and again, it involves Ramesses II. So, does this mean that Ramesses II and the Nineteenth Dynasty should be dated ca. 970 B.C. and thus, the Twenty-Second dynasty should be rolled forward 300 years, and then dated ca. 670 B.C.? There are reasons this won't work because of verifiable history from other lands, including Israel and Babylon. Alternatively, could it mean that Shoshenq of Karnak, and the inscription in question,

---

[263] For date correlation between conventional and the revised dating I propose (with help from Setterfield, Mahoney, and Rohl), add about 45 years to the standard dates, i.e., Rehoboam became King of Judah in 930 B.C. This correlation holds for when the Kingdom split as well as the ascendancy of Judah's kings.

relate to a campaign in Canaan, ca. 1260 B.C. (i.e., the date of the Battle of Kadesh, located in northern Syria) which lies in the same vicinity as the cities named at Karnak? Should the year of 970 B.C. be unhitched entirely to the inscription? If so, how does that affect the dating of other dynasties? Is this where Roehl's New Chronology comes up with "several centuries needing to be brought forward?" In any event, should we conclude that another Pharaoh and another timeframe were the subjects of this history written on Karnak's "wall of fame?" Yes! Consequently, I feel both compelled and justified to point out there are reasons to doubt that the dates of Egyptian chronology are reliable.

Figure 37 - The Egyptian-Hittite Peace Treaty aka Silver Treaty or Eternal Treaty
Istanbul Archeology Museum

Obviously, we must ask, "How does Rohl prove his claim that Ramesses II is Shoshenq?" His reasoning results from incredible investigative work: It incorporated knowledge of hieroglyphs, compared the name rings on Karnak's wall (the wall in question) with cities in Canaan [264] and connected the treaty

---

[264] The campaign identified at Karnak does not target places in (what would one day become) Judah. Instead, the "itinerary" as Rohl calls it, mostly goes through cities and lands associated with the future Kingdom of Israel (the

concluding the Battle of Kadesh signed by Ramesses and the Hittite king (Figure 37).

What's in a Pharaoh's Name? More Than You Know

The treaty is vital to the hypothesis because it records in Acadian on an extant cuneiform tablet, the names of the agreeing parties. Additionally, it so happens this treaty comprises the *first significant international agreement in the history of the world*. This matters to us because the Acadian language is *syllabic* when represented in cuneiform (written form), not *consonantal*; meaning, that it recorded vowel sounds. Consequently, we can learn how to pronounce Ramesses name identically to how it was spoken then (Note: *Ramesses, our name for him,* amounts to a Greek transliteration of his Egyptian name).

Rohl tells us Ramesses full name in Greek was Ramesses Meriamun. It would have been pronounced in Egyptian, *Riyam-ashisah-miamana*. His nickname was *Shisha*, a shortened form of his name (the same as Dave is the abbreviated form of David). And due to the change through the centuries of the letter *qoph* from a hard sound like "*cuk*" to a soft sound like "*vav*," Shisha would have been heard as "Shishak" or "Shoshenq" in the thirteenth century. But by the tenth century, it would have been transformed to "Sysvah" or "Shisha." In effect, there were two "Shishaks." At least, this is as Rohl argues the point.

Thus, the mistake can be readily understood – that is, after you go through all the factors associated with the names of the

---

Northern Kingdom). This trek would pass right by Kadesh. Plus, since we are told in the Bible that Jeroboam was allied with Shishak, it would seem more than odd if the campaign detailed at Karnak targeted the land of Jeroboam. Therefore, logically, the campaign was not the one identified in 1 Kings and 2 Chronicles. That campaign targeted what one day would become the Southern Kingdom of Judah.

Pharaohs. (For the record, the Pharoahs had many – a throne name, a birth name, and a shortened name.) One much more familiar example (sort of) would be *Tutankhamen* aka King Tut.

Unfortunately, due to a lack of clarity, Rohl doesn't entirely close the loop; so, we are left hanging. And yet, just ahead, we shall see there is a need to increase the period between the Nineteenth and Thirteenth Dynasty, for it is at that time when things get really mixed up. Perhaps it should be no surprise then, that this is precisely when the event we care the most about – the Exodus –takes place. But to get to that date, we must do as the Egyptologists do; that is, back into these dates since it is how the Bible (and Josephus) supply the information we need.

The Chronology of the Kings of Judah

The destruction of Solomon's Temple by Nebuchadnezzar of Babylon in the year 586 B.C. constitutes a near-universally agreed fixed point to commence building the Bible's Old Testament History. After that point, many sources can be queried to establish critical dates in the Bible, from Zedekiah to the Apostle John (in the New Testament).

But in keeping with the Old Testament, note that some sources propose the date is one year earlier (as shown in the following chart, Figure 38). As we proceed in fleshing out the timeline, there will be some variances, but by the end, the number of years in question will be a fraction of deviation between the Septuagint and the Masoretic Texts. That is, while we base the chronology on the testimony of the Septuagint (for the years from Abraham to Adam), it can be created using either the Septuagint or the Masoretic points of variance, mainly in regards to the duration of the Egyptian exile for the Israelites.

245

The chart conveys the standard length of this period, from 587 to 931 B.C. (or 586 B.C. to 930 B.C.), which is 344 years. The proposed corrected length of this period is 390 total years, from 586 to 976 B.C. ± 1 year. The difference from what numerous experts have established is 46 years. *This means the Israelite Kingdom, after the death of Solomon,* **splits in 976 B.C., not in 930 B.C.** Keep this in mind as we continue. This is the first significant correction to biblical chronology.

Since Solomon started building his temple in the fourth year of his reign, and his reign was 40 years in length (the same duration as the prior kings, David and Saul), Solomon began his reign in 1016 B.C. and "broke ground" for the Temple in 1012 B.C. It took seven years to finish the project, i.e., 1005 B.C.

The Challenge of Assyrian Chronology

The question arises, "Why is there any difference at all?" The answer has to do with which chronology scholars accept as the most reliable (here we go again – critics almost always chose sources outside the Bible). Most scholars believe that the Assyrian chronology is more accurate than the Bible's. So, they force the alignment of the Bible with the Assyrian's timeline. How do they do this trick? They "force" it is through creating "co-regencies" (or viceroys, where two kings reign side-by-side, or where a mother serves as co-regent with her son, as was the case with Athaliah and Joash). The longest co-regencies which compress the Jewish chronology have to do with the supposed co-regency of Azariah and Amaziah (estimated to have lasted from 790–767 B.C., ergo 22 years) as well as Manasseh with Hezekiah (similarly pegged, 697–686, 11 years).

	King of Judah	Standard Regnal Term			Favored Regnal Term (Setterfield)			Scripture Reference
		Duration of Reign	Length in Years	Overlap	Duration of Reign	Length in Years	Overlap	
1	Rehoboam	931-914	17		976-959	17		1 Kings 15:1
2	Abijah	914-911	3	0	959-956	3	0	1 Kings 15:2
3	Asa	911-870	41	0	956-916	40	0	1 Kings 15:10, 2 Chron 14:1ff
4	Jehoshaphat	870-845	25	0	916-891	25	0	1 Kings 22:42
5	Jehoram	853-842	9	8	891-886	5	8	2 Kings 8:16-17, Cf. 2 Kings 3:1
6	Ahaziah	842-841	1	0	886-885	1	0	2 Kings 8: 26
7	Athaliah	841-835	6	0	885-879	6	0	2 Kings 11:3
8	Joash	835-795	40	0	879-839	40	0	2 Kings 12:1
9	Amaziah	796-767	29	1	839-810	29	1	2 Kings14:2
10	Azariah	789-737	52	22	810-758	52	22	2 Kings 15:2
11	Jotham	737-721	16	0	758-742	16	0	2 Kings 15:33
12	Ahaz	730-715	15	9	742-726	16	9	2 Kings 16:2
13	Hezekiah	715-686	29	0	726-697	29	0	2 Kings 18:2
14	Manasseh	697-642	55	11	697-642	55	11	2 Kings 21:1
15	Amon	642-640	2	0	642-640	2	0	2 Kings 21:19
16	Josiah	640-609	31	0	640-609	31	0	2 Kings 22:1
17	Jehoahaz	609-609	1*	0	609-608	1*	0	2 Kings 23:31
18	Jehoiakim	609-598	11	0	608-597	11	0	2 Kings 23:36
19	Jehoiachin	608-598	10*	10*	597-597	0*	10*	2 Kings 24:8
20	Zedekiah	598-587	11	0	597-586	11	0	2 Kings 24:18
	Co-Regency		404	60		390	0	**Standard Regnal View** **Favored Regnal View** *Each duration was 3 months

Duration minus overlap, 404-60 = 344 Total Years (587-931)

390 Total Years (586-976)

Overlaps are "co-regency" periods – some may be artificial to align with Assyrian chronology.

NOTES: Rehoboam died in the 18th year of his reign, and so reigned 17 full years. Asa died in the 41st year of his reign and so reigned 40 full years. Adding these parts of years to the total of 6 months for Jehoahaz and Jehoiachin makes a total of about 1 extra year. The total time covered by this regnal list is thus 390 years. This is in accord with Ezekiel 4:1-5 which records that Israel's idolatry had lasted for 390 years from the Kingdom Division to the fall of Jerusalem in 586 BC. The Kingdom Division at the death of Solomon was thus 976 BC ±1 year. (Notes from Setterfield. http://www.setterfield.org/scriptchron_html#abraham)

Figure 38 - The Chronology of Judah's Kings

247

Where this thinking originates is with a scholar named *Edwin Thiele*. Unfortunately, Thiele's work on Assyrian chronology has been sacrosanct for decades. Even Evangelical scholars accept it. It would be easy to get into the weeds by delving into this subject. We don't have space to do this. Given that the matter is only one of several we must examine, and the variance is only 46 years, we will quickly parse the "history" concocted by Thiele.

To establish the time of Israel's kings, and eventually, the Exodus, we do need to press several points. First off, we turn to a helpful article from *Answers in Genesis*. Larry Pierce is its author, and it was published April 1, 2001 (no foolin'). The article's title: "Evidentialism – The Bible and Assyrian Chronology," meets the challenge posed by Thiele and Assyrian chronology head-on. To begin, Pierce summarily states:

Figure 39 - The Black Obelisk - Jehu paying Tribute to Shalmaneser III?

In the past 100 years, various reconstructions of Assyrian chronology have been used to undermine the accepted chronology of the period of the divided kingdom. Edwin Thiele's work on

Hebrew chronology – as reinterpreted in the light of Assyrian chronology – has become widely accepted by evangelicals and secular historians. However, Assyrian chronology is not as simple as Thiele would have us believe, and there is no reason to bend the Bible to fit the current reconstructions of Assyrian chronology.[265]

A more specific "problem statement" surfaces three principal points of contention:

> The problem with Biblical chronology is that it does not fit with our current understanding of Assyrian chronology. Depending on whom you read, the Biblical chronology is too long by about 40 to 50 years. The latest reconstruction by Thiele is but one of many attempts in the past 100 years to adjust the Biblical account to match the current conjectured chronology of the Assyrians. *Thiele very creatively manipulated the Biblical data to eliminate about 40 years of history.* He did this by constructing viceroy relationships to collapse the length of a king's reign by overlapping it with the king's predecessor. He is the first to have made such a detailed reconstruction of the divided kingdom using this approach, although variations

Figure 40 - The Black Obelisk: Tall, Dark, and Enemy to Biblical Chronology

---

[265] Pierce, Larry. "Evidentialism: The Bible and Assyrian Chronology," Answers in Genesis. (2001, April 1). Retrieved from https://answersingenesis.org/bible-history/evidentialism-the-bible-and-assyrian-chronology/.

on his scheme can be traced back at least 75 years before him. By this, he gave his shortened chronology much credibility. Having it published by a well-known university press, instead of by his church denomination, helped his cause considerably.

There are the three dates where Assyrian and Biblical histories are supposed to intersect. They are the essential reason for abridging the traditional biblical chronology which is longer. These dates are 841 BC, 853 BC, and 701 BC. There is no mention in the Bible of the events that supposedly happened in the years of the first two dates. Their intersection with biblical history rests entirely on secular interpretations of Assyrian records, not on biblical data.[266] [Emphasis mine]

Pierce explains that *The Black Obelisk*, discovered in Kalhu in 1846 (today's Nimrud, Iraq), provides the anchor for asserting Assyrian chronology stands above the Bible's (remember, an artifact is a hard object and not a religious text – its message is literally set in stone). According to Thiele's work, Ahab of Israel died in 853 B.C. and therefore Jehu's first year was 841 B.C. This stands in stark contrast to the Bible's more extended chronology (not compressed with "viceroys"), registering Ahab's death in 897 B.C., with Jehu commencing his reign in 885 B.C., making a difference of 44 years. The Black Obelisk purports to show Jehu bowing to Shalmaneser III (see Figure 39). Thiele admits that "there is no evidence, however, that the obelisk was actually depicting the Israelite monarch Jehu." And Pierce sarcastically comments, "So, except for the fact we are not certain of the actual date of the obelisk and who is in the picture, we are in fine shape!"[267]

---

[266] Ibid.

[267] Thiele, E. *The Mysterious Numbers of the Hebrew Kings*, University of Chicago Press, Chicago, 1951. The book was republished in 1965 by William B.

Evangelical Scholarship Falls for It

Nevertheless, Evangelicalism has vouched for the accuracy of Assyrian chronology and dropped approximately 46 years from the biblical account. Says another conservative scholar who embraced Assyrian record keepers rather than their biblical counterparts (his endorsement came in 1965):

> Assyrian records were carefully kept. The Assyrians coordinated their records with the solar year. They adopted a system of assigning to each year the name of an official, who was known as the "limmu." In addition, notation was made of outstanding political events in each year, and in some cases, reference was made to an eclipse of the sun which astronomers calculate occurred on June 15, 763 B.C. Assyriologists have been able to compile a list of these named years, which they designate "eponyms," and which cover 244 years (892-648 B.C.). These records are highly dependable and have been used by Old Testament scholars to establish dates in Hebrew History, particularly during the period of the monarchy.[268]

There are two other dates proffered by Thiele to synchronize Assyrian and biblical chronologies; 853 B.C. and 701 B.C. The first date corresponds to the Battle of Qarqar fought between Shalmaneser III and a coalition of anti-Assyrians. Once again, we may be uncovering a dating error here due to mistaking two Kings who have the same name. A king named, *A-ha-ab-bu Sir'-a-la-a-a* supplied 2,000 chariots and 10,000 men for battle, (as stated in *The Bible Dictionary*). This supposedly is Ahab, the King

---

Eerdmans Publishing Co., and in 1983, by Zondervan. Cited by Pierce, Ibid. Note: Both of these publishers are conservative and Evangelical. Note the dates of these publications. Therefore, his work is virtually "set in stone."

[268] Williams, Walter G., *Archaeology in Biblical Research* (Nashville, Tennessee: Abingdon Press, 1965) p. 121. Retrieved from Bible-History.com.

of Israel. So, what's in a name? How many kings have *Aha-ab-bu* as part of their name? Could there have been more than another king who was a member of the coalition of the willing? (Shades of two Shishaks! Sheesh!)[269] Pierce comments:

> Nebuchadnezzar's grandson (who) had at least four or five different names depending on who wrote the history! Just because you see a historian use a name that is the same as a name mentioned elsewhere by a different historian, you cannot assume both historians are referring to the same individual.[270]

However, the stronger argument against this "proof" has to do with how weak Ahab was when this operation against Shalmaneser III occurred. Pierce points out Ahab could only muster 7,000 troops (that comprised "all Israel") when Ben-hadad came against him directly, *outrageously demanding all his silver and gold, wives and children!* Ahab maxed out his resources to save himself, his family, and Israel's wealth. Given such a gloomy reality for Israel's king, Ahab didn't have storm troopers at his disposal (held in reserve, that is) for loaning to other kings, supplementing this ill-fated coalition against Assyria. (1 Kings 20:1-21) Ahab probably growled back at the request of the coalition, "Fend for yourselves!"

The third connection of 701 B.C. has to do with Sennacharib's attack on Hezekiah (2 Kings 18:13). Pierce's discussion here is extensive, and we won't go into it. I invite the reader to download his excellent 53-page PDF that "deep-dives" into the

---

[269] The analogue can be compared in today's world with the common names of Islamic persons. names like Mohammed Ali. One found the gnostic documents at Nag Hammadi in 1945, another was heavyweight champion of the world.

[270] Pierce, op. cit.

subject.[271] Suffice it to say, Pierce concurs with the *975 B.C. ± 1-year date,* for Rehoboam's coronation. Let's lock this date down.

The Bible Strikes Back

Always bear in mind: Scholars want to compress the Bible's chronology. But the Bible won't allow it. For there are more "hitching posts" that rescue the Bible's overall timeline from skeptics, so we won't misstep as we journey through its details.

Once such hitching post is the statement in Ezekiel 4:1-5, which records that *the idolatry of Israel lasted 390 years from the destruction of the Temple.* Adding 390 years to 586 B.C., we come to 976 B.C. ± 1 year when the kingdoms divided after Solomon's death. Setterfield comments,

> It is possible to cross-check that from the Scriptures. If the king lists in 1 and 2 Kings are taken at face value, using only the stated co-regencies and inter-regnal periods, then one can readily conclude the 390 years have indeed elapsed from the Kingdom Division to the destruction of the Temple.[272]

Setterfield cites two other authorities to validate this longer duration for Judah's Davidic Dynasty, from Rehoboam to Zedekiah. First, Dr. J. Sidlow Baxter confirms that the term of the Kings of Judah extends to 795 B.C.[273] The second, Dr. Lawrence Duff-Forbes, asserts that Saul was made king in 1096 ± 1 year.[274]

---

[271] Pierce's PDF, as of August 19, 2018, may be found at the following link: https://assets.answersingenesis.org/doc/articles/cm/Divided.pdf.

[272] Setterfield, op. cit. "Ancient Chronology in Scripture," p. 2. Retrieved August 20, 2018, from http://setterfield.org/scriptchron.htm.

[273] Baxter, Sidlow. *Explore the Book*, Lesson 35, Grand Rapids, Michigan: Zondervan, 1986, p. 120-121. Cited by Setterfield, op. cit,. p. 2.

[274] Duff-Forbes, Lawrence. *The Vineyard*, July 1991, p. 3. Cited by Setterfield, op. cit., p. 2.

If we assume, as the Bible tells us, that Saul and David were both kings for 40 years sequentially, and that Solomon began building the Temple in his fourth year afterward, then do the sum of 40 +40 +4 + added to *1012 B.C. ± 1* year as proposed earlier, the result is 1096 B.C. ± 1 year. Duff-Forbes contends 510 years had elapsed from the crowing of Saul (the beginning of the Monarchy) until the Temple's destruction (586 B.C. ± 1 year). The sum of 586 and 510 is 1096 B.C. As we say in the world of accounting (of which I confess I was once a part), those numbers "tie out."

Therefore, before moving on next to the period of Israel's Judges, let's drive another stake in the ground at this point. We have built the chronology of Israel from the destruction of the Temple in 586 B.C. ± 1 year, up to 1096 B.C. ± 1 year. Next, we turn to "the Judges," which is even more difficult to pin down. However, our research bears much fruit here as well.

Just How Long Was the Period of the Judges?

1 Kings 6:1, besides being one of the longer verses in the Bible, provides another hitching post. But pay attention closely:

> And it came to pass in the **four hundred and fortieth year** after the departure of the children of Israel out of Egypt, in the fourth year and second month of the reign of King Solomon over Israel, that the king commanded that they should take great and costly stones for the foundation of the house, and hewn stones. And the men of Solomon, and the men of Chiram hewed the stones, and laid them for a foundation. In the fourth year he laid the foundation of the house of the Lord, in the month Ziu, even in the second month. In the eleventh year, in the month Baal, this is the eighth month, the house was completed according to all its plan, and according to all its arrangement. (LXX)

Notice how carefully the date is established. We see that it took seven years to complete the building of Solomon's Temple (therefore, it was completed in 1005 B.C. ± 1 year.) However, the period spoken of in 1 Kings 6:1, *begins with the command to build it.* The Septuagint, from which we quoted above, states there were **440** *years from the time of the Exodus until the day King Solomon commanded the Temple be built.*

DEEP DIVE:

The Conventional Academic Dates for the Exodus and the Conquest of Canaan

This book argues the dates for the Exodus and the Conquest of Canaan occurred between 140 to 180 years *earlier* than the conventional "early date" of most conservative Evangelical academics, (my proposal is ca. **1628 B.C. to 1588 B.C**). Let's identify my theory as *Alternative C*. However, admittedly, scholars would dismiss *Alternative C* as *way too early* – even those scholars of firm Evangelical persuasion. Instead, the two common alternative periods are set forth in periods from 180 to 450 years later (closer to our present day).

This conventional *early date,* ca. **1440 to 1400 B.C.,** has been adopted by mostly conservative Christian scholars. In this viewpoint, the Exodus began in 1440 B.C. and then the "wilderness wanderings" concluded in 1400 B.C., followed by the Conquest of Canaan. (The conquest began in 1400 B.C. and transpired after that over what likely was a five to seven-year period). Let's call this conventional early date, *Alternative A.* However, a greater number of academics weighing in on the subject have adopted this *late date* for the Exodus (and the wilderness wanderings) ca. **1280 to 1240 B.C.**[275] This alternative might be deemed the "secularly accepted date" although some Evangelical

---

[275] It should be noted that there continue to be many scholars who doubt the Exodus occurred at all, i.e., they consider it only a myth.

255

scholars are also committed to this alternative. In this scenario, the Canaan conquest commenced in 1240 B.C. We'll call *Alternative B*.

Alternative A is based on the 480 years of 1 Kings 6:1, added to a beginning of Solomon's reign at 960 B.C. (Recall, my research contends his reign began 56 years earlier, 1016 B.C., with the Temple construction commencing in 1012 B.C. and completing in 1005 B.C.)

A fine article by Jonathan Burke covers the pros and cons of Alternatives, A and B.[276] These dates are based on a variety of factors. One factor is the place name of Rameses in Exodus 1:11[277] which is problematic and doesn't stand up to criticism. Another reason has to do with the similarity of the material in Deuteronomy with late second millennium B.C. Hittite international treaties based on the work of scholars Mendenhall, Kline, and Kitchen, which Wood disputes.[278] Another has to do with the archeological evidence supporting period (A) over period (B). A argues that B (the date of Jericho's destruction) does not correlate with the late date, but does with A. But this debate continues too.

A major factor in the overall debate concerns whether the era of The Judges should be accepted as 480 years or should, instead, be seen as symbolic; namely, 12 periods of 40 years. Burke cites Hoffmeier:

It has long been thought that the 480-year figure of 1 Kgs 6:1 might be a symbolic figure that derives from 12 times 40 – 40 years being a symbolic

---

[276] Burke, Jonathan. "The date of the Exodus: Part Two" Academia.edu, 2013.

[277] 'Egyptologist have long understood the reference to Rameses to refer to Pi-Ramesses, the delta metropolis built by Ramesses II, the 19th Dynasty monarch who reigned from 1279-1213 B.C.' Hoffmeier, James. 'What is the Biblical Date for the Exodus? A Response to Bryant Wood", *Journal of the Evangelical Theological Society*, *50*/2 (2007), p. 231. Wood stated that, "It was clear, then, that the name Rameses used in Exodus 1:11 is an editorial updating of an earlier name that went out of use," Wood, Bryant. "The Rise and Fall of the 13th Century Exodus-Conquest Theory," *Journal of the Evangelical Theological Society*, *48*/3 (2005), p. 478.

[278] Niehaus, Jeffrey J. "Covenant and Narrative, God and Time,*" Journal of the Evangelical Theological Society 53*/3 (2010), p. 550. However, Wood argues the biblical material is too complex to easily connect it (Wood, ibid., p. 480-481).

number for a generation — thus signifying that 12 generations had elapsed between the Exodus and Solomon's 4th year. Since men were usually married and had children by age 20-25, a period closer to 300 years would be more accurate. When one adds 300 to 967 BC, an Exodus date around 1267 BC (20 years into the reign of Ramesses II) results.' [279]

Among academics, even Evangelicals, there is a tendency to accept non-biblical data over the biblical text. Sometimes this is because of "dated" inscriptions or other empirical finds dug up by archeologists may provide "hard" evidence overriding textual assertions. However, as we saw with The Black Obelisk (Figure 39), the image of Ahab bowing before Shalmaneser III, is probably a case of mistaken identity. Supposed biblical figures appearing in non-Hebrew monuments (or mention of the Israelites in hieroglyphics[280]) aren't necessarily the final word. For those committed to the infallibility of the Bible, statements in the biblical text are far more likely to be true than suppositions and speculations made by academics, however sincere and studied their view may be. *The benefit of the doubt ought to go to the Word of God.*

A definitive statement by the judge, *Jephthah*, is found in Judges 11:26. Jephthah is confronted by the king of the sons of Ammon, who came to battle with Israel for "taking his land." After Jephthah recounts the true history of what happened when Israel entered the Holy Land (after being detoured by the Amorites – not Ammonites) who refused to let them pass through to Canaan, Jephthah asks the king of Ammon, *"While Israel lived in Heshbon and its villages, and in Aroer and its villages, and in all the cities that are on the banks of the Arnon, three hundred years, why did you not recover them within that time?"* The Ammonite king would not listen to reason, and this forced Jephthah

---

[279] Burke, op. cit. Citing Hoffmeier, ibid., p. 236.

[280] The Merneptah Stele (the thirteenth century B.C.) mentions Israel in Canaan. But does this mean Israel arrived at that time? Burke quotes Wood from the paper alluded to earlier, that Egyptologist Manfred Görg suggested the inscription dated to the thirteenth century, may have been copied from an eighteenth dynasty record (possibly from the sixteenth century B.C.), implying Israel was in Canaan long before the thirteenth century, supporting an earlier Exodus.

(with the help of the LORD) to rout the Ammonites, crushing them entirely, with Jephthah capturing their 20 cities (Judges 11:33).

As shown in Figure 41, page 259, Jephthah is estimated to have been Israel's judge from 1277–1253 B.C. If we add 300 years to his "term" of rulership, that places the Israelites in Canaan between 1577–1553, entirely in line with the overall chronology my research identifies pertaining to the commencement of the Conquest of Canaan.

The lesson learned is this: We should establish the Bible's chronology from events before and after the incident in question. Remarks in the text of the Bible must be taken seriously, and empirical findings from archeology should be tested by the text, not the other way around (we ought not to surrender inerrancy at the first sign of divergent data). Evangelicals have become too quick to compromise biblical truth, seeking to find an allegorical or metaphorical way to understand the Bible's assertions. In contrast, the Bible should be taken to present true history – more often than not. There may be exceptions (as with Matthew's chronology), but the rule is this: Trust the Bible's historical framework.

Regarding 1 Kings 6:1, the beginning year should be 1012 B.C. However, there is a problem. The Masoretic Texts and the Protestant Bibles that follow the MT, translate the number in 1 Kings 6:1 as *480 years*. Once again, we find a discrepancy *between the two versions that originated from the Hebrew scriptures.* The LXX differs from the MT by 40 years. So, which is it? Was it 440 years or 480 years? While our premise insists we follow the Septuagint, as we saw in reviewing the dates in the Genesis 11 chronology, it wouldn't be surprising to discover a scribal error was at fault in one or the other. Did this occur? Given other factors we will examine, this seems most likely. The old Hebrew (which resembled the Phoenician script), could easily lead to mistakes, such as the date when Methuselah "brought forth"

Lamech, at 187 instead of 167 years.[281] Therefore, for other factors we will cover shortly, at this point we will add only 480 years to 1012 B.C. ± 1 year, giving us the date 1492 B.C. ± 1 year.

If we look just at the numbers we have so far, the would determine the date of the Exodus to be 1492 B.C. ± 1 year. This would make the year when the conquest of Canaan occurred, (40 years after the Exodus), or 1452 B.C. However, this date for the Conquest of Canaan doesn't match the most likely time for the destruction of Jericho *identified by Archeology*. We will see the Jericho's demise appears to have happened roughly 100-130 years earlier, based on the strenuous efforts of highly regarded archeologists who did the field work. And since one of this book's objectives is to harmonize the Bible with secular Archeology whenever we can, we mustn't dismiss their conclusion. So, we appear to be left with a discrepancy of about one century.

But hold on. There is one more factor to consider. It is known as "The Omission Principle." Setterfield is not the first to identify this, but his explanation of it was the first time I had encountered this principle in my research. Setterfield notes that many years were omitted by 1 Kings 6 besides its declaration concerning how many years elapsed between the Exodus and Solomon's command to build the Temple. According to Setterfield, a total of 93 years was excluded from 1 Kings 6. However, we will see in

---

[281] This was a mistake in some LXX manuscripts. The Septuagint has Methuselah's age when Lamech was born at 167 years, while other authorities confirm it was 167. "With all of the evidence … we can firmly claim that the 167 reading for Methuselah's begetting age in Codex Alexandrinus (A) of Genesis 5:25 is an early scribal error and was not part of the original LXX translation in 282 BC." ("Methuselah's Begetting Age in Genesis 5:25 and the Primeval Chronology of the Septuagint: A Closer Look at the Textual and Historical Evidence," Henry Smith, 2017 AD.) See http://bible.ca/manuscripts/Book-of-Genesis5-25-Methuselah-begetting-Age-Lamech-187-167-years-Bible-Manuscript-Textual-Variants-Old-Testament-Septuagint-LXX-Masoretic-MT-scribal-gloss-error.htm.

Figure 41 that he misses 21 more years based on the same principle. But first, let's review Setterfield's explanation:

In 1 Kings 6:1 there is a key comment that is the basis for many chronologies. The record there, states that 480 years elapsed from the Exodus to the fourth year of the reign of Solomon when work began on the Temple. This needs to be examined carefully as other Biblical passages imply [appear to imply] that the total length of this period amounted to **573 years** [actually 594, to be clarified following]. This Scriptural conundrum is solved when all the relevant statements are examined. The book of Acts provides us with the first of these clues. There we find that the 573 years is made up of **40 wilderness years (Acts 13:18), 450 years under the Judges** (Acts 13:20), **40 years under Saul** (Acts 13:21), **40 years under David** (1 Kings 2:11), and **3 years under Solomon** before the Temple construction commenced (1 Kings 6:1). This totals 573 years, **or 93 years longer** than stated in 1 Kings 6:1.

Despite this conundrum, **the Church Fathers** had no chronological doubts! Their writings confirm that the time of the Judges was accepted as 450 years. One typical example comes from about 150 AD. when Theophilus wrote to Autolycus. He spelled out the details that from Joshua's death, after judging Israel for 32 years, to David's death, was 498 years [(450 - 32) + 40 + 40].[282] From this, one may deduce that adding full 3 years of Solomon's reign, plus 32 years under Joshua, plus 40 years in the wilderness **totals 573 years from the Exodus to the beginning of the Temple construction.** This is in complete accord with the Acts quotation.

We can assume that these Church Fathers had been instructed by the Apostles on this matter, who in turn received it from Christ. **One then wonders why there is a 93-year difference compared with I Kings 6:1.**[283] [Emphasis mine, comments in brackets mine]

---

[282] 'Theophilus to Autolycus' in *'The Ante Nicene Fathers', Book III*, Chap. 2330, A. Roberts and J. Donaldson, eds, Eerdmans Pub. Co. Cited by Setterfield.

[283] Setterfield, op. cit.

To begin with, Setterfield has overlooked (or failed to mention) the fact that the Septuagint states that there were only *440 instead of 480 years*. But moving on: Setterfield points out what he calls "the omission principle." He identifies five distinct periods in the Book of Judges where the Israelites are oppressed (because they are "out of fellowship" with the Lord). His 93 omitted years are identified in five passages below:

- 8 years under the King of Mesopotamia (Judges 3:8)
- 18 years under the King of Moab (Judges 3:14)
- 20 years under the King of Canaan (Judges 4:23)
- 7 years under the Midianites (Judges 6:1)
- 40 years under the Philistines (Judges 13:1)

However, while Setterfield's position is generally correct, my research yielded a more reliable chronology of the Judges, (generally regarded too opaque to reconcile), that *adds 21 years more to the era of the Judges as guided by this "omission principle."* Again, this additional 21-year period of oppression is overlooked by Setterfield. This includes the 3 years of Abimelech's rule, and 18 years of oppression by the Philistines and Ammon, east of the Jordan. (See also the notes at the bottom of Figure 41). The total years omitted due to being "out of fellowship" (or under oppression) was 114 years rather than 93. My depiction of the Judges' Chronology, Figure 41 on page 264, shows both the length of rule for each judge and the periods of omission that correspond to the timeframe of each judge. So, the duration from the year Temple construction began (1012 B.C.) until the Exodus was 594 years. Adding 594 to 1012, the timeline leads to the same date of 1606 B.C. for the Exodus and 1566 B.C. for the year the conquest of Canaan begins. Consequently, the years from the Israelite Kings to the Exodus places us much earlier than the accepted "early" chronology of the Exodus (Alternative "A" on page 251).

1606 B.C ± 1 year is close to the date of the Exodus, and therefore, 1566 B.C. ± 1 year could be the date that Joshua "fit the battle of Jericho." However, "The Chronology of the Judges," page 264, analyzes the various durations given for each key event and suggests a date of 1628 B.C. ± 22 years. The variance is due to two periods not explicitly defined in the Scripture: *The respective lengths of Joshua's and Samuel's rulership.* The chart provides the best estimate by reconciling various sources from my research. We will look at another critical incident in history below that leads me (and a few others) to posit the 1628 B.C. date.

Confirming the Dates: The Exodus Event & Jericho's Destruction

First, let's consider the destruction of Jericho. The primary reason that most archeologists dismiss the possibility of the Exodus at all, is because the usual timeframe granted when it might have occurred (in coincidence with Ramesses II), was ca. 1280 B.C. However, *there is no evidence for the destruction of the principal cities in Canaan at that time.* In effect, if Joshua and the Israelites were in the business of tearing down the walls of Jericho, they missed their chance hundreds of years before. In 1250 B.C., Jericho was already destroyed and was deserted for centuries. What we learn (as mentioned above) is that the destruction of the cities mentioned in the Bible, beginning with Jericho, from our vantage point was no later than 1550 B.C. This means *the cities must have been destroyed before 1550 B.C.*

In her book, *The Parting of the Sea*, Barbara J. Sivertsen reports on a 1992 conference at Brown University regarding the evidence for the Exodus. She recounts the lectures of several attending scholars who provided arguments against an Exodus event, but primarily due to the usual timeframe assigned to it

(1280 B.C., the *Late Bronze Age*). Scholars William Dever and James Weinstein, based on Archeology, stressed the lack of archeological evidence for a thirteenth or twelfth century B.C. conquest of Canaan. Either no cities were destroyed by Joshua (there was no conquest), or the Exodus didn't happen at all.

Finally, William A. Ward conveyed the gist of the mainstream opinion, asserting that the Exodus and Conquest of Canaan must be considered "as a single event." That is, if you don't have a conquest of Canaan, there is no need for an Exodus.

Citing Sivertsen's words:

> The archeological evidence is indeed unequivocal. Although there is much archeological evidence for the destruction of (several) Canaanite cities at the end of the Middle Bronze Age [**1550 B.C. or earlier**], there is little or none for their destruction when the conquest of Joshua would have occurred [assuming 1240 B.C] ...if the Exodus had taken place during the Nineteenth Dynasty (the time of Ramesses II in the Late Bronze Age).[284] [Emphasis and comments in brackets are mine]

This statement (there was decisive evidence for the destruction of the Canaanite cities) provides empirical confirmation of the conquest of Canaan, but only if the timing can be shifted to "1550 B.C" or earlier. Sivertsen's statement doesn't indicate whether 1550 B.C. is the latest or the earliest date to which the proof points. Given she is moving from 1240 B.C. (thereabouts) "backward" to 1550 B.C., it appears she means that Jericho must have been destroyed *earlier than 1550 B.C.; therefore, a* date of 1566-1586 B.C. would be considered highly likely.

---

[284] Sivertsen, Barbara J. *The Parting of the Sea: How Volcanoes, Earthquakes, and Plagues Shaped the Story of Exodus*, Princeton, New Jersey: Princeton University Press, 2009. P. 2.

CHRONOLOGY OF THE JUDGES AND THREE KINGS OF ISRAEL

Event	Starting Date B.C.	Ending Date B.C.	Years of Oppression	Years of Rule	Total Years	Bible Reference	Comments
Exodus	1628	1628	-	-	0	Numbers 32:13	This date is estimated. The range is ± 22 years.
Wilderness Wonderings	1628	1588	-	-	40	Num. 14:25-38; Deut 1:34-40	
Period of Conquest	1588	1583	-	5	5	Joshua 13:8-14; Josh 14:7 & Josh 14:10	Based on Caleb's Words. Range of 5-7 Years.
Joshua Judges from the End of the Conquest to His Death	1583	1555		28	28	Judges 2:6-7	Joshua Lived Until He Was 110. Could Be As Long As 38 Years.*
Othniel Overcomes Cushanrishathaim	1555	1507	8	40	48	Judges 3:8, 11	Othniel Delivers Israel, the Land Rests 40 years
Next 80 years in Canaan	1507	1409	18	80	98	Judges 3:30-31, Judges 5:6	Ehud and Shamgar Free Israel From Eglon
Next 40 years in Canaan	1409	1349	20	40	60	Judges 4:3-6	Deborah & Barak Free Israel From. Jabin
Gideon Judges	1349	1303	6	40	46	Judges 6:1-6; 8:28	Gideon Frees Israel From the Midianiates
Abimelech Rules	1303	1300	3	-	3	Judges 9:22	
Tola Judges	1300	1277	-	23	23	Judges 10:1-2	
Jair Judges	1299	1277	-	22	22	Judges 10:3	
Jephthah Judges	1277	1253	18	6	24	Judges 12:7	Philistines and Ammon Oppress Israel, East of the Jordan
Ibzan Udges	1253	1246	-	7	7	Judges 12:8-9	
Elon Judges	1246	1236	-	10	10	Judges 12:11	
Abdon Judges	1236	1228	-	8	8	Judges 12: 13-14	
Samson Judges	1228	1168	40	20	60	Judges 13:1, 16: 30-31	Oppression in Samson/ Eli Period.
Eli Judges	1168	1128	-	40	40	1 Samuel 4:16-18	
Ark in the Hands of the Philistines	1128	1127	1	-	1	1 Samuel 6:1	
Samuel Judges	1127	1097	-	30	30	1 Samuel 7:1-6, 13	Samuel Rules. Could Be Longer Than 30 Years.*
Samuel's Sons Judge	1097	1096		1	1	1 Samuel 8:1	Joel and Abiah (Duration Unidentified)
Saul Reigns Over Israel	1096	1056	-	40	40	Acts 13:21	
David Reigns Over Israel	1056	1016	-	40	40	2 Samuel 5:4	
Solomon Commands Temple Construction		1012	-	-	-	1 Kings 6:1	480 years plus 114 Years of Omission = 594 years or 1606 B.C.
Solomon Reigns As King	1016	976	-	40	40	2 Chronicles 9:30	1 Kings 6:1, from 1012 B.C.

NOTES:	
	Joshua Ruled Over Israel After the War of Conquest Until His Death.
	Samuel Ruled Over Israel Before Saul. This Duration Was About 30 Years.
	See article by James K. Hoffmeir, James K. "What is the BiblicalDate for the Exodus?"
	Journal of the Evangelical Theological Society 5 0/2, June, 2007, p. 227-228.

Figure 41 - The Chronology of the Judges, Multiple Sources

From the book, *Patterns of Evidence*, author Tim Mahoney confirms the same. Says Mahoney:

> The mainstream view is that the archaeological landscape for a period of several hundred years seems to yield no time when the evidence matches the Bible's account. In fact, several of the Bible's Conquest cities seem to have been completely abandoned or largely abandoned throughout the entire Late Bronze Age (conventionally dated to about 1550 – 1200 BC).[285]

Jonathan Burke, in the paper alluded to earlier, cited Evangelical scholar William Albright, a historical figure in Archeology, who contended that Kathleen Kenyon's "subsequent investigation of the [Jericho] site re-dated the destruction (argued by Garstang) to around 1500 BCE, too early for the Hebrews."[286] Albright's comment was to dismiss the "early date" (1440 B.C.) in favor of the "late date" (1280 B.C.) because the Kenyon evidence disproved the early date. However, as stated in this chapter, the real problem is that *the early date is not early enough!*

Indeed, Archeology has provided a dramatic collection of evidence, once we move the date of the Exodus and the Conquest of Canaan, back just before the end of the Middle Bronze Age (traditionally concluded about 1550 B.C). The cities demonstrably destroyed by that point in time included Jericho, Hazor, Dan (Laish), Arad, Debir, Hebron, Hormah, Bethel, Eglon, Gibeon, and Lachish. All these cities weren't just missing in action: They had been turned into ruinous heaps. Some had been burned.

---

[285] Mahoney, Timothy. *Patterns of Evidence: The Exodus* (Kindle Locations 5476-5479). Thinking Man Media. Kindle Edition.

[286] Burke, Jonathan. "The Date of the Exodus: Part One." Academia.edu. (2013). Citing William Albright, from Elwell & Beitzel, *The Baker Bible Dictionary*, 1988, p. 744.

It is most curious the manner archeologists dismiss the Exodus. Essentially, they contend that the Exodus couldn't have happened because there is no evidence for the Conquest of Canaan during the Nineteenth Dynasty (ca. 1280 B.C.). They readily admit those cities had been wiped out centuries before. To this we say, "Amen. Exactly right." *They were devastated precisely 300 years before the academic date ascribed to the Exodus by most scholars.*

When Dame Kathleen Kenyon excavated the site at Jericho from 1952 to 1958, instead of confirming the 1400 B.C. date that had been proposed by earlier work there, she concluded the year for the destruction of the city was much earlier than that, *occurring no closer to our time than 1550 B.C.* She added that Jericho had laid dormant for hundreds of years afterward. This verdict was rejected by Christians because it contradicted the accepted date for the Exodus. This rejection holds true whether we argue for the Exodus date of 1440 B.C. or 1280 B.C. A most unwise choice.

Kathleen Kenyon DBE
(1906–1978)
Archaeologist

Dame Kathleen Mary Kenyon is recognized as one of the most influential archaeologists of the 20th century. She is best known for her extensive work digging the ancient city city of Jericho. She also engaged in digs at other neolithic sites in the Fertile Crescent region. In the year 2003 the British School of Archaeology in Jerusalem was renamed the Kenyon Institute in her honor.

Figure 42 - Dame Kathleen Kenyon

An advocate for the Exodus, Bryant Wood, believes the conventional time of 1400 B.C. is correct based on pottery artifacts.[287] However, the problem remains for anyone arguing on behalf of the 1400 B.C. date, for he or she must overcome a mountain of contrary empirical evidence that won't budge: *The cities in Canaan were destroyed before 1550 B.C.*

Now for the *external* evidence (external to the Bible and the archeological discussion surrounding the Exodus): The Exodus date of no later than 1606 B.C., has been established to this author's satisfaction due to the "coincidence" of one of the most dramatic natural cataclysms of all time – the eruption of Thera. This was the Minoan eruption in 1628 B.C. This Mediterranean catastrophe during the Middle Bronze Age was estimated to have been at least ten times more powerful than the eruption of Krakatoa (Krakatoa erupted on August 26, 1883). And the island of Krakatoa literally annihilated itself. Its shockwave circled the globe multiple times as recorded at the Observatory in Greenwich, England. The sound of its four significant eruptions could be heard 3,000 miles away. The sun was blackened for two days.

---

[287] An academic article penned by James K. Hoffmeier, responds to Wood who elsewhere challenged the highly regarded scholar Kenneth Kitchen, an Evangelical, who nevertheless holds to the late date of the thirteenth century for the Exodus. Wood claims that Kitchen's argument is just a "theory" while his view is the only biblical view, and his date of 1445 B.C. is the only date the Scripture allows. Hoffmeier, who is also an Evangelical scholar of note being a professor of Old Testament at Trinity Evangelical Divinity School, agrees with Kitchen on the later date for the Exodus and scoffs at Wood's critique of Kitchen. However, none of these three scholars takes into consideration the empirical data that demonstrates the Conquest of Canaan had to have happened in the sixteenth century B.C. Kenyon's data isn't disputed, it is just ignored. Each relies on their respective historical analysis (which relies on a flawed Egyptology-based chronology as will be shown in the next chapter). Neither do any of them seem aware of others who consider the date of the Thera eruption as a decisive marker that could nail down the year of the Exodus. Likewise, all three scholars dismiss the statement in 1 Kings 6:1 (whether based on the MT or the LXX version, i.e., 480 or 440 years) as anything more than symbolic since it includes too many 40-year periods (40-years times 11 or 12). See article by James K. Hoffmeier, "What is the Biblical Date for the Exodus?" *Journal of the Evangelical Theological Society 50/2*, June 2007, p. 227-228.

Tsunamis were 120 feet high, while five cubic miles of debris were expelled into the atmosphere. Thera's eruption in the Aegean Sea is dated to 1628 B.C. based on substantiated scientific data from several sources. Consequently, it constitutes a scientifically-derived moment in time – a fixed date – principally determined by examination of radiocarbon in tree rings around the world. It is "hard evidence" verified by science.

> The eruption of the Thera volcano on the Greek Island of Santorini was a major event felt as afield as Turkey and Egypt. Not only did the explosion bury the neighboring Minoan settlement in a layer of ash and rock more than 40m deep, it has been linked with devastating rainstorms that threw ancient Egyptian society into disarray… The scientists used radiocarbon dating of the annual rings of trees that have been alive since around the time of the eruption, and this allowed them to narrow down the date.[288]

So, the date of the eruption is certain. But did it have anything to do with the events associated with the Exodus? Sivertsen's book provides a summary of evidence for the link between the plagues of the Exodus and Thera's eruption.[289] She supported her thesis by mapping the great plagues to the effects of the volcano. However, her explanation doesn't adequately serve our purposes on all counts (as an explanation for all the

---

[288] Gabbatis, Josh. "Mystery of volcanic eruption that shaped ancient Mediterranean solved using tree rings." (2018, August 22). Retrieved August 23, 2018 from https://www.msn.com/en-nz/news/world/mystery-of-volcanic-eruption-that-shaped-ancient-mediterranean-solved-using-tree-rings/ar-BBMiHUV.

[289] Because of the impact of the eruption on Thera, the Minoan civilization was all but destroyed. Based upon the witness of the Bible, peoples surrounding Thera fled. It is believed that these peoples came from Crete and Cyprus, coming ashore in the land of Canaan, perhaps at Gaza. The biblical witness is that these peoples became the Philistines and are the forbears to today's Palestinians. The eruption continues to have vast implications 3,700 years later. See the discussion in Wikipedia on Caphtor at https://en.wikipedia.org/wiki/Caphtor. See 1 Chronicles 1:11-12.

plagues) because most of the signs and wonders happened before the day of the Exodus, while the most likely impact of the eruption occurs soon after the eruption. In other words, the volcanic explosion isn't necessarily associated with the plagues. The connection lies with the remarkably devasting, virtually unprecedented volcanic cataclysm playing a significant part in the central events of the Exodus: (1) the destruction of the Egyptian army with a gigantic wave sweeping over them (but not the Israelites), and (2) the darkness through which Israel marched (thanks to the supernatural pillar of fire lighting their path). Additionally, I should point out that Sivertsen's linkage of the Exodus to the Thera catastrophe wasn't an original idea. Other scholars had expressed the same opinion. This author suggested this connection in 2010 without referncing the scholars listed here.[290]

Sivertsen provides a brief history of the line of thinking she follows. Beginning in 1964:

> A.G. Galanopoulos suggested the Minoan eruption of the Santorini (Thera) volcano in the Aegean Sea was responsible for the plagues of the Exodus and the destruction of the Egyptian army in the Sirbonis lagoon on the northeastern coast of Egypt.[291]

Sivertsen then points out that the connection between the Exodus and the Santorini eruption was covered in Dorothy Vitaliano's 1973 book, *Legends of the Earth: Their Geologic Origins.* Likewise, Ian Wilson's 1985 book, *Exodus: The True Story Behind the Biblical Account,* made the same argument as did Elizabeth

---

[290] See my book, *Decoding Doomsday.* But until completing this research, I did not have corroborative opinions or scientific evidence to support my intuitive supposition.

[291] Sivertsen, op cit., p. 7.

and Paul Barber in their work, *When They Severed Earth from Sky: How the Human Mind Shapes Myth.* In 1981, Hans Goedicke, a renowned Egyptologist who did not have access to the scientific data we have today, "made headlines… when he announced that the Exodus had occurred in 1477 (B.C.) and that the pursuing Egyptians had been drowned by a tsunami caused by the eruption of the Thera volcano."[292] We must be mindful that sea levels were likely different than today. Some of those lands exposed in the region now may have been under water then. Therefore, we can obviously theorize that the miracles of the Exodus may have been accomplished (in part) by the providence of God *using natural phenomenon.* It is not out of character for Him to do so.[293]

No doubt, the finger of God engaged in what occurred. But is the supreme king over all creation unable or unwilling to perform miracles by unleashing natural power at precisely the right moment in time to accomplish His objectives?

Indeed, we could ask, "Which is harder? A wonder directed by God's supernatural power holding back the water of the Red Sea? Or a miracle combining a series of natural disasters with other ordinary forces holding back the water for the Israelites to cross the Red Sea and releasing the seas only on the Egyptian army?"[294] Timing is everything! (Well, it almost is.)

---

[292] Sivertsen, op. cit., p. 8

[293] Some have conjectured Joshua's long day and the giant hailstones destroying the army of the Amorites (Joshua 10) may have been due to a visitation by a comet, a rogue meteor shower, or even the legendary planet Nibiru. See http://www.accuracyingenesis.com/joshua.html.

[294] Those disasters being a volcano erupting with power seldom seen in history, which then generates a tidal wave "of biblical proportions," perhaps 100 to

Sivertsen's book draws many conclusions that this author disagrees with as her research does not rely on the biblical text to interpret the meaning of the Exodus event. Nevertheless, one can argue that the most reliable confirmation of a biblical text comes from a source that rejects biblical premises. We have that confirmation here – from sources addressing the Conquest of Canaan and the Exodus from Egypt. (It should be *noted that Josephus identified the date of the Exodus as 1624 B.C., almost identical to my proposal*). I believe there is good reason to hold to the timing shown on Figure 41 as a sound estimate (give or take two decades spread across that 600-year period), since the time of Judges remains subject to much debate, and since the Bible's history during this window of time does not appear to be precise. Add to that the "the omission principle" supplementing the 480 years specified by 1 Kings 6:1 (from Solomon's command to begin building the Temple to the Exodus) and the reader can see why a range ± 22 years in the dating of these events provides a coherent timeframe and margin for error. Therefore, my conclusion is that an Exodus date in 1628 B.C. is well supported by biblical evidence, archeological evidence, and scientific proof. However, for the reader's convenience, allow me to spell out the reasons more plainly:

1. The reasoning of many other scholars regarding the eruption of Thera playing a decisive role in Israel's escape from Egypt;

2. The much-averred archeological dates in Canaan, which argues that we establish the beginning date of the Conquest of Canaan

---

200 feet high! Recall the scripture attributes the parting of the sea with natural causes, "*And Moses stretched forth his hand over the sea, and the Lord carried back the sea with a strong south wind all the night, and made the sea dry, and the water was divided.*"(Exodus 14:21, LXX)

somewhere between 1588 and 1566, (a powerful marker based on the weighty unearthed empirical evidence);

3. The research of David Rohl and Tim Mahoney who studied this matter over many years, and who demonstrated in the film and the accompanying book, *Pattern of Evidence*, that this timeframe was highly likely.

I must admit my disappointment that Mahoney and Rohl were reluctant to confirm the evidence for the Exodus (1650-1600) was where the research led them. Why were Mahoney and Rohl so shy? I believe they were hesitant to stand with their evidence because too many Evangelical scholars had adopted academic speculation and dated the Exodus no earlier than 1440 B.C. (with many still fixated on the late date of 1280 B.C.)

Figure 43 - Santorini, Greece, Modern Day
The Faint Island in the Middle of the Crater is the Cone at the Center of the Thera Caldera

Perhaps they were too cautious because it was the lesser of two arguments. Specifically, in the article cited earlier, Hoffmeier argued that *the date of the Exodus is far less critical than collecting and presenting evidence that it had happened at all!* However, my reaction to this statement is to assert that Evangelicals stand a better chance of proving that the event really happened if we can confidently establish the date when it occurred.

I would be remiss if I did not also point out one final reason why the Thera date is so logical. If we assume that the Thera eruption took place in 1628 B.C. as I venture, and the principal Israelite population lived in Goshen on the Nile Delta near the Mediterranean coast, it is almost a certainty that the Hebrews would have been entirely wiped out by a massive tidal wave from the eruption of Thera. Scientists confirm that a volcanic eruption of this magnitude would created a tidal wave hundreds of feet high that would move south-southeast from Santorini, Greece, i.e., straight for the Nile Delta. That there is no mention of the Thera eruption in the Hebrew account underscores that the land of Goshen had been evacuated earlier, and the 2 million Israelites were now many miles inland from the coastline of Goshen, where they would have been annihilated had they remained there. Instead, the tidal wave crushed the Egyptian army.

Granted, the mighty acts of God can be chalked up to mere coincidence, at least by those who will not believe no matter how much proof is presented. Nevertheless, Jews and Christians believe that God's deliverance of the Children of Israel comprised the evidence of His love for His people and Israel's vital place in the plan of God to save humanity.[295] Indeed, the God of the

---

[295] The proof that Moses, Joshua, and the loyal servants of Yahweh perpetually reference, comes through their deliverance from the army of Egypt by these mighty acts. The Exodus event is an antitype to the saving death and resurrection of the Son of God. The children of Israel walked through the depths of the water on dry ground. Given the ancient fear of the unpredictable sea along with the witness of Bible's writers who associate the depths of the sea and the earth with

Bible does not have to use purely natural means to achieve miracles. However, when one ponders the circumstances as I have, the providence of God is undoubtedly manifested after it has been established that He most often accomplishes His goals by the precise synchronization of natural events to rescue the godly. *"The Lord knows how to rescue the godly from trials, and to keep the unrighteous under punishment until the day of judgment."* (2 Peter 2:9, ESV) This is my experience.

To conclude: Given the material provided by Setterfield, Mahoney & Rohl, Josephus, the scientists familiar with the Thera eruption, and the numerous historians named here that came to the same connection as I do, 1628 B.C. stands out as the most likely date for the Exodus. I regard it settled (a *fait accompli*, if you will). Therefore, my chronology, as laid out on the various charts before this point in the book as well as afterward, is built upon this premise. All factors considered, the date of 1628 B.C. is a far stronger date for the timing of the Exodus than the conventional times put forth, since it is reliant upon a vast amount of biblical data, accepted empirical evidence through archeological findings that support it (but do not support the conventional theories), and the historical certainty of related events in the vicinity – vis-à-vis the Thera eruption – that likely played a significant role under the guidance of the providence of God.

In Part 2 of *Rebooting the Bible,* I will argue that we must identify the chronology of the Bible if we are to verify the other famous events of primeval history recorded in the Bible can be validated as historical events, can be reasonably aligned with the Archeology of Mesopotamia, and with Egyptology. That is why so

---

death, their walk through the valley of death (waters held back on both sides of them) represents salvation from death and the resurrection of the people by arriving alive ("high and dry" as it were) on the far bank.

much of this book deals with the controversies surrounding chronology.

And, as a means to transition our study, we introduced research in this chapter that Egyptology possesses a story much more detailed and well known than that of its immediate predecessor Mesopotamia. However, it remains fraught with crucial mistakes that misstate its dating by as much as 400 years over the academically accepted timeline of the Egyptian dynasties.

Therefore, the next endeavor will be to challenge the conventional wisdom (once again), regarding the chronology of Egypt. After it is brought into alignment, the biblical chronology looks very accurate indeed.

Chapter Seven:
ESTABLISHING THE EXODUS –
A CHRONOLOGY CONTROVERSY, Pt. 2

The Hyksos and the Hebrews: Asiatics in Africa

THE FOLLOWING CHART, FIGURE 44, SUMMARIZES THE MANY DATES AND EVENTS WE'VE COVERED SO FAR. HOWEVER, THERE ARE TWO OTHER MATTERS WHICH MUST BE RESOLVED regarding the events just before and after the Exodus. These other matters have to do with (1) *the Hyksos invasion of Egypt* ("When did it happen and who were they?"); and (2) the *length of Israel's sojourn*. "Was it 215 years or 430 years in duration?" "Did the sojourn occur in both Canaan and Egypt or just in Egypt?" And equally vital, "How long were the Hebrews enslaved?" It turns out the LXX helps to answer these questions.

The first issue would appear to challenge the 1628 B.C. date presented in this book as the Exodus date. *The second issue* influences the length of the Bible's timeline; that is, it deals not only with the Exodus chronology but the overall biblical timeframe. You see, dating the Exodus is the pivotal point of biblical chronology. It specifies Abraham's entry into Egypt; then it extends from Abraham "backward" to primeval biblical events. In other words, Bible history reaches from Abraham all the way to the creation of Adam as detailed in the genealogies of Genesis 5 and 11. That is why the date for the Exodus is the pivotal point in primeval biblical history, connecting the Genesis chronologies with the Kingdom of Israel and Judah.

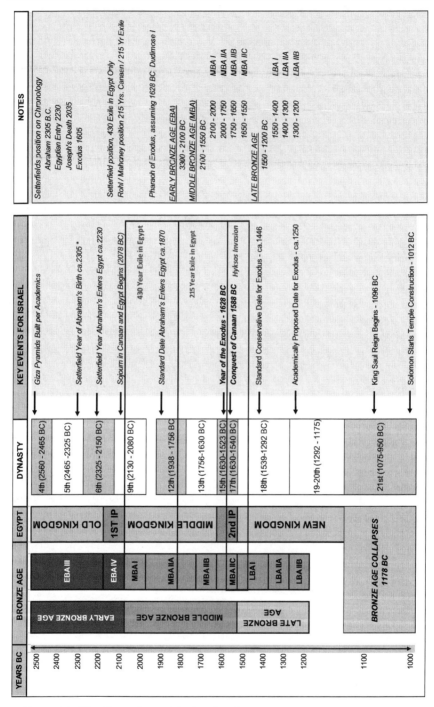

Figure 44 - The Chronology of the Exodus Controversy © S. Douglas Woodward

The first issue: Who were the Hyksos? There is much to say about them. The priest Manetho, writing during the time of the Ptolemies (within the same timeframe as the translation of the Septuagint), documented the invasion of the Hyksos. This invasion occurred during a period of Egyptian national weakness. The Hyksos were incorrectly known as the "Shepherd Kings" ("hyk," literally "hk," meant *ruler* and "sos" supposedly meant *shepherd*). However, Egyptologist James Henry Breasted (for a photo of the young Breasted see Figure 46, page 281), taught us why this epithet is wrong. The phoneme written, "sos," actually meant *countries*. So, the translation of *Hyksos* should be "the rulers of countries." If the Hyksos were Amorites as some conjecture (who had a long history of empire throughout Mesopotamia), this epithet would be correct. However, others argue they were the *Amalekites* (as identified in the Bible) who Moses encountered when Israel left Egypt (Exodus 17:8-16.)[296] Indeed, the Amalekites would remain a thorn in Israel's side for the next 500 years.

Manetho's quotation of the Hyksos invasion is oft-repeated and therefore, I ought not to break with convention here:

> There was a king of ours whose name was Timaios, in whose reign it came to pass, I know not why, that God was displeased with us… Unexpectedly, from the regions of the east, invaders of obscure race marched in confidence of victory against our land. By man force they easily seized it without striking a blow; and having overpowered the rulers of the land, they then burned our cities ruthlessly, razed to the ground the temples of the gods, and treated all the natives with a cruel hostility, massacring some and leading into slavery the wives and children of others.[297]

---

[296] See *Creation Wiki, Hyksos*. Retrieved August 27, 2018, from http://creationwiki.org/Hyksos.

[297] Breasted, James Henry. *A History of Egypt from the Earliest Times to the Persian Conquest,* 1905, p. 122. Calathus Publishing. Kindle Edition. Timaeus, is

Although lacking research from the past 100 years, James Henry Breasted made some modest but well-reasoned proposals on the Hyksos' origin at the turn of the last century:

> If we ask ourselves regarding the nationality, origin and character of this mysterious Hyksos empire, we can hazard little in reply. Manetho's tradition that they were Arabians and Phoenicians, if properly interpreted, may be correct. Such an overflow of southern Semitic emigration into Syria, as we know has since then taken place over and over again, may well have brought together these two elements; and a generation or two of successful warrior-leaders might weld them together into a rude state. The wars of the Pharaohs in Syria immediately after the expulsion of the Hyksos show the presence of civilized and highly developed states there.[298]

Figure 45 - The Hyksos Entering Egypt

Dudimose I, which was the odds-on favorite to be Pharaoh of the Exodus. Sobekhotep IV, Khaneferre, had been the Pharaoh, whose jealously of Moses caused Moses to flee Egypt to Midian. Sobekhotep III was the Pharaoh whose daughter Merris adopted the Hebrew baby, Moses (aka Prince Mouses).

[298] Ibid., p. 124.

The reader will recall the earlier discussion regarding Avaris on page 236. Avaris served as the capital of the Hyksos. Because it was built (as archeologist David Rohl argues compellingly) on top of the same area where another Asiatic group resided before them – namely, the Hebrews – Joseph and his eleven brothers had to have been there first. The distinction between the two Asiatic peoples can be determined by their respective traditions of burial. The Hebrews buried their dead with what we might regard as their "personal" animals, such as their donkey. Additionally, they laid dead family members on their side, resembling a fetal position. Finally, the pottery in their graves was modest. In contrast, Hyksos' burial traditions did not include the same type of items placed within Hebrew graves. And the buried pottery evidenced a more affluent people. After all, the Hebrews were slaves, while the Hyksos were rulers.

A minority view (famously offered by Josephus) suggests these two Asiatic groups were really one and the same. While it's true they both lived in North Africa during the Middle Kingdom, Josephus' conclusion, that the Hyksos were the Hebrews, doesn't find a great deal of support from scholars today. For instance, JewishHistory.org has this to say regarding their respective identities:

> In about the year 1700 BCE, a watershed event occurred in Egyptian history: the invasion of the Hyksos people. They successfully took over Egypt and a succession of six kings took power, known as "the Great Hyksos Pharaohs."
>
> Josephus Flavius, Jewish historian of the First Century CE and author of *The Antiquities of the Jews,* identified the Hyksos with the Hebrews. Most historians today disagree, but there are some striking similarities. First, the Hyksos people were from an alien culture and did not follow the Egyptian religion. The Hyksos Pharaohs never claimed to be gods, nor did they build for

themselves any of the tremendous monuments that later Pharaohs would. They also moved the capital of Egypt northward. Josephus points out the proximity of their capital to the land of Goshen, which is the area the Jews settled.[299]

So, in addition to the archeological evidence that the two peoples lived "one under the other" proving they were not contemporaneous citizens of the Nile Delta, we have the proof that one people were slaves and the other rulers.

There is hardly a consensus among archeologists on the dating of these various "levels" at Tell el-Dab'a. Manfred Bietak assigns dates of 1620 to 1560 B.C for the Hyksos. William Dever sees the same layer dating to 1675 to 1575 B.C. Sivertsen informs us that dating the Hyksos cannot be more specific than a range of 150 to 200 calendar years, which allows for the supposition David Rohl, Barry Setterfield, Tim Mahoney, and yours truly makes – that the Hebrews preceded the Hyksos.

Says Sivertsen:

> All of these estimates are based on approximations of the length of each pottery or occupation phase. Unfortunately, the only radiocarbon dates published for any level at Avaris/Tell el-Dab's have too wide a range (150 calendar years) for one from late in level G, 113 radiocarbon years, the equivalent to 194 calendar years, for the average of two other dates to resolve the dating controversy.[300]

---

[299] Jewish History Blog. "Hyksos or Hebrews: The Middle Kingdom of Egypt." JewishHistory.Org. Retrieved August 25, 2018, from https://www.jewish-history.org/hyksos-or-hebrews/.

It's a convenient location to mention that Sivertsen in her book, *The Parting of the Sea*, appears to agree with Josephus, going against the mainstream today, suggesting the Exodus was the same event as the Egyptians expelling the Hyksos, 100 or so years after their invasion. See Sivertsen, op. cit., p. 45.

[300] Sivertsen, Barbara J. Op. cit., p. 24.

The Meaning of the Hyksos Invasion

Additionally, we must pay attention to Manetho's statement that the Hyksos were virtually unopposed. Egypt could not defend itself. Scholars tell us that the Hyksos introduced the horse-drawn chariot. Before their innovation, Egyptian chariots were drawn by asses. (And no doubt driven by a few too.) The easy victory by the Hyksos over the Egyptians is chalked up to the chariot – not to their army having been destroyed in the Red Sea.

Another Egyptologist, Henry Hall of Oxford, writing almost 110 years ago, offered this assessment:

> Very possibly the swiftness and completeness of the conquest was due not only to the weakness and disunion of the Egyptians, but to the possession by the invaders of a new engine of war, previously unknown to the Egyptian mil-

Figure 46 - Egyptologist James Henry Breasted

itary system, the war-chariot and its horses. The chariot, drawn by asses, had been used by the Babylonians in war from time immemorial, and must have been known, at least by hearsay, to the Egyptians for centuries, but they never adopted it for use with their asses. When the horse was introduced, probably not much before 2000 B.C., into Western Asia from Iran, where it was first domesticated, it replaced the ass in the chariot, which now, with fiery steeds yoked to it, became a terrible instrument of war.[301]

Figure 47 - The Edwin Smith Papyrus, Egypt, ca. 1600 B.C.
First Translated by James Henry Breasted
The Papyrus Reveals Egyptian Medical Knowledge Was
Surprisingly More Sophisticated Than Hippocrates, 1000 Years Later

Given the collapse of Egypt, it is only logical to recognize that the Egyptian army drowning in the Red Sea, by the mighty hand of Yahweh, left the country defenseless. Barry Setterfield emphasizes this critical point:

> These Hyksos conquered Egypt "easily, without a single battle." How remarkable! Where was all the might of the Egyptian armies that had conquered Nubia a few years before. 'Without a single battle' implies that there was no Egyptian Army to fight against them. Why not? Unless Pharaoh's armies had just been

---

[301] Hall, Henry R. *The Ancient History of the Near East*, (1912), p. 155. Ballista Press. Kindle Edition.

284

destroyed in the Red Sea and there were no military personnel left. That can be the only logical conclusion one can come to. Manetho's comment is therefore an important piece of contributory evidence.[302]

David Rohl essentially offers the same insight: He states in *Patterns of Evidence*, that there was only one major collapse of Egypt during the Second Millennium B.C. and it transpired at the time of the Hyksos' invasion. Quoting him precisely, "When these foreigners invade – we call these the Hyksos rulers. When the Hyksos come in and destroy the land, the native Egyptian rule is completely suppressed. Egypt is on its knees. That's what we see in the archaeological evidence of this period. And it only happens once in 1,000 years of Egyptian history."[303]

Later, Rohl and Tim Mahoney have a cogent dialogue on the topic. It's worth citing here in its entirety:

> Rohl: "Something had happened to devastate Egypt, which made them unable to defend themselves. And these marauding hordes took over the country. And we call this the Hyksos Period. And they enslaved the Egyptians. But the point is they could have defended themselves. They had a mighty army – except for the fact that 'God' had smitten the Egyptians..."
>
> Mahoney: "How do you interpret this?"
>
> Rohl: "You look for a collapse in Egyptian civilization, and that's where you'll find Moses and the Exodus."

Then, Mahoney provides this commentary:

> I had to remind myself that Rohl is an agnostic, someone who is not sure about God and his existence, yet he still sees evidence that supports the biblical story. It made sense that this

---

[302] Setterfield, Barry. Op. cit., p. 13.

[303] Mahoney, Timothy. Op. cit., Kindle Locations 3666-3669.

singular collapse points to the most likely time to look for the Exodus out of Egypt. This kind of collapse does not occur at the time of Ramesses around 1250 BC. And Hoffmeier had said that there was no sign of collapse at the 1450 BC Exodus date either. However, once again, the fact **that this collapse happened two centuries earlier than 1450 BC** is consistent with the previous four steps of the pattern (*of evidence*, specifically 'judgment'), I had been discovering from Rohl and others.[304] [Emphasis mine]

We see from this chat between the two, that not only was the Hyksos invasion a result from the destruction of its army in the Red Sea, it was also after-and-not-before the Exodus of the Hebrews. Furthermore, Mahoney reinforces the timing (aligning with my proposed dating), that this occurs "two centuries earlier than 1450 B.C." *He is just reluctant to assert this is the case.*

How Long was the Sojourn in Egypt?

Genesis 15:13-16 comprises the pivotal passage that kicks off the discussion regarding the length of the "Sojourn" of Abraham and his descendants. The King James reads as follows, "

> God said to Abram, "Know for certain that your descendants will be strangers in a land that is not theirs, where they will be **enslaved and oppressed four hundred years**. But I will also judge the nation whom they will serve, and afterward they will come out with many possessions. As for you, you shall go to your fathers in peace; you will be buried at a good old age. Then **in the fourth generation they will return here**, for the iniquity of the Amorite is not yet complete."

The Septuagint is materially different. Genesis 15:13-16 reads:

---

[304] Ibid., Kindle Locations 3694-3702. Note that this dating is the conclusion that Rohl and Mahoney argue for, but won't rest their case on.

And it was said to Abram, "Thou shalt surely know that thy seed shall be a sojourner in a land not their own, and they shall enslave them, and afflict them, and humble them four hundred years. And the nation whomsoever they shall serve I will judge; and after this, they shall come forth hither with much property. But thou shalt depart to thy fathers in peace, nourished in a good old age. And in the fourth generation they shall return hither, for the sins of the Amorites are not yet filled up, even until now.

Barry Setterfield questions the Septuagint despite being its champion in most other places. He says:

It is certainly true that the Septuagint currently appears to give the time of 430 years as the total time of the Children of Israel **in both Canaan and Egypt**... However, the implication is that this time is counted from **the time of the entry of Abram into the Canaan** unto the Exodus. This leaves about **215 years for the sojourn in Egypt**, and many chronologists have accepted that as a fact uncritically. [305] [Emphasis added]

Setterfield asserts that the 430 years begins about the time Joseph and his brothers bring their father Jacob (Israel) *into Egypt.* The opposing view, which Tim Mahoney intimates, is that the *Sojourn* begins with *the seed* (i.e., Abrahams descendants, but specifically the birth of Isaac) – sojourning first in Canaan and then many years more when in Egypt. Indeed, we should remember that Canaan was not yet Israel's land – it had not yet been given to Abraham and his descendants. So was it the land or the seed which was the promise of the covenant?

Christians would argue that at one level Isaac is the seed. However, Paul teaches, that at another level it is Christ who is the seed. "Now the promises were made to Abraham and to his

---

[305] Setterfield, Barry. About the Exodus. Retrieved August 27, 2018, from http://setterfield.org/Egypt_and_Exodus.html.

offspring. It does not say, "And to offsprings," referring to many, but referring to one, "And to your offspring," who is Christ." (Galatians 3:16). As to the inheritance of the land, this would not occur until the Conquest of Canaan was complete.

Figure 48 – The Sacrifice of Isaac
Domenichino, Palacio de El Pardo, Madrid

In other words, the promise was made when Abraham was 70, and the seed was born when Abraham was 100 years old. But the deed to the land remained distant. It would not be handed over for four more centuries.

In any event, we still are wont to ask, "When did the Sojourn begin? How long were the Israelites enslaved?" Exodus 12:40 provides more information, but it doesn't settle the issue either:

> *Now the sojourning of the children of Israel, who dwelt in Egypt, was four hundred and thirty years.* (King James Version)

> *And the sojourning of the children of Israel, while they sojourned in the land of Egypt **and the land of Canaan**, was four hundred and thirty years.* (Septuagint)

The Masoretic Text begins running the clock for 400 years (or 430 years), when Jacob and his family entered Egypt. In contrast, the Septuagint begins the four centuries *while Abraham and his descendants still live in Canaan.* And yet another option exists: the 400 years might not start precisely when the Hebrews are enslaved, but rather after they had resided in Egypt for about 100 years. From the website, *Associates for Biblical Research*, we can obtain a smart, detailed analysis of the issue. Their summary reads:

> From possibly as early as the LXX (ca. 250–150 BC), there has been a tradition that the 430 years in Exodus 12:40 (or apparently rounded to the 400 years of Genesis 15:13) represent only 215 actual years of Israelite sojourn in Egypt, with the other 215 years representing the sojourn in Canaan. The Hebrew MT of both of the above verses, however, appears to indicate *that the total years constituted the full period of time of the sojourn in Egypt prior to the Exodus.*[306]

The "Associates" suggest there are *important implications* for determining the correct biblical chronology, as this author has already repeated on many occasions in this study:

> Depending on the interpretation given to the 400 (430) years, the events of Genesis 15 happened either during Middle Bronze Age I (2200–1950 BC) or during Middle Bronze Age IIA (1950–

---

[306] Associates for Biblical Research. The duration of the Israelite sojourn in Egypt. Retrieved August 27, 2018, from http://www.biblearchaeology.org/post/2012/01/05/The-Duration-of-the-Israelite-Sojourn-In-Egypt.aspx#Article.

1800 BC) — or more specifically, **about 2095 BC or 1880 BC**, respectively. Therefore, Abraham came to Canaan either during the Ur III Dynasty (ca. 2112–2004 BC) [from Mesopotamia] or during the First Dynasty of Babylon (ca. 1894–1595 BC).[307]

Their perspective seems to be that the covenant that *God unilaterally established with Abraham* might mark the point in time when the 400 years began. Some suggest that the covenant commenced when Isaac was born (when Abraham was 100 years old), or when the LORD last confirmed the covenant with Jacob. We know during the lives of Abraham, Isaac, and Jacob, the LORD confirmed the contract numerous times. (The Lord confirms the covenant with Abraham in Genesis 15:21, 17:1-8, 17: 9-27; with Isaac in Genesis 17:21, 28:13-22; and with Jacob in Genesis 35:9-18). Each time, the Patriarch in question marks the occasion with a monument or by naming the location with a unique name where the confirmation (and in some cases, the appearance of the LORD) took place. It appears that in most of the cases, *God's presence accompanies His promise.*

In the chart provided (see Figure 44, page 291), I propose the 400-year clock "starts" at the birth of Isaac. This also happens to be 30 years after the LORD covenanted with Abraham (when Abraham was 70 years old).[308] Thus, these two related events provide both a 400-year and a 430-year timeframe. The fact that the promise and the "make good" on the promise occur precisely at 430 and 400 years respectively (before the Exodus) provides strong justification supporting my viewpoint. Numbers matter in the biblical record.

---

[307] Ibid.

[308] There are differing views on the age when God covenanted with Abraham. 70 is my position. This seems likely to be the reason for the two distinct dates: The 430-year and 400-year durations before the covenant promise would be fulfilled.

When we need to turn to the New Testament, the ambiguity continues. Consider the statements made by Stephen as he testified before the Sanhedrin, and by Paul from his explanation regarding with whom God made His covenant. These two passages in the New Testament may support different viewpoints:

> Acts 7:6-7, *"And God spoke to this effect — that his offspring would be sojourners in a land belonging to others, who would enslave them and **afflict them four hundred years**. 'But I will judge the nation that they serve,' said God, 'and after that they shall come out and worship me in this place.'"* (ESV)

> Galatians 3:16-17, *Now **the promises were made to Abraham** and to his offspring. It does not say, "And to offsprings," referring to many, but referring to one, "And to your offspring," who is Christ. This is what I mean: the law, which **came 430 years afterward**, does not annul a covenant previously ratified by God, so as to make the promise void.* (ESV)

Note: Paul emphasizes the covenant with Abraham came 430 years before the Law was given at Mt. Sinai. If the law was given ca. 1628, the covenant was made, ca. 2058 B.C. with Abraham. Referencing "the Associates" commentary on these passages:

> The NT also appears to be divided on the subject. In Acts 7:6-7, Stephen uses ... the same wording as the Genesis passage, which appears to allocate a full and literal 400 years to the Israelite sojourn in Egypt. In Galatians 3:17, however, Paul seems to indicate that the 430 years extended from Abraham to the giving of the Law, rather than representing the totality of the sojourn in Egypt. **In this, he appears to be following the LXX of Exodus 12:40.** (Emphasis mine)

Tim Mahoney presents his position in an excellent appendix to his book, *Patterns of Evidence*, entitled, "Four Hundred Years of Slavery?" He notes that until 150 years ago (mid-nineteenth century), scholars (both Jewish and Christian) generally split the Sojourn into two segments, both equaling 215 years, comprising 430 years in total. However, more recent scholarship tends toward

400 years of slavery in Egypt, disregarding the time Abraham and his descendants lived in Canaan (and overlooking the comment of Paul in Galatians). We should recall that Abraham used that term sojourning when he was away from his homeland (Haran in Mesopotamia). And that Isaac and Jacob both choose wives from their family in Haran. They sojourned in Canaan too. Mahoney notes the term *sojourn* in several "Patriarch" passages:

> [Abraham speaking] *I am a stranger and a sojourner with you: give me a possession of a burying place with you, that I may bury my dead out of my sight.* (Gen. 23: 4 KJV)
>
> *And Jacob said to Pharaoh, "The days of the years of my sojourning are a hundred and thirty years. Few and evil have been the days of the years of my life, and they do not attain to the days of the years of the life of my fathers, in the days of their sojourning."* (Gen. 47: 9 DBY) [See also Genesis 23:4, 28:4, 47:9, & Hebrews 11:8-13)]

Mahoney also cites Jewish "sages" who indicated that both Canaan and Egypt were to be included in the 430-year sojourn:

> These sources include Josephus in the Antiquity of the Jews, Jose Ben Halafta (writer of Seder Olam Rabbah, ca. 150 AD), the Book of Jubilees (ca. 100 BC), Philo (ca. 30 AD), Demetrius (the earliest Jewish author to write in Greek, ca. 250 BC), writings found in the Dead Sea scrolls (some written about 100 BC), and the Babylonian Talmud (ca. 400 AD). The Jewish Midrash, in Genesis Rabbah, interprets Genesis 15: 13 by stating that "this means, until four hundred years after seed shall be granted to thee."
>
> Rabbi Jacob Neusner, one of the most published authors in history, commented on this: "The Israelites will not serve as slaves for four hundred years, but that figure refers to the passage of time from Isaac's birth." In the Babylonian Talmud in Megillah, it states, "And the abode of the children of Israel which they stayed in Egypt and in other lands was four hundred years."[309]

---

[309] Mahoney, Timothy. Op. cit., Kindle Locations 5388-5395.

DATE OF EVENT	LENGTH OF OCCURRENCE	DESCRIPTION OF EVENT	SCRIPTURE REFERENCE
2128 BC	500	Abraham is born. It will be 500 years until the Exodus from Egypt.	Genesis 21:5
2058 BC	430	The Covenant promises are given to Abraham, possibly in Ur or Haran. Abraham is 70 (numerically significant).	Genesis 11:31-12:4, Acts 7:2-4, Galatians 3:15-18.
2028 BC	400	Isaac is born, Abraham is 100 years old. It is 400 years to the Exodus.	Genesis 21:5
1968 BC	340	Jacob is born to Isaac. Isaac is 60. Jacob is born in Canaan. Joseph is born to Jacob as the last of his sons, when Jacob is 91-92 years old.	Genesis 25:26
1847 BC	219	Joseph becomes Vizier of Egypt (Viceroy of Pharaoh) when he is 30 years old. Jacob is approximately 121 years old when this happens.	Genesis 41:46
1838 BC	210	Jacob arrives in Egypt with his family. Joseph is 39-40. Jacob is 130.	Genesis 45:11, 47:9.
1767 BC	139	Joseph dies 71 years later at 110 years old. Levi dies 17 years after Joseph, being 137 years old, in 1750 BC - about 60 years before Moses' birth.	Genesis 50: 26, Exodus 1:6-8, 6:19
1728 BC	100	About 22 years after Levi dies, 100 years of slavery begins (the number of years of slavery isn't explicit in the scripture).	If slavery lasts 400 years, add 300 more years here.
1708 BC	80	Moses is born to Amran 80 years before the Exodus. There aren't "missing generations" in Moses' lineage : Levi, Kohath, Amran, Moses. Levi and Jacob came to Egypt, entering together, counting as one gen.	Exodus 6:16-20, 7:7. Genesis 15:16.
1628 BC	0	Exodus commences. The fourth generation after Jacob, from Levi to Moses will return to Canaan, as God's promises Abraham.	Deuteronomy 11:3-4; Genesis 15:16.

Figure 49 - Chronology of the Sojourn

Mahoney lists advocates for the "shorter chronology" who held the view that the 430 years included sojourning in Canaan as well as Egypt. This list contains many impressive names in the history of Christian theology. Recapping Mahoney's list along with his comments on Sir Isaac Newton:

> Saint Augustine, Saint Thomas Aquinas, Martin Luther, John Calvin, John Wesley, and Jonathan Edwards – also accepted this understanding. Even Sir Isaac Newton, who wrote more on the Bible than on physics and mathematics, calculated his biblical calendar in agreement with this thinking. It was only after modern translations started summarizing Exodus 14:40 in the 1800s that views regarding the length of the Israelite sojourn began to change.[310]

[Note: My chart, Figure 49, was developed based upon the table prepared by Tim Mahoney in *Patterns of Evidence*. But the years specified in this chronology are my extrapolations, not his.]

Why the Long-Sojourn (400 Years of Slavery) Fails

The core problem is that if we begin with Joseph's entry into Egypt, the period would be much longer than 430 years. To see the issue, we can benefit from a chart that zeroes in on the chronology of the 430-year Sojourn (see Figure 49) on the previous page. It provides a timeline beginning with the birth of Abraham in 2128 B.C. This culminates with the Exodus in 1628 B.C., 500 years later. [Note: The chart estimates 100 years of slavery from 1728 to 1628 B.C. If there were 400 years of slavery, we would need to add 300 years to the timeline at this point, pushing *Abraham's birth out to 2428 B.C.,* which seems out of the question.] There is also no reasonable possibility that there would be only four generations per God's promise – from Levi to Moses – if that

---

[310] Ibid., Kindle Locations 5411-5414.

period is a full 400 years in length.[311] However, if Levi died in 1750 B.C. (17 years after Joseph) and Moses was born in 1708 B.C., with generations 20-25 in length (meaning fathers become grandfathers in their 40s and great grandfathers as they approached 70 years of age), this would be perfectly reasonable. The only hitch: From Jacob to Moses is five generations. However, since Jacob and Levi entered Egypt together, only one generation need be counted. Both were born in Canaan, came at the same time, and died in Egypt.

Concerning the length of generations during this period, Mahoney makes the following statement:

> Two of the 12 sons of Jacob were grandfathers despite being in their 40s when entering Egypt. Benjamin in his mid-twenties at this same time already had 10 sons, and in Joseph's 71 years in Egypt after Jacob's entry he saw his son Ephraim's children to the third generation (Gen. 46: 12, 17, 21 and 50: 23).[312]

The children of Israel were "multiplying greatly." However, there may still be a problem. This means there were 215 years from the time of Jacob's entry into Egypt with 75 family members (according to the Septuagint and the words of Stephen in the Book of Acts), growing to approximately 2 million Israelites 215 years later. *The issue boils down to the rate of population growth*: Can a family of 75 persons create a population of about 2 million people, only 215 years later? Rates of growth would likely be well beyond present-day numbers, with family sizes likely exceeding 12 or more. But slavery shortens lives. And during one period, all male children were put to death soon after birth (hence,

---

[311] Generations in the Bible can be 100 years, but rarely so. See https://www.gotquestions.org/generation-in-the-Bible.html for a good discussion.

[312] Mahoney, Timothy. Op. cit., Kindle locations 5440-5442.

we have the story of Moses being placed in a basket in the Nile in hopes it would save his life). Consequently, it's difficult to arrive at a growth rate to achieve the population size necessary. So, did God supernaturally increase the population beyond what statistics would allow? We know that the Israelites "multiplied exceedingly." (Genesis 47:27) But is any reasonable growth rate adequate? Is there enough time in 215 years to reach 2 million Israelites? There are many factors we can't know about the situation in Egypt during the Exile; i.e., the birthing age of women, the number of twins, the size of families, and the length of life. But we do know that if family sizes involve only four offspring, the population doubles every 20 years. Just four children per family will exceed two million persons in 400 years. But would family sizes of 10 children grow to two million in 215 years with women bearing children at young ages? This seems problematic.

However, a study published in the Journal of Creation *by Robert Carter and Chris Hardy offers a sophisticated model that allows for this possibility. They note that the challenge posed for population growth within the timeframe of the "Short Sojourn" (215 years), has been used as an argument against it.*[313] *They hesitate to wholeheartedly agree. Depending upon child-bearing age, the space between children, twining, polygamy (one man with multiple wives as was the custom during this era), and the age of menopause, achieving this population size is not out of the question. "Starting with 12 founding couples, it was possible to reach 2.7 million people within the 215-year 'short' sojourn model, but only under certain, favorable parameter settings."*[314] *Figure 50 - Model for Short Sojourn, Carter and Hardy, Creation.com*

---

[313] See Minge, B., 'Short' sojourn comes up short, *Journal of Creation 21* (3), p. 62–64, 2007.

[314] The information cited here comes from the paper as published on the Creation.com website. See https://creation.com/biblical-human-population-growth-model.

below, produced for the Carter/Hardy paper, illustrates that the population can reach up to 5 million, with a child-bearing age of 17, and spacing between children of 2 to 3 years. (Many other factors are built into the model.) In a note to this author from Dr. Carter, he rightly cautioned, "Due to the great amount of ambiguity and the tremendous numbers of unknowns, one simply cannot know the population size at any specific time."[315]

In concluding this section and tying it to the overall chronology of the Bible, I should indicate that my chronology differs from that developed by Barry Setterfield. As noted earlier, Setterfield argues that the period of slavery did extend for a full 400 years. His most recent (revised) date for the Exodus is 1605 B.C. (within 1 year of one calculation provided in Figure 50). So, for Setterfield, slavery must have begun in 2005 B.C. This causes him to push out Abraham's birth earlier, into the third millennium B.C.

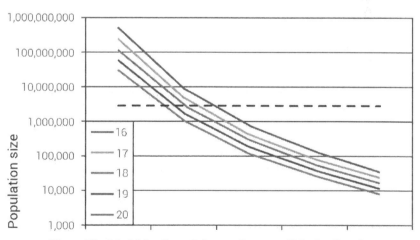

Figure 50 - Model for Short Sojourn, Carter and Hardy, Creation.com

---

[315] Personal correspondence, Dr. Robert Carter to S. Douglas Woodward, September 12, 2018. Dr. Carter is right. However, "the Israelites multiplied greatly."

The date calculated in this study for the Exodus (1628 B.C.), compared to Setterfield's analysis, varies by only 23 years (1605 B.C.). However, the divergence is much more significant when specifying Abraham's birth at 2322 B.C., as Setterfield does, whereas my calculation is 2128 B.C. (See Figure 27 on page 224.) The difference calculated for Abraham's birth is 194 years. This variance would need to be subtracted from all the date-years on this earlier chart identified above which utilized Setterfield's calculations. Considering all the dates involved, I assert the sojourning of Abraham and his family was 430 years in Canaan and Egypt, counted together, following the Septuagint.

For instance, doing the math for the most critical date: The difference between Adam's birth and what I calculate yields a year for the creation of Adam at **5616 B.C.** (Setterfield's 5810 B.C. less 194 years). *My estimate approximates what the Church Fathers set forth. They relied upon the Septuagint as their source. They held Adam's creation to have been between 5500 and 5600 B.C.*

Six Millennial Days Conclude Around 400 A.D., not 2018 A.D.

It is especially crucial that we understand the Church Fathers believed in a prophetic premise that Christ would return after 6,000 years had elapsed. However, they thought this meant he would come in the fifth or sixth century A.D., within 400-500 years of Christ's first coming. They estimated that the first coming of Jesus Christ was 5,500 years from Adam. *So, 500 years added to that 5,500 years would make a total of 6,000 years.* Thus, we see again that they supported the chronology of the LXX, not the MT. They held it would be "six days and then *the millennium day*." The *2,000 years* of the Church Age was a mystery hidden from them. The Patrons assumed the Church Age (so to speak) was part of the first 6,000 years and it was limited to 500 years. Read what Barnabas (not Paul's friend) wrote in 130 A.D.:

Now what is said at the very beginning of Creation about the Sabbath, is this: In six days God created the works of his hands and finished them on the seventh day; and he rested on that day and sanctified it. Notice particularly, my children, the significance of 'he finished them in six days.' What that means is, that He is going to bring the world to an end in six thousand years, since with Him one day means a thousand years; witness His own saying, 'Behold, a day of the Lord shall be as a thousand years. Therefore, my children, in six days – six thousand years, that is – there is going to be an end of everything. (*The Epistle of Barnabas*, 15).

Irenaeus, writing in the second century, asserted that Adam sinned on the first day and Christ died for Adam's sin on the sixth day (not the fourth day, i.e., fourth millennium, 4,004 B.C.).

And God brought to a conclusion upon the sixth day the works that He had made; and God rested upon the seventh day from all His works. This is an account of the things formerly created, as also it is a prophecy of what is to come. For the day of the Lord is as a thousand years; and in six days created things were completed: it is evident, therefore, that they will come to an end at the sixth thousand year.[316]

Hippolytus, writing early in the third century A.D. said, "And six thousand years must needs be accomplished... for 'a day with the Lord is as a thousand years.' Since, then, in six days God made all things, it follows that 6,000 years must be fulfilled."[317] Augustine, writing late in the fourth century or early in the fifth, asserted, "Fewer than 6,000 years [not 4,400 years]

---

[316] Irenaeus, *Against Heresies*, 5:23:2, from *The Ante-Nicene Fathers*, vol.1, p.557, T&T Clark Eerdmans © Reprinted 1996.

[317] Hippolytus, *The Extant Words and Fragments, On Daniel 2:4*, *The Ante-Nicene Fathers*, vol. 5, p.179, T &T Clark Eerdmans © Reprinted 1995.

have passed since man's first origin."[318] Clement of Alexandria, writing early in the third century and who held to the creation in 5592 BC stated, "For the creation of the world was concluded in six days ...Wherefore also man is said to have been made on the sixth day ... Some such thing also is indicated by the sixth hour in the scheme of salvation, in which man was made perfect."[319]

Therefore, we can state with certainty that the Church Fathers anticipated the Second Coming of Christ at the end of the sixth millenniumia (from Adam). Twenty-first-century "date setters" also predict Christ is coming "at the end of the sixth millennium." They assume, because of the Ussher dating, that the millennium begins in the twenty-first century. But they are overlooking 1,512 years of history that the LXX and the Church Fathers included as part of the biblical timeline. You see *chronology matters*. Getting it wrong, creates mistakes in other doctrines.

Plus, as we will see throughout the remainder of this study, with these revised dates, the chronology of the Scripture essentially squares with the timeline established by academia for *primeval civilization post-flood*.[320] This accomplishes one of this study's primary objectives. It *strengthens the argument for the accuracy of biblical history* and eliminates one of the reasons *scientists in Anthropology or Archeology reject the Bible's testimony*. In other words, once we realign the dates of the Bible's significant events

---

[318] Augustine, *City of God*, 12:11, translated by Henry Bettenson, p. 484 – 485, Penguin Classics © 1972.

[319] Clement of Alexandria, *The Stromata or Miscellanies*, 6:16, *The Ante-Nicene Fathers*, vol. 2, p. 512 – 513, T&T Clark Eerdmans © Reprinted March 1994

[320] Perhaps surprisingly, by and large, secular history seems to acknowledge that a great flood did occur in the fourth millennium BC affecting all (or almost all) of humanity. In the secular scenario, the great flood was localized to the Mediterranean, the Black Sea and the Persian Gulf. We will discuss this in Part 2.

in Genesis and Exodus, the earliest archeological finds in Egypt and in Mesopotamia synchronize reasonably well with what the Bible states (i.e., reveals). Academia is no longer embarrassed to suggest a flood may have occurred about 3,500 B.C. The Mesopotamian civilization begins ca. 3200 B.C; the Egyptian civilization begins ca. 3100 B.C. (I will argue closer to 2800 B.C.)

In conclusion: My position upholds the shorter chronology of the Exodus, based on the Septuagint and Paul's statement in Galatians 3:15-17. This means the Exodus took place ca. 1628 B.C., Abraham was born 500 years earlier (ca. 2128 B.C.), and God created Adam almost 3,500 years before Abraham (ca. 5616 B.C.).

Unlike the Masoretic/Ussher chronology which posits 4,000 years elapsed before the birth of Christ, this book sees a 5,600-year timeframe. *And it's validated from many different viewpoints.*

Egyptian Chronology: Does It Begin in 3100 B.C.?

Before we finish this chapter, we must take up one last matter: Egyptian chronology and what is known as the Sothic Cycle. We won't delve deeply into this subject, only to the level necessary to corroborate the chronology proposed in this book.

To begin, the reader should recall that there is considerable "flux" in dating Egyptian dynasties. There may be 200 years variance from what one Egyptologist asserts to another. Plus, the dating was originally based on some inaccurate assumptions about the Bible's "Shishak" and Egypt's "Shoshenq." We did not talk about the contention that exists regarding the overlap between dynasties and how this would likely "compress" (or shorten) the time when Egyptian history began. But this contention does exist between some Egyptologists, and the debate weakens the dating accepted by Egyptologists overall.

301

As a reminder, the academic dating of the Exodus (1250 B.C.) based upon its misinterpreting the Bible, falls way short of the evidence. Even the conventional view of conservative biblical scholars, 1450 B.C. for the Exodus, fails to synchronize with

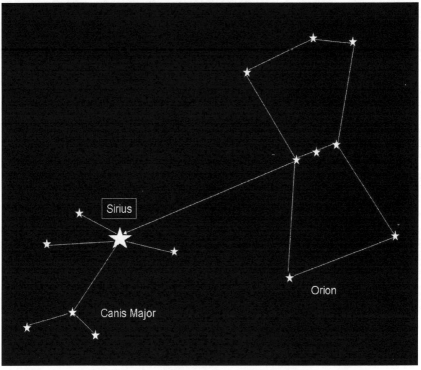

Figure 51 - Sirius, The Dog Star
The Brightest Star in the Sky, in the "Big Dog" Constellation
https://pics-about-space.com/sirius-star-constellation?p=2.

the Archeology of the Conquest of Canaan which took place before 1550 B.C. In contrast, this book concludes the Exodus occurred almost 200 years prior (1628 B.C.) based on scriptural arguments, the eruption of Thera, and finally, accepted academic archeological evidence for the Conquest of Canaan which this author believes commenced ca. 1588 B.C., concluding ca 1581.

And yet, our chronology might still be criticized by Egyptologists for one final reason: *It doesn't necessarily "sync" with*

Egyptian chronology beginning with the First Dynasty, convention- ally dated to 3100 BC. While it is generally acknowledged there was a "great flood" affecting Egypt and Mesopotamia, archeol- ogists would likely suggest that this flood occurred around the middle of the fourth millennium BC, ca. 3500 B.C. (which this book's chronology also contends). But if so, it is questionable whether there was adequate time to establish the "regimes" of Upper and Lower Egypt, and therefore, the subsequent *uniting of Upper and Lower Egypt* by the legendary Scorpion King – the first Pharaoh, Menes, (who is also generally identified as *Narmer*).

To accommodate this anticipated critique, it is best that we reduce the Egyptian timeline by another 200-300 years (from 3100 B.C. to 2800-2900 B.C.) just to be safe.[321] That was accom- plished on one end of the timeline through the mistakes pointed out early in the study and as alluded to on the prior page. How- ever, the reduction in the variance can also be established by reevaluating the beginning of the Egyptian chronology. To do this, we need to consider the validity of the so-called *Sothic Cy- cle.* This author will argue the First Dynasty began closer to 2800 B.C. rather than 3100 B.C.[322]

Why the Sothic Cycle Reveals Egypt's Dynasty No. 1

---

[321] A comment in passing regarding the Sphinx and the Pyramids at Giza. I do not believe they were built by post-flood Egyptians. This will be taken up in Part 2 where I freely speculated on "what came before" (whether we are talking about antediluvian times or possibly even before the special creation of Adam and Eve which I hold to be ca. 5616 BC.)

[322] Biblical historians argue that Nimrod began the civilizations of Egypt, As- syria, and Babylon (the latter two comprising Mesopotamia). For this biblical view to synchronize with both Egyptology and Archeology, the First Dynasty had to commence closer to 2800 B.C. This section demonstrates why it did.

What is the Sothic Cycle – the calendric method most likely employed by the Egyptian Pharaohs from time immemorial? And how does it establish the probable date for the commencement of the First Dynasty in Egypt?

There is a considerable amount written about this topic. And there is a reasonable amount of controversy among the experts concerning whether it was in fact employed by the Egyptians. Once again, I follow the lead of Barry Setterfield in this matter as he has provided a strong argument to support the view that the First Dynasty took place with the commencement of the first Sothic Cycle, which can be dated considerably later (closer to our time) than 3100 B.C.

Ancient calendric systems were often based on a 360-day year, but at some point, they came to observe that the cycle of Earth's seasons was based on a 365-day calendar, plus a smidge. That smidge was almost ¼ of a day. And most of these systems devised various means to keep the calendar working correctly, to track accurately planting and harvest. It was serious business. Getting those dates wrong could mean your population dies from starvation. Consequently, it was essential to work out the calendar.

The ancient "Stonehenges" of the world were zeroed in on the winter and summer solstice, and perhaps more importantly, the two equinoxes (one about 9-21 and the other about 3-21), as these were almost perfectly aligned with planting and harvesting. Yes, they predicted eclipses too, but eclipses weren't matters of life and death (unless you were scheduled to be sacrificed on the altar to convince the Sun to return after the eclipse).

One of the curiosities of our earth (and the calendar we have that tracks the rhythm of our world) is how it does two things virtually simultaneously over a year.

First, it follows the shifting of the axis of our earth as it faces to or away from the Sun. This acknowledged tilt creates the seasons, and it references the Earth's position in respect to the Sun. And this tilt fully repeats itself annually as we move around the Sun. It occurs in 365.2422 days. It is called the *Tropical Year*. Secondly, the Earth rotates around the Sun in 365.2564 days (looking at the ecliptic). This is known as the *Sidereal Year*. The Sidereal Year references the Earth in respect to the stars.

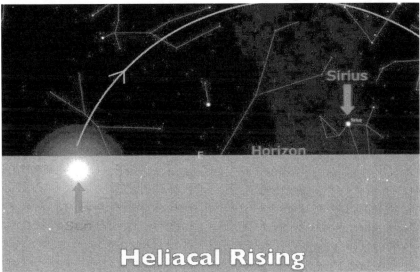

Figure 52 - The Heliacal Rising of Sirius

It's fascinating to me that these two movements line up almost perfectly. I'm sure Sir Isaac Newton could explain why this alignment occurs the way it does. But I'm at a loss. This difference is subtle, about one hour a year. Over a year, the earth does a lap around the Sun while its movement "up and down" along the way creates our seasons. Just to make the story complete (although it isn't relevant to the Sothic Cycle), there is one other factor known as the Procession of the Equinox, which takes into account our planet's wobble on its axis of rotation. This movement causes us to move backward from the direction of our orbit. The wobble (or spin) takes 25,920 years to make one full rotation in its movement. This movement is called *the Great Year* by the Mayans. We learned about this long-term spinning phenomenon during the 2012 craze. The wobble causes the rotation of the constellations in their position in the sky from our point of view. We hear about the 12 "houses" of the Zodiac and our movement from one house to another. "The Age of Aquarius" refers to this phenomenon. The transition of each of the 12 houses takes 2,160 years. This movement doesn't slow down like a top does. It is perpetual.

Combined, these three movements are complicated. It's another reason why I'm not an astronomer. (My lack of mathematical skill constitutes another. Math gives me a headache.)

The Egyptians Were Serious About Sirius

The Egyptians had a much different way of looking at the calendar. They were concerned with the star *Sirius*. At some point, (and we will disclose that point in a few paragraphs), the star Sirius would arise just moments before the Sun appeared at the dawn of the day. This is known as the "helical rising of Sirius." All stars atop the "ecliptic" will have a helical rising (think of an imaginary line that runs from horizon to horizon splitting the middle of the Milky Way Galaxy – from our point of view, that is). In Sirius' case, given it's not perfectly on the ecliptic, it takes 1,461 years before this position repeats itself. This repeat performance we call "the Sothic Cycle." It's called *Sothic* because *Sothic* is the Greek name for Sirius. Apparently, the Greeks enjoyed the first right of refusal to name a lot of things.

But unlike the Romans (and most other cultures), the Egyptians were committed to tracking time – keeping Sirius at the center of time. Given that Sirius is associated with Isis and she is at the center of their pantheon of Egypt's gods, it isn't too surprising. Supposedly, when Sirius arose, since it was already a part of the "Canis Major" constellation, i.e., the "Big Dog," the Dog Days of Summer were to begin then. What was necessary for the Egyptians, however, was it meant *that the Nile would flood.* So, if you were a farmer in the Nile region, it would be an essential thing to know. And yet, this circumstance was right for only 121.75 years of this Sothic cycle. [323] What Setterfield does through his research, is to identify when the heliacal risings of Sirius occurred during the past. He summarizes the importance of the Sothic Cycle to the dating of the First Dynasty this way:

> The inception of the calendar based on the Sothis star and Nile flooding would therefore have commenced the Sothic Cycle on the first day of the first Egyptian month. We know one Cycle ended in 139 AD. We know each Cycle took 1457 ± 4 years to complete. If we therefore subtract two Cycles or 2914 ± 8 years from 139 AD., we arrive at the date of inception of the calendar. That was 2775 ± 8 BC, or sometime in the period from 2767 BC to 2783 BC. On grounds explored elsewhere, this date accords with the minimum obtained for the commencement of Dynasty 1.
>
> For example, J. Baines and J. Malek in the 'Atlas of Ancient Egypt', p. 36, (*TimeLife* 1994), point out that the error in date for the 1st Dynasty may be as much as 150 years and gives its inception as 2920 BC ± 150 years. The lower end of this range, 2770 BC

---

[323] The phrase, "dog days of summer" actually comes from the so-called "dog star" Sirius appearing in the summertime. But it does not arise during the month of July, except for 121.75 years every 1461 years (1/12th of 1461). Since the *dog days* shift and no longer accurately predict the flooding of the Nile, the Egyptians needed smarter timekeeping to cover the other 11/12ths of the 1461-year cycle.

for the start of the 1st Dynasty, is in good accord with the Sothic Cycle data. This can hardly be coincidence as Dynasty 1 could not function without the calendar [It would seem so], nor could a calendar be introduced some way into the Cycle. All three (the calendar, the Cycle, and the 1st Dynasty) had to be introduced simultaneously. [Therefore] a date for the commencement of 1st Dynasty about 2770 BC is indicated. [Comments mine] [324]

According to Setterfield, the Pharaohs were under oath to continue to keep the Sothic Cycle and maintain a Sothic calendar. Of course, they eventually had to devise a time-keeping system that reflected 365.25 days while also realizing that the Dog Days of Summer were going to shift significantly, every 122 years.

According to Calendar.Wiki.com, Eduard Meyer worked out the dates for the "Sothic" years. Meyers argued that the first was observed in 4241 B.C.; the second in 2781 B.C. (Setterfield's date was 2770 to 2783); the third, 1461 years later, in 1,290 B.C.; and finally, 139 A.D. (after everyone could care less and stopped counting). Today, scholars dismiss the 4241 B.C. date as way too early, but give some credence to 2781 B.C. If Setterfield is right, (1) this date was the first observation of the heliacal rising of Sirius tied to founding their religious calendar; and (2) this was the beginning of the First Dynasty as identified by Manetho (writing around 250 B.C.). Therefore, the beginning of the Egyptian pharaohs (post-unification by *Menes*, aka *Narmer*), occurred at least 300 years before the academic world asserts (not much before 2800 B.C., instead of the "accepted date" of 3100 B.C.)

---

[324] Setterfield, Sothic Cycle, op. cit.

This point is important when arguing that the Pyramids of Giza were built *after* the Great Flood (assuming the Ussher timeline of 2305 B.C. for Noah loading up his ark). If the reader agrees with my suggested dating of the Flood ca. 3,358 B.C. and the Tower of Babel incident about 3150 B.C., then the biblical account and archeological research are nearly identical concerning ancient dating. Consequently, the Sothic Date remains vital to establish the 300-400 duration from the beginning of Egypt's Dynasties back to the Tower of Babel. As we will see in Part 2, *this nicely aligns the Bible and Archeology with this pivotal point in the history of humankind.*

We must recall all the factors that make any precise timing of the Egyptian Pharaohs *suspect*. The Sothic dating lacks incontrovertible proof. However, given the logic and the research of various scholars, including Barry Setterfield whom I hold in high regard, it remains credible. Figure 53 on page 309 provides the revised biblical chronology based upon "fixing the date" of the Exodus at 1628 B.C. and the 500 years prior from the Exodus to the birth of Abraham. With these points set, we can follow the genealogies/chronologies all the way back to Adam.

Concerning the "main events," we know that Shem was 100 when the Great Flood occurred, and so he was born 3459 B.C. Hence, *Noah's Flood was 3359 B.C.* The date for the Tower of Babel event can be estimated to have taken place about *200-250 years after the Flood* primarily due to referencing the corrected date of the Egyptian First Dynasty and the estimates archeologists who study Mesopotamia assign to the Flood (about the thirty-fourth or thirty-fifth century B.C. – which will be examined in Part 2). Another factor taken into consideration is the necessary population to participate in the raising of the Tower of Babel. About 200-250 years would be required for adequate population growth.

The subsequent "Dividing of the Nations" (tied to Peleg) requires considerable discussion. We will begin Part 2 of *Rebooting the Bible* delving into this intriguing topic. A little earth science will be necessary to work out the timing of this event. And the Creation (all of it or only Adam and Eve, depending upon your view of the age of the earth), took place in our Gregorian year of 5616 B.C. (give or take only a few years).

Conclusion: Part 1 of Rebooting the Bible

Thus, we conclude Part 1 with a list of the critical dates of the Bible summarized below. All times coming before the completion of Solomon's Temple should be understood as approximate – with no earlier or later time outside of a range *of plus or minus 22 years*. Again, this range is caused by the uncertainty of the duration of Joshua's and Samuel's rulership in Canaan: Joshua who began the period known as "The Judges" after the Conquest; and Samuel who concluded the period of The Judges, transferring rulership to Israel's first king, Saul ca. 1096 B.C.

- The Temple of Solomon: Completed 1005 B.C.
- The Conquest of Canaan: Commenced 1588 B.C.
- The Exodus: 1628 B.C.
- The Birth of Isaac: 2028 B.C.
- The Birth of Abraham: 2128 B.C.
- The "Dividing" of the Nations: Peleg 2829 B.C.
- The Tower of Babel: (Estimated) 3159 B.C.
- The Flood of Noah: 3359 B.C.
- The Creation of Adam and Eve: 5616 B.C.

But I encourage you to read the appendices of the book that follow as they supply other information vital to the context of this study.

BIBLICAL CHRONOLOGY FROM ADAM TO JOSEPH (LXX)

Patriarch	Son	Begetting Age	Son's Birth AC	Son's Birth BC	Lifespan (Years)	Lifespan (Dates BC)
CREATION			5616 B.C.			
Adam	Seth	230	230	5386	930	5616-4686
Seth	Enosh	205	435	5181	912	5386-4474
Enosh	Kenan	190	625	4991	905	5181-4276
Kenan	Mahalalel	170	795	4821	910	4991-4081
Mahalalel	Jared	165	960	4656	895	4821-3929
Jared	Enoch	162	1122	4494	962	4656-3694
Enoch	Methuselah	165	1287	4329	365	4494-4129
Methuselah	Lamech	187	1474	4142	969	4329-3360
Lamech	Noah	188	1656	3954	777	4142-3365
Noah	Shem	500	2158	3459	950	3959-3009
THE FLOOD	2257 Yrs After Creation, about 3359 B.C.					
Shem	Arpachshad	100	2258	3358	600	3458-2858
Arpachshad	Cainan	135	2393	3223	535	3358-2523
Cainan	Shelah	130	2523	3093	460	3223-2763
Shelah	Eber	130	2653	2963	433	3093-2660
Eber	Peleg	134	2787	2829	404	2963-2559
Peleg	Reu	130	2917	2699	339	2829-2490
Reu	Serug	132	3049	2567	339	2699-2360
Serug	Nahor	130	3179	2437	330	2567-2237
Nahor	Terah	179	3358	2258	208	2437-2229
Terah	Abraham	130	3488	2128	205	2258-2053
Abraham	Isaac	100	3588	2028	175	2128-1953
Isaac	Jacob	60	3648	1968	180	2028-1848
Jacob	Joseph	91	3739	1877	147	1968-1821

NOTES: EXPLANATION

MT Differences due to Akiba's corruption of proto-MT text circa 100 A.D.

Methuselah's difference is due to scribal error (see Smith's article)

Lamech's variance is due to a copyist error in the LXX

Figure 53 - Biblical Chronology, Woodward's Proposed Dates

311

APPENDICES

APPENDIX 1:
A REVIEW OF THE
PREFACE TO THE KING JAMES BIBLE

APPENDIX 2:
THE LETTER OF ARISTEAS

APPENDIX 3:
THE BOOKS OF THE
SEPTUAGINT COMPARED WITH THE
CONVENTIONAL BOOKS OF THE MT

APPENDIX 4:
TALMUDIC JUDAISM – WHY IT DESERVES
HONOR

APPENDIX 5:
THE PRESERVATION OF THE
BIBLICAL TEXT

APPENDIX 6:
DRAFT OUTLINE FOR PART 2

APPENDIX 1:
A REVIEW OF THE
PREFACE TO THE KING JAMES BIBLE

Why the Preface Should Be Considered

IN 1611, THE TRANSLATORS OF THE KING JAMES VERSION (KJV) OF THE BIBLE BELIEVED IT WAS ESSENTIAL TO EXPLAIN TO THE READERS WHY THERE SHOULD BE ANOTHER ENGLISH translation of the Scripture. Many Bibles had already been translated into the King's English. The Church of England previously utilized the Great Bible and the Bishop's Bible. But the translators, with the blessing of King James, came together to improve upon what had been accomplished before. Their remarks to the reader were, in part, to justify this new version, but also to explain their reasons why another Bible was a good idea.

Like modern translators today, they had no illusions. The dedicated clergy and laity were not praying for another translation, feeling that their current Bible, The Bishop's Bible, was enough. There is no doubt that most parishioners loved their Bible and were not anxious to entertain yet another version. Change is usually rejected rather than accepted. The translators note that this is especially so when anyone is dealing with sacred matters of faith. And this is so because it took over one hundred years (if not longer), before the KJV became widely accepted. The preface records numerous statements from the translators as to how they expected many would accuse them with mortal sin, altering the Bible that the laity had come to use, memorize, and guide their spiritual lives.

315

To begin with, the translators emphasized that the Bible should be readable by the ordinary person in his or her native language. God raises up scholars with great learning and insight into ancient languages, notably Greek and Hebrew, in order to ensure that the rendering of a modern native language translation is as accurate as can be hoped. For there are so many choices in selecting words (or phrases), finding the right ones which best convey the word from the original text is challenging. We see this plainly when we look at a concordance such as Strong's. The same Hebrew word, for instance, may be translated into a dozen different English words. The context generally becomes the determining factor for making the selection.

The issue of what a new translation means relative to the old implies that the old was flawed. To this, the translators stated that "nothing is begun and perfected at the same time." They stated that the previous translators would, by in large, praise the work of the new translators for the Word of God once delivered to the Saints should always be elevated to the highest level of quality that the elements available to scholars afford. The translators did not argue that the older translations were less the Word of God than the KJV. They compared the translation effort to communicating the speech of King James (in English) to others understanding only French, German, Dutch, Italian, or Latin. While the words employed in some such translation would not be in English, the speech nevertheless would remain the speech of King James. Likewise, God's word was made known through the previous translations, and so it will be in the KJV. God's Word transcends the printed book no matter how well the words are composed or ordered. God's Spirit always provides a mediating impact upon our minds and hearts. This process we might call "illumination."

The translators compared their situation to that of Jerome who had translated the Catholic Vulgate. It was a Latin translation mostly from the Hebrew. But Jerome's effort was not "locked up" and unavailable for correction or improvement – for it had been subject to revision many times. The scholars who colleagued together for many months to give birth to the KJV anticipated that neither would their version be locked up and beyond the reach of future translators to improve and "update" their words to the vernacular of that future day.

Which Words Were the Right Words?

The translators provided marginal notes to inform the reader what choices had been made (with other options identified) to convey the original. They were not always sure which word was the best choice, but they did their best to arrive at a consensus among the 47 experts who worked on this translation. After all, it was Augustine who said that "a variety of translations is profitable for finding out the sense of the Scriptures."

Bill Combs, a professor at Detroit Baptist Theological Seminary, made these points clear in a series of articles on the DBTS website. He made note: "Prior to the KJV, there had been many English translations of Bible: Wycliffe (1382), Tyndale (NT, 1526), Coverdale (1535), Matthew's Bible (1537), the Great Bible (1539), the Geneva Bible (1560), the Bishops' Bible (1568), and the Douai-Rheims (1609–10). [325] The many translations speak not of the insufficiency of the previous versions, but the

---

[325] Combs, Bill. "The Embarrassing Preface to the *King James Version*." DBTS.edu. April 9, 2012. Retrieved November 15, 2018, from http://www.dbts.edu/2012/04/09/the-embarrassing-preface-to-the-king-james-version/.

recognition that there are many audiences with different preferences whose educational experiences and dialects vary.

Combo quoted a pithy although lengthy passage from the KJV Preface. For clarity, I will paraphrase this portion of the Preface. (Readers are encouraged to review The Preface themselves but will find the vocabulary and style difficult – hence the paraphrase here, and an object lesson in why modern versions are a necessary endeavor to equip the Saints for good works.

While there is zeal to do something that does good for everyone, whether we come up with it ourselves or improve upon what was done previously, we know that offering up our work will be greeted with a cold reception. For no matter how good we esteem our work to be, others will find fault even if the flaw they point out is trivial – or no flaw is found at all. We all know this situation to be the way life is – something altogether new is almost always condemned as a step down rather than a step up.

But King James knows, in part because he has rare wisdom supplied to him by God as well as having achieved an incomparable level of education, that whoever attempts to accomplish something beneficial for the public, will nevertheless find him or herself seated on a stage to be mocked by all with an unforgiving abundance of tongue lashing. Our king knows that it isn't smart to meddle with anyone's religious practice let alone to suggest an alternative way for them to conduct their privileged office (i.e., "Mind your own business!"). This is true on both counts even if they hold nothing dear regarding either one.

Already, many are outspoken (with no sign of ceasing) in complaint about the translations we have had on hand for many years, or others that have barely been considered with little more than a perusal, asking why the Church could be so deceived, paying good money for the prior translations about to be shelved. Why was the version not worthy any longer? Was it wrong when it was created? What is it that needs fixing? Why were people mis-led and made to believe that the prior version was the proper translation? What makes you think this version, the KJV, can escape these same criticisms? (In fact, we can be sure it won't.)

Is More Polishing a Good Idea?

And so, to complete the thought, allow me to share the actual wording of the translators for comparison:

> *Yet for all that, as nothing is begun and perfected at the same time, and the latter thoughts are thought to be the wiser: so, if we building upon their foundation that went before us, and being holpen by their labours, do endeavour to make that better which they left so good; no man, we are sure, hath cause to mislike us; they, we persuade ourselves, if they were alive, would thank us.*

Combs conveys that this is the answer to those who insist that the KJV should not be changed neither should other translations be ventured. All translations are completed by flawed human beings. The translators would have applauded the efforts to make their words more accessible to modern ears in the centuries ahead. "For by this means it cometh to pass, that whatsoever is sound already... the same will shine as gold more brightly; being rubbed and polished; also, if anything be halting, or superfluous, or not so agreeable to the original, the same may be corrected, and the truth set in place."

For Combs, "It is obvious the KJV translators would be horrified at the thought their work was perfect and would be the first to commend later improvements and corrections of their work."

Nevertheless, devotees to the King James Version that believe it is exclusively the Word of God, are unlikely to be persuaded their view is wrongheaded even if King James and the

47 translators were to arise from the dead and tell them so. They would still contend that the opinion of these 48 men does not matter – only their finished work does. And they are satisfied that God agrees with this unflinching esteem for the King James Version because tradition has taught them so. Therefore, any opinion about the inspiration of Scripture, finally considered, must assuredly discern that 500 years ago God's Holy Spirit exclusively inspired this English Bible the 47 translated, utilizing their expertise but more the directing control of the Spirit down to the letter. Nevertheless, when it came time for them to reflect on their work and inform the KJV reader what guidance they would give for putting this new translation into practice, the scholars' opinion mattered not at all. For God – apparently –did not inspire their opinion regarding their work just finished. Otherwise they would have known that what they had completed was perfection and therefore, should never be revisited ever again.

APPENDIX 2:
THE LETTER OF ARISTEAS
HIGHLIGHTS

Introduction

THE LETTER OF ARISTEAS IS A PRIZED LEGENDARY WORK WRITTEN IN GREEK, MOST LIKELY BEFORE THE MACCABEAN WAR AGAINST THE WICKED ANTIOCHUS EPIPHANES IV (therefore, circa 175 B.C.), although some experts argue a date closer to 130 B.C. [326] It tells the story of how the Septuagint was created by 72 Jewish scholars who traveled to Alexandria, Egypt at the behest of Ptolemy Philadelphus (285-247 B.C.) The story relates that these 72 "elders" were comprised of six men from each of the original 12 Israelite tribes. They completed their work in 72 days (completing the Pentateuch and possibly the books of Joshua and Judges). Miraculously, through working separately, the elders translated the text, and when finished, the text miraculously was precisely the same for all 72 versions.

This work is considered *pseudepigrapha* since Aristeas is regarded as a fictional character. It should be noted, however, that Josephus considered the book a fair account, and some Christian fathers such as Justin Martyr defended the story as historically accurate. Justin had traveled to Alexandria (ca. 150 A.D.) and witnessed the small quarters of the elders on Pharos,

---

[326] "It is therefore best to follow M. Hadas and date the Letter around the year 130 B.C. Wendland assumes that it was composed between 97 and 93 B.C. Willrich and Graetz suggest the reign of Caligula, but this dating is too late, since Aristeas presumes that the island of Pharos is inhabited, whereas Caesar had made it uninhabitable in 63 B.C." (Rost, Leonhard, *Judaism Outside the Hebrew Canon*, Nashville, TN: Abingdon, 1976, p. 102)

321

the island of the great lighthouse of Alexandria, made uninhabitable by Julius Caesar because of his war with Pompey (63 B.C.) Like many legends, this work of literature mixes truth with fable. Even to the casual eye, it reminds us of Plato writing his *Dialogues* concerning Socrates (through which we know what we know about Socrates). The dialogue was instrumental in creating the conversation as a form for philosophical thought and its presentation. This form is known as the "Socratic dialogue." A major portion of the text is devoted to 72 questions King Ptolemy asks the elders. (Justin would use the format himself in his "Dialogue with Trypho.")

The Letter of Aristeas begins somewhat akin to the Gospel of Luke, as the author is presenting information for the reader supposedly through an epistle documenting what transpired when this epic series of events took place. Aristeas begins his letter with praise for his brother who loves the pursuit of *Sophia* (wisdom):

> Philokratés, a noteworthy narrative has been compiled of a meeting which we had with Eleazar, the chief priest of the Judeans, arising from the great importance which you attached to hearing a personal account of our mission, its content and purpose. By detailing each aspect, I have tried to present you a clear exposition of it, realizing your love-of-learning. (Aristeas 1:1)

Recall that Luke, Paul's traveling companion and secretary, was a learned Greek physician who (many judged) penned the "best" Greek in the New Testament (his native tongue). Luke begins his work writing to his reader, *Theophilus* (i.e., lover of God):

> Forasmuch as many have taken in hand to set forth in order a declaration of those things which are most surely believed among us, Even as they delivered them unto us, which from the beginning were eyewitnesses, and ministers of the word; It seemed good to me also, having had perfect understanding of all

322

things from the very first, to write unto thee in order, most excellent Theophilus. That thou mightest know the certainty of those things, wherein thou hast been instructed. (Luke 1:1-4, KJV)

Like Luke, the letter seeks to be persuasive. In a technical sense, both are works of propaganda, although Luke's writing happens to be true history. There are historical errors in the Letter of Aristeas, perhaps since it was likely seeking to be politically correct. For instance, Ptolemy's war against Antigonus, verse 180 (occurring in 258 B.C.), was a *defeat not a victory.*

Nevertheless, scholar Emil Schürer concludes:

> In every respect then it is the circumstances of the Ptolemaic age that are presupposed. If the author has only artificially reproduced them, this is done with a certainty and a refinement which cannot be assumed in the case of a pseudonymous author living after it. Hence the opinion, that the book originated not later than 200 B.C. is justified.[327]

Debate continues about the reason the book was written. Some see it as an attempt to persuade Hellenistic Jews that the Septuagint was, like the original Hebrew books of the Bible, a result of supernatural inspiration. There is an argument for this, but it clearly includes "interpretation" of God's Word as the translators in Alexandria understood it.

The book concludes with Ptolemy and all the people in his court pledging never to change a single word of the book, for it was inspired by the Great God. "Since this version has been made beautifully and sacredly, and in every respect accurately,

---

[327] Schürer, Eric. (*The Literature of the Jewish People in the Time of Jesus*, pp. 309-310)

it is only fair that this should remain exactly as it is, and that there should be no revision." (verse 310) However, as stated in Appendix 5 of this book, God's method of preserving the text includes the work of a scholar who meticulously studies the texts to determine its most likely original wording. Aristeas was not, we should acknowledge, either a theologian or a real historian.

Another possible reason for the book was to improve the reputation of Jews to the Gentile world since the vaunted king, Ptolemy II Philadelphus, was the sponsor and active participant in the creation of the Septuagint. It is probable that anti-Semitism was at work in Alexandria and across the Ptolemaic Empire. The apocryphal book, 3 Maccabees, which had nothing to do with the war against Antiochus Epiphanes IV, is included in the Septuagint; thus, it is included in the Catholic and Orthodox Bible. Its story discusses the persecution of the Jews in Alexandria after Ptolemy IV, Philopator (222 to 205 B.C). Philopator returned to Egypt through Jerusalem after defeating Antiochus Epiphanes III in 217 B.C. at the Battle of Raphia. Philopator was rebuffed when he attempted to enter the Holy of Holies by the Temple Priests. Upon returning to Alexandria, he was furious. Recall that the city had been a haven for Jews since the time the town was founded by Alexander the Great, about one hundred years before Philopator. The angry king sought to round-up all the Jews in Egypt and put them to death in Alexandria's Hippodrome. 3 Maccabees tells the story of their miraculous salvation. Given this incident and the fact that anti-Semitism seems to spring up most anywhere the Jews reside, one wonders if The Letter of Aristeas was written sometime before this time of persecution, anticipating that the Jews of Alexandria were soon to lose their privileges, and much worse.

The highlights presented here, seek to convey the manner of the writing and document the significant portions of the story. Of particular interest is the "travel log" of the Jerusalem visit when Aristeas goes seeking the 72 scholars from Eleazar the Priest (verses 107-120). This portion of the story is considered a possible bit of plagiarism from a lost writing of an ancient writer named Hecate. Nevertheless, the story, while perhaps a legend, remains intriguing and worth reading. It seems a reasonable bet that some portion of the story, as Justin Martyr maintained, is based upon historical incidents and that leaders of the library at Alexandria were eager to obtain a copy of the Hebrew Bible in Greek so it might be available to scholars there. Although

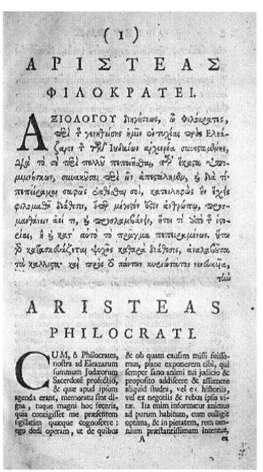

Figure 54 - Greek and Latin Versions of The Letter of Aristeas

it must be admitted that it isn't settled whether this was the primary reason for the endeavor or it was merely to benefit the Egyptian Jews who sought a copy of the Bible in the Greek language they now spoke fluently. Recall Hebrew was all but dead to them living far away in Egypt.

The Letter of Aristeas to Philokratés

CHAPTER 1

1 Philokratés, a noteworthy narrative has been compiled of a meeting which we had with Eleazar, the chief priest of the Judeans, arising from the great importance which you attached to hearing a personal account of our mission, its content, and purpose. By detailing each aspect, I have tried to present you a clear exposition of it, realizing your love-of-learning, **2** which is a great quality in any human who has tried continually to increase his learning and understanding, whether from the histories of others or even by actual experience…

9 On his appointment as keeper of the king's library, Démétrios of Phaléron undertook many different negotiations aimed at collecting, if possible, all the books in the inhabited earth. And by purchase and translation, he brought the king's plan to a successful conclusion, as far as lay in his power. **10** Therefore, on one occasion, when we were present, he was asked, "How many tens of thousands of books are there?" He spoke, "Over two hundred thousand, O king. But I shall take urgent steps in the immediate future to increase the total to five hundred thousand. Now a message has been brought to me that the lawbooks of the Judeans are worthy of translation and inclusion in your royal library." **11** "What is there to prevent you from doing this?" he spoke. "Everything for your needs has been put at your disposal." But Démétrios spoke, "Translation is needed. For they use letters characteristic of the language of the Judeans, exactly as Egyptians use the formation of their letters in accordance with their own language. But the Judeans are assumed to use Syrian language, but this is not so; instead, it is another form of language." Now the king, in answer to each point, ordered that a letter be written to the Judean chief-priest, so that the previously-mentioned project might be carried out…

(VERSES 12 THROUGH 20 OMITTED)

CHAPTER 2

21 But also regarding the copy of the command, I think that its insertion will be not unprofitable. For the king's magnificence will also be more clearly manifested by it, as God gives him strength to bring this salvation to vast multitudes. **22** Now it was as follows:

> By order of the king: everyone who served our father's expeditions in the regions of Syria and Phoiniké, and who, in their advance upon the country of the Judeans, became masters of any Judean bodies whom they transported into either the city or the country, or sold to someone else (but also, any such captives who were there prior to the advance or were subsequently brought in): anyone who holds such persons are required to release them at once, receiving twenty drachmas as the price per individual. Indeed, in the case of soldiers, such money will be added to their salaries; but in the case of the remainder, from the royal bank. **23** For we believe, that these prisoners were taken contrary to our father's will, and in a manner against all fairness; but, that both the destruction of their country, and the transportation of the Judeans into Egypt, was a hasty act of military rashness. For the spoil which fell to the soldiers along the plain was sufficient for them. For this reason, the enslavement of these humans is absolutely unreasonable. **24** Therefore, we have a reputation of dispensing righteousness to all humans, but, all the more, to those who are enslaved without good reason; and our overall aim is to promote both the righteousness and the piety in all things. Therefore, we have ordered that all Judean bodies in slavery everywhere in the kingdom, for whatever reason,

shall be released, and that their owners receive the payment laid down above, and that no one shall act leisurely in these matters. But within three days following the publication of this command, the owners shall furnish registers of slaves to those appointed over these matters and give immediate details of these individuals. **25** For we have also concluded, that it is in the interest of ourselves and our affairs that this matter shall be accomplished. But anyone who wishes may bring a message to me concerning those who refuse to be compliant, on the understanding that he will assume the office of the accused if he was shown to be liable; but the possessions of such men shall be appropriated into the royal bank…

28 Now when this had been completed, he directed Démétrios to report on the transcription of the Judean books. For all measures were taken by these kings by means of ordinances and in great security, and with no trace of negligence nor carelessness. And for this reason, I have inserted the copies of the report and of the letters, as well as the number of presents sent and the condition of each, because each of them was outstanding in magnificence and skill.

29 Now the copy of the report is as follows:

Démétrios to the Great King: Your order, O king, concerned the collection of missing books needed to complete the library, and of items which fell short of the requisite condition. And since I have given highest priority and attention to these matters, I now have the following report to lay before you: **30** Books of the law of the Judeans, together with a few others, are missing from the library. For these works are written in Hebraic characters and language. But according to the report of the experts, they have been transcribed somewhat carelessly and not as they should be; for they have never been made with any sort of royal foresight.

31 Now it is necessary that these works should also be made into an accurate version for your library, because this legislation, as could be expected from its divine nature, is also very philosophical and uncontaminated. For this reason, both writers and poets and the whole multitude of historians have been reluctant to refer to the previously-mentioned books, and to the men who have lived and are living in accordance with them, because their conception of life is so pure and solemn, as Hekataios of Abdéra declares. **32** Therefore, if you approve, O king, a letter shall be written to the chief-priest at Jerusalem, asking him to dispatch men of the most beautiful lives and who are elders, skilled in matters pertaining to their law, six in number from each tribe, in order that after probing the text agreed by the majority, and having achieved an accurate translation, we may produce an outstanding version in a manner worthy, even of the contents and of your purpose. May you be prosperous in every way!

(VERSES 33 AND 34 OMITTED)

35 King Ptolemais to Eleazar the chief-priest, greetings and good health. It is a fact that many of the Judeans settled in our country after being uprooted from Jerusalem by the Persians during the time of their mastery, but even more yet came with our father into Egypt as prisoners. **36** He put many of them into the soldiery on larger salaries; but similarly, he, having also judged the veterans to be trustworthy, set up fortresses which he handed over to them, to prevent the Egyptians from feeling any fear on their account. But having also received the kingdom, we adopt a more humane attitude to all our subjects, but more especially to your citizens. **37** We have freed more than a hundred thousand prisoners, paying to their captors the price in silver proportionate to their honor. We also make amends for any damage caused by the violence of the crowd. We decided to do this as a pious obligation, making it as a thank-offering to the Greatest God, who has

329

preserved the kingdom for us in peace and strongest glory throughout the whole inhabited earth. Also, those who are in the prime of their age, we have drafted into the army, but those who are also able to be attached to me, being worthy of trust in our household, we have put in charge of some positions. **38** But it is our wish to grant favors to them and to all the Judeans throughout the inhabited earth, and to future generations. Therefore, we have decided that your law shall be translated into Hellenic characters from what you call the Hebraic characters, in order that they should also take their place with us in our library with the other royal books. **39** Therefore, you will act beautifully, and in a manner worthy of our eagerness, by selecting and dispatching elders of exemplary lives, experienced in the law and who are able to translate it, six from each tribe, so that an agreed version may be found from the large majority, in view of the great importance of the matters under consideration. For we believe that the completion of this project will win us great glory. **40** Now we have sent off on these things: Andreas the chief-bodyguard and Aristeas, men whom I hold in honor, to confer with you. And with them, they bring first-fruits of my votive-offerings for the temple, and 100 talents of silver for sacrifices and the other requirements. Now write to us on any matters you wish, and your requests will be gratified; and you will be performing an act worthy of a friendship, for what you choose will be carried out with utmost speed. Farewell.

41 In reply to this letter, Eleazar wrote in acceptance as follows:

Eleazar the chief-priest sends greetings to his genuine friend King Ptolemais. Good health both to you and to your sister Queen Arsinoé, and to your children; if that is so, it would be beautiful, and as we wish. Now we also are in good health. **42** On receipt of your letter we rejoiced greatly because of your purpose and beautiful counsel. And we gathered together the whole multitude, reading it to them, that they might know about your piety toward our God. But we also showed them the vessels which you sent, twenty of gold and thirty of silver, five cups, and a table for offering, and 100 talents of silver for the performance of sacrifices and the furnishing of the temple requirements. **43** These gifts were brought by two men held in honor by you, Andreas and Aristeas, men who are beautiful and good, and outstanding in discipline, and worthy in every respect of your conduct and righteousness. And these men communicated your messages to us, and they received a reply from me in agreement with what you wrote. **44** For everything which is to your advantage, even if it is unusual, we will carry out; for this is a sign of friendship and love. For you have even bestowed great and unexpected benefits upon our citizens in many ways. **45** Therefore, we offered sacrifices without delay for you, and your sister, and your children, and your friends. And the whole multitude prayed, that your plans might prosper continually, and that God, the Lord of all, might preserve your kingdom in peace with glory, and that the translation of the holy law might prove advantageous to you and be carried out successfully. **46** Now in the presence of the whole assembly we selected elders, beautiful and good men, six from each tribe, whom we have sent with the law in their possession. Therefore, once the translation of the books is complete, it will be a beautiful-deed, O righteous king, if you order, that these men be restored to us again in safety. Farewell.

47 Now the names of the men are as follows:

First tribe: Joseph, Hezekiah, Zechariah, Johanan, Hezekiah, Elisha.

Second tribe: Judah, Simon, Samuel, Adai, Mattithiah, Eschlemiah.

Third tribe: Nehemiah, Joseph, Theodosios, Basaiah, Orniah, Dakis.

48 *Fourth tribe*: Jonathan, Abrai, Elisha, Hananiah, Zechariah, Hilkiah.

Fifth tribe: Isaac, Jacob, Jeshua, Shabbethai, Simon, Levi.

49 *Sixth* tribe: Judah, Joseph, Simon, Zechariah, Samuel, Shelemiah.

Seventh tribe: Shabbethai, Zedekiah, Jacob, Isaac, Jesiah, Natthai.

Eighth tribe: Theodosios, Jason, Jeshua, Theodotos, Johanan, Jonathan.

Ninth tribe: Theophilos, Abram, Arsam, Jason, Endemiah, Daniel;

50 *Tenth tribe:* Jeremiah, Eleazar, Zechariah, Benaiah, Elisha, Dathai.

Eleventh tribe: Samuel, Joseph, Judah, Jonathan, Caleb, Dositheos .

Twelfth tribe: Isael, Johanan, Theodosios, Arsam, Abietes, Ezekiel.

They were seventy-two in all.

And this indeed was the answer given by Eleazar's party in reply to the king's letter...

(CHAPTER 3 OMITTED)

CHAPTER 4

83 Now what follows embraces the road which we took to Eleazar. Now first I will describe the layout of the whole country. For when we drew near the region, we saw the city built in the middle of the whole land of the Judeans, on a mountain which extended to a great height.

84 Now the peak had been furnished with the temple, which is preeminent above all. And there were three enclosing walls, but they were over seventy cubits in their magnitude, and the width was proportionate, and the length of the structure of the house was also. Everything was built with a magnificence and expense which excelled in every respect...

96 Now it was an occasion of great consternation to us when we saw Eleazar engaged in his public-service, with both his vestments and his glory, which was revealed in the tunic in which he was vested and in the stones around him. For golden bells surround the hem at his feet, making a very special sound. But alongside each of them are tassels adorned with flowers, which are of marvelous colors.

97 Now he was clad in a resplendent magnificent belt, woven in the most beautiful colors. But on his breast, he wears what is called an oracle, to which are attached twelve stones of different kinds, glued together with gold, giving the names of the tribal-chiefs according to their original order, each stone flashing its own natural distinctive color — quite indescribable.

98 Now on his head he has what is called the tiara, but on this the inimitable turban, the royal diadem having the name of God in relief on the front in the middle in holy characters on a golden leaf, ineffable in glory. The wearer is considered worthy of wearing these vestments during the public-services.

99 Now the appearance of these things instills one with fear and disorder, so that a man would think he had entered the outside world. And I emphatically assert, that every human who comes near the spectacle of what I have described will experience indescribable consternation and marvel, his very mind transformed by the holy arrangement on every single detail...

(CHAPTERS 5 AND 6 OMITTED)

CHAPTER 7

172 Now Eleazar offered a sacrifice, and selected the men, and furnished an abundance of gifts for the king. He then sent us forth on our journey with a large escort. **173** Now when we reached Alexandria, a message of our arrival was given to the king. But on being introduced to the court, both Andreas and I paid our affections to the king and presented the letters from Eleazar.

174 Now the king, anxious to meet the men who had been sent, directed that all the other court officials be dismissed, and that these humans be summoned. **175** The unprecedented nature of this step was very clear to all, because it was an established procedure that important useful visitors should be granted an audience with the king on the fifth day after their arrival, while those sent from kings or important cities, only with difficulty, secure admission to the court within thirty days. But he deemed the present arrivals to be worthy of greater honor, and he held the one who sent them to him in high regard. So, he dismissed all the officials whose presence he considered superfluous and remained walking among the elders until he had greeted all of them.

176 Therefore, they arrived with the gifts which had been sent with them, and with the fine skins on which the legislation had been written in gold in Judean characters. The parchment had been marvelously prepared, and their joining together was constructed so as to be imperceptible. As soon as the king saw the men, he proceeded to ask questions about the books.

177 Now when they had removed the parchments out of their coverings and unrolled them, he paused for a long time, bowed down about seven times, and spoke, "Men, I indeed offer my thanks to you, but even more to him who sent you, but most of all to the God whose oracles these are."

178 Now all of them, both visitors and the others who were present, spoke together with one voice, "God save the king!" At this the king was moved to tears, so deeply was he filled with joy. For the intensity of the soul and the overwhelming of the honor received, do force men to tears in the moment of good fortune.

179 Now the king, after directing the materials to be put back in their places, immediately greeted the men, saying, "It is right, O God-revering men, first to grant favor to the documents for whose sake I have summoned you here, and, after that, to extend to you the right hand of friendship. This explains my first action.

180 Now I regard this day of your arrival as of great importance, and it shall be specially marked year by year throughout my life, for by a happy chance it coincides with the anniversary of the victory of the sea-battle against Antigonos. And for this reason, it will be my wish to dine with you this day.

181 Now everything of which you partake," he spoke, "will be served in compliance with your habits; it will be served to me as well as to you." Now after they expressed their pleasure, the king directed the most beautiful apartments to be given them near the citadel, and the preparations for the drinking-party to be made.

(CHAPTERS 8 THROUGH 13 OMITTED)

CHAPTER 14

301 Now three days afterward, Démétrios took the men with him. And they traversed the seven-stadia-long dam across the sea toward the island, and crossed the bridge, and went into the northern districts. There he gathered them in a house which had been duly furnished near the beach. It was a distinguished building and in a secluded situation. He invited the men to carry out the work of translation. Everything they would need was handsomely provided.

302 Now they set to completing their several tasks, reaching agreement among themselves on each by comparing versions. Now this was how the result of their agreement was made into a suitable copy by Démétrios. **303** And, indeed their session lasted until the ninth hour. But after this, they were released for the care of their bodies. Everything they desired was furnished for them on a lavish scale. **304** But even apart from all this, Dōrotheos also provided for them the same preparations as were made for the king himself—for this was an order which he had received from the king. Now daily, in the early morning, they attended the court; and after making their salutations to the king, they retired to their own region.

305 Now following the custom of all the Judeans, they washed their hands in the sea, as they might pray to God. Then they devoted themselves to the reading and the translation of each passage.

306 Now I also asked this question, "What is their purpose in washing their hands before praying?" Now they explained, that it is evidence that they have done no evil, for all activity is done by means of the hands. This is how they beautifully and sacredly refer everything to the righteousness and the truth.

307 Now, as we have previously-stated, they met together daily in their region (which was pleasantly situated for its calmness and brightness), proceeding to fulfill their prescribed task. But the outcome was such that in seventy-two days the translation work was completed, as if such a result was achieved by some predetermination. **308** But when it was completed, Démétrios gathered together the multitude of the Judeans in the region where the translation had also been finished. He read it publicly to everyone, and in the presence of the translators, who also received a great reception from the multitude, because of the great good things which they had conferred upon them. **309** But they also bestowed warm praise upon Démétrios, beseeching him, now that he had transcribed the whole law, to present a copy to their leaders.

310 Now after the scrolls had been recognized, the priests stood up, along with the elders from among the translators and from the representatives of the body of citizens, and with the leaders of the multitude, speaking, "Since this version has been made beautifully and sacredly, and in every respect accurately, it is only fair that this should remain exactly as it is, and that there should be no revision."

311 Now after everyone approved of what they stated, they directed that a curse should be pronounced, as was their custom, on anyone who should revise it by any addition, or by change to any part of the written text, or by any deletion either. This was a very beautiful precaution, to ensure that the words be preserved unchanged for all the future time.

312 Now when the events were also reported to the king, he rejoiced greatly. For it seemed that the purpose which he shared had been safely accomplished. Now the entire version was also read by him, and he marveled profoundly at the mind of the lawgiver. And he spoke to Démétrios, "How is it that none of the historians or poets have ever thought it was worth their while to allude to such a wonderful work?"

313 Now he declared, "Because the legislation is solemn and of divine origin. And because some of those who made the attempt were struck by God, they refrained from their design…"

(VERSES 314 THROUGH 316 OMITTED)

317 Now when the king had received Démétrios' account on these matters (as I previously told), he bowed down to them, directing for great care to be taken of the books and to keep them pure. **318** But he also invited the translators to visit him often after their return to Judah. "For it was only right," he spoke, "that they should now be sent home." But when they returned, he would, as was proper, treat them as friends, and they would receive the greatest gifts from him.

319 Now he directed preparations to be made for their departure and treated the men magnificently. For he presented to each one: three robes of the finest materials, and two talents of gold, and a small-cup worth a talent, and all the furnishings for a set of three couches. **320** But he also sent to Eleazar, along with their luggage, ten silver-footed couches, and all their necessary accessories, and a small-cup worth thirty talents, and ten robes, and purple cloth, and a resplendent crown, and one hundred pieces of finest linen, and bowls, and dishes, and two golden cups for a votive-offering. **321** But he also wrote an invitation stating, that if any of the men desired to return to him, there would be no impediment, for he counted it a great privilege to enjoy the society of such disciplined men, and he would rather invest his wealth generously in such men, and not on vanities.

322 Now there you have my narrative, Philokratés, exactly-
as I professed. For I think that these matters will delight you
more than the books of the mythologists. For you are devoted
to the study of those things which are able to benefit the mind,
and to them you devote the greater time. But I will also try to
write down the remainder of what is worthwhile, in order that
in going through it you may achieve the very beautiful reward
of your purpose.

THE BOOKS OF THE SEPTUAGINT COMPARED WITH THE CONVENTIONAL BOOKS OF THE MT

(The variances noted in this list are very high level.)

MASORETIC TEXT (MT)	SEPTUAGINT (LXX)	COMMENTS ON KEY DIFFERENCES
Genesis	Genesis	Chronologies of Genesis 5 and 11 are variant.
Exodus	Exodus	
Leviticus	Leviticus	
Numbers	Numbers	
Deuteronomy	Deuteronomy	
Joshua	Joshua	
Judges	Joshua	
Ruth	Ruth	
1 Samuel	1 Kings	1 Kings 6:1 – 440 instead of 480 years from the Exodus to the beginning of Temple work.
2 Samuel	2 Kings	
1 Kings	3 Kings	
2 Kings	4 Kings	
1 Chronicles	1 Chronicles	
2 Chronicles	2 Chronicles	
Ezra	1 Ezra 2 Ezra	Parts of 2 Chron. and Nehem. are found in the text. A prayer of Ezra is included.
Nehemiah	Nehemiah	

Ester	Tobit	Tobit and Judith are not historical books but tell enjoyable stories teaching biblical truths.
	Judith	
	Ester	
	1 Maccabees	1 and 2 Maccabees tell the story of the fight for independence from The Seleucids in the second century.
	2 Maccabees	
	3 Maccabees	
		Book 3 tells the story of the attempted genocide of the Jews of Alexandria.
		There is a 4 Maccabees usually excluded from the LXX.
Job	Psalms	Several psalms are combined or are split. One additional short psalm of David (151) is also included.
Psalms	Jobs	Job is longer in the Septuagint.
Proverbs	Proverbs	There are many variations in the Proverbs.
Ecclesiastes	Ecclesiastes	
Song of Solomon	Song of Songs	
	Wisdom of Solomon	
	Wisdom of Sirach	
Isaiah		
Jeremiah		See comment for Jeremiah in LXX
Lamentations		
Ezekiel		

Daniel		See comment for Daniel in LXX
Hosea	Hosea	
Joel	Amos	
Amos	Micah	
Obadiah	Joel	
Jonah	Obadiah	
Micah	Jonah	
Nahum	Nahum	
Habakkuk	Habakkuk	
Zephaniah	Zephaniah	
Haggai	Haggai	
Zechariah	Zechariah	
Malachi	Malachi	
	Isaiah	
	Jeremiah	Jeremiah is approximately 25% shorter in the LXX.
	Baruch	A story of a Jewish village that repents.
	Lamentations of Jeremiah Epistle of Jeremiah	A one-chapter book. A letter to the captives of Judah as they are carried away to Babylon.
	Ezekiel	
	Daniel Susanna Bel and the Dragon	Ordered differently than Daniel in Masoretic. The original book of Daniel was changed out to Theodotion's version in the third or fourth century.

APPENDIX 4:
WHY CHRISTIANS SHOULD HONOR THE JEWISH TALMUD

Who Are the Jews?

W HAT CHRISTIANS BELIEVE ABOUT JUDAISM IS HIGHLY DISTORTED IF NOT DISTURBING. THE JUDAISM WE THINK WE KNOW IS THE JEWISH RELIGION OF THE OLD Testament with its emphasis upon the Torah and Temple worship. We might know that what we call the Old Testament is composed of three categories: The Law, the Prophets, and the Writings. We know that Abraham and Moses are honored as the founders of the Jewish faith. And we believe that the Prophets of God revealed to His people many things about the Messiah and the world to come. We don't understand very much about the Temple, except it was at the center of their religion. We assume that with the destruction of the Temple in 70 A.D., the nature of Jewish religion changed. And yet, we know little about what happened afterward. And what we do know is tainted with twisted facts.

Some of us believe the Jewish religion and its people continued in an unbroken legacy. The Jews didn't "die out." The race continued while the religion experienced a dramatic resurgence in the third century. We admit the Jews have "wandered" for almost two thousand years after the time of Christ. But others believe that Israel, the northern 10 tribes, were "lost" to history and dispersed globally. Where they were lost, or whether they genuinely disappeared has become the stuff of legendary speculation regarding who they are today. Some say they are the British, or more precisely, the Anglo-Americans as if this gives English-speaking nations a stake in

345

the promises made to Israel. However, the historical proof for this belief is thin to say the least.

Nevertheless, this speculation amounts to only one plank of several asserting a denial that the Jews exist anymore. Many suppose that Jews are "so-called" Jews only because they lack any racial link to "Jewishness" whatsoever. One can find many arguments against the Khazars, the Ashkenazi, and other "fake" Jews. Many books have been written – some scholarly, some polemical rants – degrading those who seek to call themselves Jews.[328] Going against the flow of Christian Zionists, author Texe Marrs has based several his books on challenging the identity of Jews. Here is a sample of his position:

> The newest DNA scientific studies, showing that the people known as the Jews of Israel—and, indeed Jews all over the world—are, in fact, of Khazar, not Israelite origins, is (sic) backed by the earlier work of historians.

> These historians found that their scholarly books and reports were immediately attacked by Zionists desperate to maintain the fiction the Jews could trace their heritage all the way back to Abraham.

> The Zionists knew the truth—that they are not a race but a composite of many races. They had to keep up the myth that they were a homogenous race kept together by religion and community interests for 5,000 years. Only in this way could the Zionist Jews claim to be the seed of Abraham. Only as "Israelites" could the Jews claim possession to land where they and their ancestors had never been.[329]

---

[328] *The Invention of the Jewish People*, by Shomo Sand, 2009, and Arthur Koestler, *The thirteenth Tribe*, 1976 re-issue.

[329] Marrs, Texe. *How the Racial Hoax of the Jews Was Finally Exposed.* Retrieved from http://www.texemarrs.com/042013/racial_hoax_exposed_article.htm.

This teaching underlies some, but not all, of the attacks on the Jews of today. Many attacks are directed at the State of Israel due to its ill-treatment of the Palestinians. And a sea change (i.e., a profound change in perspective) has occurred over the past decade or so in Evangelicalism. It is true that up to now "Bible-believing" Christians supported the notion that Jews should be granted their own homeland.[330] This controversial opinion became an inexorable "fact" after the Holocaust. While a small number of Holocaust deniers express this unbelievable point of view, the most relevant issue emerging today is a different interpretation of Bible prophecy that no longer sees the primacy of Israel's return to the Holy Land as the single most important sign of the soon return of Jesus Christ. After all, the Jews in Israel aren't "born again" and many if not most aren't religious at all.

Consequently, younger biblically-oriented Christians, as well as many activists in mainstream, denominational churches, denounce Israel as an illegitimate nation that practices apartheid and should be dissolved. Apparently overlooked is the historical basis for Israel that consists in three essential accomplished facts: The "Balfour Declaration" (November 2, 1917), the United Nations mandate to partition Trans-Jordan to create

---

This perspective is rebutted in Freedman's book which we will take up. See *The Talmud: A Biography*, pp. 89-90. Entering into this controversy lies far outside our scope here.

[330] This statement ignores the "minority" view of the so-called Covenant Reformed Theology that sees the Church replacing Israel as the fulfillment of God's Old Testament promises. The majority view derives from the emergence of Dispensationalism bred in England beginning in the 1830s. However, history of Christian support for "Zionism" actually begins several hundred years before J.N. Darby and Dispensationalism in what was known as English "Restorationism." See William Watson, *Dispensationalism Before Darby*. Watson's book corrects the all-too-common falsehood that Darby led the first Christian movement to support the Pre-Tribulation rapture and the support of Israel.

347

Israel (November 29, 1947), and the recognition of its government by virtually all nations in the world (Arab countries being the exception). However, this author's view remains true to the original course: *Israel is a sovereign nation even if it has unjustly treated Palestinians.* We should easily recall that Russia, Germany, China, and many other countries continued to be sovereign states despite atrocities a thousand times worse than what has transpired or alleged to have happened, in Israel.

So, is there a case that racial Jews still exist? However strong the arguments against the continuity of Judaism and the connection to the land of Palestine, historically the evidence for the Jews is unassailable – evidence which stems from the existence of the Talmud and its development predominantly in Babylon, among the Jewish community existing there. It was comprised of two groups: the first group included the majority of Jews remaining in Babylon after Zerubbabel had led a contingent back to Judah in 539 B.C. The second contingent were those Jews emigrating to Babylon almost 675 years later at the time of the so-called Hadriadic persecutions, in response to the Bar Kokhba rebellion of 135 A.D. If Israel in fact consists primarily of Jews with racial links to the ancient past, the Talmud and not just the Torah are hugely responsible for this amazing fact.

The Precursor to the Talmud: The Mishnah

After the Temple was destroyed, one could say that the Jewish faith split into two paths *both led by Pharisees*. The first path was led by Paul of Tarsus, of the tribe of Benjamin, self-described as a "Pharisee of Pharisees" (Philippians 3:5), along with the other Jewish Apostles who followed Jesus of Nazareth. The second path was led by a Pharisee named John, son of Zakkai (Yohanan Ben Zakkai). Paul's story readers of this book know well. Zakkai we do not know. But his survival from the assault of Jerusalem led to the formation of academies for the continuation of the Pharisaic movement.[331] Zakkai escaped from the clutches of the Zealots by playing dead. He was carried out of Jerusalem by his disciples. Once away from the city, he "arose" from the coffin into which his followers laid him and immediately paid a visit to Vespasian, the commander of the Roman army. Vespasian, soon to be Caesar (69-79 A.D.), granted Zakkai his request to allow the religion of the Jews to be saved. The academies were created at Javneh (Jamnia in Greek). Soon, the Pharisees became known solely as sages or teachers, i.e., rabbis.

As documented early in this book, one of the star pupils of the Javneh academy was Josef ben Akiva (R. Akiba). Several notable Pharisees compiled the Mishnah, the collection of all the laws of the Torah and the Oral Tradition (so-called) that would be written down to explain (or alter, depending upon your point of view) the 613 Torah laws. This process occurred not through "instructor-led" curriculum but in discussions between younger and older members of the community (reminiscent of Jesus, at 12-years of age, discussing the Torah with the scholars in Herod's Temple). Freedman explains:

> It seems the method of teaching was for the students to sit in on the discussions of the older scholars, who were collaborating to collect and clarify the entire body of Jewish law, creating a belief system and legal code that no future group of dissenters, whether Sadducee or anyone else, could come along and challenge.[332]

---

[331] The Sadducees and the Sanhedrin were dissolved once the Temple was destroyed. Harry Freedman (whose book, *The Talmud: A Biography* I will reference here numerous times), states: "The rebuilding of Judaism, and the emergence of Christianity, which was taking place in the same place at exactly the same time, can be directly attributed to the vision and skill of two people: Paul for the Christians and Yohanan ben Zakkai for the Jews." Freedman, op. cit., p. 17.

[332] Ibid., p. 20.

A principal player in the compilation and creation of the law book known as the Mishnah was Eleazar ben Azariah. Upon his election, legend has it that the gates of the academy were thrown open and 700 new students joined. But not all was happiness. Rabbi Akiba was instrumental in the process that followed helping to solve a bitter dispute between two rival leaders of the newly formed rabbinic community. However, "Akiva is the best known and most highly regarded of all the rabbis. Legends and stories about him abound. Unfortunately, this makes it hard to know his true-life history, which is concealed somewhere beneath layers of folklore and fable."[333] After Akiba was put to death in Rome for his support of the rebellion led by Bar Kokhba (135 A.D.), Akiba's pupil, Meir, was responsible for most of the final version of the Mishnah which included a previous Mishnah written by Akiba. A noteworthy descendant of Hillel and Gamaliel undertook the final collation of the laws and recorded opinions expressed in the discussions. This person was Rabbi Judah, the *Nasi* (i.e., Hebrew for *prince*). Freedman relates:

> When Judah finished his Mishnah, the process of recording the Oral Law was nearly at an end. The Mishnah became accepted as authentic, comprehensive, and authoritative. Indeed, in some circles studying Rabbi's Mishnah was so holy a task it became an acceptable substitute for the now-defunct sacrifices.[334]

Hence, the study of the commentaries to become a scholar of Jewish Law was fully ingrained in the new "normative" Judaism. According to Freedman, the Mishnah is "a stand-alone work that's

---

[333] Ibid., p. 23. Freedman comments that Akiva ranks with the other prominent Jewish leaders and scholars (Moses, Isaiah, Maimonides, Spinoza. "He dominates the whole scene of Jewish history from the period of the Second Isaiah, about 540 B.C.E. until the rise of the Spanish school of philosophers, about 1100 C.E." (p. 24)

[334] Ibid., p. 27.

often read independently of the Talmud. It's systematic, terse, and direct in its language." The Talmud includes lengthy discussions that can jump to other topics than the principal one of the *tractates* (tractates means "treatise or essay"). The method for following the discourses is somewhat akin to jumping around via hyperlinks on the Internet. The Mishnah limits its exposition on the Torah to summarizing only the primary points of view. Once finished, the Mishnah served as the basis for the intense discussions among the students at academies in both Palestine and Babylon for the next 300 years. In fact, the Talmud certainly owes its origin to the discursive process established with the formation of the Mishnah. This process generated an intensive method of what might be called, *rabbinic dialectic.* At one level, this process of studying, discussing, and recording the discussions in the academies, primarily in Babylon, became the glue that held Judaism together. The trained sages became leaders of the Jewish communities as they grew and spread. Thus, the rabbi became the leader and authority of these communities. "Ask the Rabbi" (like we learned in the movie, *Fiddler on the Roof*), was at the heart of practical Judaism. And so, it was the Talmud that catalyzed the teachings and *traditions* of Judaism.

Somewhat ironically, the most critical city in the world to preserve Judaism was now, in fact, Babylon – with its pagan astrology and mystery religion – the emblematic enemy of what Jerusalem had historically symbolized as the hub of Jewish life and mainspring of its Yahwist religion.[335] Some might comment

---

[335] See Zavada, Jack, "Babylon Was a Symbol for Sin and Rebellion," March 17, 2017, at https://www.thoughtco.com/history-of-babylon-3867031.

that the new Judaism thriving in Babylon is itself an indication that God was not behind what became of Judaism. Perhaps.

The Talmud – A Very Short History

Babylon became a relatively quiet and safe place for the growth of revised Judaism. The Parthian Empire gave way to the Sassanid Empire in 226 A.D. The Sassanids pushed their Zoroastrian religion as a means to solidify their rule and society (akin to what Constantine sought to do with Christianity). The challenges to Judaism were minor compared to the continued persecutions in what remained of Roman Palestine. More Jews fled to Babylon. The mathematical and astronomical knowledge which flourished there found its way into the Talmud and became a part of Jewish scholarship. Such allusions to these sciences are located throughout the Talmud. Freedman comments, "The Talmud is replete with passages on these subjects, from calculations of the size of the earth and the thickness of the sky to legends about demons and medicinal cures."[336] One of the most important factors allowing Judaism to persist amidst rival cultures and secular governments, (in contradistinction to Sharia Law of Islam which seeks to displace "the law of the land"), is what Freedman calls "a landmark ruling … *dina malchuta dina*, that in all areas of civil and monetary law the law of the state is the law."[337] Jewish law prevailed in religious doctrine, whereas any conflict in civil law would not be challenged by Judaism.

---

[336] Ibid., p. 38.
[337] Ibid., 45.

The *Gemara* (Aramaic for teaching)[338] purportedly concluded "at the close of the teaching," along with a loose compilation of the discursive material in Babylon, being completed ca. 500 A.D. But turning this loosely woven material into a multi-volume book continued for at least another 300 years. Some scholars suggest that much of the material of the Talmud was handed down from generation to generation throughout this time. And yet, eventually, the Talmud was formed into a (somewhat) coherent and completed whole.[339] Freedman surmises that "there must have been many of them, who pulled the whole thing together but have altogether disappeared from view."[340] So almost nothing is known about the final editing process.

In 633, Mohammed's religion conquered Babylon. Soon afterward, a new city emerged: *Baghdad*. The Sassanids would give way to the Umayyads. In 750, the Umayyads gave way to the Abbasids. It should be stated the Abbasids were a form of Islam that the modern world could live with. For the Abbasids, learning was the highest virtue: "The ink of the scholar is more holy than the blood of a martyr." Baghdad itself would stimulate the

---

[338] Gemara became an alternative way to speak of the Talmud when the name *Talmud* became the focus of censorship or when the Talmud was outlawed, which was frequent throughout the two past millennia.

[339] Whether there is truly a "method to the madness" of the organization of the Talmud, is itself a source of debate. Jacob Neusner, in his foreword to Abraham Cohen's book, *Everyman's Talmud*, indicates that Cohen saw the Talmud as a random collection of wisdom, whereas Neusner sees order amidst what Cohen saw as chaos. "In fact, we have learned what Cohen, along with his generation, did not realize, which is that the Talmud as a whole is cogent, doing some few things over and over again, it conforms to a few simple rules of rhetoric, including choice of language for discrete purposes, and that fact attests to the coherent viewpoint of the authorship at the end – the people who put it all together as we have – because it speaks, over all, in a single way, in a uniform voice." Neusner, from Cohen, Abraham. *Everyman's Talmud: The Major Teachings of the Rabbinic Sages*. New York: Schocken Books.1949. p. xix.

[340] Ibid., p. 52.

writings we know as *"The One Thousand and One (Arabian) Nights."* What is seldom understood by most everyone is the influence that Islam and rabbinic Judaism had on one another.

Freedman points this out with these well-chosen words:

> Both Islam and Judaism are religions which minutely regulate every aspect of the believer's life. They're each based on a God-given written document – the *Torah* for Judaism and the *Qu'ran* for Islam. These divine texts are each interpreted and expanded upon by an oral tradition – the *Talmud* and the *Hadith* respectively... The Jewish system of law is called *halacha*, the Islamic system is called *shar'ia*. Both names mean a "pathway' or a 'way to go.' Unlike Christianity, the laws and beliefs in Islam and Judaism are derived through a process of reasoning and scholarship; there are no councils or synods to rule on doctrine, ethics or behavior.[341]

Freedman goes on to convey, surprisingly to Christians in the twenty-first century, the similitude of Islam and Judaism respecting the sanctity of human life: "The Qu'ran states that 'We decreed upon the Children of Israel that whoever kills a soul... it is as if he had slain mankind entirely. And whoever saves one – it is as if he had saved mankind entirely."[342] A ninth century Talmudist (Pirkoi ben Baboi), asserted that under Islam, Babylon's academies were safe from imprisonment, forced conversions, or plunder. Likewise, the Abbasids protected the Jewish communities from the "Romans and Greeks." With the Abbasids, as ironically as that may seem, we see Islam as the protector of Judaism.

Because the communities of Jews and Muslims were spread far apart, Freedman points out that edicts were the means of communicating matters upon which their respective peoples

---

[341] Ibid., p. 59.
[342] Qu'ran, Sura v.32, cited by Freedman, op. cit., p. 58. Would that all Muslims today embraced these teachings and unfailingly practiced them.

should keep in sync with the "orthodoxy" espoused by their religious leaders. These edicts were labeled *Teshuvot* by Jews and *Fatwas* by Muslims. Such communiqués kept their devout communities from wandering too far from permissable paths.

Nevertheless, one sect that did not concur with the Teshuvot, (and continues unto today), is the *Karaites*. There Jews rejected the Teshuvot and Rabbinic Judaism along with its written, oral law and vast commentaries (aka the *Mishnah* and the *Talmud* respectively). Like the Sadducees, the Karaites rejected out of hand that Moses had handed down an oral law in addition to the written law. For the rabbis believed there was an official (authoritative) line of succession from Moses to Joshua, from Joshua to the Elders, then on to the Prophets, and finally to Ezra's Great Assembly,[343] constituting a secretive (gnostic-like) knowledge maintained by a scholarly elite. The charge against the Talmud by the Karaites (a view which seems highly reasonable to the Christian world) is that the many differences of *opinions undermine the idea of a single oral law handed down by Moses*. Since there were many opinions expressed in the Talmud, apparently there was no clear and unambiguous wisdom passed down. Instead, Karaites believe that reason instead of "Talmudic laws fencing off the Torah's laws from abrogation, should *interpolate* the Torah for guidance to the children of God in this life. *The Torah alone is authoritative, not rabbis and not the Talmud*. The orthodox Christian surely doesn't disagree with the Karaite's position.

Moving on: No telling of the story of the Talmud is complete without mention of Maimonides (1138-1204) and his work, the

---

[343] *Aboth 1.1*, Cited by Cohen, Abraham. *Everyman's Talmud: The Major Teachings of the Rabbinic Sages*. New York: Schocken Books.1949. p. xxxvi.

Mishnah Torah, completed in Cairo when he was 45 years of age. *The Mishnah Torah* was accused by his opponents as an alternative to the Talmud. The *Mishnah Torah* comprised 14 volumes of precise interpretations (if not exact prescriptions) of the law. Of particular interest is the fact that Maimonides, aka Ramban, wrote only this work (among many compositions) *in Hebrew* and

Figure 55 - Maimonides in the U.S. House of Representatives

included interpretation of the laws governing the Temple. Apparently, Maimonides anticipated a future third temple would be built. At face value, his work appears to reject Rabbinic Judaism; however, there is little else to substantiate his exact opinion regarding the Talmud. Despite such criticism, Maimonides remains the greatest Jewish scholar of Medieval times.

The Christian Attacks on the Jews and the Talmud

Persecutions (pogroms) of Jews were always close at hand after the time of Ramban. There are too many to recount. Christians often outlawed the Talmud and forced the Jews to leave their homes and fortunes due to their unwillingness to convert to Christianity. Lies of "blood libel" were told and falsely alleged to exist within the Talmud. Jews were often accused of kidnapping and ritually sacrificing the children of Christians, using their blood to bake Passover bread. Such allegations always seemed to be the trump card played whenever a city or nation-state wished to rid itself of the Jews.[344]

However, the methods often changed. In many cases, apologetics became the focus of interactions between Christian scholars and Jewish sages. One person stands out like this "pivot point" in the relationship between the Jewish system of interpretation and the Christian one. His name was Peter Abelard (1079-1142). His most famous attribute was his love affair

---

[344] One thinks of the Alhambra Edict on March 31, 1492 giving the Jews four months to leave Spain or convert - Columbus left for America four months later, two days after the deadline, on August 3, 1492). The pressure that Christians asserted on the Jews to conform, assimilate, and convert is the dominant element of the history of the interaction of the two belief systems with few respites such as *Restorationism* in England in the seventeenth century and *Dispensationalism*, also in England, in the nineteenth century. The latter was the instrumental influence in America's Christian Zionism in the twentieth and twenty-first centuries. The *Scofield Bible's* treatment of Bible prophecy is often cited as the principal cause for the widespread belief that Jews returning to the Holy Land signal the coming of the Messiah (and Second Coming of Christ). As indicated earlier, this summary view of where Evangelicals stand is under attack today from many sides.

with a student, Héloïse, which came to a tragic end with Peter becoming a castrated monk, and Héloïse ordered to a nunnery. Notwithstanding the fame of this colorful matter, our interest is his role as a polemicist. He came amidst a new realization by scholarly Christians that coercion and threats were not effective tools of evangelism. It was felt a new approach must be attempted. Freedman states:

Figure 56 - The Crusaders Discover the 'True' Cross

> The Christians were beginning to realize the significance of the Talmud to the Jews, and to understand that if they wanted to prove the Jews wrong, they would need to do it by refuting the Talmud, not by bringing arguments from the Bible. The Jews would not accept Christian interpretations of the Old Testament. They had their own, which were stored in the Talmud.[345]

Freedman indicates that it was Peter's life-long attempt "to show both Muslims and Jews the errors of their ways (which) mark the beginning of an onslaught on both religions over the next one hundred years." One immediately thinks of the Crusades which determined that the sword and not scholarship

---

[345] Ibid., p. 112.

would be the way to deal with Jews and Muslims. Indeed, killing Jews reached its zenith when the Crusaders conquered Jerusalem over five weeks from June 7th to July 15, 1099, during the lifetime of Maimonides.

One crucial incident during this low point in human history, involved yet another Peter, in this incident Peter the Hermit, whose sermons in the Valley of Jehoshaphat near the garden of Gethsemane on the Mount of Olives, sent the Crusaders into a frenzied zeal. Soon, the Crusader's siege would conclude in the slaughter thousands of Jews and Muslims, who fought side by side defending Jerusalem. Some eyewitness accounts said that blood was up to the ankles of the Franks (to clarify: Crusaders were Germanic Saxons of Europe), with corpses strewn throughout Jerusalem. It is estimated that 40,000 Jews were slain along with 20,000 Muslims.

Despite these "lachrymose" times, the Talmud continued to serve as the centerpiece of Jewish religion and understanding. Freedman relates the view of American historian Salo Baron (1895-1989) who argued that in spite of the times of hostilities, the Jewish community succeeded in leading "creative lives, learning, working, reading, teaching, raising families and promoting the way of life they believed in."[346] In his own words, Freedman concurs, contending that the Talmud's followers "have explored the deepest intellectual oceans, traversed broad plains of knowledge and ideas, created and sustained communities, and attained a clear and uncompromising sense of personal identity and self-knowledge."[347] Freedman likewise reiterates that *learning was the heart and soul of Jewishness.*

---

[346] Ibid., p 112.
[347] Ibid., p. 112.

Books were the lifeblood of Jewish life; the people may have been as poor as any in the Middle Ages, but they had pride in their learning. Their books were often all they had. Study was an end in itself and the highest aspiration of any Jewish parent was that their son would become a rabbinic scholar, an authority in Talmud. They wouldn't have given up their holy books without a fight, many of those fights would have ended in bloodshed and tragedy.[348]

Summarizing several other "lowlights" of the war against the Jews and the Talmud (which preceded the Reformation):

- In 1244, Pope Innocent IV encouraged King Louis in Paris to burn all copies of the Talmud. After three years, the law was altered allowing the Talmud in a Jewish home, but it must be censored from any portion deemed antithetical to Christianity.

- Louis' successor, Philip the Fair, expelled the Jews in 1306 along with the Templars in 1307. Both were likely attacked because of financial reasons (Philip was seriously in debt to both Jews and the *Templars* – the first global bank). The Jews returned in 1315, but by 1319 all copies of the Talmud in France had been burned.

- Many Jews in Spain converted to Christianity during the century leading up to the Alhambra Edict. The converts were called the *conversos*. These Jews acknowledged Christ as the Messiah but continued to follow Talmudic law. In 1480, the Inquisition was instituted in Spain to purge the Talmud from the *conversos*. By 1492, Spain had had enough. Ferdinand and Isabella expelled the Jews. "There was no sight more pitiable… there was not a Christian who did not feel their pain."[349] Nonetheless, Christians could not or would not stand up against the expulsion.

---

[348] Ibid., p. 117.

[349] Felipe Fernandez-Armesto, *1492: The year Our World Began.* London: Bloomsbury, 2009, p. 87. Cited by Freedman, op. cit., p. 132.

The Reformation and Its Impact on the Jews

Martin Luther famously nailed 95 theses to the Wittenberg Door in 1517. His document was not much more than an invitation to discuss the grievances he had against the Roman Church. But the sound of this nail pounding was soon heard across Europe. And with it began the Protestant Reformation. Of concern to this author is the fact that Scripture and Scripture alone (*sola scriptura*) stood out as the pivotal position of the Reformers. It was this principle that led the Reformers back to the Hebrew Bible, believing the only reliable source to uphold biblical authority, had to be the Hebrew version of the Old Testament. *But before one can study Hebrew, one must be able to read Hebrew.* This would eventually generate a group of Christians who learned Hebrew, and therefore, were called *Christian Hebraists.* Just before Luther's declaration in Wittenberg, an Alsace native Conrad Pellican, developed a Hebrew book of grammar in 1501 two years after he began studying Hebrew (and when he was only 22 years old). Another fellow following a similar path was Johannes Reuchlin. Reuchlin was interested in mysticism generally, but Jewish mysticism in the Kabbalah specifically. Not long after completing his own Hebrew book of grammar (which became the instruction standard after that), he became a student of the Kabbalah and authored the classic, *On the Art of Kabbalah.*

A third Christian Hebraists, who stands in stark contrast to the first two mentioned above, Josef Pfefferkorn, learned Hebrew with a singular intent: *To declare war on the Talmud.* Soon Reuchlin and Pfefferkorn would lock horns leading to a many-year debate costing both sides considerable sums. Reuchlin defended the value of the Talmud believing it offered additional evidence for the value and truth of biblical religion. Pfefferkorn slammed Reuchlin with vitriolic arguments – eventually causing Pfefferkorn to lose face with the King. Thanks to Pope Leo X's interest in the Kabbalah, Reuchlin would be vindicated and

Pfefferkorn silenced. The fallout of this conflict was Pope Leo's granting approval to publish the Talmud on Gutenberg's revolutionary 1439 invention, the printing press.[350] Just as Gutenberg's machine helped to standardize the wording of many manuscripts, the Talmud benefitted too. For as its circulation increased, the Talmud gained a positive reputation among many.

The Talmud and the Development of Political Science

At the same time, and quite to the benefit of both Christianity and Rabbinic Judaism, political thought was developing into its own distinctive discipline. And it is here, as Christians, we should honor the Talmud. You see, *the Hebrew Bible plus the Talmud provide considerable support for the ideal of the republic, selected personal freedoms, and the modern nation-state.* At that time, some intellectuals began to realize that God had designed a political constitution to guide the lives as well as the religion of the children of Israel – and the Talmud amplified this view.[351]

The Dutch scholar, Hugo Grotius (1583-1645), was a pioneer in this new discipline. He believed that the Hebrew Sanhedrin – which had authority over only civil law (and not religious) – provided a biblical precedent for what we now call "the separation of church and state." Plus, Grotius was a Calvinist. Netherlands' separation from Catholic Spain was, for him, proof that God worked a providential miracle demonstrating the correctness of the Calvinist (and more broadly, Protestant) position.

A friend of Grotius, Petrus Cunaeus, became a leading figure at Leiden University. His vital work on the ownership of

---

[350] The first publication of the Talmud was accomplished in Venice by Daniel Bomberg in 1523. Virtually all subsequent issues used the same pagination.

[351] Freedman, op. cit., p. 149.

property – specifically land ownership – borrowed heavily from the writings of Maimonides. Cunaeus concluded that Ramban's work provided the basis for an equitable society. However, there was a downside. Grotius and Cunaeus considered the Jewish Karaites more intelligent than the Talmudists since they did not embrace the Talmud and the concept of Oral Law. Additionally, Grotius believed that the Hebrews should settle in Holland, but only because he felt the Calvinist Church in the Netherlands would be more effective in converting the Jews.

Another lawyer, John Selden in England, became an essential figure in recognition of the Talmud by Christians. Selden became infamous for disputing the legitimacy of tithes. He argued that the tithes received by the Israelite priests were not a divine, God-given right. Therefore, the clergy of the Church of England was not entitled to tithes either. As you can imagine, his assertion set off a firestorm in the Church. Without the biblical mandate for tithing, the clergy couldn't insist any longer that Christian parishioners pay tithes to the Church. Not long afterward, Selden found himself crosswise with the English King after insulting the monarch's spokesperson in the Parliament. Selden wound up in the Tower of London. Facing an endless time in prison, Selden asked a friend to bring him a copy of the Talmud from the Library at Westminster Abbey. This afforded Seldon the time to learn Hebrew and gain a knowledge of the Talmud rivaling even the most astute Hebrew sage. He composed six scholarly works, including a 2,000-page tome on Hebraic jurisprudence. Seldon's books were to "influence a generation of British political thinkers ... Isaac Newton, Milton, Ben Jonson, and Hobbes."[352] Freedman observes that Seldon,

---

[352] Ibid., p. 155.

despite not being a Jew, still ranks as one of the top scholars on the Talmud. Finally, the Talmud had won friends.

The Talmud's Legacy for Christians

While Calvinist Christians on the Continent, in Switzerland and the Netherlands, increasingly argued that Judaism was replaced by the Church and inherited the blessings promised to Abraham and his descendants, Englishmen in the Church held a different understanding of the Bible and the connection between Jews and Christians. Both England and America were destined to become home to Christian Zionism. As touched on earlier, Restorationism of the 1600s and 1700s led to Dispensationalism in the 1800s. This Biblicist point of view would become a dominant facet of American Evangelicalism in the twentieth century. Freedman notes an example of the more conciliatory mood among Christians toward the Talmud in our time:

> George Foot Moore, a Presbyterian pastor, and Professor of the History of Religion at Harvard, concentrated on the Bible and on the origins and theology of religion. He wrote a three-volume work on Judaism during the period that the Talmud was gestating (in the first three centuries of the Christian era). Many of his works are studded with Talmudic references.[353]

Indeed, the founding of this nation may not have been expressly Christian, but Judaic-Christian principles were at the forefront of the political philosophy that gave rise to the Declaration of Independence, the American Revolution, and the United States Constitution. The Torah and the Talmud played no small part in creating the groundwork for our nation's foundation. In

---

[353] Moore, George Foot. *Judaism in the First Three Centuries of the Christian Era: The Age of Tannaim, 3 volumes.* Cambridge, MA: Harvard University Press, 1927). Cited by Freedman, op. cit., p. 205.

so doing, despite the disagreement Christianity has with Rabbinic Judaism over whether Jesus was the Messiah, Christians should regard the Talmud not only as one of history's most celebrated pieces of scholarly composition but as contributing to a nation-state that promises to both Jews and Christians a society whose Constitution guarantees freedom of religion to its citizens.

Conclusion – Do Jews Know God 'Personally?'

Christianity teaches a dynamic form of knowing God intimately, classically understood as *mysticism* in theological terms, because we believe Jesus Christ comes to live within us through the agency of the Holy Spirit. There are scores of verses that teach us this truth. Here are but two that come quickly to mind: *"To them, God chose to make known how great among the Gentiles are the riches of the glory of this mystery, which is Christ in (us) – the hope of glory."* (Colossians 1:27) *"I have been crucified with Christ. It is no longer I who live, but Christ who lives in me."* (Galatians 2:20a)

However, it is not accurate to say that Jews solely relate to God by adhering to Mosaic Law. They also believe that they can mystically *know* God. Talmudic truth separates its teachings into the *Halachah* and the *Haggadah*. The Halachah points out the rules of living a godly life and constitutes the means by which the Jewish community retains its Jewishness, keeping it distinct from the non-Jewish world in which it lives. But the Haggadah teaches that there is more to Judaism than just following a legalistic code. Abraham Cohen comments,

> Even if it were possible to isolate the *Halachah* from the other elements in the Talmud, it would still be a mistake to envisage it as a system of dry legalism devoice of all spiritual content, as its critics invariably allege… *Haggadah* (Narration), therefore, signifies the non-legal sections of Rabbinic literature, and is equally important as the other for a correct understanding of the world of thought

which generations of teachers lovingly evolved. Striking through the contract between Halachah and Haggadah, they complement each other, spring from the same root, and aim at the same goal. "Is it your desire to know Him Who spake and the world came into being? Learn the Haggadah; for from it *you will come to know the Holy One*, blessed be He, and cleave to His ways."[354]

While Christians would not be satisfied by Judaism's method for how to know God, Christianity's towering truth grew from Jewish roots in which *spirituality combined living a godly life and knowing God in a personal way.* These two aspects of the spiritual life are both essential and neither can be compromised. They flow from the Word of God as given to His people.

And finally, while this book has been highly critical of rabbinic alterations to the Bible and seeking to hide those passages of Scripture that clearly present the nature, mission, and identity of the Messiah, the criticism targets what transpired in the second century. To be sure, Christians and Jews do not believe the same things about Jesus Christ and this has created an enormous chasm between us. I maintain these differences matter – for time and eternity. Nevertheless, the theological foundation for both religions obviously share a common source. And in a world hostile to any notion of Judeo-Christian truth, an alliance remains an indispensable witness to the God of the Bible by standing opposed, locked arm in arm, against the forces of evil that threaten our world. It is in this spirit that I submit this book, hopeful that an authentic witness of what the Scripture truly says, will sanctify life and bring new light into the world.

---

[354] Cohen, op. cit., p. lii. Citing Sifré Deut. 49:85a.

APPENDIX 5:
THE PRESERVATION OF THE BIBLICAL TEXT

"He who would read the New Testament must know Koine;
but he who would understand the New Testament
must know the Septuagint."

– Sidney Jellicoe[355]

Inspiration and Preservation of the Text – How So?

THE MOST ESSENTIAL QUESTIONS WE MUST ADDRESS IF WE ARE TO BELIEVE THAT GOD VOUCHSAFED HIS WORD TO THE CHURCH THROUGH THE GREEK SEPTUAGINT, ARE these: "DID He inspire *this translation of His Word* as well as the Hebrew autographs?" Or, "Were the words from the Septuagint simply part of the process of God's promise to preserve the text?" And, "When those words were quoted and included in the New Testament, did this make only those specific words, God's words?" Or is our notion of what "the Word of God" means, too narrowly conceived? Is God's Word found in other places?

For Evangelicals, biblical inspiration means that God ensured the original writings in the canonical scriptures were without error, even though He worked through fallible human authors – yet, without violating their free will or overwhelming their human capacities. He saw to it that the original Hebrew writings were without defect. But did He also secure the Greek LXX such that it was free from error? Does it matter if the plenary (complete) inspiration of the Hebrew *alone* was inspired?

---

[355] Sidney Jellicoe, "Septuagint Studies in the Current Century," *Journal of Biblical Literature 88* (1969): p. 199.

The doctrine of the preservation of the text means that God's Word is preserved for us, through the ages, so that every generation can enjoy the same privilege – God's revelation to us. We read: "*The words of the Lord are pure words: as silver tried in a furnace of earth, purified seven times. Thou shalt keep them, O LORD, thou shalt preserve them from this generation forever*" (Psalm 12:6-7).

The inspiration of the text has often been mischaracterized as God superintending the writing of the biblical author, working in a stream of words, without revisions, edits, or proofing. No secretary could have been involved who might have inserted a phrase or corrected a misspelling. Neither could the work be set aside for a period and then taken up again…or, so it seemed. However, this "all at once" inspiration stands only one stop short of dictation. It is akin to "automatic writing" in the world of the paranormal. It seems much too magical to be believable – and not at all in keeping with the notion that God worked through human authors using the best of their rational faculties.

As it pertains to the *preservation* of the text, the common conception presumes that no mistakes of any kind could creep into biblical words at any point in history. *The words must be as precise as they were when first written.* However, while this might seem like the perfect way to keep the Word of God pure, obviously, this idea is unrealistic and improbable.

And yet, the idea that God inspired the King James Version of the Bible in English in 1611, such that it had no errors, is how an ill-informed fundamentalist notion of inspiration works. Likewise, for the theologically undereducated, the *preservation of the text* means that no errors will infiltrate the text – ever. Therefore, an "inspired" KJV would seemingly circumvent *both* opportunities for mistakes to contaminate the pure Word of God. With a perfect KJV – inspired in the autographs by the Holy Spirit

368

and safeguarded from careless transmission through the ages as has become resident within the KJV, we can be assured that God has preserved his Word perfectly – in English at least. If correct, we should presume God is an Englishman.[356] We should surely pity the non-Anglo-Saxon world. God speaks to imperfectly.

Of course, as we reviewed at the outset of this study, the KJV has been revised numerous times, as has the *Received Text* New Testament of Erasmus, as has the Hebrew Old Testament both before and after the work of the Masoretes. And, it is admitted, whatever benefits the LXX has, inerrancy isn't one of them. But does this mean some manner of God's preserving work failed? The Orthodox Church claims the LXX is inerrant through *the on-going ministration of the Church*. This is an exciting notion of which I am predisposed to learn more about, but I must leave it to the Orthodox Church to advance this claim.

Obviously, it is incoherent to adopt a hermeneutic of "KJV only." And yet, can we believe that while God did inspire the autographs without error, He nonetheless preserved the text from generation to generation even though shortcomings (errors and omissions) found their way into His Word? If so, how?

We will consider in this chapter that the inspiration of God and the preservation of His Word are concepts that must be expanded beyond the simple-minded conceptions of what they usually mean. There is more to it than we know. The Septuagint and its contribution to God's revelation make this clear. For the "secret sauce" as I might casually term it, is the all-encompassing reality of the *providence of God*. Indeed, I believe it is this doctrine,

---

[356] R.F. Delderfield wrote an historical novel with this title in 1970. Published by Sourcebooks Landmark. There is a reference to this absurd notion in the comedic Gilbert and Sullivan opera, *HMS Pinafore.* There are several hundred nations that might object to this assertion. The French would be chief among them.

working alongside the principles of inspiration and preservation, that has given us the Bible. God's Word, as He defines it (not necessarily as we would define it), continues to be preserved through our Scripture. The full depth of how we should conceptualize this truth is beyond the scope of this small paper. However, our modest goal is to discuss that of which we can rest assured: *The providence of God working in and through the processes of both inspiration and preservation cause the LORD to reveal Himself to His people.*

Jeremy Sexton and Henry B. Smith Jr., in the article referenced earlier in this book, "Primeval Chronology Restored: Revisiting the Genealogies of Genesis 5 and 11," surface this very same question and make several key points that help supply a useful context for the dialogue on preservation. The specific quote below brings this out as it pertains to the LXX chronology:

> While we maintain that the MT is generally reliable, the doctrine of preservation does not demand that only the MT preserves the OT. Scripture contains many promises that God will preserve His Word, but it does not specify exactly how He will do so. God does not promise to preserve the Scriptures in only one textual tradition. Bible-believing Christians are at liberty to consider the compelling text-critical arguments for the numbers in LXX Genesis 5 and 11.[357]

The issue for Evangelicals which seems to allude us is how God preserves the text. Does He invoke an invisible work of the Holy Spirit to influence the minds of men? In affirming the *inspiration* of the original autographs of the authors, we believe that the answer is "Yes." 2 Timothy 3:16 states, *"All Scripture is breathed out by God and profitable for teaching, for reproof, for correction, and for*

---

[357] Sexton, Jeremy, and Smith, Henry B. Jr., "Primeval Chronology Restored: Revising the Genealogies of Genesis 5 and 11." *Bible and Spade* 29.2 (2016).

training in righteousness." This process isn't like occultic auto-matic writing (aka a "stream of unconsciousness"). There are no reputable Evangelical scholars who argue God dictated either the Old or New Testament.[358] Visions and dreams – Yes. But dictation – No. How inspiration occurs is a mystery unto itself.

Providence and the Preservation of the Text

Biblical inspiration has always been challenged to explain how divine and human interaction occurs in such a way that the words put on paper, reflect what God wants to be said without compromising the elements that influence all human writers (education, culture, understanding, insight, and preferences in word choices). The Evangelical viewpoint states this categori-cally. And it remains definite even if our perspective lacks pre-cision in its description. Humankind and the Divine come to-gether to compose Scripture in such a way that God's purpose has been served. He has revealed Himself and His will. Whether we are dealing with the initial inspiration of the bibli-cal author or the ongoing preservation of God's Word, the un-derlying assurance remains that what is said is what God wants to be said. *This means that inspiration and preservation demand the providence of God.* This providence – the oversight and control of what transpires – is too often underappreciated when it comes to biblical inspiration.

Benjamin Warfield, one of the most influential voices of bib-lical inspiration, had this to say about inspiration that under-scores God's providence which preserves His word:

---

[358] Interestingly, Orthodox Jews do believe in the dictation theory, at least as it pertains to the Pentateuch. I learned this from a personal conversation with Rabbi Daniel Lapin.

The Church, then, has held from the beginning that the Bible is the Word of God in such a sense that its words, though written by men and bearing indelibly impressed upon them the marks of their human origin, were written, nevertheless, under such an influence of the Holy Ghost as to be also the words of God, the adequate expression of His mind and will. It has always recognized that this conception of co-authorship implies that the Spirit's superintendence extends to the choice of the words by the human authors (verbal inspiration) and preserves its product from everything inconsistent with a divine authorship—thus securing, among other things, that entire truthfulness which is everywhere presupposed in and asserted for Scripture by the Biblical writers (inerrancy). Whatever minor variations may now and again have entered in to the mode of the statement, this has always been the core of the Church doctrine of inspiration.[359]

Commentators Grubbs and Drum explain, "While being primarily concerned with the Holy Spirit's work as 'co-author' of the text, Warfield connected the work of the Spirit *through inspiration with the human author's 'choice of words'* and the *preservation of those words.*"[360] [Emphasis mine]

While less emphatic about the 'God-breathed' nature of the Spirit's work, Theologian Wayne Grudem rests upon *the providence of God* as a cornerstone of His view on biblical inspiration:

In cases where the ordinary human personality and writing style of the author were prominently involved, as seems the case with the major part of Scripture, all that we are able to say is that

---

[359] Benjamin Breckinridge Warfield, *The Inspiration and Authority of the Bible* (ed. Samuel Craig). Philadelphia, PA: Presbyterian & Reformed, 1948, p. 420.

[360] Grubbs, Norris C., and Drum, Curtis Scott. "What Does Theology Have to Do with The Bible? A Call for The Expansion of The Doctrine of Inspiration." *Journal of the Evangelical Theological Society 53/1* (March 2010), p. 65-79.

God's providential oversight and direction of the life of each author was such that their personalities, their backgrounds and training, their abilities to evaluate events in the world around them, their access to historical data, their judgment with regard to the accuracy of information, and their individual circumstances when they wrote, were all exactly what God wanted them to be, so that when they actually came to the point of putting pen to paper, the words were fully their own words but also fully the words that God wanted them to write, words that God would also claim as his own.[361] [Emphasis mine]

When discussing these issues with Dr. Michael S. Heiser over email, he recommended Grudem's explanation as similar to his own thinking. However, he indicated he would supplement Grudem's passage with this one from Dr. Stanley J. Grenz, emphasizing the work of the Holy Spirit: "That work of the Holy Spirit (which influences) the authors and compilers of Scripture to produce writings which adequately reflect what God desired to communicate to us."[362] I entirely agree.

The Chicago Statement on Inerrancy

When stalwart Evangelical leaders gathered together several decades ago to arrive at a consensus concerning what could be affirmed about inspiration and preservation (and implicitly about the providence of God), they concluded with a substantive statement on the inerrancy of the Bible. Several official articles or assertions resulted. Looking at four of these articles from this statement of faith, we see inerrancy is fully averred:

---

[361] Grudem, Wayne. *Systematic Theology*, Grand Rapids, MI: Zondervan. 1995. p. 81.

[362] Grenz, Stanley J. *Theology for the Community of God*, Vancouver, B.C.: Regent College Publishing, published jointly with Eerdmans, 2000, p. 498.

- **Article VII** – We affirm that inspiration was the work in which God by His Spirit, through human writers, gave us His Word. The origin of Scripture is divine. *The mode of divine inspiration remains largely a mystery to us.* We deny that inspiration can be reduced to human insight, or to heightened states of consciousness of any kind.

- **Article VIII** – We affirm that God in His Work of inspiration utilized the distinctive personalities and literary styles of the writers whom He had chosen and prepared. We deny that God, in causing these writers to use the very words that He chose, overrode their personalities.

- **Article IX** - We affirm that inspiration, though not conferring omniscience, guaranteed true and trustworthy utterance on all matters of which the Biblical authors were moved to speak and write. We deny that the finitude or fallenness of these writers, by necessity or otherwise, introduced distortion or falsehood into God's Word.

- **Article X** – We affirm that inspiration, strictly speaking, applies only to the autographic text of Scripture, **which in the providence of God** can be ascertained from available manuscripts with great accuracy. We further affirm that copies and translations of Scripture are the Word of God to the extent that they faithfully represent the original. We deny that any essential element of the Christian faith is affected by the absence of the autographs. We further deny that this absence renders the assertion of Biblical inerrancy invalid or irrelevant.[363] [Emphasis mine]

Indeed, Evangelicals argue *that the mind of God and the mind of man collaborated to produce the Word of God.* The incarnation of the Logos (the Word) in Jesus Christ provides the perfect picture and biblical precedent. The manifestation of God in Christ, aka the incarnation, as hammered out in the *Chalcedonian Creed*

---

[363] International Conference on Biblical Inerrancy, "The Chicago Statement on Biblical Inerrancy," in *Inerrancy* (ed. Norman Geisler). Grand Rapids, MI: Zondervan, 1979, p. 494.

374

in 451 A.D.,[364] affirmed this foundational truth of the Church, that the human nature and divine nature were both in Jesus Christ, yet were not "co-mingled" or combined, but remained separate and distinct while fully present in one person. They were distinct but united in such a way that Jesus Christ was an "integrated" personality (as they might say in psycho-analysis) but was both truly human and truly divine. This is known as an *antinomy*,[365] a mystery of the Christian faith.

All Evangelicals are persuaded that God *inspired the work of composition* when the Bible was first penned. But seldom are Evangelicals sure that God also works through human agents to preserve His word. But He does. He employs the amazing detective work of textual critics as a means to this end. The providence of God usually *uses textual criticism to preserve the text* with discoveries of new texts or fragments that may provide new "readings" to help us better understand and appreciate what the original author said. God does not do this all at once. It is an ongoing process. The preservation of the text, like the inspiration of the text, is a "mutual project" of God working providentially through the agency of men. Just as composition and investigation are different processes, God's efforts differ in how these outcomes are realized. But this doesn't mean that God is any less involved, providentially, in making them both come to pass. This does not imply that inspiration and

---

[364] "This creed was adopted at the Fourth Ecumenical Council, held at Chalcedon, located in what is now Turkey, in 451, as a response to certain heretical views concerning the nature of Christ. It established the orthodox view that Christ has two natures (human and divine) that are unified in one person." See https://carm.org/christianity/creeds-and-confessions/chalcedonian-creed-451-ad. Few know that the splintering of the Church began soon after this council meeting.

[365] "A contradiction between two beliefs or conclusions that are in themselves reasonable; a paradox." *Oxford Dictionary Online.*

preservation are precisely alike. Likewise, we can readily conclude how the ongoing research of the Septuagint's text helps us purify the Bible, to return to us the original autographs.

Dr. Heiser also pointed me to the article by Grubbs and Drum quoted earlier, setting forth the case that the current conceptualization of inspiration (and preservation as well, I believe), needs a more expansive understanding than what evangelical scholars have been willing to grant during the past century. Citing the Grubbs and Drum article to support my point that our view of inspiration and preservation is too narrow:

> One obvious need ... is for scholars to seek to account for the wide range of material represented in the Bible when describing inspiration. While one can properly describe elements of the Bible as having been written by one man with little or no revision or collection needed, clearly other portions of the Bible will not fit into this paradigm. A careful consideration of the complexity of the biblical texts will guard scholars from making statements about inspiration that simply are not true for all of the Bible.
>
> The most important implication ... is that the traditional definitions of inspiration need to be expanded in order to account for issues such as collection, revision, and multiple authorship. While the traditional understandings of inspiration with their emphasis on the authors are helpful and theologically correct, the various genres and content of the biblical text require a broader view of this important issue. Perhaps a larger stress on the process rather than just the writer would provide an avenue for going forward.[366]

And I would add, scholars should calibrate the place of the Septuagint in supporting the preservation of the biblical text.

---

[366] Grubbs, Norris C., and Drum, Curtis Scott, op. cit.

We delve into several examples next that should make this requirement plain to the reader.

Does the LXX Ever Fill in the Gaps Left by the MT?

Timothy E. Miller in his article "An Evangelical Apology for the Septuagint" (which I highly recommend for those wishing to dive deeper into this subject) regarding the LXX states, "For evangelicals, *the textual-critical implications* are perhaps most significant." [Emphasis mine] Indeed, since the LXX reflects the Hebrew as it stood over 2,500 years ago, why can't it help us understand what the original Hebrew communicated? Clearly, it can.

Miller believes Evangelicals worry about the LXX because of their concerns regarding the inspiration of scripture. Still, he contends there is no conflict between holding the LXX in high regard as God inspired, just as with the MT. [367] In fact, having the LXX as a second voice to the MT is invaluable. Miller explains:

> This question is even more difficult considering the differences between the MT and the LXX. While there are some inconsequential differences (e.g., the order of the books), there are also more significant differences. The Jeremiah text of the LXX is an eighth shorter than its MT counterpart, while Job is a sixth shorter in the LXX. Apocryphal additions provide Esther with 103 extra verses in the LXX, while providing multiple chapters of additional material to Daniel (The History of Susanna, Bel and the Dragon, and the Song of the Three Children). *Samuel and Kings are so different from the MT that some scholars believe they are built on an earlier, and perhaps better text.* These differences understandably challenge evangelical interpreters for whom the Scripture is the final rule for faith and practice.[368] [Emphasis mine]

---

[367] Miller, Timothy E. "An Evangelical Apology for the Septuagint," *Detroit Baptist Seminary Journal, DBSJ 22* (2017), p.40-41.

[368] Ibid., p. 41.

An excellent example of how the LXX can "fill in some gaps" existing today in the MT, is found in Robert Charles Hill's translation of *St. John Chrysostom's Commentary on the Psalms, Vol. 2*:

> Though our (MT) text has one verse (13) missing, which the LXX supplies, (it is) an inclusion confirmed by the Hebrew manuscripts discovered at the Dead Sea." (DSS) This is the verse occurring in the LXX and a Hebrew MS (manuscript) found at Qumran; it is not in the Masoretic Hebrew text of this alphabetic psalm at the point where we would expect a verse beginning with the Letter *nun*.[369]

This Psalm is an "acrostic" – each verse is to begin with a letter from the Hebrew alphabet in the proper sequence. One verse that should begin with the Hebrew letter "nun" isn't included in the MT, but it is in the LXX. Without the LXX supplementing what was missing in the MT, the text would be incomplete. So, I must ask two rhetorical questions: "Isn't this a perfect example of the preservation of the text? Isn't the fact we have both handy a God-given provision?"[370]

Yet another fine example is presented by Miller.[371]

> When asked what the LXX can provide for evangelicals today, many would primarily recognize its potential for textual criticism of the MT. This use is appropriate in light of three factors. First, the Hebrew text was not fixed until early in the Christian era [i.e., at Jamnia]. Thus, the LXX, which was translated centuries before, provides some level of evidence for the Hebrew text used by the

---

[369] Hill, Robert Charles. *Translation of St. John Chrysostom's Commentary on the Psalms, Vol. 2*, Brookline, MA: Holy Cross Orthodox Press, 1998, p. 343-344.

[370] I might add, isn't it an example the MT isn't inerrant as we have it today?"

[371] Miller argues that the Church *shouldn't* reverse course and prefer the LXX over the MT, but the LXX should still play a vital role in textual criticism and enable us to retrieve what has been lost in the Masoretic Text.

translators. [Two different versions widely separated by distance and great lengths of time, which are almost identical, prove each other to be generally valid.] Indeed, Gentry reminds us that "the Septuagint remains in many cases the earliest witness to the text of the OT and therefore of immense significance and value."[372] *Second, the manuscripts discovered in the Dead Sea region verify that some early Hebrew texts match the renderings in the LXX better than the MT* (though many of the Hebrew manuscripts align with the MT).[373] [Emphasis and comments mine]

Miller continues:

Third, there are readings in the LXX that appear superior to the renderings in the MT. Only two examples of the superiority of a LXX reading over the MT reading will be examined because of the limitation of space. First, in 2 Samuel 6:5 the MT indicates that the musicians were playing with "fir trees," but the LXX reads "tuned instruments." The Holman Christian Standard Bible (HCSB) renders this "fir-wood instruments," seeking to make the best of the Hebrew. But since the reading of the MT can be explained by metathesis (switching of letters) in the original Hebrew, it is preferable to see this as a case where the LXX preserves the original text.[374]

A second example derives from Genesis 4:8, where the MT reading is preserved in the text of the ESV, "Cain spoke to Abel his brother. And when they were in the field..." In a footnote, the ESV indicates that the Septuagint and Samaritan Pentateuch read "Cain spoke to Abel his brother, 'Let us go out to the field.' And when they were in the field..." While the MT reading is possible,

---

[372] Gentry, Peter J. "Septuagint and the Text of the Old Testament," *Bulletin for Biblical Research 16.2* (2006), p. 193-194. Cited by Miller, op. cit., p. 46.

[373] Harrison, Everett Falconer. "The Importance of the Septuagint for Biblical Studies [Part 1]," *Bibliotheca Sacra 112*, October 1955. p. 352. Cited by Miller, op. cit., p. 46.

[374] Peters, Melvin K. H. "Why Study the Septuagint?" *The Biblical Archaeologist, Vol. 49*, No. 3, September 1986, p. 179. Cited by Miller, op. cit., p. 46.

the LXX reading is preferable not only because the text flows more naturally, but also because a corruption of the Hebrew text is easily explainable as a haplographic error, where an early copier accidently skipped over that series of words because the Hebrew word for *field* is repeated.[375] [Comments mine]

Did the LXX "Correct" a MT Misunderstanding?

Dr. Heiser points out another flaw in the MT that the LXX explains. In a blog for Logos Bible Software, Heiser provides a fascinating example of how the LXX provides a "fix" for a MT "mix-up" in a passage found at Deuteronomy 33:1-2.

Hebrew Text from Masoretic	Greek Text from Septuagint
¹This is the blessing with which Moses, the man of God, blessed the Israelites before his death.	¹This is the blessing with which Moses, the man of God, blessed the Israelites before his death.
² He said: Yahweh came from Sinai, and He shone upon them from Seir. He appeared in radiance from Mount Paran, and **approached from Ribeboth-Kodesh, from his right lightning flashed at them.**	² He said: The LORD came from Sinai, and He shone to us from Seir; He made haste from Mount Paran **with ten thousands of Kadesh, his angels with him**.
³ Indeed, **he loved the people, all his holy ones at your hand**. And they followed at your feet; he bears your words,	³ And **He had pity on his people, and all the holy ones were under your hands; and they were under you**; and he received his words,
⁴ the law which Moses commanded us, an inheritance for the assembly of Jacob.	⁴ the law which Moses charged us, an inheritance to the assemblies of Jacob.

Table 1 - Deuteronomy 33:1-2, LXX and MT Comparison

---

[375] Miller, op. cit., p. 46.

Says Heiser, "I thought it might be helpful to provide a practical example where the Septuagint explains what *seems* to be a New Testament theological blunder. I'm betting most of us are interested in that sort of thing!"[376]

Heiser first provides a literal rendering of the Hebrew from the Masoretic Text (Heiser is, after all, a noted scholar in ancient Semitic languages) along with an English translation of the Septuagint (he once taught Greek in his spare time too). This comparison is presented in Table 1 above.

Dr. Heiser points out that whereas the "holy ones" in the MT appear to be talking about *the Israelite people*, the LXX seems to speak of them as *God's angels*. Verse three in the MT appears to be reinforcing "the people" with "all His holy ones at His hand" (they are the same, i.e., "the people are His holy ones at His hand"). However, the LXX comes across differently. Here there are people upon which the LORD had pity, and then, separately, there are the angels – His holy ones – both of which were with God (i.e., "He had pity on his people who were under (His) hands; *and* all the holy ones were under (Him)." In Verse 4 of the MT, there is only the assembly of Jacob (singular) while in verse 4 of the LXX, there are "assemblies" (plural). This seems to follow logically since, in the LXX's verse 2, there are ten thousand of Kadesh (God's angels) with the LORD. In this verse, *Kodesh* and *Kadesh* appear to be causing confusion. But who was confused? The Masoretes inscribing the MT? Or the Alexandrian scholars when translating the LXX? Which one's right? The Hebrew MT *provides a place name.* The Septuagint includes something of an *annotation when expressing the origin of the giving of the Law of God* (aka the *correct* meaning). Then, Heiser refers

---

[376] Heiser, Michael S. "Why Use the Septuagint?" *LogosTalk*. Retrieved from https://blog.logos.com/2007/12/why_use_the_septuagint/.

us to three passages in the New Testament that convey that the Mosaic Law was given by angels (*aggeloi* in the Greek). We are led to ask, "Did the New Testament misread the Hebrew MT? Or was it simply using the Greek? Were Stephen, Paul, and the writer to the Hebrews wrong when they conveyed to their audiences the law of Moses was delivered by angels?"

Read the following three passages while noting that these are supplied by the King James Version *whose New Testament conflicts with its Old Testament,* (i.e., the NT Greek Textus Receptus conflicting with the OT Hebrew Masoretic Text):

- Acts 7:52-53 – *Which of the prophets have not your fathers persecuted? And they have slain them which shewed before of the coming of the Just One; of whom ye have been now the betrayers and murderers: Who have received the law by the **disposition of angels** and have not kept it.*

- Hebrews 2:1-2a – *Therefore, we ought to give the more earnest heed to the things which we have heard, lest at any time we should let them slip. For if the **word spoken by angels** was steadfast...*

- Galatians 3:19 – *Wherefore then serveth the law? It was added because of transgressions, till the seed should come to whom the promise was made; and it **was ordained by angels** in the hand of a mediator.*

Heiser (I believe, rightly) concludes:

Simply put, if you stick to the traditional Masoretic Hebrew text for your Old Testament, there is no place that the New Testament writers could have drawn such an idea. The closest you come to that is in Psalm 68:17. While that verse has a multitude of angelic beings at Sinai, it says zilch about the Law. The point is that the New Testament references have provided fodder for biblical critics who want the New Testament to be guilty of either an outright error in thought, or just contriving a doctrinal point out of thin air. The Septuagint shows us that those perspectives are just simply incorrect. The New Testament writers weren't nitwits or dishonest. They were using the Septuagint.[377]

Heiser, in this instance he cites, what is going on is more than supplying a missing verse or straightening out a mistranslation of the Hebrew. Here, the LXX's "translation" *appears to supply the doctrinally correct meaning of the passage in Deuteronomy 33:1-2* that was the position taken by Stephen and Paul and the New Testament. Consequently, *we can discover the LXX is contributing more than correcting a misspelling.* Something was being expressed in the LXX that was unclear in the MT, and this makes a difference in what we are told about how the Law of God was given to humankind. Could this "find" have been providential? And more broadly speaking, might this illustrate that God's preservation of scripture includes work performed *on its translation?* Was the LXX's clarification a providential occurrence? Wasn't this a case of God preserving the text?

St. Augustine is willing to go further than today's Evangelicals would allow. He argues that inspiration *could include the translation of the LXX as well as the original Hebrew.* The truth can be found *by considering both versions carefully.* Noting the similarities and the differences might make the truth plain. That is, God's Word may be discovered in reconciling the MT with the LXX. From his classic work, *The City of God* (18.43.1), Augustine offered these surprising, but important thoughts:

> If, then, as it behooves us, we behold nothing else in these Scriptures than what the Spirit of God has spoken through men, if anything is in the Hebrew copies and is not in the version of

---

[377] Ibid.

the Seventy, the Spirit of God did not choose to say it through them, but only through the prophets. But whatever is in the Septuagint and not in the Hebrew copies, the same Spirit chose rather to say through the latter, thus showing that both were prophets. For in that manner He spoke as He chose, some things through Isaiah, some through Jeremiah, some through several prophets, or else the same thing through this prophet and through that. Further, whatever is found in both editions, that one and the same Spirit willed to say through both, but so as that the former preceded in prophesying, and the latter followed in prophetically interpreting them; because, as the one Spirit of peace was in the former when they spoke true and concordant words, so the selfsame one Spirit hath appeared in the latter, when, without mutual conference they yet interpreted all things as if with one mouth.

For Augustine, the LXX was more than a translation. It was a divinely inspired *interpretation* of what the original meant. No doubt when translating a text, interpreting it is part of the deal. In this case, God's work incorporates interpretation too.

Unifying Providence, Inspiration, and Preservation

Yet, another bit of assistance Dr. Heiser gave me at my request was identifying a dissertation that might address the specific issue of the inspiration of the Bible, its preservation, and *the role the providence of God plays in its preservation*. In listening to a podcast of his on the topic, it became clear to me that Heiser had a more nuanced understanding of these matters than did I (now, that is not really so surprising). Subsequently, I asked him if he had anything he might have written to expand upon his oral viewpoint that captured his position on the preservation of the text. Several article references in this appendix came from that request, as well as the following dissertation completed by R.J.J. Frost, *The Doctrine of Scripture and the Providence of God*. Dr.

Heiser recommended I look at it (he was not endorsing it but thought it might be helpful for me to examine). Frost's dissertation is not publicly available to my knowledge. Nonetheless, it is exceptional. And I did read the entire work by Frost. As one might suppose from reading a good dissertation, the examination of the subject far exceeded expectations and provided much useful scholarship.

To close out this subject, it seems appropriate to share just a taste of his exceptional research and analysis on the topic. His study on how the providence of God molds and shapes a prophet of God supplies a perfect illustration (an analog to be more specific) on the way that the LORD works in revealing His Word to us. I quote an extended portion of his conclusion:

> Providence in the service of special revelation was scrutinized [in the dissertation] more closely by probing the providential preparation of Moses to speak the Word of God. We began with Exodus 1 and 2, where the theme of the preserving and guiding hand of God over the early life of the prophet is established. It comes to something of a climax at Moses' commissioning, where God promises His ongoing formative presence and guidance (Deut 4:10-16). The providence of God proves effective, and at the end of his life Moses is eulogized as a prophet (Deut 34:10). Before he dies, he leaves Israel with the institution of prophecy which carries in its constitution the notion of providential preparation (Deut 18:15). Jesus Himself, as the antitype to Moses, enjoyed the same providential preparation (Acts 3.22-26). Reading Exodus 1 and 2 as establishing the pattern of providence over prophecy finds further confirmation in Stephen's speech (Acts 7:17-40). Luke shows how providence governed all three periods of Moses' life and prophetic ministry. The writer to the Hebrew shows the same from the human perspective. He encourages the reader to understand the life and ministry of Moses as an

expression of faith in the providence of God (Heb. 11:23-28, 39-40). The pattern established in Moses is extended to the line of prophets from Samuel to Jesus (1 Sam 2:21, 26; 3:19; Luke 1:80; 2:40, 52; Matt 1-2). Tracing the theme of providential preparation for the ministry of the prophetic word compelled the conclusion that providence serves special revelation.

It remained to test the idea that providence serves scripture itself. For that we turned to four passages. In the account of Josiah in 1 and 2 Kings Josiah's reform program and the fulfilment of the prophecy against Jeroboam are both bound up in the discovery of the Book of the Law. These bare facts combine with the details of the account and invite the reader to ascribe the discovery and preservation of the Book not to chance, fate or human ingenuity, but to the ordering hand of providence over history. Similarly, in Jeremiah 36, when King Jehoiakim destroys the scroll, it is the providential hand of God that hides the prophet and preserves the written Word. Romans 15:4 was presented as an exemplar of the common New Testament idea that the Old Testament scriptures were intended by God for later generations. Since the intent is divine, wherever the idea appears it necessarily implies the providential preservation of the scriptures.

Finally, in Galatians 1:15-16, we revisited the theme of the providential preparation of the prophets. Here it applied to the apostle Paul, who was providentially ordained and prepared for a ministry of gospel proclamation that included the written Word. The weight of these examples was compounded by the fact that they followed examples of providence in the service of redemption and special revelation. The cumulative weight of the evidence brought us to conclude that providence also serves scripture.[378]

---

[378] Frost, RJJ. *The Doctrine of Scripture and the Providence of God.* Dissertation. October 2014, p. 150-151.

Conclusion

As the breadth of the study presented in *Rebooting the Bible – Part 1* illustrates, God demonstrates His sovereign abilities to work in ways beyond what we would anticipate. Moses, the other prophets of God, and the Apostles of Christ conveyed the Word of the LORD in no small part due to how He had prepared them. The light of God's Word shone through them and their words which had become His words. Indeed, this light was refracted through the episodes, the trials, and the triumphs of His emissaries. *"Long ago, at many times and in many ways, God spoke to our fathers by the prophets"* (Hebrews 1:1). The method by which He spoke and the way he prepared these vessels which would voice His revelation, often outmaneuver our sacrosanct preconceptions. "Your God is too small," as J.B. Phillips once advised. And so it is with the Septuagint.

Our misconceptions and our ignorance have kept us from discovering missing pieces of the picture. The Septuagint is a crucial provision God has made for us in these last days to purify the text and, if you will, *reboot the Bible*. There are some big problems in several selections of the Old Testament that we must reconsider. Remember, I am not saying the LXX should necessarily replace the MT-based versions of the Bible. However, there are more than a few Theologians today who are arguing for its "reinstatement."[379] But undoubtedly it should occupy a sacred place in the life of the Church and one of the more powerful text-critical tools for the Bible scholar. For we seek the

---

[379] Mogens Müller, Professor of NT at the University of Copenhagen is one such example. W. Edward Glenny asserts, "For these reasons Müller believes it was a fatal mistake for the Church to put aside the LXX in favor of the Hebrew-Aramaic text." Müller, *The First Bible of the Church*, p. 116. Cited by Glenny, W. Edward, "The Septuagint and Biblical Theology." *Themelios* 41.2 (2016): p. 263-278.

text that represents as closely as possible what was revealed by God to the writer when his composition was originally written. And by the way, I do take heart that many scholars who do text-critical work, argue that for all practical purposes, *what we have is what they wrote.* The surfeit of copies (over 6,000 manuscripts and still counting), along with some of the best minds in Christendom, have given us this gift.

What we have learned about the Bible and its history is unexpected for most Christians. Perhaps we have allowed the existence of the LXX to frighten us up to now, worrying that it might cloud the doctrine of inspiration. Indeed, there is no shortage of Bible teachers that say the Septuagint is a corrupted understanding of God's Word, which should only be provided to humanity through the Hebrew language. Or maybe, we were just set in our ways. But what we have learned is that its history and its texts reaffirm our faith and God's methods and mannerisms in presenting Himself to us. Evangelicals have allowed this treasure to be suppressed for 15 centuries. It is time to correct this lapse on our parts. We've neglected the Bible of the early Church, the Bible that served it for half a millennium, and which supplied the Old Testament cherished by the first Christians and quoted almost exclusively by New Testament authors. It is time we shine a light on the LXX again, to enliven our study of the Bible and to learn lessons it may yet teach us about the truth God *"has delivered once and for all to the Saints"* (Jude 1:3). There are holes in our understanding of the Bible that the Septuagint can fill in. Let us embrace this opportunity to learn new things about the history of our scriptures, our faith, and our Savior, Jesus Christ.

My final word of advice: Get a Septuagint! There are still more treasures embedded in its pages to be uncovered which can help us "set the record straight." It's a team effort. Engage!

DRAFT OUTLINE FOR PART 2 OF
Rebooting the Bible

(Subject to change as research continues).

Chapter Eight:
PELEG, THE DIVIDING OF NATIONS, & THE ASSIGNMENT OF LESSER ELOHIM

Who Was Peleg?

The Dividing on the Nations: What Are the Alternatives for Its Meaning?

The Book of Enoch: Worthy Pseudepigrapha

The Divine Counsel and Its Place in the Economy of God

Assigning the Lesser Elohim to Rule Over the Nations

One Step Further Back: The Table of Nations

The Family of Man: Ham, Shem, and Japheth

A Leap to Pre-History: Egypt, Assyria, and Babylon

Chapter Nine:
NIMROD, THE TOWER OF BABEL, AND PREHISTORY IN MESOPOTAMIA

Nimrod: The First King in the Post-Diluvian World?

Mesopotamian Pre-History: Now it All Fits

Error #1: Alexander Hislop and *The Two Babylons*

Error #2: The Book of Jasher

Error #3: The Book of Jubilees

Timeline Charts: Contrasting MT & LXX Timelines

The Christian Speculation on Nimrod

Goodgame: The Second Coming of the Antichrist

Chapter Ten:
NOAH'S FLOOD: DISCLOSING THE HIDDEN SECRETS OF HUMANITY

The Historicity of the Flood

The Great Debate: Global vs. Regional Flood

Who Was Noah and Why Should We Care?

Angelic Infiltration of Humanity: The Nephilim

Michael Heiser: *Reversing Hermon*

Salvation from Sin and the Effects of Sin

One Great Flood: One Giant Leap for Mankind

Chapter Eleven:
THE CREATION: HUMANITY'S FALL & THE FUTURE RESTORATION OF EDEN

Breaking the Link Between Ussher's Timeline & The Creation of Adam, Eve, and the World

The Young Earth and the Six Days of Creation

Intelligent Design vs. Creationism

The Gap Theory: Is It Still Viable?

The Main Points of the Drama in the Garden

Eschatology and the Future Eden

The Future Glorification of Humanity

Chapter Twelve:
ALTERNATE HISTORY: COULD THERE BE ANOTHER STORY BEFORE EDEN?

Academic Reshuffling and Humanity's Beginning

Were There "High Civilisations" Before Genesis 1:2?

Alternate History and the Great Stone Monuments

Cataclysm in 10,800 B.C.: Prep for the Next Aeon?

David Flynn and the Secret History of Mars

A Challenge for the Next Generation of Apologists

Casting Call: Becoming Part of the Greatest Drama

BIBLIOGRAPHY

Abegg, Martin, Flint, Peter, Ulrich, Eugene. *The Dead Sea Scrolls Bible*. New York: Harper One, 1999.

Aharoni,Y. *Israel Exploration Journal, 11* (1961), pp.22-23.

Anstey, M. *The Romance of Bible Chronology: An Exposition of the Meaning, and a Demonstration of the Truth, of Every Chronological Statement Contained in the Hebrew Text of the Old Testament.* London, United Kingdom: Marshall Bros., 1913.

Archaeology Study Bible, English Standard Version, Wheaton, IL: Crossway, 2017.

Associates for Biblical Research. "The duration of the Israelite sojourn in Egypt." Retrieved from http://www.biblearchaeology.org/post/ 2012/01/05/The-Duration-of-the-Israelite-Sojourn-In-Egypt.aspx#Article.

Augustine, *City of God*, 12:11, translated by Henry Bettenson, p. 484 – 485, Penguin Classics © 1972.

Baumgarten, J.M. "The Unwritten Law in the Pre-Rabbinic Period," *JSJ, Vol.III*, Oct. 1972, p. 15.

Bauer, Susan Wise. *The History of the Ancient World: From the Earliest Accounts to the Fall of Rome.* New York: W.W. Norton, 2007.

Baxter, Sidlow. *Explore the Book, Lesson 35*, Grand Rapids, Michigan: Zondervan, 1986, p. 120-121.

Beckwith, R.T. *Calendar and Chronology, Jewish and Christian: Biblical, Intertestamental and Patristic Studies.* Leiden, The Netherlands: Brill, 1996.

Berkovits, Eliezer. *Not in Heaven: The Nature and Function of Halakha*, Ktav Publishing Co., NY, 1983.

Black, Jeremy, & Green, Anthony. *Gods, Demons, and Symbols of Ancient Mesopotamia: An Illustrated Dictionary.* Austin, TX: University of Texas Press, 1992.

Boatner, Col. Mark M. "The American Revolution: Some Myths, Moot Points & Misconceptions," *American History Illustrated, Vol. III*, #4, July 1968, P. 20.

Breasted, James Henry. *A History of Egypt from the Earliest Times to the Persian Conquest*, 1905, Calathus Publishing. Kindle Edition.

Brenton, Lancelot, *The Septuagint Version of the Old Testament, according to the Vatican Text, Translated into English.* London: Samuel Bagster, 1844.

Brenton, Sir Lancelot Charles Lee, "An Historical Account of the Septuagint Version," from *The Septuagint Version of the Old Testament, according to the Vatican Text*, Translated into English. London: Samuel Bagster, 1844.

Bruce, F.F. *The Books and the Parchment*, Fleming H. Revell Co. 1984.

Carter, Robert. "Biblical human population growth model." Creation.com. Retrieved https://creation.com/biblical-human-population-growth-model, 2018.

Carter, Robert. Personal correspondence to this author. September 12, 2018.

Charles, R.H. The Book of Jubilees. CreateSpace Independent Publishing Platform, 2018.

Champollion. Jean-Francois. *Précis du système hiéroglyphique des anciens Égyptiens. French version. Elibron Classics,* Original, Paris, 1828. Republished by Adamant Media Corporation, 2006.

Church, J.R. *Daniel Reveals the Bloodline of the Antichrist.* Oklahoma City, OK: Prophecy Publications, 2010.

Clement of Alexandria, *The Stromata or Miscellanies, 6:16, The Ante-Nicene Fathers, vol. 2,* p. 512 – 513. T&T Clark Eerdmans © Reprinted March 1994.

Cohen, Shay J.D., "The Significance of Yavneh: Pharisees, Rabbis, and the End of Jewish Sectarianism," *Hebrew Union College Annual 55,* 1984, p. 40.

Collins, Andrew. *From the Ashes of Angels: The Forbidden Legacy of a Fallen Race.* Greenwich Village: Bear Company, 1997.

Colavito, Jason. *Faking History: Essays on Aliens, Atlantis, Monsters, and More.* Albany, NY: JasonColavito.com Books, 2013.

Combs, Bill. "Dean Burgon and the Revised Version" Retrieved from http://www.dbts.edu/2012/03/21/dean-burgon-and-the-revised-version/

Cornford, A.M. *Genesis and the Rahab Conspiracy.* UK: Xlibris Corporation, 2012.

Colavito, Jason. *The Cult of Alien Gods: H.P. Lovecraft and Extraterrestrial Pop Culture.* Prometheus Books, 2005.

Cremo, Michael A. and Thompson, Richard L. *The Hidden History of the Human Race.* Bhaktivedanta Book Publishing, 1999.

Craige, Peter C. *Ugarit and The Old Testament.* Grand Rapids, MI: Wm. B. Eerdman's Publishing Co., 1983.

393

Creation Wiki, "Hyksos." Retrieved from http://creation-wiki.org/Hyksos.

David E. Aune, "Orthodoxy in First Century Judaism? A Response to N. J. McEleny," *JSJ, Vol VII,* No. 1, June 1976, p. 3.

Dewhurst, Richard J. *The Ancient Giants Who Ruled America: The Missing Skeletons and the Great Smithsonian Cover-Up.* Toronto: Bear & Company, 2013.

de Santillana, Giorgio, & von Dechend, Hertha. *Hamlet's Mill: An Essay Investigating the Origins of Human Knowledge and Its Transmission Through Myth.* Jaffrey, NH: David R. Godine Publishing, 1969.

Deffenbaugh, Bob. "The Origins of Jesus Christ." Bible.org. Retrieved from https://bible.org/seriespage/origins-jesus-christ-matthew-11-25.

Dhont, Marieke. "Towards a Comprehensive Explanation for the Stylistic Diversity of the Septuagint Corpus." See https://www.academia.edu/ 36258376/ Towards_a_Comprehensive_Explanation_for_the_Stylistic_Diversity_of_the_Septuagint_Corpus.

Dill, Steven. *In the Beginnings, The Story of the Original Earth, Its Destruction, and Its Restoration.* Maitland, FL: Xulon, 2010.

Dio's Rome, Volume 5, Book 68, para. 32.

Donnelly, Ignatius. Atlantis: *The Antediluvian World.* New York: Dover Publications, Inc. 1976. Originally Published by Harper Brothers, 1882.

Donin, Hayim Halevy. *To Be a Jew.* New York: Basic Books, 1991.

Duff-Forbes, Lawrence. The Vineyard, July 1991.

Dyer, Charles. *Future Babylon: The Biblical Arguments for Rebuilding Babylon*. Taos, NM; Dispensational Publishing House, Inc. 2017.

Edersheim, Alfred. *Bible History: Old Testament. Seven Volumes*. Published: 1876-1887.

Elwell, Douglas. *The Riddle of the Sphinx*. Mysterious World Press, 1998.

Elman, Yaakov. "R. Zadok HaKohen on the History of Halakha," *Tradition: A Journal of Orthodox Jewish Thoughts, Vol. 21, No. 4*, p. 15.

Eusebius, *Chronicon Pascale*, cited in Yadin, op. cit., p. 258.

F.H.A. Scrivener, *Six Lectures on the Text of the New Testament and the Ancient Manuscripts Which Contain It: Chiefly Addressed to Those Who Do Not Read Greek*. Cambridge, MA: Deighton, Bell, and Co., 1875.

Farrell, Joseph P. and de Hart, Scott D. *The Grid of the Gods: The Aftermath of the Cosmic War and the Physics of the Pyramid Peoples*. Kempton, IL: Adventures Unlimited, 2011.

Farrell, Joseph P. *The Cosmic War: Interplanetary Warfare, Modern Physics, and Ancient Texts*. Kempton, IL: Adventures Unlimited, 2007.

Farrell, Joseph P. *The Giza Death Star*, Kempton, IL: Adventures Unlimited Press, 2001.

Finkelstein, Louis. *Akiba: Scholar, Saint, and Martyr*. Atheneum, NY, 1978, p. 156. Originally published by Jason Aaronson Inc., 1936.

Foerster, Brien. *Aftershock: The Ancient Cataclysm That Erased Human History*. Self-published. 2016

Freeman, Henry. *Sumerians: A History from Beginning to End.* Hourly History Limited, 2016.

Freedman, D. N. "The Masoretic Text and the Qumran Scrolls: A Study in Orthography," Textus 2 (1962): 87-102, reprinted in QHBT, 196-211.

Freedman, Harry. *The Talmud: A Biography.* London: Bloomsbury Continuum, 2014.

Gabbatis, Josh. "Mystery of volcanic eruption that shaped the ancient Mediterranean solved using tree rings." (2018, August 22). Retrieved from https://www.msn.com/en-nz/news/world/mystery-of-volcanic-eruption-that-shaped-ancient-mediterranean-solved-using-tree-rings/ar-BBMiHUV.

"Generations in the Bible." GotQuestions. See https://www.gotquestions.org/generation-in-the-Bible.html. 2018.

Gentry, Peter J. "Septuagint and the Text of the Old Testament," *Bulletin for Biblical Research 16.2* (2006), p. 193-194.

Glenny, W. Edward. "The Septuagint and Biblical Theology." *Themelios 41.2* (2016), p. 263-78

Gilbert, Derek P. *The Great Inception: Satan's Psyops From Eden to Armageddon.* Crane, MO: Defender Publishing, 2017.

Ginzberg in *The Jewish Encyclopedia, Vol. I,* p. 305-306, citing Je. Shek. 5:1, 48c.

Ginzberg, *Encyclopedia Judaica, Vol. 2.* p. 489-490.

Godawa, Brian. *Psalm 82: The Divine Council of the Gods, the Judgment of the Watchers and the Inheritance of Nations.* Los Angeles, CA: Embedded Pictures Publishing, 2018.

396

Godawa, Brian. *When Giants Were Upon the Earth: The Watchers, the Nephilim, and the Biblical Cosmic War of the Seed*. Los Angeles: Embedded Pictures Publishing. 2014.

Goodspeed, George Stephen. *A History of the Babylonians and Assyrians*. Lecturable, 2013.

Goodgame, Peter. *The Second Coming of the Antichrist,* Crane, Mo: Defender Books. (2012)

Goodenow, Smith Bartlett, *Bible Chronology Carefully Unfolded*. New York: Fleming H. Revell, 1896.

Gordon, Cyrus H. "Almah in Isaiah 7:14," *The Journal of Bible & Religion, Vol. 21* (April 1953), p. 106. See https://jewsforjesus.org/ publications /issues/issues-v09-n01/almah-virgin-or-young-maiden/

Gray, Jonathan. *The Forbidden Secret: How to Survive What the Elite Have Planned for You*. Teach Services, 2011.

Gray, Jonathan. *Dead Men's Secrets - Tantalizing Hints of a Lost Super Race*. Teach Services, Inc., 2014.

Green, William H., "Primeval Chronology," *Bibliotheca Sacra, April 1890*, p. 285-303. Retrieved from http://www.genevaninstitute.org/syllabus/unit-two-theology-proper/lesson-5-the-decree-of-creation/primeval-chronology-by-dr-william-henry-green/.

Grenz, Stanley J. *Theology for the Community of God,* Vancouver, B.C.: Regent College Publishing, published jointly with Eerdmans, 2000, p. 498.

Gruber, Daniel. *Rabbi Akiba's Messiah: The Origins of Rabbinic Authority*. Elijah Publishing. Kindle Edition. 2012.

Hall, Henry R. *The Ancient History of the Near East*. First published, 1913 by Metheuen & Co. Ltd. Ballista Press, 2018.

Harrison, Everett Falconer. "The Importance of the Septuagint for Biblical Studies [Part 1]," *Bibliotheca Sacra 112*, October 1955. p. 352.

Hapgood, Charles H. *Maps of the Ancient Sea Kings*. Kempton, IL: Adventures Unlimited, 1997.

Hart, Will. *The Genesis Race: Our Extraterrestrial DNA and the True Origins of the Species*. Rochester, VT: Bear& Company, 2003.

Hales, William. 1830. *A New Analysis of Chronology and Geography, History and Prophecy. Vol. 1. Chronology and Geography*. London, United Kingdom: C.J.G. and F. Rivington.

Hall, Henry R. *The Ancient History of the Near East*, Ballista Press. Kindle Edition, 1912.

Hancock, Graham. *Magicians of the Gods*. New York: Thomas Dunne Books, 2015.

Hancock, Graham. *Fingerprints of the Gods*. Three Rivers Press, 1996.

Henry, Hugh, and Dyke, Daniel J. *God of the Gaps: Gaps in Biblical Genealogies Make It Impossible to Calculate the Date of Creation*. Second Edition. Mars Hill Center, 2016.

Heiser, Michael S. *The Unseen Realm*. Bellingham, WA: Lexham Press. 2015.

Heiser, Michael S. *Reversing Hermon: Enoch, The Watchers, & The Forgotten Mission of Jesus Christ*. Crane, MO: Defender Publishing, 2017.

Hislop, Alexander. *The Two Babylons: The Only Fully Complete 7th Edition*. London: Houlston and Wright. Originally Published, 1871.

Hippolytus, *The Extant Works and Fragments, On Daniel 2:4, The Ante-Nicene Fathers, vol. 5*, p.179, T &T Clark Eerdmans © Reprinted 1995.

Hodge, Brodie. *Tower of Babel: The Cultural History of Our Ancestors*. Green Forest, AR: Master Books, Division of New Leaf Publishing Group, Inc., 2013.

Hoffmeier, James K. "What is the Biblical Date for the Exodus?" *Journal of the Evangelical Theological Society 50 /2*, June 2007, p. 227-228.

Holden, Theodore A., and McLachlan, Troy D. *Cosmos in Collision: The Prehistory of Our Solar System and of Modern Man*. Theodore A. Holden (Publisher), 2013.

Horn, S.H. "The Old Testament Text in Antiquity," *Ministry*, (November 1987), p. 6.

Hornung, Eric, et al. *Ancient Egyptian Chronology – Handbook of Oriental Studies I. Vol. 83*, Leiden, 2006, p. 13.

Hugo Mantel, "The Causes of the Bar Kokhba Revolt," *JQR, #3-4*, Philadelphia, 1968, p. 278.

Hutchings, Noah. *The Great Pyramid*. Crane, MO: Defender Publishing, 2011.

Irenaeus, *Against Heresies, 5:23:2, from The Ante-Nicene Fathers, vol.1*, p.557, T&T Clark Eerdmans © Reprinted 1996.

Jewish History Blog. "Hyksos or Hebrews: The Middle Kingdom of Egypt." JewishHistory.Org. Retrieved from https://www.jewishhistory.org/hyksos-or-hebrews/

Jobes, K.H. & Silva, M. *Invitation to the Septuagint,* Baker Academic, 2000.

Jones, Floyd Nolen. *The Chronology of the Old Testament.* Green Forest, AR: Master Books, A Division of New Leaf Publishing Group, 1993.

Josephus, Flavius. *Against Apion 1.1.* Retrieved from http://penelope.uchicago.edu/josephus/apion-1.html.

Josephus, Flavius. *Complete Works and Historical Background. Annotated Classics.* Kindle Edition.

Judaism Despite Christianity, Edited by Eugen Rosenstock-Huessy, U. of Alabama Press, University, Alabama, 1969, p. 159.

Kaiser Jr., Walter C., ed. *Classical Evangelical Essays in Old Testament Interpretation.* Grand Rapids, MI: Baker, 1971.

Kauble, David. *Creation, Time, and the Coming Nephilim.* Self-published, 2013.

Knight, Christopher, and Butler, Alan. *Civilization One: The World is Not as You Thought It Was.* London: Watkins Publishing, 2005.

Knight, Christopher, and Butler, Alan. *Who Built the Moon?* London: Watkins Publishing, 2006.

Kramer, Samuel N. *Sumerian Mythology (Illustrated).* Originally Published 1944, Revised Edition.1961.

Kriwaczek, Paul. *Babylon: Mesopotamia and the Birth of Civilization.* New York: Thomas Dunne Books, 2012.

Langford, Jack W. *The Gap is Not a Theory!* Xlibris Corporation, 2011.

Lake, Michael. *The Sheeriyth Imperative: Empowering the Remnant to Overcome the Gates of Hell*. Crane, MO: Defender Publishing, 2016.

Lake, Michael. *The Shinar Directive: Preparing the Way for the Son of Perdition*. Crane, MO: Defender Publishing, 2011.

Longenecker, Richard N. *Biblical Exegesis in the Apostolic Period*. Eerdmans, Grand Rapids: 1975, p. 143.

Lynn, Heather. *Land of the Watcher*. Cleveland, OH: The Midnight Crescent Publishing Company, 2015.

Mahoney, Timothy. *Patterns of Evidence: The Exodus*. Thinking Man Media. Kindle Edition.

Maimonides, Moses. *Mishneh Torah*, (Yad Hazakah), Ed. Philip Birnbaum, Hebrew, New York, 1985, p. 327.

Matrix Disclosure. 2018. "THOTH (known as Enoch or Saurid): The builder of great pyramid?" See https://www.matrixdisclosure.com/thoth-enoch-saurid-great-pyramid-egypt/

McLachlan, Troy D. *The Saturn Death Cult*. Self-published. 2011.

McGuckin, John A. *The Westminster Handbook to Origen*, Louisville, KY: John Knox Press, 1978.

Mei, Armando. (2015, January 28). "36,400 BC: The historical time of the Zep Tepi theory." *Ancient Origins*. Retrieved from https://www.ancient-origins.net/ancient-places-africa/36400-bc-historical-time-zep-tepi-theory-002617.

Merrill, Steven C. *Nimrod: Darkness in the Cradle of Civilization*. Xulon Press, 2004.

Miller, Timothy E. "An Evangelical Apology for the Septuagint," *Detroit Baptist Seminary Journal, DBSJ* 22 (2017), p.40-41.

Minge, B., "'Short' sojourn comes up short," *Journal of Creation 21*(3), p. 62–64, 2007.

Moreland, James Porter, and Craig, William Lane. *Philosophical Foundations for a Christian Worldview*. Downers Grove, IL: InterVarsity Press, 2017.

Muller, M: *The First Bible of the Church,* Sheffield, U.K.: Sheffield Academic Press, 1996.

Neusner, Jacob. *A Life of Yohanan ben Zakkai, Ca. 1-80 C.E.,* Studia Post-Biblica, Leiden, 1970, p. 25.

Neusner, Jacob. *Early Rabbinic Judaism*, p. 27.

Nida, Eugene A. *Toward a Science of Translating*. Leiden: E.J. Brill, 1964.

Orlinsky, Harry. "The Masoretic Text: A Critical Evaluation," from *The Canon and Masorah of the Hebrew Bible*, ed. Sid Z. Leiman, Ktav Publishing House, NY, 1974, p. 852.

Fagan, Brian M. *The Seventy Great Mysteries of the Ancient World: Unlocking the Secrets of Past Civilizations*. New York: Thames and Hudson. 2001.

Pember, G.H. *Earth's Earliest Ages and Their Connection with Modern Spiritualism and Theosophy*. Crane, MO: Defender Books, 2012.

Penglase, Charles. *Greek Myths and Mesopotamia: Parallels and Influence in the Homeric Hymns and Hesiod.* London: Routledge, 1944.

Peters, Melvin K. H. "Why Study the Septuagint?" *The Biblical Archaeologist, Vol. 49,* No. 3, September 1986, p. 179.

Picknett, Lynn. *The Stargate Conspiracy: The Truth about Extraterrestrial Life and the Mysteries of Ancient Egypt.* New York: Berkley Publishing Group, 1999.

Pierce, Larry. (2001, April 1). "Evidentialism: The Bible and Assyrian Chronology," *Answers in Genesis.* Retrieved from https://answersingenesis.org/bible-history/evidentialism-the-bible-and-assyrian-chronology/.

Pierce, Larry. "Ussher's timeline for the divided kingdom." *Answers in Genesis.* Retrieved from https://assets.answersingenesis.org/doc/articles/cm/Divided.pdf

Reeves, Ryan M., and Hill, Charles E. *Know How We Got Our Bible.* Grand Rapids, MI: Zondervan, 2018.

Religions of the World: The Religion of Ancient Mesopotamia. Charles River Editors, 2015.

Richardson, Joel. *Mystery Babylon: Unlocking the Bible's Greatest Prophetic Mystery.* WND Books, 2017.

Roberts, J.M., and Odd Arne Westad. *The History of the World, Sixth Edition.* New York: Oxford University Press, 2013

Ross, Hugh. *The Creator and the Cosmos: How the Latest Discoveries Reveal God.* Grand Rapids, MI. Baker Books, 2018.

Ross, Hugh. *Improbable Planet: How Earth Became Humanity's Home.* Grand Rapids, MI: Baker Books, 2016.

Ross, Hugh. *Navigating Genesis: A Scientist's Journey through Genesis 1-11.* Covina, CA: Reasons to Believe, 2014.

Rost, Leonhard, *Judaism Outside the Hebrew Canon*, Nashville, TN: Abingdon, 1976, p. 102.

Rohl, David. "The Biblical Exodus: Fairytale or Historical Fact? [Video file]. YouTube. (Search keyword: David Rohl).

Rohl, David. *From Eden to Exile: The 5,000-Year History of the People of the Bible*. Lebanon, TN: Greenleaf Press, 2002.

Rudd, Steve. "The Septuagint LXX Greek Old Testament and Tanakh." Bible.ca. 2017. Retrieved November 30, 2018, from http://www.bible.ca/manuscripts/Septuagint-LXX-Greek-Old-Testment-Tanakh-ancient-Synagogues-first-century-church-PtolemyII-282-246BC.htm.

Rutherford, H. Platt Jr. *The Forgotten Books of Eden*. Self-published, 2012.

Salvesen, Alison. *Symmachus in the Pentateuch, JSSM 15* (Manchester: University of Manchester, 1991), p. 296-297.

Samuel, Moses. *The Book of Jasher*. Self-published. No date.

Schaefer, Peter. *Jesus in the Talmud*. Princeton, NJ: Princeton University Press, 2009.

Scheider, Tammi J. *An Introduction to Ancient Mesopotamian Religion*. Grand Rapids, MI: Wm. B. Eerdmans Publishing Co., 2011.

Schürer, Eric. *The Literature of the Jewish People in the Time of Jesus*, pp. 309-310.

Scranton, Laird. *The Velikovsky Heresies. Worlds in Collision and Ancient Catastrophes Revisited*. Toronto: Bear & Company, 2012.

Schoch, Robert M. *Forgotten Civilization: The Role of Solar Outbursts in Our Past and Future*. Rochester VT: Inner Traditions, 2012.

Schoch, Robert M., and Bauval, Robert. *Origins of the Sphinx: Celestial Guardian of Prek-Pharaonic Civilization*. Rochester, VT: Inner Traditions, 2017.

Schaeffer, Francis. *Escape from Reason*. Downers Grove, IL: Inter-Varsity Press. 1968.

Schürer, Eric. *The Literature of the Jewish People in the Time of Jesus,* p. 309-310.

Schwab, R. Simon. *Comparative Jewish Chronology*. Retrieved from https://www.scribd.com. p. 188.

Setterfield, Barry. "The Alexandrian Septuagint History," March 2010. Retrieved from http://setterfield.org/Septuagint_History.html.

Setterfield, Barry. "Ancient Chronology from Scripture," 1999. Retrieved April 28, 2018, from http://www.setterfield.org/scriptchron.htm.

Setterfield, Barry. "History of the Septuagint." Retrieved April 28, 2018, from www.setterfield.org/Septuagint.History.html.

Setterfield, Barry. "About the Exodus." Retrieved 2018 from http://setterfield.org/Egypt_and_Exodus.html.

Sexton, Jeremy. "Who was born when Enosh was 90? A Semantic reevaluation of William Henry Green's Chronological Gaps." *Westminster Theological Journal 77* (2015), p. 193-218.

Sexton, Jeremy, and Smith, Henry B. Jr., "Primeval Chronology Restored: Revising the Genealogies of Genesis 5 and 11." Bible and Spade 29.2 (2016).

Shanks, Hershel. "4QSama - The Difficult Life of a Dead Sea Scroll," *Biblical Archaeology Review, Vol 33*. No 3, May/June 2007, p. 66-70.

Sitchin, Zecharia. *There Were Giants Upon the Earth: God, Demigods, and Human Ancestry: The Evidence of Alien DNA*. Rochester, VT: Bear & Company, 2010.

Sivertsen, Barbara J. *The Parting of the Sea: How Volcanoes, Earth-quakes, and Plagues Shaped the Story of Exodus,* Princeton, New Jersey: Princeton University Press, 2009.

Skiba, Rob. *Genesis and the Synchronized, Biblically Endorsed, Extra-Biblical Texts.* Kings Gate Media, 2013.

Smith, George. *The Chaldean Account of Genesis (Illustrated).* London: Thomas Scott, 1876.

Smith, Henry B. "Methuselah's Begetting Age in Genesis 5:25 and the Primeval Chronology of the Septuagint: A Closer Look at the Textual and Historical Evidence." *Answer's Research Journal 10* (2017) p. 169-179.

Snoke, David. *A Biblical Case for an Old Earth.* Grand Rapids, MI: Baker Books, 2006.

"St. Athanasius." *Christian Classics Ethereal Library.* Retrieved from http://www.ccel.org/ccel/athanasius.

Stauffer, Doug. *One Book Stands Alone: How to Believe the Bible.* Millbrook, AL: McCowen Mills Publishing, 2013.

Stecker, Michael A. "The Thirty Dynasties of Egypt." Retrieved October 28, 2018, from http://mstecker.com/pages/egyptdyn_fp.htm.

Swete, H.B., *Introduction to the Old Testament in Greek, Christian Classics Ethereal Library.* 1989. Reprinted with permission, Cambridge University Press, 1914. First Edition, 1900.

The Orthodox Study Bible. Nashville, TN. Thomas Nelson, 2008.

The Ancient Canaanites: The History of the Civilizations That Lived in Canaan Before the Israelites. Charles River Editors, 2016.

The Jewish Encyclopedia, Vol. I, p. 305-306, citing Jer. Shek. 5:1, 48c.

The Letter of Aristeas. See http://www.ccel.org/c/charles/ot-pseudepig/aristeas.htm

'Theophilus to Autolycus' in *The Ante Nicene Fathers, Book III,* Chap. 2330, A. Roberts and J. Donaldson, eds, Wm. B. Eerdmans Publishing Co.

Thiele, E. *The Mysterious Numbers of the Hebrew Kings,* University of Chicago Press, Chicago, 1951. The book was republished in 1965 by William B. Eerdmans Publishing Co., and in 1983, by Zondervan.

"Tischendorf and the Discovery of the Codex Sinaiticus." Video. YouTube, https://youtu.be/LVSzBGXXL1Y.

Tov, Emanuel. *Exploring the Origins of the Bible,* Baker Academic, Craig A. Evans and Emanuel Tov, editors, 2008.

Ur: The History and Legacy of the Ancient Sumerian Capital. Charles River Editors. 2015.

VanderKam, James, *The Dead Sea Scrolls Today,* rev. ed. Grand Rapids, MI. Eerdmans, 2010.

Walton, John H. *The Lost World of Genesis One: Ancient Cosmology and the Origins Debate.* Downers Grove, IL: InterVarsity Press, 2010.

Wacholder, B.Z. *Eupolemus: A Study of Judaeo-Greek Literature.* Cincinnati, OH: Hebrew Union College Press, 1974.

Waltke and O'Connor, Introduction to Biblical Hebrew Syntax. Warsaw, IN: The Pennsylvania State University Press (Eisenbrauns), 1990.

Warfield, Benjamin B., "On the Antiquity and Unity of the Human Race," *Princeton Theological Review* 9/(1), 1911. p. 1-25.

Watson, William C. *Dispensationalism Before Darby: Seventeenth-Century and Eighteenth-Century English Apocalypticism.* Silverton, OR: Lampion Press, 2015.

Wegner, Paul D. *The Journey from Texts to Translation*, Baker Academic, 1999.

Whiteford, Fr. John, "The Septuagint and the Masoretic Text, retrieved July 6, 2018, from http://orthochristian.com/81224.html

Wikipedia. "Shoshenq I." Retrieved from https://en.wikipedia.org/wiki/Shoshenq_I

Williams, Walter G., *Archaeology in Biblical Research* (Nashville, Tennessee: Abingdon Press, 1965) p. 121. Retrieved from Bible-History.com.

Woodward, S. Douglas. *The Revealing: Unlocking Hidden Truths on the Glory of God's Children*, co-written with Gary Huffman, Oklahoma City, OK: Faith Happens Books, LLC. (2017)

Woodward, S. Douglas. *The Next Great War in the Middle East.* Oklahoma City, OK: Faith Happens Books, 2016.

Yadin, Israel. *Exploration Journal, 11* (1961), p.40.

Acknowledgments

There are many persons to thank for their help, feedback, and support in the creation of this book and my ministry generally.

Early on, Dr. Michael S. Heiser provided some constructive input regarding the inspiration of the scripture and the preservation of the text. He referenced a series of articles for me to study, which I did, and found them to be of great help. He also searched for and found for my review, a 2014 dissertation by R.J.J. Frost on the scripture and providence of God which helped to solidify my own thinking on the subject. Dr. Heiser is a fantastic and helpful resource.

Thanks to Daniel Wright who not only developed an incredible cover design, but helped with copy wording, image ideas, and some great tips on resources. He's a good thinker too. Daniel, you rock!

I am grateful for so many friends who encourage me to do this laborious work. Pastor Douglas Riggs (and wife Laurie), Dr. Preston Bailey, Pastor Clark Carlton, Stacy, and his church in Colorado Springs has hosted me on two occasions and provided incredible support for my ministry. Other friends I must mention here: Anna Swain and Ann Christopher (along with their hubbies, Erich and Kevin respectively), Audrey and Brian Vanderkley, John Haller, Kim Hanke, Michael Horsey, Dr. William Doubek, Mike Geiger, Mike Perkins, and especially my traveling companion on many trips to conferences, Patricia Miljan, her husband Rain, and their son, Kristofer. For those that don't know about it, I'll let you in on a little secret: We have a running joke about "the flat earth" and Patricia never ceases to find ways to continue the fun by poking something under my nose that makes me groan. She isn't a flat-earther, but she loves to upset my serenity frequently with this oddity. It's a theory that so many who defend the literal truth of the Bible have, which I can't understand (it's the twenty-first century after all!) I believe in many conspiracies, but this is one I can't abide. Sorry.

I also need to thank those who have been a great help by inviting me to appear on their radio programs. At the top of the list is Derek Gilbert (and wife Sharon), who entertains me on "A View from the Bunker" when I have a new title to promote. Derek is an awesome interviewer and has become an excellent author in his own right (as well as a TV anchorman. Step aside, Ron Burgundy!) Others to mention in this regard: Stacy Lynn and Randall Harp, Doug and Joe Hagmann, Larry Spargimino, Dr. Mike Spaulding, Tony Koretz "down under," Pastor Caspar McCloud, Chad Schaffer, Pastor Douglas Hamp, Gonz Shimura and Basil Rosewater, Margie and Jarry Cole, Kristen Gilmore, Dr. Michael Lake, John B. Wells, the Cosmic Cowboy – Daniel Ott, and the Omega Man – Shannon Ray Davis. And Linda Kay Barnett at Prophecy in the News. There are many others I'm forgetting. Forgive me for my memory lapse.

Thanks to my writing partners (every so often): Gary Huffman, Douglas Krieger, and Dene McGriff, Anthony Patch, Gonz Shimura, Josh Peck, Benjamin Baruch, and Jeff Nyquist. I appreciate your support and in-depth discussion on matters of import!

Thanks to all my followers on Facebook and my website, faith-happens.com. Without you, this effort wouldn't be worth it.

Thanks to my wife Donna, who allows me to clutter up our apartment with books sitting everywhere, doing my best absent-minded professor act. As I described to my college class recently, it's because I'm an author that our living space looks like a library hit by a tornado. Maybe one day I will have a separate office again! Please Lord. It's what I want for Christmas. Thanks to my kids Corinne, Nicholas, and Jessica. I love you all and appreciate your kindness in letting me quote the Bible seemingly randomly, while also pointing out biblical tidbits and historical trivia. I can't help myself. This stuff is packed so tightly in my head it just has to escape sometimes. And mainly, thanks for giving Donna and me the greatest gift: Grandchildren! How I love Brody and Beowulf. They are our bright lights in a dark world.

410

Index

B

C

I

J

[Index created with **TExtract** / www.Texyz.com]

ABOUT THE AUTHOR

S. Douglas Woodward, Th.M., MA in Finance (to be completed, May 2019), is 64 years old. He grew up in Oklahoma City, where he lives once again, after working in Boston for 6 years and Seattle for 21. Doug's experience lies primarily in business information technology and financial management where he has served as an executive for Oracle, Microsoft, and a Partner at Ernst & Young LLP. He also founded his own consultancy for young companies, Smart Starters, which he managed for 10 years, before becoming Entrepreneur-in-Residence at the University of Oklahoma, Price School of Business, where he has taught classes in entrepreneurship for five years.

Over the past seven years, Doug has become a nationally recognized author having written fourteen books on the topics of America's spiritual history, eschatology, theology, and geopolitics. His books of note include *The Final Babylon, Decoding Doomsday, Power Quest (Books One and Two), Lying Wonders of the Red Planet, The Revealing, The Next Great War in the Middle East,* and *Revising Reality. Rebooting the Bible* is number fifteen.

He frequently appears on radio and television programs having been interviewed on over 100 different occasions on several dozen different shows. Additionally, he speaks at conferences concerning the multiplicity of topics about which he writes.

Doug has two amazing adult children, an incredible daughter-in-law, two fabulous grandsons, and a beautiful wife, Donna, with whom he celebrates over 43 years of marriage.

Made in the USA
Lexington, KY
04 November 2019